THE REMARKABLE LIVES OF
BILL DEEDES

THE REMARKABLE LIVES OF
BILL DEEDES

STEPHEN ROBINSON

Little, Brown

LITTLE, BROWN

First published in Great Britain in 2008 by Little, Brown

Copyright © Stephen Robinson 2008

The moral right of the author has been asserted.

A CIP catalogue record for this book
. is available from the British Library.

ISBN 978-0-316-73033-4

Typeset in Sabon by M Rules
Printed and bound in Great Britain by
Clays Ltd, St Ives plc

Little, Brown
An imprint of
Little, Brown Book Group
100 Victoria Embankment
London EC4Y 0DY

An Hachette Livre UK Company
www.hachettelivre.co.uk

www.littlebrown.co.uk

To A. T. R. R.
who didn't live quite long enough to read this.

Contents

Preface

The journalist in Bill Deedes had wanted his memorial service to be held in the hacks' church, St Bride's in Fleet Street, but in the end his life was celebrated in the most martial of settings, at the Guards Chapel, Wellington Barracks, on a crisp autumn day. With unconvincing self-deprecation, Deedes had told his son Jeremy that the cramped St Bride's would be more than ample for the modest crowd that could be expected to turn out to mark the passing of a ninety-four-year-old newspaper reporter. Bill was overruled and, inevitably, even the much larger Guards Chapel struggled to contain the throng of seven hundred who managed to secure entrance to the ticket-only service.

At first glance the service might have seemed a rather grand, establishment affair. The Queen and Princess Alexandra sent representatives; the Lord-Lieutenant for Greater London and Baroness Thatcher were there, and so was David Cameron, whom Deedes thought had deserved a little more support than he got from the *Telegraph* in his first months as Tory leader. All the charities Deedes had championed over the years sent officials, many of them personal friends. His old regiment, the King's Royal Rifle Corps, was properly represented and there was a vast contingent of present and former *Telegraph* staff and other journalists drawn from more widely around Fleet Street. Then there were people who, on their application for tickets, honestly stated they had never met W. F. Deedes, but wanted to attend because they were devoted readers of his work.

Deedes might have lost the argument over the location of the memorial service, but he prevailed in setting its tone. Jeremy

Deedes nodded at his father's Abyssinian adventures by reading from Evelyn Waugh's *Scoop*; Lucy Deedes, Bill's youngest child, read from *A Crime Wave at Blandings* by another of their father's favourite authors, P. G. Wodehouse. Charles Moore, the former *Telegraph* editor, gave an address of perfect pitch, recalling that Deedes had asked him to speak up for him 'because you know the funny side'. So Moore fondly teased him, for his bright red socks, his 1930s suits, and his famous malapropisms – 'I smell the finger of the Labour party in this one' – before concluding that it was impossible even to think about Bill without smiling.

Deedes loved a joke, and he saw no reason why there shouldn't be a few on the other side of the grave. So after a trumpeter sounded Last Post and Reveille, the Regimental Band of the Grenadier Guards struck up 'Nkosi Sikelel' iAfrika', the freedom song that became South Africa's national anthem. It was an incongruous last request from a man who, as a backbench Tory MP in the 1960s, had spoken up for old Rhodesia, but then he was the first to acknowledge that ideological consistency had never been the hallmark of his political career.

That memorial service, on 26 November 2007, might be regarded as my last encounter with Bill Deedes. The first came in 1986 when I joined the *Daily Telegraph* and he escorted me to my first experience at that theatre of the absurd, the King & Keys, the ghastliest pub in all Fleet Street. This was just after he had ceased being editor and was embarking on the last, glorious phase of his career. Thereafter he proved to be the most delightful journalistic ally, taking me for dinner during his frequent travels while I was based abroad for the paper, and always giving me lunch at Paradiso e Inferno, a trattoria in the Strand which he favoured because it had successfully resisted all culinary trends to have emerged since the early 1970s, when I was in London on leave. Thus I had known Deedes for eighteen years when I wrote to him in 2004 asking permission to embark on his biography. He responded as he always did when a matter of importance had to be discussed: he booked his usual downstairs booth at Paradiso. Over pink gins, Parma ham, melon balls and whitebait, he gave his blessing to the project, on the grounds that it was probably better I did it 'rather than some hooligan from the *Guardian*'. He warned me that I would find 'no choir boys, or tarts from Maida Vale' rattling around in his cupboards, and sadly he was right about that. He imposed a single condition upon me, that the book appear after his death. This was partly because in his lifetime Deedes wanted to be regarded as a working journalist rather than a national treasure, and he was never reconciled to the modern habit of journalists writing about each other.

But I think he insisted on the posthumous condition also because he knew any biography would delve into personal and family matters, which he had no wish to be aired while he was around. His autobiography, *Dear Bill*, was magisterially unrevealing about his family and his feelings on a number of subjects, including his father's squandering of the vast family fortune and the terminal illness of his second son, Julius. The inadequacies of that autobiography left gaps in his story that I hope, with this authorised biography, to fill.

One of the pleasures in writing this book was the universal co-operation I encountered when researching his life. Almost everyone adored Deedes, or – if they didn't know him personally – the *idea* of him. Friends and colleagues from his many lives in journalism, war, politics and humanitarian relief all spoke to me freely and generously.

Deedes had a Victorian attitude to record keeping and I began my researches with the vast archive he had accumulated during his long life, beginning with prep school reports from the 1920s and concluding with records of his trips to Africa and elsewhere in the new millennium. In the intervening years he kept the strangest things: letters from his tailor in the 1930s; boarding passes from flights taken in the 1970s; receipts for underwear purchased in the 1990s. He did not keep a diary as such, but it was his practice to make contemporaneous notes of important or interesting events and of all foreign trips, and then to file them. The archive was massive, but not, I came to suspect, entirely comprehensive. I don't think he set about weeding the archive when he gave permission for me to write his biography. Rather, I suspect, hostile letters or records of family difficulties were discarded at the time, while anything that was pleasant or complimentary was kept. That was the nature of his personality, for he had no interest in conducting feuds, settling scores, or dwelling on unhappy personal episodes.

It is difficult to write the biography of a close colleague, particularly one who was still alive when the majority of the research was carried out. I have tried to be objective and not overly influenced by our adventures over the years in Africa, America and Asia. Rereading the manuscript in preparation for publication, I was surprised that I had had the temerity to appear sometimes critical of his behaviour. I hope his family, and his legions of fans, will not be offended by this impertinence. Because I knew him as a colleague over the last two decades of his life, I occasionally intrude into the narrative that follows, and I hope the reader will indulge brief cameo appearances.

I set out to write this book not just because Deedes's life was interesting in itself, but because his career spanned most of the great events of the twentieth century. He was there, or thereabouts, sometimes as a participant, but usually as an observer, with a reporter's studied detachment. Throughout his life, Deedes proved elusive to his political and journalistic colleagues, even to his own children, who paid the price for his stringent sense of public duty and his devoted loyalty to the *Telegraph*. I revered Deedes as a journalist and treasured him as a colleague, but I never penetrated the layers of emotional reserve while he was alive, partly, I think, because he was better at engaging with humanity in the round rather than with the individual. I hope with this biography that even if I have failed to penetrate the Deedesian reserve, I have managed to navigate my way around it.

I should like to thank the following people who assisted me in the writing of this book, either by agreeing to be interviewed or by providing background information such as letters, photographs, or unpublished memoirs.

Preface

Ian Aitken; Araminta, Lady Aldington; Anne Allport; Frances Banks; Anne Barrow of the Ashford Conservative Association; Rita Boswell, the Harrow School archivist; Ethna Bradbury; Craig Brown; Caroline Burnaby-Atkins; John Butterwick; John Carlin; Lord Carrington; Jane Clark; Michael Cockerell; Victoria Combe; Penny Cranford; Sue Davey; Anna Deedes; George Deedes; Jeremy Deedes; Kate Fassett; Margaret, Lady FitzWalter; Kim Fletcher; Simon Foster; Richard Frost; the late Lord Gilmour; Stephen Glover; Roy Greenslade; Cassandra Hall; Jonathan Hall; Sir Max Hastings; Selina Hastings; Tim Heald; Simon Heffer; Ian Hislop; Andrew Hutchinson; Richard Ingrams; Boris Johnson; the late Frank Johnson; Ian Jones; Lord Latymer; Sue Lawley; the Reverend Richard Love; Peter Macdiarmid; Professor Judith Marsh of St George's Hospital, Tooting; Sinclair McKay; the late Stephen McWatters; Charlie Methven; Drummond Money-Coutts; Rosie Money-Coutts; Sophia Money-Coutts; Charles Moore; Sally Muggeridge; George Newkey-Burden; Dorina Paparritor; Edward Pearce; the late Hermione Phipps; Simon Prior-Palmer; David Profumo; the late Lord Rawlinson; Tom Rhodes; Alec Russell; Sue Ryan; Lord Ryder; Sarah Sands; Louise Simester; Sir Donald Sinden; Kate Summerscale; Derek Taylor Thompson; Carol Thatcher; Dick Tower; Abbie Trayler-Smith; Ion Trewin; Marilyn Tweddle; David Twiston Davies; Alan Watkins; Alexander Waugh; Frances Welch; Sir Peregrine Worsthorne; Mariya Zlatinova.

I am grateful to the staff at the London Library, the British Library, the National Archives at Kew and the Bodleian at Oxford, which holds the Conservative Party archive. My mother, Barbara Robinson, originally suggested to me that I should write this biography. David Miller, my agent, never wavered in his enthusiasm for the project, nor in his commitment to convivial lunches in the best tradition of old Fleet Street. Michael Kallenbach and Robert Taylor kindly lent me their cottage in Wiltshire at a crucial moment. Ursula Mackenzie at Little, Brown saw the point of the book from the very beginning and offered support even when she relinquished direct control of it after she was made head of the company; Steve Guise took over the project with great authority and application, assisted all the way by Kerry Chapple. Zoë Gullen proved herself to be a meticulous and appropriately demanding copy-editor.

My old Johannesburg colleague Christopher Munnion kindly read the Abyssinia chapters, bringing his immense experience of reporting from Africa to bear. Paul Hill provided me with a detailed and evocative account of the sheer weirdness of the working day at the old *Telegraph* office. Christopher Howse, almost as fast and much more learned than Google, did me the immense kindness of reading the entire manuscript, making many excellent suggestions and saving me from several howlers. Nicholas Garland offered wise advice throughout, read many of the chapters and proposed improvements with the candour of a true friend. His unflagging encouragement from beginning to end was an incalculable help.

From the outset I received nothing but cooperation from the extended Deedes family, including Bill's sisters, children and grandchildren. I must first thank Bill Deedes, for allowing me to go through the diaries and filing cabinets chronicling his life. Once he had given me the go-ahead he never sought to impede my researches, even when he grew nervous that I was spending more time interviewing his children than reading his speeches from his days as junior Housing minister.

Lucy Deedes lived with her father for the last three years of his life, helping to look after him and giving him the encouragement he needed to keep writing his weekly column to the very end. She proved to be a great comfort and support to him, but also to his biographer, offering me hospitality, support and friendship during countless visits to Aldington.

My greatest debt is to my wife, Lorna, a wise counsel and expert editor, who read the manuscript and imposed many improvements while heavily pregnant with our second child. To her – and to Florence and Percy, good sleepers, the pair of them – I owe more than I can express.

London, January 2008

CHAPTER 1

BOYHOOD IN A CASTLE

'The castle was the master of our lives.'

Over the centuries, his ancestors had owned huge tracts of Kent, but William Francis Deedes was born on 1 June 1913 in a nursing home in Hampstead, North London. Once his mother had recovered from the birth, they were taken back to Symnells, an Elizabethan hall house in the south-east Kent village of Aldington, which his parents had occupied since their marriage eleven months earlier. It is an interesting house that was extended and made to seem grander in the late eighteenth century by the addition of a pink stucco façade. The rooms are large, with high ceilings and ancient beams. The young family was happy there, living comfortably on an income of nine hundred pounds a year from landholdings, which allowed for an indoor staff of five, plus two gardeners to tend the two and a half acres surrounding the house. Symnells is haunted by Eliza, the daughter of a Victorian servant girl who, according to Aldington lore, drowned in a pond behind the house. Eliza is a sweet-natured ghost and she never bothered the Deedeses. Three daughters followed Bill: Frances in 1915, Hermione in 1918 and Margaret in 1923.

Early photographs show a happy, handsome boy, often surrounded by his adoring younger sisters. Aldington, which was then surrounded by quarries for the mining of Kentish ragstone,

1

was not a picture postcard village, but life was good there in Bill's first five years, despite the horrors of trench warfare across the Channel. On days when the wind blew from France, the distant sound of the guns could be heard. One of Bill's earliest memories was being taken up to the flat roof of Saltwood Castle,* before the family lived there, and watching two German planes flying towards London, slicing through the defensive searchlights.

Though the spelling of the name varied for a hundred years or so, the Deedeses settled in the Weald of Kent sometime in the first half of the fifteenth century. Appropriately enough, given the trade Bill was to choose for himself, his earliest confirmed ancestor, Robert Deeds, worked as a printing apprentice alongside William Caxton during the reign of Edward IV. *Burke's Landed Gentry* confirms the lineage only as far back as Thomas Deedes, who was buried at Dover in 1603. The foundation of the Deedes fortune was wool, which they later converted into land as generations of the family accumulated large holdings through marriage alliances and opportunistic acquisitions.

At the time of Bill's birth in 1913, it was still possible to walk the six miles from Aldington to Hythe on land entirely owned by the family, but there was no disguising that the family's fortune was on the wane. The estates were under pressure from falling land values and rising taxes and, within a few years, much of the land had been sold and what remained was heavily mortgaged.

Bill's father, Herbert William,† was born in 1881, went to Eton, and then, aged nineteen, to South Africa to fight in the Boer War. Most of the key decisions in Herbert's life were taken by his formidable mother, Rose Elinor, and she was determined that Herbert, and his younger brother, Wyndham, should maintain the family's

---

* Bill's great-great-grandfather, another William Deedes, acquired Saltwood Castle at the end of the eighteenth century. The main line of the family found it unsuitable as a home, so it tended to be occupied by distant relatives and retainers.

† Within the family as a child he was known as Bunnie, but for outsiders he preferred to be known by his second name, William. To avoid confusion with his son he shall be referred to as Herbert.

military tradition. Her husband, Colonel Herbert Deedes, was born in 1836 and went to Harrow before joining the family regiment, the 60th Rifles. He served with distinction through the Indian Mutiny and was active in the capture of Delhi and Lucknow. Rose was also born of a celebrated military family, as the daughter of Major-General L. Barrow, CB.

Rose had encouraged both her sons to go straight from school to the last great imperial adventure in South Africa. For Wyndham, this had marked the beginning of a brilliant military career: he went on to serve in the First World War, achieving the rank of Brigadier-General at the age of thirty-six and was eight times mentioned in dispatches. Despite these considerable 'establishment' achievements, and a subsequent knighthood, Wyndham always regarded himself as left wing and in the 1930s he withdrew from public life to do social work with the poor in the East End of London.

For Herbert, the South African experience had been wrenching. He had been unhappy enough at Eton, but military life, chasing down Boer commandoes and incarcerating their women and children, was much worse, and he manifestly under-performed in comparison with his younger brother. He was not wounded by Boer marksmen, but South Africa nevertheless took a terrible toll on the callow subaltern. He picked up some sort of bacterial stomach condition which was never properly diagnosed, and which plagued him for the rest of his life.* His experience also left him mentally fraught and, now loathing the British Empire and all it stood for, turned him into a highly eccentric sort of socialist.

Bill's mother had all the qualities her husband lacked: gentle humour, a softness and common sense. She was born Melesina Gladys Chenevix Trench, the second daughter of a grand Irish Protestant family. Known mostly by her second name, Gladys, she married Herbert at Holy Trinity Church, Sloane Street in 1912.

---

* It might have been a form of typhoid, which killed five times more British soldiers in South Africa than were killed by Boer action.

She was serious but not austere, with an Edwardian attitude to public service. In later years she ran a centre for poor women in Hythe, where they could drop in and seek advice on pregnancy, raising children and other domestic matters. Gladys became a Justice of the Peace, the first woman to achieve this rank in east Kent. She had a deep religious faith, and every morning the children would kneel before her as she led them in prayer and Bible readings.

Bill and his sisters were partially shielded from their cantankerous father by their beloved nanny Ethel Sinden, known as 'Effie', who ran their early lives and presided over a happy nursery. As the eldest child and the only boy, Bill would lead the play in the garden at Symnells, build camps and put up tents, and then allow the girls to come inside. There was plenty to explore and lots of birds' nests to raid for eggs. Gladys kept beehives and chickens, and the children would help out with both.

Church on Sundays was mandatory for the children, but Herbert would almost always excuse himself, protesting that he was 'not up to it'. Sometimes Gladys would take the children to Saltwood Church, though the family favoured the parish church in Hythe, where the window in the south transept is known as the Deedes window and various ancestors are commemorated in grand plaques. There was also a Deedes pew, second from the front, which was always respectfully left vacant by the rest of the congregation.

Bill loved to play the fool in church, boyishly challenging his mother's faith. One of his tricks was guaranteed to reduce his sisters to helpless giggles. They would wait breathlessly for Psalm 65 to be read: 'My misdeeds prevail against me: O be thou merciful unto our sins.' At that point, Bill would lean forward and gesture manically down the family pew to his sisters, leading the silent laughter at the hilarity of the play upon the family name. 'We were hysterical,' Margaret recalled.

Bill was a happy boy, at least in the innocent early years before he was old enough to understand the family's financial problems and the toll they were taking on his parents. Family holidays were modest but happy, and were usually taken around the coast at Westgate-on-Sea, where they would spend a few days in a boarding house. They would also go down to the sea at Hythe, and Bill would plunge in while the girls paddled, their skirts tucked into their knickers. One day, when the girls said the water was too cold, Bill snatched their sun hats and swam out beyond the surf with them piled on top of his head. The girls enjoyed watching their big brother horse around. Bill was always leader of the pack; they loved to go blackberrying together, and Bill would balance the full baskets on his head until Effie screamed at him to put them down.

The running of Symnells was left entirely to Gladys, with no contribution from Herbert in either the house or garden. As was then customary, Bill was brought up as a nursery child, forming extremely close bonds with Effie and his sisters, and being presented to his parents at set times of the day and eating separately from them. But it was not an oppressively formal household, and the mental instability and depressive tendencies that afflicted Herbert in later years did not then dominate family life. There was a cook and a cook's maid, but there was no butler, or any male indoor staff. Herbert and Gladys rarely entertained, because he was prone to take to his bed at short notice, citing stomach trouble or a migraine.

As was normal for their time and class, the girls did not go to school, but were educated at home by a series of governesses and tutors. Bill was sent away to Wellington House, a prep school at Westgate-on-Sea run by a kindly headmaster, the Reverend P. C. Underhill. Described by a contemporary as 'a genial giant of a man', Underhill would allow the boys to come to his study after prep, where he would read aloud from John Buchan, kindling in Bill a lifelong love of his writing.

Wellington House attracted the sons of the Kent gentry and the successful commercial classes, and by the standards of private schools of the time it was a humane and cheerful establishment. Underhill had rowed for Oxford, so there was an emphasis on healthy games in the bracing sea air. Bill became a handy cricketer and enjoyed all ball games.

He thrived at Wellington House, settling in with very little homesickness. In later life he would talk of himself as lacking 'intellectual equipment' and would say that he was a failure at school. The latter point was unfounded: his end of term reports showed him to be at the top of the class, or close to it. There were occasional canings for bad behaviour at the school, though Bill himself was never beaten. Matron had a soft spot for him, and called him Willie, though he discouraged the other boys from doing so. Instead, he was known by his family and friends as William or Will; it was not until he began work in London in 1931 that he was called Bill, the name that stuck with him for the rest of his life.

Distracted by games and his studies, Bill had no idea that a crisis was brewing as his grandmother Rose plotted to place the family on a social footing she thought appropriate to their ancestry. Indeed, late in his long life, Bill Deedes would divide his childhood into two distinct phases. From birth to the age of six, life was carefree, and that sense of fun is reflected in the family photographs from this period showing him as a cheerful boy at play. From the age of six to sixteen, his life was blighted by his father's increasingly erratic behaviour which was exacerbated from 1919, when they made a disastrous move to the ancestral castle at Saltwood.

At some point while her two sons were away in South Africa Rose had set herself an ambitious project. She wanted nothing less than to restore the family to the status it had enjoyed at the beginning of the nineteenth century, and for Herbert to be installed as the young squire of these holdings. Her intentions had been made clear by her elaborate plans for Herbert's homecoming from the Boer War and his coming of age. Some four hundred children were invited to the Saltwood church hall to celebrate the twenty-first birthday of the squire on 27 October 1902. They were entertained by a troupe called the Snowball Minstrels, who sang a dozen comic numbers including 'Razors in the Air' and 'The Whistling Coon'. For a family already deep in the financial mire, it could have been considered recklessly extravagant, even if the birthday boy had been able to attend. But Herbert was conspicuously absent from his own birthday party, still stuck in Malta with his battalion on their way back from Cape Town.

His absence was not allowed to spoil the festivities, which were reported in breathless detail by Kent newspapers. 'Monday was a red-letter day in the annals of the history of the pretty village of Saltwood,' reported the *Hythe and Sandgate Standard*, 'the occasion being the coming of age of the eldest son of Mrs Herbert Deedes.' The *Standard* noted that the 'young squire' was sadly absent, but that it had cast no shadow across a splendid day brilliantly organised by Mrs Deedes. Each of the four hundred young guests was given a bag of sweets, and left with a special keepsake as though they had attended a royal jubilee – a stiff card with a photograph of Herbert superimposed on the top left corner alongside the family's punning motto, *Facta non Verba* (Deeds not Words).

When Herbert did finally make it home the following month, the welcome orchestrated by his mother was predictably extravagant: huge banners were draped across the gates of Saltwood Castle declaring the family motto, as well as that of his regiment, *Celer et Audax* (Swift and Bold). The children's party had been a rehearsal for the main event on the night of 24 November, a huge dinner for Saltwood's tenants, local dignitaries and anyone who was anyone in east Kent. Some six hundred guests were invited to the party in gaily decorated marquees erected on the lawn of the inner bailey.

Only the men sat down for dinner; the ladies joined them afterwards for the speeches and more festivities. The men were fed *Gigot de Mouton Legume à la Postling* (Postling was a neighbouring parish) and they finished off with Pudding 'Deeds not Words'.

As the *Hythe Reporter* put it, this was entertainment in a 'most regal manner', and from the reports in this and other local newspapers it is clear that Rose orchestrated the entire event, and indeed the media coverage. Her speech to her guests was rapturously received. The *Hythe Reporter* noted: 'In clear, sweet, and pathetic tones she touched a tender chord in the hearts of all.'

Following Herbert and Gladys's wedding in 1912, Rose made another effort to propel them towards Saltwood Castle by organising an elaborate 'homecoming' to the castle which the 'squire' had no intention of taking on. An open carriage was sent to pick up them up from Sandling Junction and transport them the mile to the castle. Instead of a horse, Rose had persuaded the estate staff to pull the carriage into the castle on ropes, where another triumphal arch had been erected to welcome them 'home'.

The *Folkestone Herald* carried an excitable account illustrated with a photograph showing a scene of feudal absurdity: schoolchildren are penned behind crowd control ropes, holding flags and staring towards the carriage, which is being driven by a coachman in a top hat. The local constable stands stiffly to attention as he supervises the flat-capped estate workers grappling with the ropes, pulling the carriage towards the castle in which the young squire has never lived. There is also a close-up of the couple. The new Mrs Deedes is pretty in a feathered hat, her face betraying a cautious happiness and a certain bemusement as she smiles at the welcoming party. Her husband, dressed in a dark city suit and Homburg, stares morosely into the middle distance. With relief, Herbert and Gladys retreated to Symnells, where they happily began their married life together, but if the couple thought they had escaped the burdens of the family castle they were mistaken.

The financial fortunes of the Deedeses had been declining since the middle of the nineteenth century and the repeal of the Corn Laws, but the final spasm of decay was triggered by a simple misfortune. The flu epidemic of the winter of 1918–19, the lethal coda to the First World War, carried off Mrs Halifax Wyatt,

Bill's great aunt and the chatelaine of Saltwood Castle. Saltwood had been in the family since the end of the eighteenth century, but it was regarded as unsuitable as a family residence, so the main Deedes line preferred another large house and estate, Sandling Park, which had to be sold in 1897.

The death of Mrs Wyatt gave Rose her chance. Never mind that Bill's father had had no experience of farming or estate management, nor had shown any inclination to take on the Saltwood estates, or actually live in the castle. By force of personality she persuaded her first-born son to take on the dilapidated castle, its leaking roofs and cracked foundations, plus the four maiden Deedes aunts who lived there. It was in poor condition, but it was nevertheless a majestic structure, parts of which dated back to the Norman Conquest. Though the drawbridge had long since collapsed, the castle was protected by a moat and massive walls of Kentish rag stone. Within the inner bailey, there was a large chapel, completely ruined, and a great hall which had no roof. The living area was contained within and around the vast central tower, with its flat roof and views down to the Channel a mile and a half away. To the castle were attached seventy-three acres of surrounding land, five cottages and Castle Lodge, the dower house.

This was what Herbert Deedes reluctantly took on in 1919. Symnells, the family home, was sold for a song to a local doctor and they moved into the castle's crumbling fabric. 'It turned out to be a sorry decision,' Bill Deedes noted in his autobiography, *Dear Bill*, with an understatement extreme even by his capacity for downplaying calamity. The move was ruinous, in all senses of the word.

Though many young boys would love the idea of living in a proper castle, it had no appeal for Bill. His mother's mood and health quickly declined when the scale of their error became apparent. No money had been spent on the castle since the early 1880s, when it was inhabited by another William Deedes, Herbert's uncle, and it had since fallen into disrepair.

Whereas Symnells was cosy and manageable, the castle was dank and forbidding. There was electricity in the vicinity of Hythe, but the castle itself was not connected to the grid. The rooms were instead lit by candles and oil lamps, which meant that the family lived in permanent terror of fire. In winter, there was no way to keep the living areas warm, except by lighting fires in every room. Damp rose unchecked from the medieval foundations; the castle's flat roofs, which in earlier times would have given good warning of advancing armies, were not up to the task of keeping the rain out. Try as they might, the staff could not keep the moisture out, and the walls ran with water.

The physical decrepitude of the castle was bad enough, but Herbert soon found he had inherited other liabilities along with the rising damp, leaky roofs and crumbling masonry. The four maiden aunts in the dower house needed to be fed and clothed, and to have their doctors' bills paid when they fell ill. Soon after they took up residence, the doctor called and prescribed one of the aunts half a bottle of champagne a day to assist her convalescence from a stubborn illness.

As master of Saltwood, Herbert found himself at the centre of a large network of tenants and tenant farmers, all of whom came to him as first resort to settle problems or seek favours. Shy and diffident at the best of times, he was disastrously miscast for this role. When tenants fell behind with their rent, Herbert would generally tell them not to worry too much and would try to absorb the loss of income within the estate accounts.

Some people in Kent regard Saltwood Castle as jinxed because of its part in an infamous episode of English history, the murder of St Thomas à Becket in 1170. Various structures had been on the site since before the reign of King Canute, when it was made over by Haldene, a Saxon thane, to the monks of Christ Church, Canterbury. A century after the Norman Conquest, it was rebuilt by Henry of Essex, but when he disgraced himself with an act of conspicuous cowardice while carrying the King's colours during a skirmish with the Welsh in

1163, Henry II seized all his possessions and made Saltwood over to Ranulf de Broc, a particular foe of Becket's.

De Broc had turned Saltwood into a centre of opposition to Becket, and the crisis came to a head after the Archbishop's return from France in 1170, when the King made it clear that he would not honour past pledges to restore secular properties to the See. Becket responded by suspending those bishops most loyal to Henry. When Henry lamented how the 'sluggard wretches and cowards' who peopled his court would not lift a finger to deliver him from this turbulent priest, it was no surprise that the four knights who answered the royal call headed for Saltwood after crossing the Channel separately. They reached Saltwood Castle on the evening of 28 December and sat up late into the night with de Broc, planning their murderous deed, supposedly with the candles snuffed so as not to see the others' guilty faces. The next morning the knights set off on horseback for Canterbury Cathedral and accomplished their bloody mission at nightfall, before fleeing back to the castle. Since that episode, Saltwood has suffered several damaging earthquakes which weakened the ancient structure, adding to the upkeep for subsequent owners, including the Deedes family.*

The new life at Saltwood would have been a challenge even if Herbert Deedes had been suited to shouldering the burdens of running an old-fashioned estate, but he was not. First, he did not approve of private land ownership, certainly not on the scale of the thousands of heavily mortgaged acres he had notionally inherited on his father's death. Second, he was not psychologically suited to dealing with the estate's tenants or the staff he was forced to employ. And third, his health, never robust since his time in South Africa, began to decline in the castle. Herbert was by nature extravagant, and began spending on non-essentials. He bought his mother a house above Saltwood church, and had it

---

* The castle suffered further damage as recently as 2007, when an earthquake caused the foundations to shake and a ceiling in one of the towers to come down.

remodelled. Huge, ancient trees were expensively cut down to open up the view of the castle from the village and, most absurdly of all, a hard tennis court was built, though rarely used.

Soon Herbert's mental state began to deteriorate along with his physical health. Margaret, the youngest daughter, likened their childhood in the castle to the world of the sisters portrayed in Nancy Mitford's *The Pursuit of Love*, with her father resembling Fa – increasingly dotty and bad-tempered. Because the three daughters were educated at home, they were more exposed than Bill to their father's mood swings. Margaret, though deeply fond of her father, remembered him as 'very irascible; we were continually dodging the flak'. He felt the cold acutely and took to dressing eccentrically to counter it. Indoors, he would wear an overcoat and wool-knit hat, and in winter he would attach hot water bottles to a length of string tied around his waist. One moment he would be talking to the family, the next he would descend into a deep funk and turn his chair around in the drawing-room to face the wall. Sometimes his sulks would last for three days, when he would refuse to say a word.

Bill and his sisters were as loyal to their father as they could be, but there was no denying how odd he became. Bill reluctantly conceded in later life that from the time he had any memories of him, his father was 'never quite compos', and that as his frustration with life mounted he was prone to terrible temper tantrums and mood swings so violent that they bordered on the schizophrenic. He resorted to extreme measures to deal with his ill health, purging himself at Saltwood with regular enemas. 'Father was a broken reed, physically and mentally,' Deedes said later. 'He was in a state of mutiny against life.' He had at least two serious mental breakdowns, one shortly after the Boer War.

Herbert was driven most of all by a hatred of the British Empire, which was a result of his experiences in South Africa. He would read voraciously, writing extensive notes in pencil in the margins, and then would write – usually without answer – to politicians and dictators. He supported Mussolini, was impressed by Stalin, and for several years thought Hitler showed promise. He had no social life, and was certainly not a figure in the county. His main social interaction was with his barber, Mr Carr, who would come to the castle to shave him and cut his hair.

Sometimes Bill would try to indulge his father with an anarchic gesture meant to please him. To celebrate Ramsay MacDonald's formation of the first Labour administration in 1924, he wore a red rosette on his blazer at Wellington House, much to the headmaster's bemusement. On another occasion, young Bill caused a stir by playing 'The Red Flag' on the piano while the Dean of Canterbury was paying a courtesy visit to the castle. Usually his father's efforts to show reciprocal affection to his son ended in disaster. Family events would be planned, but then Herbert would duck out of them, claiming that he was feeling poorly. He would frequently take to his bed during the day, where he would lie with the curtains closed. Herbert could also be hopelessly impractical. Bill got into trouble at Harrow when his father made a rare visit, taking him to the King's Head, a notorious pub in the town, where the pair were spotted. In later years he would unthinkingly hand his young grandchildren glasses of beer or sherry.

The three girls at least had companionship, but young Bill found life in the castle isolating. He would laboriously cut and roll a cricket strip – complete with proper painted markings – on the lawn of the inner bailey. 'It was pure fancy,' Deedes noted in his autobiography, 'there was no one to play cricket with; but I liked to imagine there might be. Castles are lonely places, and Saltwood, with its moat and portcullis and thick walls, looked fairly unapproachable. Young friends did not feel drawn to it or me.'

The castle was beginning to cause Herbert and Gladys stress as their finances deteriorated; they could keep afloat only by selling off more and more land. The Deedes landholdings extended far beyond the ancestral redoubt of Saltwood, inland towards Aldington and beyond. Bill Deedes was never sure how much land was sold, but estimated the holdings disposed of by his father at about five thousand acres.

Many of the unprepossessing houses around Aldington were built on land sold cheaply by Herbert Deedes in the 1920s. The sale of a strip of land stretching from Saltwood Castle towards the coast caused a bitter row with Lord Wakefield, who had made a fortune in the oil industry and used some of it to build a grand house on a promontory overlooking Hythe. The house was blessed with fabulous, unspoilt views to the coast until Herbert sold the land below the promontory for the development of ugly modern villas for the town's rising lower-middle class. The houses, which still stand today, have lurid red-tiled roofs, so the road became known locally as Lobster Row, and Herbert was never forgiven for the blot he placed upon the Hythe landscape.

Despite the feverish rate and scale of his land sales, Herbert could not repair the holes in the family finances. Under pressure from Gladys, he spent heavily in doomed efforts to make the castle habitable for a young family. Various teams of builders were employed and were paid for their services with the proceeds of the land sales. But the castle could not be made comfortable.

Gladys longed for the cosiness of Symnells and came to resent her husband for caving in to his mother and moving the family into an obviously unsuitable structure. They quarrelled, and she would cry, while Herbert talked vaguely and despairingly of selling up and emigrating to Australia to escape the tenants and the builders' bills. The health of Gladys and Frances, dogged by respiratory ailments, was causing acute alarm. As the bills mounted, Herbert finally accepted the inevitable, faced up to his mother, and took the decision to sell Saltwood.

Knight, Frank & Rutley were commissioned to auction the castle, and a date was set for 23 July 1925 at its headquarters in Hanover Square. The estate agent's prospectus offered the castle and its seventy-three acres as an 'admirably adapted modern country residence', which – given the Deedes family's miserable experience over the previous six years – was a blatant untruth. The accommodation was described as four reception rooms,

14

tower room, sixteen bed- and dressing rooms, two turret rooms and a single bathroom. A week before the scheduled auction, Herbert reached a private deal to sell to a local Hythe resident. The price agreed was only £10,750, which suggests that Herbert had made another bad financial call. As the estate agent's details made clear, the sale price was just over double the sum of five thousand pounds that had recently been 'expended on general improvements'. Therefore, the real price achieved was under six thousand pounds, a terrible return even allowing for the depredations of inflation. Bill's uncle Wyndham later estimated that in the decade up to 1930 Herbert had burnt his way through about seventy thousand pounds – some £3.15 million in current value.

Nevertheless, the family felt a collective sense of relief. 'The castle was the master of our lives,' Bill Deedes recalled. 'Saltwood was the intruding element – it was a great relief to get rid of the bloody thing.' His father, however, must have felt a terrible sense of humiliation at his failure to make the castle work. Once again he tried to persuade his wife that they should move to Australia and start a new life, but she refused. Increasingly Gladys sought solace in the devoted Effie Sinden, with whom she could at least have sensible conversations. Effie was loved unreservedly by all the children, not just for what she had done for them but for serving as a prop to their mother, whose only other company was her increasingly erratic and demoralised husband.

One lovely summer's day in 2005, Deedes reluctantly agreed that I should drive him and his youngest daughter, Lucy, the short distance from his home in Aldington to Saltwood Castle. He had been on edge all day and on arrival he refused to get out of the car, protesting that he was feeling unwell. He only relented when our hostess, Jane Clark – the widow of Alan Clark, the Tory MP and diarist – protested that she had made rock cakes in his honour.

Mrs Clark took Lucy and me on a tour of the castle and the grounds while Deedes sat defiantly in the morning room. By this stage of his life, he could walk only uncertainly with sticks, so would have been unable to get around the upper levels without assistance. When we came back, uplifted by the astonishing grandeur of the castle and its grounds, he looked miserable and cross. I asked him what he had been doing during his solitary hour in his childhood home. 'Listening to my mother crying,' he replied.

CHAPTER 2

SCHOOL ON THE HILL

*'I have today had to dismiss six boys. They were found
behind the tombstones with women of the serving class.'*

W ith the proceeds of the castle's sale in the bank, and with his
family in urgent need of recuperation from the trauma of
Saltwood, Herbert Deedes did what came naturally to him: he spent
more money. Once Gladys had ruled out any suggestion of emigrating to Australia, they settled on the cold, dry air of Switzerland
as the best way of clearing out the family's lungs and, despite his
socialist principles, he transported his family across the continent in
extravagant style at the beginning of 1926. Agents from Thomas
Cook were employed to ease the family's passage by rail from
London to the south of France, and from there onwards to Geneva.
Porters were handed tips which, Bill later recalled, were 'lavish to the
point of eccentricity'. His father signed a year's lease on a chalet in
the winter resort of Les Avants, above Lake Geneva and across the
valley from Caux. There the family indulged joyfully in the simple
pleasures they had been denied as reluctant masters of Saltwood.*

---

* The house was later bought for eleven thousand pounds by Noel Coward, who was
seeking a Swiss domicile and a less punishing tax regime. The Deedes connection was
maintained because Coward also lived in the village of Aldington as a neighbour of
WFD. When Deedes was an MP the two of them would occasionally share the first-
class compartment to Ashford from London. Coward would invariably greet Deedes
with the clunking double entendre: 'Ah, the Member!' Deedes, who had relatively
relaxed views about homosexuals for a man of his age, but who was never entirely
comfortable in the company of camp men, noted of Coward, 'His handshake left just
the faintest whiff of musk in the palm of one's right hand.'

Bill led his sisters in a packed programme of games and exercise. By day they skied, luged and skated in the crisp mountain air, and Frances's and Gladys's health began to improve. Bill started to keep a diary, fragments of which survive, confirming a fascination with the weather that was still evident in his *Daily Telegraph* columns eighty years later. Each day's entry began with a brief summary of weather conditions, which – in the mountains above Lake Geneva in January – tended to focus on the snow.

On 4 January the twelve-year-old diarist noted that it 'snowed all day', before revealing that he had 'made the aquatance with Bosswall's Life Of Johnson'. With faulty spelling, and clearly struggling with the Remington manual typewriter he had purloined, Bill pronounced Boswell a neglected talent. 'People always say that Bosswall was a shadow of Johnson, and was quite content to stay as such. I think he was a jolly good one. Ask yourself, would Johnson have been able to write a life of Bosswall, like Bosswall wrote the life of him, I think not. By the way, while on the subject of Johnson and his works, how did he manage to compile that dictionary all by himself? Nowerdays men do the same in big lots, and find it difficult enough, it's rather a marvel. Still Johnson was a marvel, so I leave it at that.' He copied out chunks of *Paradise Lost*, and learnt them by heart ('Milton was a marvel'). The mood was gay, but there were occasional indications of the children's awkward relationship with their father. Bill noted that one day after tea, he had 'a long talk with Daddy, but I cannot for the life of me remember what it was about'.

In his diary, there were occasional hints of his father's unreliability. One day Herbert suddenly announced he was moving on to Milan, 'but I am glad to say he changed his mind'. Bill was already showing the first signs of prolific writing: not content with his daily diary entries, he founded the *Deedes Family Gazette*, appointing himself editor and chief contributor and corralling his sisters into helping out. The first issue appeared on 23 January, a day on which there was 'snow all day'.

Frances painted the cover, and several short stories appeared inside. 'An excellent piece of blank verse by Hermione, and another splendid one by Frances, made the Mag the success it deserved . . . after a family tea together we went on to finish it, a good day's work,' Bill noted in his diary.

The children's relief at escaping the dank castle is palpable in Bill's account of their time in Switzerland. Bill, Frances and Hermione put on an ambitious theatrical production for their parents, starting with performances from Shakespeare. Bill completed his reading satisfactorily, but on taking the stage Frances descended into a giggling fit, provoked by Hermione making 'hideous contortions with her face'. The show then descended into complete farce: 'To put the final touch, the curtain cord snapped, and a side curtain callapsed [*sic*], it was a time.'

They were a happy family again, just as they had been in Symnells before the move into the castle. Bill clearly wanted to get closer to his father, but it was a struggle. One day he persuaded the girls to stay in all morning so they could collaborate on an essay for their father entitled 'The Fall of Snow'. Bill was proud of their work, 'and I am glad to say that Daddy was delighted with the results'. But because of his weak health and hypochondriac tendencies, Herbert would not join the children in their outdoor games, and even conversations did not go far. He was only forty-four years old at the beginning of their sojourn in Switzerland, but in Bill's diaries Herbert emerges as a much older, and extremely remote, figure. Bill had much more success with engaging his mother, who was calm and loving with all four of the children

At the age of twelve, Bill was also the most acute critic of his own writing, apologising in his journal for always recording his morning's skiing and skating. On one occasion he notes they had turkey for supper: 'Though I do not as a general rule make a habbit [*sic*] if possible of mentioning food in my diary, occasions such as this special one seem to need a little attention.'

By the end of the year, Herbert had managed to spend a good proportion of the money raised by the Saltwood sale and Bill had to prepare to leave the happy family cocoon to begin at Harrow School in the easter term of 1927. It is not entirely clear why Harrow was selected for him. In later life, Bill would say he was too dim to get into Eton, where his father and uncle Wyndham had gone, or Winchester, the school favoured for the boys in his mother's family. But in his final year at Wellington House he was placed fifth in the school order, rated first-class in classics, English and French, and second-class in mathematics. Nor were his distinctions purely academic: he was a school captain, or prefect. On that basis alone, and excluding the important fact that he was the son and nephew of Old Etonians, it is difficult to imagine how he could not have fulfilled the school's entry qualifications of the mid-1920s. The more likely explanation is that Herbert vetoed Eton because he had been unhappy there or because of some inchoate socialist objection, and that Harrow was selected because Bill's grandfather had been there.

Bill's mother took him to Harrow on the Metropolitan Line train at the beginning of his first term. Beyond their fear of the new school, both were nervous they would get lost, for neither of them knew London well. Bill, a cheerful but slightly anxious thirteen-year-old, spent most of the journey trying not to cry, for he knew it would set his mother off too. Their morale was not improved by his knowledge, from hearing his parents quarrel, that his mother did not regard Harrow as a suitable establishment for her only son.

A large homosexual circle had been uncovered in 1925, eighteen months before Bill was to begin there. When news leaked out about how extensive had been the ring of adolescent sodomy, and how masters had apparently turned a blind eye, Harrow's reputation hit a low. The deeply religious Gladys Deedes was appalled when she belatedly heard of the scandal, and tried unsuccessfully to persuade her husband that Bill should go elsewhere.

While his prep school had been advanced for its time in its generally gentle and civilised outlook, Harrow was relatively barbarous, even by the standards of public schools of the 1920s. The memory of the Great War hung oppressively over the school, which was understandable given that, of the 2917 Harrovians who served, 690 of them were wounded and a further 644 – 22 per cent – were killed. Corps was compulsory for all boys over fifteen, and parades were twice a week, on Wednesday afternoons and Friday mornings. 'Slacking at Corps' was a serious offence, and the automatic punishment a brisk beating.

Fagging was intrinsic to school life, and would remain so for many years after Deedes left. Fagging tasks ranged from warming the lavatory seat or making toast to polishing the senior boy's Corps belt. Its benefits were described by one of the masters, C. H. P. Mayo, in 1928: 'Those who hope to rule must first learn to obey . . . to learn to obey as a fag is part of the routine that is the essence of the English Public School system.' Fagging rituals were, however, often a cover for homosexual activities between the boys.

There were occasional scandals involving masters and boys; sometimes the master would quietly move on to another posting, but usually it would be resolved with a 'quiet word' from the headmaster. Harrow, then and more recently, has had the reputation among other public schools for being a 'queer school'. Cecil Beaton, an Old Harrovian, recalled that sodomy was rampant in some houses in the 1920s, and the playwright Terence Rattigan, a contemporary of Bill's, was a notoriously camp flirt, who had already established homosexual liaisons in London.

As late as the 1950s, when Harrow masters debated whether to abandon the practice in one house of the juniors swimming naked, an opponent of change was emboldened to point out – with the authority of the true connoisseur – that 'a young boy in swimming trunks [is] more erotically attractive to older boys than if he was in the nude'.

As Deedes stressed with some pride in later life, Harrow also had its share of heterosexual scandals. Just before the outbreak of the First World War, Percy Buck, the director of music and a father of five, began a passionate affair with the nineteen-year-old daughter of a housemaster, George Townsend Warner. But that was not the end of Townsend Warner's humiliation – his wife ended up marrying one of the Harrovians whom her husband had instructed in the complexities of the game of fives. Harrow was deeply shaken by a bigger scandal in the year before Deedes arrived: a group of seven seniors had motored down to central London and were caught by police in the company of loose women in a nightclub. The arresting officers ensured the incident reached the newspapers, and the impact was worse because the group of miscreants included the head of school and two monitors. Four left the school immediately, including the head of school. One was spared on the most cynical of grounds: a handy cricketer, he was needed for the all-important annual cricket match against Eton at Lord's the following term.

There was yet another sex scandal in Deedes's final year, as mournfully relayed by Dr Cyril Norwood, the headmaster, in his end-of-term address. Years later Harrovians of that era, on coming together during the War or at social functions, would reduce each other to hysterical laughter by impersonating Norwood's faintly Cockney accent in announcing the scandalous event to school assembly: 'I have today had to dismiss six boys. They were found behind the tombstones with women of the serving class.'

Despite the absence of any medical or scientific evidence to support the theory, public school masters of the era assumed that vigorous sporting activity would dampen the sexual urges of adolescent boys. Harrow was a hearty school, though Deedes's time there coincided with the phased abandonment of Harrow Football, a highly physical soccer-rugger hybrid whose rules were understood only by the masters and boys of the school. The annual two-day cricket fixture against Eton at Lord's was the high point of the school year, partly because it bolstered Harrow's diminishing claim to be the second grandest public school in the land. Deedes recalled going in the summer of his first year, as well as his anxious search for a tailor who could produce a silk waistcoat befitting the grandeur of the event. Harrow ceased to function during the Eton match, and the boys were given two days off for the game, and two days to recover. Before the Second World War it was considered rather off-side if the game did not conclude with a mass brawl between the rival supporters in front of the members' pavilion. Memories of these hooligan episodes of his youth were one reason why Deedes, many years later, failed to join fellow *Telegraph* columnists in condemning the 'yob culture'. He had a lot of experience of it before he left his teen years, even if in his case the yobs wore fancy waistcoats and drank champagne rather than lager.

Sport was taken very seriously by the boys, and even more so by the masters. When Anthony Part, a future permanent secretary, left the school in 1934 his housemaster's final report began thus: 'Although he has not fulfilled his early promise at games, he did become twelfth man to the School Cricket XI. He also won a scholarship to Trinity College, Cambridge.'

Deedes had been placed in the house called the Knoll which was run by J. H. Hollingsworth, a captain in the Great War who had won a DSC in 1918. In those days, Harrow housemasters ran the boarding houses as private businesses, charging the parents separately for accommodation. Most earned a good income, because numbers at the school had risen by some 40 per cent in the decade before Deedes's arrival. This meant that several of the houses, including the Knoll, had become crumbling warrens, overcrowded and unsanitary, and that the housemasters had little financial incentive to make long-term capital improvements when they could generate short-term income by packing the boys in. Deedes never minded physical squalor, whether in the ruins of Saltwood Castle, or subsequently under Army conditions. He did recall in later life, however, that the washing facilities in the Knoll were rudimentary, and that there were no inside lavatories. But he clung to small comforts, remembering the kindness of the Knoll's butler, who would allow him and his friends to play darts in his pantry.

Like all new boys starting at boarding school, Deedes's first concern was to learn the rituals that governed life there. There was a Victorian slang to master: 'groize' was a swot, 'tosh' was a bath and 'eccer' was sport. Younger boys were not allowed to roll their umbrellas or visit boys in other boarding houses. Though lessons were centrally organised, the individual houses were largely autonomous and were the centre of the boys' social existence. Rivalry between the houses, both on the sports field and in the academic realm, was intense. Harrow was a tribal institution with tribal rituals. The birth of a master's son (but not a daughter) meant a half-holiday for the whole school. The new wives of masters were expected to wear their wedding dresses on their arrival at school.

Many years later Deedes recalled that he found Harrow deeply intimidating after the cosiness of his prep school. He lacked confidence as a boy, an affliction no doubt exacerbated by his father's uncertain health and financial precariousness. 'I was unmanly, I was a late starter,' he said of himself at this time. Thus he found himself in his first year in a state of perpetual terror of doing the wrong thing and inviting ridicule, or even a beating, for violating the elaborate code of etiquette. Harrow had abandoned tail-coats in the Great War, switching to grey flannels and blue blazers, or 'bluers'. The bluer might have been informal by the standards of many public schools at the time, but the buttoning was a critical part of Harrow's ceremony. First year boys had to have all three buttons done up; second years were entitled to open the bottom button, and third years and above were allowed to open the top button too.

Like all juniors, Deedes was attached as a fag to a fagmaster, a senior boy for whom he had to perform menial tasks. On his first day he was warned that burning his fagmaster's toast was a beatable offence, and canings were frequent for a wide range of transgressions. Deedes was caned only once – he forgot why – and never by a master, which was unusual for the time. His capacity for navigating his way around trouble, a skill that was to stand him in good stead in adult life, was in early evidence.

Until 1965, Harrow headmasters kept the Punishment Book, recording all the beatings they undertook and noting down any of the serious scandals in the houses, or boys who had to leave in a hurry for the usual, unmentionable reason. To thwart nosey Old Harrovians, the book is now sealed and cannot be read by outsiders, but there is no mention of Deedes in it.*

In the 1920s Harrow still enjoyed a certain cachet, and was producing Tory politicians at an impressive rate – Baldwin and Churchill were only two of that era. But Harrow, unlike Eton, was also by this time attracting many sons of the nouveaux riches or, as Deedes would put it later, 'there was a higher proportion of them than was sensible'. While the landed struggled to maintain their estates in the face of falling land values and poor agricultural prices, some of the parents of the first-generation Harrovians had done very well financially in the War. The father of one of Deedes's friends at the Knoll had made a fortune out of supplying asphalt to the Army. There was clearly tension between the diminishing school population of aristocrats and gentry, on the one hand, and the boys whose fees were paid out of the proceeds of 'trade'. The masters, too, were not shy of entering the debate, and there were frequent rows in the common room over the high number of Jewish boys being admitted.

If Deedes was slightly uncomfortably around the sons of new business tycoons – he had never met their sort before in rural Kent – he was also too shy and lacking in confidence to mix with the pretentious young aristocrats who swaggered around. He also recalled there were quite a few 'coloured chaps', which was novel for him and which he found he rather enjoyed. At one point he shared a study with an Emir 'of somewhere or other'. Deedes

---

* The author was not granted access to the Punishment Book, but Rita Boswell, the Harrow School archivist, agreed to search it for any reference to Deedes and confirmed there was none.

was vague about Middle East geography but, always a bit of a dandy, he had perfect recall of the young Emir's fabulous collection of tailored silk shirts.

Deedes may have performed better than average at prep school, but he cannot be said to have made much impact at Harrow. The only record of any competitive sporting activity that survived in the school magazine, the *Harrovian*, was his appearance in a house match for the Knoll against Moretons in a game of Harrow Football in the spring term of 1928. Deedes played as one of the halves, and the Knoll lost heavily. He played cricket in the summer, but he made no great mark in house matches or fixtures against other schools. Deedes's youngest sister, Margaret, recalled their mother opening his school reports and copies of the *Harrovian* hoping to read of her son's achievements. 'I remember her being rather sad, when every boy had done something, and there was no mention of Bill.'

It is possible he would have begun to do much better in his fourth year at the school. But his father's recklessness deprived him of this chance to shine. Herbert had decided that land was for fools, and that the future lay in stocks and shares. With no experience of the markets, and without taking any proper advice, he sold off all the remaining land holdings and embraced the great bull market of the late 1920s. He piled into all sorts of stocks, some highly speculative, such as a holding in Mexican oils. And then, when Wall Street crashed in October 1929, he was completely wiped out. The final reserves of some 450 years of careful accumulation of Deedes capital were squandered in a few reckless and uninformed gambles.

Even Wyndham, who had been a reliable source of subsidy and had generally stepped in to clear up the mess created by his elder brother's financial incompetence, was unable or unwilling to help out. It is possible that he was so cross with his brother that this time he refused to pull out his chequebook. Bill Deedes knew little about the darkening international financial situation, and nothing of his father's stock exchange gambles. So it was a terrible shock to receive a letter from his mother one morning, telling him he would have to come home.

In later life, Deedes would claim to have only the faintest memory of this episode, but it seems more likely he was willing himself to forget it. There must have been some sense of recrimination at home, if not from Bill himself, then from his mother towards his father, for their son's school career seemed to have been wrecked by foolish investments. In his autobiography, Deedes dismissed his three unhappy years at Harrow, and his abrupt departure, in a sentence: 'I made some good friends there, but was never particularly happy nor successful at work or games.' That memory is only partially accurate, for in fact he later spoke of the deep unhappiness and loneliness he experienced on his arrival at the age of thirteen, and for most of the next three years. Despite his claim to have made 'some good friends', he did not remain in long-term contact with any of his Harrow contemporaries, except John Profumo, and that was only because they were thrown together in the House of Commons while trying to contain the scandal that took Profumo's name. Not for the first time, in his abbreviated assessment of his time in Harrow, Deedes was showing his life-long facility for blocking unhappy memories out of his compartmentalised life.

According to the school records, Deedes's academic record was modest, but by no means disastrous. Some boys at boarding school thrive only in their final year once they have conquered the loneliness and lack of confidence that go with being junior in a large institution. So it is impossible to know if Herbert had cost Bill an opportunity to go up to Oxford or Cambridge, where about 40 per cent of Harrow boys found places. In his final year he was placed at the top of the third of four academic divisions, which suggests he would have had a fighting chance of securing a university place if he had managed to maintain momentum, though he would certainly not have been scholarship material. Instead he departed after three years, having left only the slightest imprint on an institution to which he remained largely indifferent for the rest of his life.

He returned to his family in their rented house on Marine Parade in Hythe, and was taught by a tutor who pushed him hard enough for him to pass his school certificate – which he returned to Harrow to sit – with credits.

Even if he had been able to stay the course at Harrow, Deedes would not have come out at the other end particularly well-educated, because it was not an intellectual, or even an academic school. But by the age of sixteen he had acquired something of more value than a good formal education. From his Irish mother he had inherited a natural charm, an absence of pomposity and an innate kindness; from Effie Sinden's nursery he emerged with impeccable manners and an allied intolerance of lateness or any manifestation of boorishness. And at Harrow, for all its philistine tendencies, he learnt self-reliance. He was not as badly equipped to face the world as it may have seemed. Not for the last time, Bill Deedes was to emerge from a period of adversity only to land firmly on his feet.

CHAPTER 3

CUB REPORTER

'My number had come up, though in circumstances which
many will condemn today as a deplorable example of
privilege, nepotism, elitism – there is hardly a word strong
enough to condemn it.'

It started with the Indian rope trick. When reports reached the *Morning Post* newsroom in late June 1931 that the trick had been successfully performed in Cheltenham before the International Brotherhood of Magicians, it seemed a story perfectly suited for the new boy who had just turned eighteen, and who was so lacking in experience that he didn't even merit a salary. Commendably, Deedes knocked the story down. He had no option, because the man who was supposed to have performed the trick – Professor Bofeys – confessed it was hokum. His assistant, the renowned conjuror Jasper Maskelyne, concurred. 'The whole thing is pure illusion,' Deedes quoted him as saying, 'and although we, together with many others, have given demonstrations of part of the story, the real Indian rope trick has never been performed or witnessed by anyone.'

Normally when a reporter hands in a story in which he has described an event as not actually having happened, sub-editors are liable to place it on the 'spike', where it rests unpublished until it is discarded. Perhaps it was a slow news day at the *Morning*

29

Post; possibly the news editor wanted to encourage his new recruit, who was about a third of the age of most of the other reporters. Whatever the reason, Deedes's three-quarter-of-a-century journalistic career was born with an eight-paragraph story, under the headline INDIAN ROPE TRICK, and the somewhat optimistic sub-headline, REPORTED TO HAVE BEEN GIVEN IN ENGLAND. More than simple pride was at stake: because he was untested, Deedes had been employed 'on space', which meant he was paid only for what got into the paper.

Deedes had blundered into a career in journalism entirely by chance. He recovered from the shock of his abrupt departure from Harrow by spending an agreeable eighteen months in Hythe. He quickly mastered the art of typing at Miss Clough's Secretarial School in Folkestone, and his golf game was soon showing promise. But eventually he had found himself under some pressure from his parents to find gainful employment. His well-connected uncle, Wyndham, was deputed to help out and, only because of the typing, the notion took hold that he might try journalism. Wyndham, who was already paying for most of the family rent and for the girls' tutors, took his nephew to talk to an acquaintance, John Reith, director-general of the BBC. Reith decided that Deedes, then still seventeen, was of no use to the Corporation.

Undeterred, Wyndham set up an interview with Guy Pollock, the managing editor of the *Morning Post*, an ancient true-blue Conservative paper aimed at the aristocracy and gentry. Pollock had craved a gun on a shoot run by another Deedes uncle, Lionel Knight, on his estate in Hampshire. When Knight obliged, Pollock asked if there was anything he could do to return the favour. The uncle mentioned that his nephew had not worked since leaving Harrow in chaotic circumstances the year before. Deedes was summoned to interview in late May, shortly before his eighteenth birthday. The *Morning Post*, financially stretched at the best of times, was short of reporting cover going into the summer so the interview turned out to be a formality: Deedes was told that if he could start the following Monday morning the job was his. 'My number had come up, though in circumstances which many will condemn today as a deplorable example of privilege, nepotism, elitism – there is hardly a word strong enough to condemn it,' Deedes noted in his autobiography.

Wyndham, having secured his nephew a job, then offered him a room in the large house he was occupying in Bethnal Green. After distinguished service in the Boer War and First World War, Brigadier-General Sir Wyndham Deedes, KBE, CMG, DSO had served as an administrator. He was military attaché in Constantinople from 1918 to 1919, then director-general of public security in Egypt for two years, before serving in a similar capacity in Palestine. Then he abruptly withdrew from official public service, retiring to perform social work in one of London's more deprived areas, although in recognition of his high rank he was not expected to slum it. He was granted a large house in Victoria Park Square, which had once been the Bishop of Stepney's palace. It was a substantial home, with six bedrooms and a private chapel that was used as a storeroom. Bethnal Green was then, as now, an unglamorous part of London, but being on the east side of town it was at least convenient for Fleet Street, which could be reached within twenty minutes by bus through the City's then-uncongested streets.

Once again Deedes's young life was turned upside down. After the happy months with his sisters in Hythe, he had to start work in a city he hardly knew. He might have spent three years at school on the northern fringes of the city, but he had only come into the centre for the annual Eton–Harrow cricket match at Lord's. Of the mysterious working class and immigrant quarters to the east of London, or the newspaper haunts around Fleet Street, journalism's newest recruit was entirely ignorant.

Entry into journalism has always been haphazard, but Deedes's position was unusual in that he was joining a national newspaper without any experience whatsoever – no internship on the *Folkestone Herald*, no dummy runs on undergraduate journals.

His new home life was strained, too. It was kind of his uncle Wyndham to take care of him, but he was an austere and somewhat prissy man, no more loving and approachable than his brother. More uncomfortable still was the presence of Bill's grandmother Rose, who acted as housekeeper-cum-consort for her younger son, accompanying him on official engagements. Bill knew enough about her responsibility for the Saltwood disaster to be wary of her, and he knew his own mother would never forgive her for what she had put the family through.

On the night before his starting day, Bill had an acute attack of anxiety, and realised that he had been so nervous before his job interview that he had no memory of how to get to the offices of the *Morning Post*, which was in Tudor Street, just south of Fleet Street. Rather than risk arriving late for the first day of his working life, he had to endure the humiliation of his grandmother accompanying him on the bus. She presented him to the doorman and left, rather in the manner of a mother handing over her son to matron on his first day at boarding school. All through his time at Harrow, Deedes had been nervous and acutely lacking in confidence, and those demons haunted him again as he climbed the stairs to the newsroom.

His first impression was how very old everyone seemed to be. There were a couple of relative youngsters, but none nearly so callow as he. Ian Colvin was closer to his age and, like Deedes, a winner in the nepotism stakes, for he was the son of the *Post*'s main leader writer.* Another was J. C. Trewin, an aspiring drama critic who was regarded as a good 'colour' writer when a more descriptive or wry tone was required by the news editor. But most of the staff were in their fifties or sixties, veterans as journalists or soldiers of the First World War. H. A. Gwynne, the *Morning Post*'s formidable Welsh editor, had covered the Boer War for

---

* Impressive as it was for two Colvins to be working at the *Morning Post*, the Deedeses later trumped that record, scoring a nepotism cross-generational triple crown when Deedes, his son Jeremy (managing director) and grandson Henry (diary reporter) simultaneously worked for the *Daily Telegraph* in 2003.

Reuters alongside Winston Churchill, who was then writing for the *Morning Post*. Even by the standards of the day, it was a formal environment and the staff did not mix much between departments. According to one member of staff, the reporters were 'treated as gentlemen' and therefore expected to give their best. 'There was no harshness and no nigger-driving.' Deedes looked back to his six years on the *Morning Post* as halcyon days, rather as some grown men wax lyrical about their best years at their Oxbridge college. For him, the *Morning Post* was the university he would never attend because of his family's financial collapse. By the standards of the rest of Fleet Street, it was a tiny concern, with no more than ten reporters, so the atmosphere was cosy and supportive. The thinness of the news operation offered an ambitious new recruit an early opportunity to shine, and once his nervousness subsided Deedes sensed it could indeed prove a lucky break.

Many years later, when colleagues stood in a Fleet Street bar with Deedes and remarked on his extraordinary professional longevity, talk would turn to the world around him when he embarked on his career. That world of 1931 certainly seems remote from the first decade of the twenty-first century. Herbert Hoover was in the White House; Ramsay MacDonald split the Labour Party by forming the National Government. In America, where Prohibition was still in force, Al Capone was sent to prison, the Empire State Building was topped out and 'The Star-Spangled Banner' was designated the national anthem. *Cavalcade* by Noel Coward had its premiere at Drury Lane, George Formby emerged as a star and Sergei Rachmaninov's music was banned in the USSR for being 'decadent'. It was a big year for films, with the release of Charlie Chaplin's *City Lights*, *Frankenstein* starring Boris Karloff, and *Mata Hari* with Greta Garbo. Arnold Bennett and Thomas Edison died.

Britain was more rural, and London less dominant over the rest of the country. What later came to be called the media, centred in London, held far less sway. Only three million households had a wireless licence, and the circulations of quality newspapers such as *The Times*, and the *Daily Telegraph* were modest by today's standards. The mid-market papers, the *Daily Express* and the *Daily Mail*, at circulations of 1.7 million and 1.8 million respectively, were growing but remained far below their future peaks. The *Daily Mirror*, the working man's paper, was selling around seven hundred thousand and its circulation was about to take off. Almost all national newspapers in the 1930s were written and printed in a small hub around Fleet Street. Printing mass-circulation papers was an industrial process, requiring furnaces to produce molten lead for the printing plates. Vast reels of paper had to be brought into the heart of London, and the papers taken out again for dispatch around the country by rail.

On the day Bill Deedes joined the *Morning Post*, the consequences of the 1929 Crash were still rippling around the globe. Factories were closing, trade was contracting and unemployment rising. Britain was forced off the Gold Standard, and on the continent totalitarianism was beginning to take hold. The *Morning Post* was not blind to these social and economic trends, but it never really appeared to understand how they would undermine its financial well-being. It preferred to think of its past rather than of potential future problems. Certainly, no paper could boast so dazzling and catholic a range of contributors. Over the decades of its long life, Coleridge and Disraeli wrote its leaders, Wordsworth contributed sonnets and Charles Lamb elaborated jokes at sixpence a time. Thomas Hardy contributed poems, as – inevitably – did Rudyard Kipling, who captured 'the very odours of Empire' and therefore also sat on the board of directors.

In 1900 Winston Churchill, then twenty-five, had covered the Boer War for the *Morning Post*, which seemed delighted that its correspondent had taken his Mauser pistol along and could occasionally put down his notebook and help out the British forces against the Afrikaner guerrillas. He was captured by the Boers during an attack on a British armoured train, after taking a leading role in the British defensive operation. He escaped from military prison – allegedly while on parole – and upon reaching what is now Maputo, Churchill filed to the *Morning Post* the most famous and self-aggrandising dispatch in the paper's long history: 'I am very weak but I am free. I have lost many pounds but I am lighter in heart. I shall also avail myself of every opportunity from this moment to urge with earnestness an unflinching and uncompromising prosecution of the war.'

The *Morning Post* was first for King, Country and Empire, and in the 1930s it attacked Irish republicanism with the vigour with which it once disdained Irish Catholicism. It was strongly pro-French and anti-Bolshevik, but always difficult to pigeonhole because of a certain ideological skittishness that kept its critics on their toes. It demanded the National Government do more for the unemployed in Distressed Areas, campaigned for a national education system and could never see the point of free trade.

By the time Deedes joined, the *Post*'s great days were already behind it, and it was selling under a hundred thousand copies a day. Gwynne was determined that the *Post*'s loss of commercial success should not be reflected in any loosening of the paper's robust political outlook and strident right-wing views. Founded in 1772, the paper was not just the oldest national newspaper, but – as it declared below the masthead – 'The Empire's Senior Daily'. Its first editor, Henry Bate, 'journalist, duellist, dramatist, prebendary of Ely, and formidable pugilist, art critic, and breeder of greyhounds', set the tone for the paper's fighting spirit which it never lost, even as its fortunes flickered and its influence waned.

Its outlook was old-fashioned, its news columns dreary, its leaders occasionally eccentric. The advertisements of that era, at least, offer a snapshot of the emerging consumer society through the widening economic distress. Guinness was good for you, Kensitas cigarettes, a shilling for twenty, were guaranteed not to 'hurt, affect or irritate your throat'. The streets of London were still blessedly free of traffic despite the efforts of the motor industry to turn driving into a mass pursuit. A Bantam Singer, 'the most advanced small car', could be bought in 1935 for £120, a raincoat from Aquascutum for two-and-a-half guineas. The Union Castle line advertised passage to Cape Town for £90 first class, £30 tourist. A house in Oxfordshire with three reception rooms and eight bedrooms was offered at £2000, while a mansion flat in West Hampstead could be rented for £105 a year. In the mid 1930s a professional man's annual salary could buy a family home. Before the mass immigration that followed the Second World War, foreigners tended to stick out in London. The *Morning Post* reported a rally of 1500 waiters in Hyde Park, protesting against the influx of Italian staff in the catering industry. They gathered under a banner that declared: 'We were British in 1914; You be British now'. The demonstration was orderly, the *Post* reported, 'and attracted slight public attention'.

This was the world into which the longest Fleet Street career of them all was launched, though Deedes was so green he was put under the wing of more experienced men for on-the-job training. His first assignment was to accompany the chief reporter, S. R. Pawley, on a two-penny tram ride to Elephant & Castle to interview the owner of a timber yard. The trade was suffering from what the *Morning Post* referred to as the 'red timber menace' – the Soviet Union's dumping of cheap wood on the international market to the disadvantage of European producers. Deedes somewhat impertinently suggested to Pawley that it was not the most exciting story in the world; the veteran newsman put the young pup in his place, informing him that it was not for him to judge, and that the issue of red timber was very important to *Morning Post* readers.

Deedes quickly settled into the Stygian surrounds of the Tudor Street reporters' room, a cramped, airless cabin, which was stiflingly hot in summer. J. C. Trewin described it thus: 'A cluster of desks and swivel-chairs; a green baize notice-board pocked with drawing-pins; a telephone-booth, its walls scored with a palimpsest of names, dates, numbers; an electric wall-clock, that raced when you were straining to catch an edition, and lagged on those dim, forgotten evenings of Sunday late duty.'

The office may have lacked glamour, but the *Post*'s small team of reporters provided a network of tutors and lunchtime drinking companions for Deedes. The reporters would drift in towards eleven o'clock, check the news wires and regional correspondents' cables, then await a commission from the news editor, Mervyn Ellis. Assuming they did not have to go out of town on a story, they would head to one or other of the several pubs within easy walking distance of Tudor Street. The White Swan, next to Temple, was the preferred *Morning Post* pub. Apart from the occasional drink provided by his father, Deedes had no experience of alcohol before he came to Fleet Street, but he was a quick learner, acquiring a taste for mild and bitter at 7d a pint. The reporters would drink two or three pints at lunchtime, and more in the evening, which Deedes later conceded, without much emphasis, 'was far too much, I suppose'.* Ellis, an abstainer from alcohol who had seen too many journalists succumb to the bottle and beer keg over the years, would lecture his young reporters about the need – as he put it – to 'stay clean on the teapot'. The gang of reporters who repaired to the White Swan took his instruction seriously, solemnly raising a toast, 'clean on the teapot', each time they set about another round.

Though most journalists indulged the *Morning Post* in its political quirkiness, one episode in its long history was difficult to brush aside, even after taking account of the ambient anti-Semitism of much of British public life between the wars, and before the Holocaust imposed restraints on what might be said in polite company. The *Morning Post* was a driving force behind the dissemination in the English-speaking world of *The Protocols of the Elders of Zion*, the crass anti-Semitic forgery that purported to reveal how an international Judeo-Communist conspiracy was

---

* Because of *Private Eye*'s spoof 'Dear Bill' letters from Denis Thatcher, Deedes acquired a reputation as a big Fleet Street drinker. In truth, though he drank with lunch and dinner throughout his career, and winced when he saw a journalist nursing a glass of fizzy water, he indulged moderately by the standards of many colleagues and was never seen impaired in the office.

masterminding a takeover of the world. Victor Marsden, a committed anti-Semite who was married to a Russian, had been the *Morning Post*'s correspondent in Tsarist Russia and was briefly locked up by the Bolsheviks after the October Revolution. The *Protocols* were supposedly passed to, translated and edited by an obscure Tsarist official called Serge Nilus, who claimed they had been recovered from the (non-existent) Zionist global headquarters in France. Marsden, an accomplished linguist, set about translating them from the Russian into English after his expulsion from Bolshevik Russia, and they found their way to H. A. Gwynne in early 1920.

There followed an intense debate within the *Morning Post* about whether to publish. The argument was complicated because several *Post* staffers, including the chief leader writer, Ian Colvin, the foreign editor and Gwynne himself, were already writing a companion book to be published after the *Post*'s serialisation, and so stood to profit should the *Protocols* prove to be sensational. Henry Peacock, the *Post*'s business manager, was alarmed when he heard that Gwynne intended to publish the *Protocols* not just as a news story but as a major serialisation. He wrote to the paper's owner, Lord Bathurst, reassuring him that he was 'no lover of the Jews, indeed the older I get the less I like the characteristics of the race'. But he told Lord Bathurst that the *Protocols* were obvious 'moonshine' and that publication would 'shatter the reputation of the *Morning Post* as a serious organ of public opinion and we should be made a laughing stock'. To concentrate Lord Bathurst's mind, Peacock emphasised how advertisers in London might not be so indulgent of a blatant display of anti-Semitism as the *Morning Post*'s country readers. Appealing to his sense of commercial self-interest as much as to his journalistic integrity, Peacock suggested that publication of the *Protocols* could create a situation in which 'the prosperity of the paper is jeopardised and may be destroyed'.

In the absence of any clear direction from the proprietor, Gwynne responded to Peacock's objection by stressing that he stood by the *Protocols'* authenticity, but adding another point in a covering note: 'We have had the reputation for being anti-Jew for three years and *we have flourished.*' Gwynne stressed he was not against all Jews, only those who are 'determined to obtain domination over the world'. He pleaded with the proprietor to be allowed to alert readers to the scale of the problem the world faced. 'Are we, holding these opinions, to stand by and let the Jew work his wicked will on the British Empire, simply because we are afraid of reprisals?' Gwynne won the argument over Peacock, and the *Protocols* were published as a series of seventeen articles between 12 and 30 July 1920, with heavy promotion.

Within weeks the *Protocols* were proved to be a lurid forgery, to the satisfaction of everyone but Gwynne and a handful of the *Morning Post*'s most mulish readers. Gwynne survived as editor, despite the terrible humiliation he had brought upon the paper, and even though he had withheld evidence that cast doubt on their authenticity from the proprietor in advance of publication. When the *Morning Post*'s archivist was called upon to write a piece celebrating the paper's 150th anniversary in January 1922, he pointed to the paper's role in publishing the *Protocols* 'in which were laid bare the causes of the present World Unrest', as if they had never been shown to be bogus.

If H. A. Gwynne was embarrassed by the journalistic fiasco he had masterminded, he never publicly acknowledged it. He remained in the editor's chair for another seventeen years until the *Morning Post* expired. Deedes joined the Post only eleven years after publication of the *Protocols*, so memory of the episode must still have been raw for many of the staff. But he never mentioned the furore when he discussed his blissful early days in the trade.

Deedes may have secured his job by chance and through nepotism, but he quickly proved himself to be a capable reporter, despite his youth and unworldliness. No matter was too trivial to escape his attention: a four-paragraph item suggested that the skill of newly fashionable beauticians, combined with modern concerns about over-exposure to the sun's rays, meant freckles on ladies' skin were facing oblivion. There were reports from cat shows, a speculative piece about the dismal prospects for the hop-picking season in Kent due to inclement weather, a rabbit festival in Bethnal Green and the case of a reader who complained that the Inland Revenue planned to tax the view from his home.*

He applied himself to all these stories with rigour and no little flair, and within a few months he was earning two or three pounds a week 'on space', an adequate income for a young, single man whose bed and board were covered by his beneficent uncle. In October 1932, sixteen months after he started work, Deedes's progress was recognised by his formal promotion to the staff, albeit in the lowly official role as junior assistant to the news editor at a salary of five guineas a week. This was no mean achievement, because the *Morning Post* was sliding deeper into the financial mire. Earlier that year Guy Pollock, the managing editor and Deedes's first journalistic benefactor, oversaw the sacking of twelve staff as a cost-cutting measure and added his own name to the list of leavers.

With his promotion to a staff position, Deedes knew he was now on his way and his reward was ever-more important assignments. His first real splash was a gruesomely detailed report about lions at Whipsnade Zoo mauling to death a man who had tried to retrieve a visitor's hat from their enclosure. In those days the front page of an upmarket newspaper was covered in classified advertising and the main news of the day appeared on a right-hand inside page, normally page eleven, and increasingly Deedes began to fill this slot.

He was already marked down as something of a dandy around the office on account of his well-cut suits from the family's tailor, Huntsman, in Savile Row. He was the natural candidate to be sent to Royal Ascot, where his assessment of the standard of gentle-

---

* In 2006, almost identical stories appeared in the press about greedy councils squeezing hard-pressed council-tax-payers who were being penalised for their pleasant views.

men's dress on a rainy day was withering: 'It was impossible to avoid the impression that many more present could have graced the paddock and more expensive stands in the formal attire of morning coat and dark trousers, had they so desired; and that a damp day cannot really be held to excuse the unusually large number of lounge suits that were to be seen on those who by now must know that Ascot, if it is worthy of a visit, is, at the same time, worthy of correct dress.' Reporters who could turn a phrase were allowed a surprising degree of latitude in editorialising their news copy, particularly when highlighting lapses in a gentleman's conduct, or excessive behaviour by leftists, at home or abroad.

Deedes's career was on a steady upward trajectory, his confidence growing and his writing style improving, when he suffered his first major setback in early 1935. Appropriately enough, given his role in a future Macmillan government as Cabinet minister responsible for information, he fell victim to political spin. He made the mistake of taking as truth a story that was being floated by the spokesman of Sir Kingsley Wood, the postmaster general. Deedes met Sir Kingsley's press man, Braebmer, and trusted him when he suggested the cost of posting a letter would be slashed by a halfpenny from 1½d. It was sensational stuff, the ultimate consumer story, and the *Morning Post* splashed it with real impact. 'Penny Post in Two Months' the headline confidently declared, and for extra effect it ran across three columns rather than the normal two. Deedes reported that with the Post Office making a profit of ten million pounds a year, the radical postmaster general was determined to make the cut before King George V's silver jubilee in two months' time. Not only did it have a direct bearing on the personal budget of every reader, there was a strong patriotic angle too, making it the perfect *Morning Post* story.

Breakfast in Victoria Park Square that morning must have been a lively affair, with congratulations all round for the young reporter's scoop. But by the time Deedes reported for duty at Tudor Street problems had emerged. The story was being adamantly denied by the very man who had leaked it. Braebmer, the prototype of the modern spin-doctor, had given what journalists know as a bum steer: possibly his intention had been to float the idea on Wood's behalf and see what the reaction would be. In this case, it seems the Treasury squashed the idea, realising that Sir Kingsley Wood was contemplating shutting down a lucrative stealth tax in the form of the Post Office's vast annual surplus. The afternoon papers knocked down the Deedes scoop, reporting Sir Kingsley's firm denial. Deedes was summoned to see H. A. Gwynne to explain himself. He feared the worst as he stood outside the office like a naughty schoolboy waiting to be caned. In fact, Gwynne was decent, muttering to Deedes that it 'was just the rub of the green'. The editor's detractors would argue that as the man who had ruined the *Post*'s reputation with the *Protocols*, he was scarcely in a position to discipline Deedes. So he escaped censure, and as the international situation deteriorated the young reporter, now with four years' experience under his belt, was ready for his next big adventure.

CHAPTER 4

OUT OF TOWN JOB

*'The warriors, who had marched through the night stark
naked – to ensure their invisibility in the darkness – met
with little resistance.'*

In later life, Deedes would tell fellow journalists that the only
reason the *Morning Post* picked him for the Abyssinian assignment was that he was young and single, and therefore cheap to
insure. There may have been some truth to this. But, still, it was
a singular achievement for a relative novice, only recently turned
twenty-two, to be sent to cover the biggest foreign story of the
year and one that was to pitch him against some of the most
famous characters of British and American journalism. Four years
of filing reports of the Indian rope trick and sloppy standards of
dress at Royal Ascot had yielded impressive journalistic fruit.

The origins of the Abyssinian war lay in Italy's bit-part in the
European states' nineteenth-century scramble for Africa. Never a
great player in the continent, Italy was aggrieved that it was not
given a larger share of Germany's African colonies under the
Treaty of Versailles. Italians yearned to avenge this slight, as well
as the shameful defeat at Adowa in 1896, when native forces
killed 4500 Italian soldiers, many of whom – in popular mythol-
ogy, at least – were castrated by a mob of Danakil tribesmen who
were reputed to present potential brides with the testicles of slain

invaders. With Mussolini's accession to power in 1922, the need to present Italy as a rising, avenging force became imperative: from 1925, the Fascist leadership began devising plans to absorb Abyssinia into Italy's modest and largely worthless African empire, thus linking the two existing possessions of Eritrea to the north and Italian Somaliland to the south. By the beginning of 1935, as the League of Nations dithered over the breakdown of collective security, invasion seemed inevitable.

Most of Fleet Street had already ordered their star writers to Addis Ababa by the time Deedes was summoned to see the editor one hot August day. The *Morning Post*, in dire financial straits, had put off as long as possible the decision to send a reporter, but as rival papers began splashing increasingly overblown reports of the countdown to the Fascist invasion it realised it would have to take on the costs in order to protect its reputation as a serious newspaper.

Gwynne had covered the Boer War, so he would no doubt have been impressed that Deedes's father and his uncle Wyndham had both served in South Africa. Deedes's familiarity with military matters may well have been a factor in his selection as the *Morning Post*'s special correspondent. The editor provided avuncular advice to his young reporter, emphasising that a dead correspondent was useless to his newspaper and stressing the benefits of a finger of whisky in a water bottle to neutralise nasty bugs. Edward Russell, the austere managing editor, sent a note with his best wishes, before adding: 'If the Emperor tells you – as he told me years ago – that the London policemen are marvellous you needn't bother to cable it.'

Accepting the assignment was a financial bonanza. In addition to his regular salary, Deedes was assured that all his expenses in Abyssinia would be met and that he would get a special hardship bonus of twenty pounds a month, which would accumulate in his bank account while he was away. Moreover, he would equip himself for all eventualities at the company's expense, and though Gwynne urged him to 'observe due economy', Deedes did not stint when he found himself in the tropical outfitting department at Austin Reed in Regent Street.

Deedes conceded that he let rip on a 'lively shopping spree', and was sanguine when Evelyn Waugh delightedly seized upon this to such devastating comic effect in *Scoop*. There was no time to visit Huntsman, his regular tailor, so for the first time in his young adult life he acquired a suit off the peg. In fact, he bought three of them on the *Morning Post*'s account: well-made, silk-lined tropical suits with safari jacket front pockets. Until the end of his life, the jacket from one of these suits hung on his bedroom door, still a perfect fit.

In addition to the suits, Deedes picked out six safari shirts, four pairs of riding breeches (two summer, two winter), a double-brimmed sun hat and a sola topi, as well as long boots to deter mosquitoes at sunset. Deedes did not know how to ride, but the breeches were deemed important because it was assumed that, in the event of an Italian invasion, the only way out of Addis would be on horseback. To convey all this, plus more regular clothing, a camp bed and bedding roll and his typewriter, he bought two large metal uniform cases and a cedarwood trunk – zinc-lined to repel the legendarily voracious Abyssinian ant – with the legend W F DEEDES stencilled on the lid.* After Austin Reed, Deedes proceeded to the Army & Navy Stores, which boasted a specialist tropical pharmacy. From there he loaded up with large, sealed blocks of dark chocolate – emergency supplies in the event of a protracted siege. He also picked out mosquito nets and a tropical medicine chest packed with quinine tablets, which he was to swallow in vast quantities throughout his time in Abyssinia.

Gwynne sent Deedes a long letter warning him – presciently – that the logistics of filing copy would pose the biggest problem. He suggested that the correspondents come to an agreement to arrange 'a system of runners', a whiff of what was to come in

---

* The trunk remained in the cellar of Deedes's home until his death, and was used to store some of the unused and unloved family silver.

45

Evelyn Waugh's portrayal, in *Scoop*, of William Boot's selection of six hockey and six polo sticks, intended – as he explained to Cruttwell, the shop assistant – 'for my dispatches, you know'. Certainly 'kaffir runners', as they were known, were used extensively in the Boer War by journalists and soldiers, and while it would be nice to imagine athletic Africans sprinting through the bush carrying specially cloven hockey sticks from a London department store, it seems unlikely that the system would have been used in the Abyssinian theatre.

When Waugh made fun of Deedes's luggage in his creation of William Boot, he did exaggerate: there was no collapsible canoe, cigar humidor, astrolabe, nor cane for whacking snakes. But Waugh overlooked some of Deedes's other effects. The man from the *Morning Post* had the foresight, for instance, to take a white tie and tail-coat for formal functions, a decision vindicated by his invitation to Emperor Haile Selassie's press banquet. Waugh attended the same event, but inappropriately fitted out in black tie, while many of the other correspondents struggled to find so much as a dark lounge suit. Sadly Deedes, a meticulous record-keeper all his life, did not retain the receipts from Austin Reed so it is not known how much of the *Morning Post*'s dwindling reserves were exhausted on his shopping spree. But we do know that his luggage comprised seven separate pieces, and that attached to his first batch of expenses sent back to the office from Addis was a letter apologising to the foreign editor for the cost of 297 pounds of luggage charged at excess rate.

When Deedes set off for Abyssinia from his uncle Wyndham's house in Bethnal Green, two taxis had to be summoned for the journey to Victoria Station, one for the young reporter, another for his luggage. From there, Deedes took the boat train to Calais, then a fast train to Marseilles where he boarded the Messageries Maritimes steamer, the *General Metzinger*. Despite his new purchases, Deedes wore his favourite London outfit, a double-breasted Huntsman suit, dark with chalk stripe, medium-weight.

He was comfortable enough in the second-class cabin he shared with a man he described as a Turkish merchant called Alfred Roche. The ship teemed with adventurers and spies, all determined to cash in on the looming international crisis. In a letter to his mother dated 2 September 1935, Deedes described an encounter with a devout Nazi, much stricken with seasickness, who had deserted from the German army and – somewhat quixotically – planned to join up with the non-existent Abyssinian Air Force. There was also a Mexican who claimed to have led revolutionary forces in Cuba and elsewhere in the Americas. 'Fortunately both are travelling 3rd so I don't have to see much of them,' Deedes reassured his mother.

Life on board ship was pleasant enough, with plenty of rich French food, which was worked off by brisk strolls and games of deck golf. The only problem was the stifling heat and humidity. Deedes confessed to his mother in his next letter, dated 7 September, that with the temperature now more than 100° Fahrenheit, 'we have descended to eating every meal in shirt sleeves' and that he and most of his fellow passengers no longer dressed for dinner.

When the *General Metzinger* docked at Port Said to pick up supplies and new passengers, Deedes scored a mini-scoop, courtesy of his uncle Wyndham, who happened to know the Commandant of Police. Deedes reported the moment the ship arrived to his mother in breathless terms, suggesting that he might have been cooped up too long reading P. G. Wodehouse, whose novels were read and passed between the English passengers. 'As we docked, a frightfully smart looking English chappie in a gorgeous fez and whatnottery leaped up to me, being saluted right and left, and bore me in triumph off the ship.'

More importantly, the official gave Deedes access to the confidential written records of the traffic passing through the Suez Canal, so he was able to file his first dispatch back to London based on hard data, not the rumours upon which most journalists relied. Newspapers in the 1930s were stringently mean in granting bylines to named correspondents, and Deedes had never before been honoured with one. But set loose on his first assignment as a war correspondent, he appeared for the first time, as he remained for the rest of his life in print whenever his name was used, as W. F. Deedes. Thus on 6 September was born the most enduring by-line in journalism, under the headline:

RUSH OF SHIPS
THROUGH SUEZ
15,000 Italians a Week

The words that followed were not shaped into a traditional journalist's news intro, but couched in a casual, conversational style: 'I learn from an excellent source that October 20 is regarded as a likely date for the opening of hostilities in Abyssinia.' Deedes was right in assuming that war was inevitable given the men and *matériel* being rushed through the Canal, though reckless to cite a specific date for the start of the war, which in fact began on 3 October. But he was relieved to have filed his first piece: his debut war dispatch was barely four hundred words long, and comfortably contained by the *Morning Post* sub-editors within a single column. To put it in cricketing terms, as Deedes might have done, it was runs on the board. And because editors back in London were anxious to catch up with rival papers, which were already trumpeting the dispatches of their top men, Deedes the junior reporter was given star billing as though he were an established and famous war correspondent. For the rest of his time in Abyssinia all of his dispatches, however brief or mundane, were credited to the byline W. F. Deedes and garlanded with his elevated designation as '*Morning Post* Special Correspondent'.

Several journalists joined the ship at Port Said, ensuring that the remainder of the voyage would be lively. Conspicuous among them was Hubert J. Knickerbocker, the splendidly grand American reporter from Hearst Newspapers, who was said to receive his salary in gold bullion and who later achieved a little piece of journalistic immortality on account of an expense claim relating to a stay at the Savoy during the Second World War: 'To entertaining generals, etc.: $10,000.' Grand he may have been, but Knickerbocker took the young Deedes under his wing, reassuring him about the task ahead and offering him tips about the business of foreign corresponding.*

Deedes was clearly exhilarated by his first 'out of town job' – as Corker called such foreign jaunts in *Scoop* – and sent pen portraits of the more colourful characters on board ship back to his mother. The letters were excitedly passed to his three sisters, who were eagerly following his progress across the globe. The cast of on-board characters get follow-up mentions in Deedes's letters. The would-be Nazi aviator is so struck by seasickness that he cannot leave his cabin. 'Of like kidney is the Japanese war correspondent,' Deedes wrote to Mama. 'His English is shaky, his French and other lingees nix . . . When I came down after lunch he was sucking down cold tea, sobbing away, "Verra, verra hot."'

Deedes had no complaints (though his typing was faulty) as the *Metzinger* steamed south through the stifling heat of the Red Sea to the east African port of Djibouti. 'There are now five English journalists, six French, 1 Belgium [*sic*], 1 Japanese, 1 Spanish and a few camp followers, all due for Jibouti [*sic*] and later Addis. Life is much brighter with the Fleet Street chaps on board.'

On landing at Djibouti, Deedes scouted around the fetid port town, interviewed the governor, then fired off his second cable to the *Morning Post*, which was not his finest effort. Betraying his lack of experience – or perhaps merely showing an essential journalistic honesty – he opted to emphasise to his readers his own ignorance of what was going on, and the local people's utter indifference to the

---

* Deedes did not forget Knickerbocker's kindness, and many years later was delighted to hear from his daughter when she visited London. Conscious that Knickerbockers did things in style, Deedes decided against his normal lunching haunt, the rather dingy Paradiso on the Strand, and took her across the road to the Savoy Grill, which had been recently and controversially refurbished to the dismay of its traditional clientele. Deedes was appalled by the changes: the food, the camp young waiters and, most of all, the bill of £150. It was the last time he set foot in the Savoy Grill.

events around them. His cable, dated 9 September, appeared in the *Morning Post* on 11 September, the day Deedes arrived in Addis Ababa. 'In the total absence of any reliable news by newspapers, radio, or other means of modern communications,' it began, 'the population of this town awaits developments in astonishing tranquillity for those so near the scene of possible conflict.' Had he written that intro in London, a wise *Morning Post* hand might have explained to the young reporter over a beer or two that it was better not to alert the reader to the journalist's ignorance.

The only transport in to Addis Ababa in those days was along the French-built railway, starting at Djibouti. Deedes was lucky, as the representative of an impoverished newspaper, that Knickerbocker had secured the *wagon-lit* and then generously invited Deedes to join him in the private compartment for the two-day journey. Knickerbocker, who spoke in a Texas drawl and wore cowboy boots and a Stetson, was an engaging travelling companion, with a large stock of foreign correspondents' tall stories. While the other passengers sweltered in the public carriages, Deedes sat in relative comfort sipping chilled Vichy water as they made their way through the steaming interior. The carriages were supposed to be self-cooling, with wooden-slatted sides designed to keep air flowing, while resisting spears thrown by local tribesmen. Nevertheless, the heat and humidity were appalling, especially during the frequent stops when cattle wandered on to the line.

The climate changed abruptly as the train climbed towards the capital, and Deedes quickly cast aside his tropical gear as the air cooled, reverting to his familiar Huntsman suit, which he was to wear almost for his entire stay. Addis Ababa lies at 8500 feet and was therefore cool and rainy for much of Deedes's time there. He described the climate to his mother as the train climbed on to the plateau forty miles from the capital. 'It was pretty cold about this time and very wet. Rain? I've never seen such stuff. Clouds just broke up and distributed water over the mountains. Scenery not so different from Switzerland, only on a bigger scale and bits of it really queer.'

The arrival of the Djibouti train was always something of an event in news-starved Addis and, in the absence of other leads to pursue, journalists tended to head to the railway station to see which adventurers and journalists were arriving. It was on that evening at the station that Deedes and Evelyn Waugh met for the first time. Deedes made little impression on Waugh on that or on subsequent encounters. But neither did Deedes seem particularly impressed by the fashionable novelist. Waugh was by then a considerable figure on the London literary scene – *A Handful of Dust* had been published the year before, to acclaim – but in his letters home to his mother, Deedes is not moved to describe him in any detail. That may be because he thought a woman living in dramatically reduced circumstances in a quiet seaside town in Kent would have little interest in literary matters. But in his passing references to Waugh, Deedes spoke of him as the man from the *Daily Mail*, and not as a literary figure.

Also present at the railway station was Stuart Emeny of the *News Chronicle*, an old Fleet Street pal of Deedes since the pair of them worked together on the Brighton Trunk Murders, two of the most sensational murder cases of the 1930s.

Deedes was met by a man he refers to only as Salmon, who had been serving as the *Morning Post*'s stringer, or part-time fixer-cum-correspondent, until the staff man's arrival. Salmon had greased the wheels at the Customs Office, so Deedes's luggage could be speedily hauled off the train by a team of porters. Waugh would have watched the transfer as the journalists exchanged gossip, so it is safe to assume that the legend of William Boot's luggage was born there, at the Addis Ababa railway station, on the early evening of 11 September 1935, as the cedarwood trunk, the uniform cases, the tropical medicine chest and the outsize bed-roll were squeezed into a waiting Chrysler taxi.

Any romantic expectations about Addis Ababa were instantly dashed when Deedes caught sight of the capital. It was a shabby, dusty town, peopled with lepers, eunuchs and slaves. The dirt roads ran in muddy torrents during the frequent downpours of the rainy season. The handful of businesses catering for Westerners were run by Indian entrepreneurs, or the tiny rump of Europeans with strange stories to tell. The standard form of building was mud-and-wattle walls topped by corrugated iron roofs. By far the most lucrative venture in town was the cable station, owned by Emperor Haile Selassie himself, and when he fled into exile the following year with hoards of cash, much of the fortune had been provided by journalists forced to pay the exorbitant 2s 6d a word cabling rate.

Deedes spent the first night at the relatively luxurious Hotel d'Europe, but it was five miles out of Addis and far from the main body of the international press pack. He was grateful the next day when a share of a room could be found for him at the Deutsches Haus, a modest but comfortable *pension*, where Waugh, Emeny and Patrick Balfour of the *Evening Standard* had already established themselves. Addis was heaving with foreigners, and rooms to suit Europeans were hard to find. Most of the hundred or so journalists in the city were billeted four to a room at the Imperial Hotel next door, so Deedes was living in relative comfort, and was handily placed to pop round to pick up gossip. Crucially, both establishments were within a couple of hundred yards of the cable station, the journalists' only link to their offices and to the outside world.

The Deutsches Haus was run by a genial colonial German couple, Herr and Frau Heft, who had been forced out of Tanganyika when Germany lost her African possessions under the Treaty of Versailles. Waugh described the establishment in vivid detail, and was much taken by its location at the centre of the Addis prostitution trade. The roads on either side were full of whores' houses. 'Cotton curtains hung over the entrances which were drawn back when the inhabitants were disengaged, to reveal a windowless interior, a wood fire, a bed and usually a few naked children and goats.'

The only drawback was the hotel's proximity to a tannery, which Waugh claimed was run by a Russian prince. When the wind gusted in the wrong direction, Deedes and Waugh would be forced by the appalling smell to abandon their quarters and reassemble in another part of town. The front gates of the *pension* were guarded by a grizzled native warrior who carried a seven-foot spear, and further security was provided by a pair of aggressive geese, which viciously pecked all comers, regardless of ethnic origin. A pig that wandered around the grounds was eventually slaughtered by Herr Heft, who made a delicious range of sausages and pâté.

Addis's extreme altitude played havoc with the constitutions of the visiting press pack, especially those who failed to heed warnings to reduce their intake of alcohol. But Deedes was already reaping the benefits of his formidable constitution. 'The atmosphere hasn't yet affected me a scrap,' he reported to his mother, 'though some people have been badly laid up. I eat like several horses and sleep twelve hours a night. Stores are getting a bit short in the town, and though there is plenty of game and stuff for us, we shall soon be going short on delicatessen or whatever it is.'

The bigger problem for the journalists was the utter lack of news. Over the years, reporters covering the build-up to various wars have written a tremendous amount of rubbish, and Abyssinia was no exception. Deedes was candid: 'There's no news at all. Everyone hares around all day, pays out thousands of thalers to spies and chaps and gets nothing.' The problem for the journalists was that they were all in the wrong place, stuck in a capital city where the authorities refused to release any significant information, hundreds of miles from the borders where the Italian forces were massing, observed by cannier journalists who had had themselves accredited with the invading forces. Apart from Waugh and a couple of other dissidents, the foreign press corps was so pro-Abyssinian that the ad hoc correspondents' association suggested to the Emperor's officials that censorship should be introduced to prevent the Italians getting vital information. This in itself was absurd, because none of the journalists cooped up in Addis had any idea what was going on; and it was to rebound disastrously later, when the Abyssinians found censorship to their liking and imposed a news blackout that meant journalists could not wire even the most banal titbits.

As was to be the case throughout his subsequent career, when Deedes was in doubt about what to report he wrote in detail about the weather. 'Despite confident predictions to the contrary, torrential rains, bringing as much as one and half inches in one day, continue to sweep the upland plateaux and mountains the whole length of Abyssinia,' he filed on 13 September, before adding, with the same dangerous specificity he had shown in predicting the war would start on 20 October: 'It is expected that they will continue for exactly another fortnight – until Sept 27.'

The foul weather was not without significance, because it impeded any early Italian invasion, but such reports were scarcely what Deedes's editors in London would have wanted in return for their considerable financial outlay. In one letter to his mother he estimated the cost of keeping him going in Addis was amounting to £150 a week, a staggering £6900 or so in today's money. No wonder the young reporter felt under intense pressure to perform to the standards of the journalistic stars around him, from both Fleet Street and America.

From Deedes's point of view, there was another problem. The *Morning Post*'s diplomatic correspondent, G. A. Martelli, had cannily exploited his Italian origins to get himself embedded with the Fascist forces in Eritrea as they prepared to invade from the north. As Deedes was filing cables at 2/6 a word, speculating on how long the rainy season would last, Martelli was touring the northern front and sending colourful copy back to London.

Martelli was able to report the significant detail that the Italians had massed two hundred planes ready for uncontested bombing raids against Abyssinian targets. 'I am the first British journalist to whom permission to undertake such an inspection has been conceded,' Martelli wrote breathlessly. His dispatch was obsequious and self-serving, but there was no disguising that it was interesting and exclusive, and far superior to anything the *Morning Post*'s other special correspondent had yet filed from Addis.

Deedes was aware of his colleague's presence in what he regarded as his theatre, and it must have haunted him, knowing that what he and the other journalists in Addis were filing amounted to nothing very much.* In truth, there was only one real scoop of the Abyssinian war, and that had broken on 31 August, eleven days before Deedes arrived in Addis. He therefore was entirely blameless in missing the story; that could not have been said of Evelyn Waugh, who was in Abyssinia but not in Addis. Waugh's humiliation over missing this scoop, much more than Deedes's Bertie Woosterish manner and extravagant luggage requirements, was the true inspiration for *Scoop* because it was in this novel that Waugh got his revenge on those who had beaten him to the story.

The worst thing for Waugh was that it should have been his exclusive. When he travelled to Abyssinia ahead of Deedes, a mysterious Englishman named Francis Rickett boarded the ship at Port Said, immediately arousing the suspicions of Waugh. He claimed he was carrying funds raised by the Coptic Church for use by the Red Cross in Abyssinia. Crewmen kept bringing Rickett, who was the master of the Craven Hunt, shore-to-ship coded telegrams that he claimed were from his huntsman. ('He says the prospects for cubbin' are excellent.') Waugh was a good enough journalist to see through Rickett's absurd cover, but insufficiently assiduous to land the story.

Rather than cultivate Rickett and keep a close eye on him, Waugh wrote casually to Penelope Betjeman, asking her to check up on her Berkshire neighbour but misspelling his name as 'Rickets'.

---

* Many years later, Deedes admitted he had a certain contempt for Martelli. 'I thought, "you're with the bullies, on the safe side, and you can get out. I can't, I'm stuck here."' Deedes did concede, however, that Martelli was a good reporter.

Waugh told her not to use his name in her investigation, and to try to establish whether Rickett worked for Vickers or Imperial Chemicals, or perhaps even for British intelligence. 'Be a good girl about this and I will reward you with a fine fuck when I get back.'

The final sentence was almost certainly a joke, or wishful thinking on Waugh's part: he had long lusted after Penelope Chetwode, before and after her marriage to John Betjeman two years earlier, but she always made clear that she found him unattractive and disliked the schoolboy obscenities in his letters to her (though the pair long remained correspondents and friends).* Letters to and from Addis took at least a fortnight each way, so it was absurd for Waugh to follow up his suspicions about Rickett by letter. Had he wired his office and got a *Daily Mail* reporter to check Rickett's bona fides, he might have got somewhere. Instead, Waugh headed off to the ancient town of Harar with Patrick Balfour of the *Evening Standard*, leaving the legendary figure of Sir Percival Phillips, knighted for his services to government propaganda during the Great War, to pick up the scraps and fashion them into an exclusive for the paper he had joined only the year before, the *Daily Telegraph*. With the full financial power of the *Telegraph* behind him, Phillips ran an elaborate network of spies and stringers who reported back to him in his hotel suite, which he rarely left. He was a highly professional operator as well as a vivid writer, and one who doggedly worked Rickett until he gave him, and Jim Mills, a wily old-style reporter from the Associated Press news wire, the only real news story of the war.

The sub-editors in London did their star reporter proud in clearing out the main news platform, page eleven, for the three

---

* Waugh's biographer Selina Hastings says that she is satisfied there was no affair, though Waugh was determined to maintain there was for many years afterwards. One evening, when introducing his future wife to his parents, Auberon Waugh casually asked his father at dinner if he liked Penelope Betjeman. Waugh replied, 'If you are asking me if I have fucked her, the answer is "yes".'

thousand words Philips had wired at 2/6 a word, urgent rate.* 'ABYSSINIA'S £10,000,000 DEAL WITH BRITISH AND US INTERESTS' ran the top headline in the *Telegraph* of 31 August, announcing that Rickett had effectively bought up the oil and mineral rights to half the country. 'A few strokes of an ordinary black fountain-pen this morning performed the most momentous and far-reaching act in the history of Ethiopia, bringing her out from the Middle Ages and setting her fairly on the road of the twentieth century,' Phillips's dispatch began. As Deedes conceded many years later, through slightly gritted teeth, Phillips's intro could not be faulted.

It was a sensational story, for it meant, on the face of it, that London and Washington were now co-opted into the protection of Abyssinian sovereignty. Haile Selassie, sensing that almost nothing could save him from the impending Italian invasion, had seemingly played a clever card, throwing in his lot with the company Rickett claimed to represent, the dubiously named African Exploitation and Development Corporation. The corporation, no trace of which could be found in London despite its pretensions to being an Anglo-American operation, was registered in the US state of Delaware. It was certainly in no position to exploit Abyssinia's oil reserves, even assuming they could be found. There was fury in Rome at the Emperor's ploy, and consternation in London and Washington, where officials immediately distanced themselves from the deal and urged Haile Selassie to rescind it.

Before long the contract was to fall apart, but in the meantime the *Daily Telegraph* milked their scoop for all it was worth. The issue of Monday, 2 September was largely concerned with the international reaction to the story. 'WORLD STARTLED BY ABYSSINIAN DEAL' ran the top headline. A sub-headline trumpeted 'ANOTHER SPECIAL MESSAGE FROM SIR PERCIVAL PHILLIPS'.

---

* The non-urgent rate was 1/3 a word, but took several days.

The *Telegraph* was really twisting the knife into its rivals, particularly the *Daily Mail*, where Phillips had worked until only the year before, when he fell out with Lord Rothermere. Deedes, at this point, was still on the high seas, steaming towards Djibouti, but there was no excuse for Waugh, who had opted to go to Harar with Patrick Balfour. It was their bad luck that they had together secured a respectable mini-scoop there about the incarceration of a noble French couple, Count and Countess Maurice de Roquefeuil du Bousquet. They had been arrested by the authorities after the countess tried to pass a roll of film, concealed in her armpit, to the Italian consul in Harar. When a cable reached him there from the *Mail*, Waugh assumed it would be a 'herogram' from the office, congratulating him on a story he thought would be right up their street. But instead it read: 'BADLY LEFT OIL CONCESSION SUGGEST YOU RETURN ADDIS IMMEDIATELY.' This is the sort of communication that sends the toughest foreign correspondent into decline. All the excitement of a foreign trip evaporates in the moment of realisation that a rival has got the story, and that the next few days will be spent in that most ignominious journalistic endeavour – catching up with someone else's scoop.

After his undignified order back to Addis, Waugh reacted by flaunting his contempt for the *Daily Mail*, ostentatiously using their abusive telegrams as a spill for his post-breakfast cigar at the Deutsches Haus. But Deedes, for one, was convinced that his failures cut him deeply, creating the sense of resentment that provided the impetus for *Scoop*. The Phillips exclusive, reworked so that the hapless William Boot triumphs despite himself, provided the plot too. Most foreign correspondents having a bad time with the office take revenge by drinking extravagantly at the hotel bar on their foreign desk's account. Waugh sought solace in his hotel room, plotting his novel about journalism and writing home to his grand friends, rubbishing the trade he had expediently entered to subsidise his novel-writing. 'The journalists are lousy – competitive, hysterical, lying,' he complained to Katharine

Asquith. 'It makes me unhappy to be one of them but that will soon be O.K. as the *Daily Mail* don't like the messages I send them and I don't like what they send me . . .'

It must have been especially galling for Waugh, because he was one of the few members of the travelling press pack who knew anything about Abyssinia, having covered Haile Selassie's coronation for *The Times* in 1930. Waugh's vigorous narrative style and eye for detail were well suited to that sort of occasion and to that sort of newspaper, but less so to the absurdities of reporting a war from a capital all but sealed off from any real news, and for a paper like the *Daily Mail*. Waugh was banned from the British legation because he had drawn heavily on it for farcical scenes in *Black Mischief*, and he made no effort to cultivate Abyssinian sources, whom he regarded (not without justification) as inept and mendacious. They in turn were suspicious of him, on account of his being – as he put it in a letter to Diana Cooper – 'slappers with the wops'.

Though Waugh shared the *Mail*'s raucous pro-Italian sympathies, it was scarcely the sort of paper his friends would have read. Arthur Waugh, the novelist's father, had been horrified to hear of his commission from such a vulgar employer, writing to a friend that Evelyn had signed up with 'that abominable rag the *Daily Mail*'. Waugh was conscious that the friends in London whom he wished to impress would have taken a similar view.

Waugh secured another strong story from his great source, the Italian minister Count Vinci, who leaked to him exclusively the news that the Italian diplomatic delegation was to leave Addis. This was sensational stuff for, as Waugh correctly divined, this was the trigger for the Italian invasion. But he elected to file the story in Latin to prevent the wireless operators selling it on to other correspondents. As Waugh should have guessed, there were no classicists on the *Mail*'s foreign desk, so the apparently meaningless cable was assumed to be one of the novelist's little jokes and the story was spiked. Despite this failure, Waugh's biographer

Selina Hastings notes that he was not as inept as others have suggested, and that the *Mail* published more than sixty of his cables in a three-month period in 1935. He certainly wasn't idle, and worked hard to secure the two scoops that failed to make their way into the *Daily Mail*.

The loss to the *Mail*'s foreign desk was the gain of *Scoop* enthusiasts as Waugh concentrated on getting his own back on a trade he despised. There have been other funny novels about journalism – *Towards the End of the Morning* by Michael Frayn is more subtly observed than *Scoop* – but no one has yet matched Waugh's brilliant dialogue or his savage satire in the characterisation of Corker, Pigge et al.

> On Monday afternoon, I was in East Sheen breaking the news to a widow of her husband's death leap with a champion girl cyclist – the wrong widow as it turned out; the husband came back from business while I was there and cut up very nasty. Next day the Chief has me in and says, 'Corker, you're off to Ishmaelia.'
>
> 'Out of town job?' I asked.
>
> 'East Africa,' he said, just like that, 'pack your traps.'
>
> 'What's the story?' I asked.
>
> 'Well,' he said, 'a lot of niggers having a war. I don't see anything in it myself, but the other agencies are sending feature men, so we've got to do something.'

Encapsulated in that exchange of dialogue are the main characteristics Waugh identified in journalists: they are ignorant, incurious and common. Yet a copy of *Scoop* is as likely to be in a foreign correspondent's luggage as a local guidebook, and it is quoted *ad nauseam* by journalists bellied up in bars around the world. Even today, once a 'fireman' is handed his travelling instructions by the foreign desk, the chances are as he strides out of the newsroom bound for the airport, he will be muttering to his envious colleagues: 'Out of town job.'

*

The Abyssinian war, with its exorbitant wiring rates, was the heyday of 'cablese' – an often impenetrable means of communication between office and correspondent using as few words as possible. Because cables were charged by the word, and at half a crown urgent rate, five shillings could be saved by turning 'as long as' into SLONGS. The *Morning Post* had its own code, which Deedes was required to memorise. AALAND meant 'Going, expect delay before next message'; ELBA was 'Please cable more money'. SKELETON meant: the following cable is highly abbreviated, please plump it up in the office. Most of Deedes's cables were sent under the SKELETON advisory, and put into fuller narrative prose by J. C. Trewin, a *Morning Post* reporter who later became a famous theatre critic.*

Thus pleasantries were rarely observed in these exchanges with the office. Despite his shortcomings as a war correspondent, Waugh quickly mastered cablese. When badgered by the *Mail* to follow up a rival's colourful – but fictional – report about nurses being blown up in an Italian bombing raid at a non-existent hospital in Adowa, he took great delight in cabling back 'NURSES UNUPBLOWN' – a masterpiece of enraged concision, and a bargain at only five shillings.

In mid-September, when Deedes came on stream for the *Morning Post*, Sir Percival Phillips was still setting the pace. Phillips's rivals in Addis were growing suspicious of the impressive detail in his colour writing, because they knew he rarely left his suite at the Imperial Hotel. Eventually they discovered his secret weapon – an obscure travel book called *In the Country of the Blue Nile* by Colonel C. F. Rey, from which Phillips quoted liberally and without attribution. O. D. Gallagher of the *Daily Express* had received a stream of increasingly desperate call-backs from his foreign desk: 'PHILLIPS IN TELEGRAPH SAYS

---

* 'My "skeletons" became belles letters', Deedes noted in his autobiography, adding guiltily that Trewin dressed his bald dispatches in peacock's feathers without any public credit.

ABYSSINIAN SPEARSMEN MASSING ON TIGRE FRONT STOP WHAT FOLLOW UP EXYOU.'

The press pack knew perfectly well that it was quite impossible for Phillips to know whether the spearsmen were massing, or indeed if the Emperor's warriors carried spears. But rather than rubbish his rival's dispatches, Gallagher decided to fight fire with fire and procured his own copy of the Rey book. The results were instant and gratifying: 'PHILLIPS BRILLIANT IN TELEGRAPH BUT YOU EXCEL HIM STOP KEEP IT UP.'

Deedes did not keep the cables sent to him in Addis by the *Morning Post*, which might indicate they betrayed a certain impatience with his copy. Over the years, any disobliging letters tended to be weeded out of the voluminous Deedes filing system. In one letter which does survive (dated 5 November), he apologises to Shannon, the foreign editor of the *Morning Post*, for the 'rather lamentable quality of my cables', which suggests gentle rebukes might have come across the wire from London. It is certainly true, as Deedes freely acknowledged many years later, that his early copy tended to dwell too much on commonplace observations about Addis Ababa. There was little to write about because no one in the capital knew what was going on, and the Italians were in full control of the timing of their invasion. Patrick Balfour said that journalists in Addis were as well placed to describe the war on the northern and southern fronts as a Londoner would have been able to report the Jacobite uprising in Scotland in 1745.

Deedes's cuttings suggest that after a few weeks in Addis he realised that the most scrupulous journalistic techniques would yield little. He got the message of what was required, either directly from his foreign desk or by the example of his colleagues' antics. By 8 October, five days after the Italians launched the invasion, Deedes was emboldened to report in some detail a dramatic counter-attack by the Abyssinian forces on the northern front. In common with the rest of the Addis-confined press pack, Deedes was entirely ignorant of what was going on in the regional centre of Adigrat, where there were no communications. But citing 'reliable reports which I have received today' – almost certainly the press spokesman at the imperial palace – Deedes conjured up a splendid image of a commander, Ras Seyoum, leading his men into Adigrat at dawn. 'The warriors, who had marched through the night stark naked – to ensure their invisibility in the darkness – met with little resistance.' Reflecting their delight with the Deedes dispatch, the sub-editors splashed it the next day beneath the dramatic headline: 'ADIGRAT RECAPTURED BY NAKED WARRIORS'.

This was the sort of detail the London press craved, for it reinforced the prevailing view that Ethiopia, never colonised by the white man, was a nation of disparate savage tribes with a disturbing weakness for eating uncooked meat and hanging the testicles of their slain enemies around their necks. In spite of this perception, most of Fleet Street supported Abyssinian independence in theory, and disapproved of the Italian aggression. The *Daily Mail* was the main exception to this, as was the *Morning Post*, though somewhat less stridently. The *Post*'s leaders lampooned the League of Nations, failed to take the notion of Abyssinian sovereignty seriously and opposed the imposition of sanctions against Rome but nevertheless rightly predicted that Mussolini was insane to commit so many men and so much treasure to a worthless colonial possession. In taking this view, the *Morning Post* was strongly influenced by Winston Churchill, who was close to the editor, Gwynne, on this and many other issues. It was obvious that the ragtag Abyssinian tribesman would be unable to hold back the mechanised Italian forces, but both men knew, from personal experience, how difficult it had proved for the might of the British army to subdue a determined guerrilla rebellion during the Boer War. Britain and France were both keen to strike a shabby deal with Italy, to satisfy her ambitions with a trade-off of Abyssinian territory, but Mussolini seemed deaf to any suggestion of compromise. Churchill, playing the role of a friendly critic, offered a prescient warning.

'To cast an army of nearly a quarter million men,' he wrote, 'embodying the flower of Italian manhood, upon a barren shore two thousand miles from home, without the goodwill of the whole world, and without the command of the sea, and then in this position embark upon what may well be a series of campaigns against a people and in regions which no conqueror in four thousand years ever thought it worthwhile to subdue, is to give hostages to fortune unparalleled in all history.'

To his credit, Deedes did not allow the prejudices of his masters in London to shade his reports. Like most correspondents in Addis Ababa, his sympathies lay strongly with the Abyssinians, though after three months he was deeply frustrated by their endless unfulfilled promises to the reporters that they would be allowed to travel to the front. Deedes saw Haile Selassie as an heroic and honourable man who realised that, by avoiding the European colonisation experienced by the rest of the continent, Abyssinia had not yet entered the twentieth century, or indeed the nineteenth century.

A Deedes profile of Selassie, which appeared in the *Morning Post* on 8 October, cast little new light on the Emperor. Deedes pointed out that, despite the vast array of potted biographies that had appeared, 'he is still almost unknown'. He then offered this unequivocal endorsement, which would have bewildered a great many of the paper's ultra-conservative readers: 'The Emperor of this essentially uncivilised country has maintained his balance, his dignity, and his grip.' That may have been true up to a point, although the assessment does exclude the germane fact that his country was at that very moment of publication being overrun by foreign invaders.*

Deedes met Haile Selassie in Addis Ababa only once, and very briefly, on the night the Emperor threw a press banquet at the new palace. Deedes sent a vivid account of the evening to his mother,

---

* To be fair to Deedes, the article had been written at least a fortnight before it appeared in the *Morning Post* for he was under instructions to save cabling costs by sending feature-length pieces by mail.

but in those days it would not have occurred to a journalist from a respectable newspaper to exploit a social occasion to fire off a colour piece for publication. The banquet was at the new palace, a dreary concrete construction likened by Evelyn Waugh to the 'villa of a retired Midland magnate'. This was not surprising, as the palace was closely modelled on the Norfolk home of Lord Noel-Buxton, which the Emperor had seen on a visit to Britain in 1924. But there were some striking flourishes, including the pride of twenty lions that roamed the grounds, and whose roars could be heard across much of the capital and kept the journalists awake at night. The interior decorations were supplied by the London store Waring & Gillow, and the overall effect was fashionable but not cosy.*

The lights went out five times during the dinner, causing problems for the servants, who wore splendid uniforms of gold, scarlet and green, set off by white knee-length stockings and patent-leather pumps. The servants spun around the room bearing vast silver salvers, offering the thirsty journalists large cocktails. The place-cards were extravagantly engraved, and the gold knives and forks bore the imperial crest. Each time the lights went out, the Emperor betrayed not a flicker of irritation or embarrassment: servants dashed into the banqueting room carrying paraffin lamps so that conversations were not interrupted.

'Terrific meal of fairly European quality, rather foul wines of Ethiopian quality,' Deedes reported to his mother. Resplendent in full white tie, he was expectant when courtiers summoned him from the table for a one-to-one chat with Haile Selassie. But any hopes of a scoop, or indeed of hearing his favourable opinion of London policemen, were dashed. The Emperor spoke reasonable English and rather better French, but by nature he was retiring and monosyllabic. Deedes's recollection of the conversation was as follows:

---

* Every stick of furniture, every piece of carpet, was to be systematically carried off by mobs of looters when the Emperor left the capital the following year, and Addis descended into anarchy.

'I am glad you have come to our land.'
'I am glad to be in your land, Emperor.'

Though the dinner ended early, the evening descended into something of an undergraduate riot on account of the combination of the altitude and tetch, a vile-tasting concoction based upon fermented honey. Several correspondents were locked into their rooms at the Imperial. George Steer, the *Times* correspondent, had his door nailed closed and missed a train out of Addis the following morning while waiting for a carpenter who was summoned to free him. Deedes does not dwell on this aspect of the evening's events, but it seems a reasonable bet that he and Waugh – who loathed Steer – were part of the mob that carried out the sabotage. Deedes did, however, report to his mother that Stuart Emeny 'forgot himself so far as to throw a large rock through the Imperial window'.

In the same letter home, Deedes reported another violent incident. 'Sunday we had a frightful smash. Ground wet and our native driver round [*sic*] slap into an Ethiop. Ethiop sent for several sixes.' The driver organised for a friend to cart the poor pedestrian – who may or may not have survived – to hospital, while a policeman 'apologised to white men for trouble caused to white men'.

By the unexacting standards of the 1930s, Deedes was liberal on matters of race. These were the days, after all, when Oxford hearties would stand on Broad Street chanting: 'Bloody Balliol, bring out your black men.' Waugh, the bourgeois minor public schoolboy, fills his letters and journals with gratuitous references to 'niggers' and 'wops'.[*] To Diana Cooper, who did not share his crypto-Fascist sympathies, Waugh wrote that he had 'got to hate the Ethiopians more each day goodness they are lousy', before expressing the hope that the Italians 'gas them to buggery'.

---

[*] Those words would have been used freely by the English talking among themselves in 1930s; Waugh, though, tended to use them, particularly the latter, with calculated contempt.

Several reporters bought monkeys from local traders to relieve the boredom of life in Addis, but only Waugh went as far as to buy a baboon and name it after the local Abyssinian archbishop.* Deedes, the Old Harrovian, in all his letters home to his parents and to the office, does not use a single racial epithet. Waugh viewed the war in terms of a superior civilisation conquering savage hordes. For Deedes, it was about aggression, injustice and the collapse of post-Versailles collective security. From what Deedes said about his mother in later years, one senses she would have thought racial labels were unkind, and therefore unnecessary and slightly common.

Deedes remained in fine health throughout his time in Addis, unlike most of the other correspondents who succumbed to bouts of dysentery and malaria. He took a weekly hot bath at the Hotel d'Europe where the Emperor also bathed, there being no proper facilities in the unfinished palace. Deedes was unaffected by the high altitude, though as a precaution against colds he had accepted the advice of more experienced hands and started drinking at least one large whisky in the evening. Hitherto a mild and bitter man, he told his mother he found it 'tiresome, as I don't like whisky, but it keeps one from catching a chill'. Thus began, in the frigid, damp climate of the Abyssinian capital, a solemn ceremony of a whisky and soda at sundown, which Deedes – convinced to the end of his long life of its health benefits – never abandoned.

The Italians launched their assault on 3 October, but the hundred-strong press corps in Addis was entirely ignorant of the news, which was broken to the world by reporters embedded with the invading forces. They had dramatic stories to tell – the first skirmishes at the front, the first bombing raids. The media contingent in Addis was once again reduced to the dreaded role of reporting reaction and local colour. For instance, after the imperial officials

---

* Small monkeys could be bought for as little as 3d, Deedes told his mother. Waugh soon grew bored with his baboon, claiming it spent most of the day masturbating in the garden of the Deutsches Haus.

released a proclamation announcing the full mobilisation of all Abyssinian fighting men, Deedes jumped into his rented Chrysler and ordered his Sikh driver to head at full speed to the British legation for some informed reaction. Sir Sidney Barton, the minister, had not been told of this key development by his government or by the Abyssinians, so Deedes had the satisfaction of being able to fill him in.

In his reports over the next few days Deedes's clear sympathies towards the Abyssinian cause became even more pronounced. Two days after the invasion, he filed a report dismissing the significance of early Italian advances. Under the headline 'ABYSSINIANS NOT DOWNHEARTED', Deedes's intro read: 'No alarm has been caused by the news from the North that Adowa has fallen at last,' and then speculated that the invaders may well have fallen into a cunning military trap set by the great military strategist Haile Selassie. 'I was informed today by a responsible Minister that the progress of the fighting so far has been entirely in accord with official expectations.'

Looking objectively at Deedes's dispatches seven decades after the events he describes, many of them read as nothing more sophisticated than fairly witless propaganda. 'Simply, humbly, and with great dignity,' he reported on 11 November, 'the Emperor and Empress offered thanks on the occasion of the fifth anniversary of their accession to the throne.' But it is also easy to see why he would have sided so obviously with the lost cause of independent imperial rule. By disposition, Deedes tended to support the underdog against the big battalions, and as a twenty-two-year-old on his first trip to Africa he was appalled that a blameless and primitive native culture should fall under the heel of the unsympathetic white man. There was another factor at play: he tended to respect authority and trusted the officials with whom he found himself at any given point. World-weariness and scepticism informed Waugh's writings about Africa, but they were not part of Deedes's outlook. He was, after all, a decade younger, unworldly and trusting. His reference above to the Abyssinian 'responsible Minister' is typical Deedes: on one level it is sweetly naive, because all of the officials in Addis were corrupt or incompetent; but it also betrays early symptoms of what one journalistic colleague later used to refer to as Deedes's 'subaltern's mind' – a certain credulity, a reluctance to confront authority, an English aversion to making a scene.

Despite their different personalities, political views and the ten-year age gap, Waugh and Deedes spent a lot of time together in Abyssinia. Apart from both boarding at the Deutsches Haus, they would frequently join the press crowd at the two Addis cinema clubs, Le Perroquet and Mon Ciné, which showed old American films and had large bar areas that doubled as nightclubs. Deedes would try to keep pace with Waugh's consumption, but was defeated by his preferred drink, a dubious cocktail of cognac and crème de menthe. One night Deedes witnessed Esmé Barton, the daughter of the British minister, dash a glass of champagne in Waugh's face at Le Perroquet in revenge for his having lampooned her, thinly disguised, as Prudence Courteney in *Black Mischief*.*

The Barton daughters, Esmé and her older sister Marion, were a spirited pair who kept the nightlife in Addis interesting with their 'poppet list' of eligible young men about town. Marion eloped with a virile Italian horseman and married him in Rome, then set up home with him in the remote Abyssinian town of Debra Marcos, where her husband served as consul. Shortly after the birth of their first child, Marion began a brisk affair with another Italian diplomat, which reached a peak of passion in August 1935, just as the international press pack was arriving in Addis. Her husband reacted to her infidelity in spectacular fashion, shooting himself in the chest. The press delicately reported that he had injured himself accidentally while shooting game with his pistol. But Sir Sidney Barton was furious with his daughter for

---

* Esme later became the second wife of George Steer, the *Times* correspondent in Addis, whom Waugh particularly loathed.

making such a spectacle of herself and did not speak to her again until he was on his deathbed.

As the likelihood of an invasion increased, the nightlife in Addis became ever more lively. Deedes was on hand late one night when Waugh and Knickerbocker squared up to each other after the American let slip, at the end of a long session of poker, that Waugh and Aldous Huxley were his two favourite writers. Waugh, who loathed Huxley's writing and was always quick to take offence with Americans, regarded this as a gross impertinence that could only be settled the old-fashioned way. Deedes held Knickerbocker's spectacles as the American grappled briefly with Waugh on the lawn of the Imperial Hotel, but no serious punches were thrown before honour was satisfied.

Knickerbocker, however, added insult to injury by taking fifty dollars from Waugh, and ten from Deedes, by casually wagering them over dinner one evening that he could get within fifteen miles of the fighting. The very next day he set off in a chartered plane, flew around the front, taking fifty photographs and three hundred yards of film, and, most thrillingly, took a bullet in the wing over Adowa. The Rickett scoop aside, this was undoubtedly the top stunt of the war and Deedes never learned how Knickerbocker had managed to procure a plane or get clearance to fly.

Days became intolerably tedious in the capital as the journalists realised they were never going to find out what was going on at the southern and northern fronts. Most days they would wake up with thick hangovers made worse by high-altitude grogginess. Breakfast would be a leisurely affair and then they would begin the round of daily calls, to the palace and the various legations. Waugh, who could ride well, taught Deedes the basics, partly for something to fill the day but also as an alternative way out of the capital should the railway line to Djibouti be bombed by the Italians. There was a not unreasonable assumption among the small expatriate contingent in Abyssinia that large-scale air raids or a bloody Italian march on the capital would trigger a massacre of whites in Addis Ababa. Sir Sidney Barton was nervous that the British mission could be attacked and, though he was much lampooned by Waugh and others for his caution, he had the foresight to instruct London to send a protective force of 140 Sikhs and three British officers, a precaution amply justified in 1936 when serious rioting erupted as the Emperor fled. Deedes and Waugh were far less inclined to panic than many of their colleagues, but both of them realised it was possible that they would have to escape in a hurry.

The tedium of life in Addis had become intolerable by November, so Waugh, Emeny and Deedes plotted a trip to Dese, whither it was assumed the Emperor would transfer his court when the Italian forces got too close to the capital. That way, Deedes could honour his commitment to the *Morning Post*, which was adamant he should stay close to 'headquarters'. As Deedes recounted to his mother, the trip to Dese got off to a disastrous start before it began, when the Abyssinian driver spent his advance on wages on tetch and a gun, went on a rampage around town, shot up a brothel and was locked up in prison. Waugh, Emeny and Deedes finally set off to find the war front with a new driver. They left town with six servants, in a Chevrolet lorry flying a Union flag and with the names of their three newspapers painted on the side. They assumed orders would be sent down the line to recall them, so as a precaution they snipped the telephone line – an uncharacteristically reckless act for Deedes – which ran the course of the dirt track linking Addis to Dese.

Some fifty miles out of the capital they hit their first roadblock. They learned later that Haile Selassie had personally ordered this press convoy be stopped, but the local chief, showing commendable independence of mind and taking account of Abyssinia's somewhat devolved system of government, said that as the three correspondents' papers were in order they must be allowed to proceed. The journalists' luck ran out further up the road, when frantic messages from the Imperial Palace finally got through. The trio spent an uncomfortable night under canvas, guarded by soldiers – 'armed chaps, very decrepit indeed, but armed . . . and formed a jolly semi-circle round our tent', as Deedes described it to his mother. As the soldiers menacingly clicked their rifle bolts, the reporters ate well and drank whisky under the stars, before heading back to Addis, under duress, the next morning. Waugh refused to accept Deedes's protestations that he was not a bridge player, and was then unforgiving when it turned out he really couldn't play. Deedes vowed that if he made it back safely to Addis he would never play bridge again. He kept that promise for the rest of his life.

The journey back to the capital was dispiriting: they had been thwarted in their ambition to hear a shot fired in anger, but Deedes still milked it in best Fleet Street tradition. 'OUR CORRESPONDENT HELD PRISONER' declared one of the four headlines above his 18 November dispatch. 'TWENTY HOURS TRYING TO TELEPHONE' read another, making much of the inadequacies of the Abyssinian infrastructure. 'After three adventurous and somewhat hazardous days in the interior,' Deedes began his report, 'I succeeded in penetrating 100 miles north in the only journalist's caravan which has so far left Addis Ababa in this direction.' Deedes was also able to report, based on a local source he encountered, on a mutinous skirmish within the Abyssinian forces between the crack armed troops and the more traditional tribal warriors who carried only spears and were jealous of their rivals' superior kit. Characteristically, Deedes was concerned in a way that Waugh certainly would not have been that the Palace would be angry with the journalists for their independent action. But he was able to reassure his mother that 'the British Legation was delighted', and that over at the Palace the Emperor 'thought it a goodish show and laughed a bit, so we are all right'.

The *Morning Post* did its best to project its special correspondent's derring-do, but Fleet Street's appetite for the Abyssinian story was already diminishing. Most of the correspondents were being recalled as the expense claims and cable bills rolled in. Deedes made one more trip out of the capital to Harar, in the east, where he was nauseated to see the scarred Abyssinian victims of the Italian mustard-gas bombing raids. This was the first time – but not the last – in a lifetime's reporting of war that he realised that civilians tended to become the lasting victims when armies fight.

While in Harar, on 30 November, Deedes received a cable from his office, which must have come as a relief: 'What about coming home?' He needed no second bidding; he could be home for Christmas. Mervyn Ellis, news editor of the *Morning Post*, wrote to Deedes's father at Marine Parade in Hythe to tell him his son had been recalled. 'Please understand that his coming home does not in any way imply the slightest dissatisfaction with his work . . . His stuff has been excellent, and he has kept his head in very difficult circumstances.'

The latter point was undoubtedly true. For a young man of just twenty-two, who had never travelled outside Europe, Deedes had shown commendable fortitude and initiative, holding his own against much older, more experienced and more cynical Fleet Street hands in an alien and difficult African environment. But in truth his coverage, though adequate, was rarely inspired. He did not conspicuously fail, as Waugh had done, but he cannot be said to have had a good campaign, like Phillips of the *Daily Telegraph*, or Steer of *The Times*, whose exclusives were shamefully under-played by his editors in London. Even so, Deedes had reason to feel pretty satisfied with himself when he boarded the boat home at Djibouti on 8 December. The young man who had been forced to leave school in humiliating family circumstances, and whose hopes of going to university had been dashed because of financial disaster, had secured an extraordinary three-month crash course in journalism and in life. He had met such legendary American correspondents as Knickerbocker, and learnt at their knee. He had seen the first test of the post-First World War order, the rise of Fascism, poison gas attacks and their hideous consequences.

He had boarded with the most fashionable young English novelist of the interwar years, and travelled towards war zones with him. In later life Deedes would say that the best thing that ever happened to him was that his father had squandered the thousands of acres that should rightly have been passed to him, thus forcing him to get a job and embrace the twentieth century, and to seek an education in Abyssinia far superior to anything his contemporaries found at university.

CHAPTER 5

AT WAR WITH WAUGH

'Waugh was a natural shit . . . he knew he was a pig, he
knew of his awfulness, which is why he clung to his
Roman Catholicism as it was something he hoped would
redeem him.'

One of the oddities of Waugh's non-fiction writing about Abyssinia is that Deedes does not merit a single mention. Apart from Patrick Balfour, Deedes spent as much time as anyone with Waugh in the three months from mid-August 1935. Yet there is no reference to Deedes in Waugh's letters from Abyssinia, no acknowledgement that he might have found an ideal hero for a comic novel about journalism. None of Waugh's diaries from this period survives. His grandson, Alexander Waugh, believes he probably destroyed them after incorporating the parts he needed into *Scoop* and *Waugh in Abyssinia,* his non-fiction (though not entirely truthful) book about his experiences.

Stuart Emeny, whom Waugh actively disliked, features in *Waugh in Abyssinia* as 'the Radical'. He earned Waugh's contempt partly because of his suspect left-wing views, but also on account of his striking lack of physical courage, which Deedes also observed, but more indulgently. Emeny was a fusser, who worried about the smallest insect bite and headed to the hills outside Addis Ababa the moment war was declared, fearing Italian air raids. Waugh also heartily disliked George Steer, the *Times*'s South African-born correspondent, who – like Deedes – had ill-disguised sympathies for the Abyssinian cause, and went on to achieve fame for breaking the story of German responsibility for the atrocity at Guernica in April 1937. Small and slight, Steer was described by Waugh alternately as 'a zealous young colonial reporter' and 'a very gay South African dwarf'.

Waugh may have been jealous of Steer because he was working for *The Times*, which had sent him to cover the Emperor's coronation five years earlier, and was the sort of newspaper his friends read. Steer was having a conspicuously good Abyssinian war, exploiting his excellent contacts with the palace, which ensured that he was granted exclusive interviews with Haile Selassie and given special leave to travel outside the capital.

Steer supposedly owed his unique access to a joke played on him by his fellow South African, the *Daily Express* man O. D. Gallagher. Gallagher slipped a fake cable, purporting to come from Lord Astor, then owner of *The Times*, into his bundle of messages from London. 'NATION PROUD YOUR WORK STOP CARRY ON IN NAME YOUR KING AND COUNTRY.' The message was intercepted by palace spies, who were so impressed by Steer's status that Haile Selassie ordered he be given the run of every ministry.

Nicholas Rankin, Steer's biographer, suggests there could have been another reason for Waugh's antipathy. Steer might have been short in stature and colonial in origin, but he had been to Winchester and Christ Church, Oxford, rather than Waugh's minor public school, Lancing, and his unfashionable college, Hertford. Steer, a brilliant scholar, took a double first in Greats, whereas Waugh had scraped a third in history.

Late in life Deedes would say that he took it as a compliment that he escaped being savaged in Waugh's letters home, or in *Waugh in Abyssinia*. Nevertheless, he seemed slightly bewildered, and perhaps a little hurt, that Waugh had rated his role in Abyssinia so minor as not to deserve any mention at all. Selina

Hastings, Waugh's biographer, suggests Deedes was 'too young and probably too un-neurotic properly to engage Waugh's attention'. Certainly, ten years Waugh's junior, Deedes was far removed from Waugh's world and very different from the sophisticated literary–aristocratic circle in which Waugh moved in London. During his time in Abyssinia, Waugh was much preoccupied with securing an annulment of his marriage to his unfaithful first wife so he could marry Laura Herbert. None of this he discussed with his young colleague from the *Morning Post*, even when they were drinking heavily and in danger from jumpy Abyssinian soldiers during their night together under canvas, circumstances in which journalists abroad tend to open up to one another. Waugh was sexually frustrated, eyeing the ugly Abyssinian prostitutes ruefully while keeping his distance and complaining in a letter that he had been abstinent since leaving London. Deedes seemed undisturbed by sexual yearnings, and was almost certainly entirely inexperienced with women.

The notion that Deedes was the inspiration for Boot followed him around for his entire career. In a BBC film based on his family memoir *Fathers and Sons*, Alexander Waugh asserted that Boot was closely modelled on Deedes, but he provided no evidence from the family archive to support this claim. It is not clear when the idea took root, and who promoted it. Evelyn Waugh certainly never did anything to encourage it. His son Auberon displayed much more warmth towards Deedes than his father ever had, based on their working together in the early 1960s on the *Telegraph*'s Peterborough column. 'I have never known a man with less side to him – always cheerful, always friendly, always polite, always one of the boys threatened by authority from above,' Auberon Waugh wrote in his autobiography, *Will This Do?*

In that book, Auberon Waugh suggested erroneously that Deedes and his father had together covered the coronation of Haile Selassie in 1930. He also described Deedes as a cub reporter on the *Morning Post*, which was not an accurate reflection of his standing on the paper by 1935. 'My father's novel about journalists was his [Deedes's] Bible,' Auberon Waugh recalled. He added that his father had always referred to him as 'Young Deedes' and, rather to his surprise, Auberon found that that was precisely how the former junior minister and holder of the MC was known around the *Telegraph* office in the 1960s.

Though Waugh father and son had clearly discussed Deedes, Evelyn did not tell Auberon that he was the model for William Boot. That does not of itself prove Deedes was not, but it would seem odd that Evelyn did not mention it to his son if it were the case, when Auberon started working at the *Telegraph*. As for Deedes, over the years he rebutted suggestions that he was the inspiration for Boot, yet he did so in a way that did nothing to discourage the speculation. He seemed to enjoy the riddle, for it added to his celebrity, and was a jolly good joke. When his books were published, the notion that Deedes was Boot was left hanging in the air. 'Many assume him to be the model for Boot in Evelyn Waugh's classic novel *Scoop*,' reads the flyleaf to his autobiography, *Dear Bill*, offering plenty of encouragement for those who wished to believe it.

There is no doubt that Waugh would have found Deedes's famous Abyssinian luggage hilarious. In some respects, Waugh's description of William Boot's home, Boot Magna Hall, with its pleasing sense of genteel decay and the numerous old retainers and dependants, sounds like Saltwood Castle in the days before the Deedes family were forced to sell up. Boot's Uncle Theodore stares through the morning-room window and sings: 'Change and decay in all around I see.' On the basis of what his children subsequently said, it is quite possible to imagine Deedes's own father singing exactly the same line (from the hymn 'Abide with Me'). With his burning social aspirations, Waugh must have been quite intrigued that Deedes had grown up in a castle and was from an ancient Kentish family.

On the other hand, Deedes was unlike Boot in many more obvious ways than he was similar. By the time he left for

Abyssinia in the summer of 1935, Deedes was a young man about town, a party-goer, living in the East End of London, with four years of experience in journalism under his belt. He would scarcely have known where to start if required to write a weekly instalment of 'Lush Places'. There is a photograph of Deedes taken as he prepares to leave for Abyssinia, with his giant bed-roll visible at the bottom of the picture. He stares confidently into the camera, looking sophisticated and metropolitan, not timid and tweedy like a *Scoop* reader's image of William Boot. Ever the dandy, Deedes is positively rakish in the double-breasted suit that was unexpectedly to see so much service in chilly Addis Ababa.

It is difficult to sustain the notion that William Deedes was in any important sense the *model* for William Boot. It is much easier to conclude that the sight of Deedes and his quarter-ton mound of luggage at Addis Ababa railway station inspired Waugh in the direction of his brilliant comic creation. Deedes's eager youthfulness can be seen in Boot, but in truth that is all the young man from the *Morning Post* brought to the hero of *Scoop*.

Towards the end of the novel, Waugh introduces the character of Bateson, an eager young cub reporter on the *Beast* sent to meet Boot's train at Victoria station. Bateson announces he is only 'on space' at the *Beast*, the terms on which Deedes had joined the *Morning Post* and a phrase he used frequently in later years. Bateson makes much of having obtained a diploma in journalism from a correspondence course; Deedes had gone to secretarial college to learn to type before beginning his career. Bateson is anxious to use his expense account for the first time, so persuades Boot to join him for a drink. Bateson orders whisky, the spirit young Deedes had learned to consume in Addis Ababa to ward off chills. Bateson is in love with the idea of being a journalist: 'It's a great profession, isn't it?' he exclaims to the weary, non-committal Boot. This is exactly what Deedes thought from the beginning of his career until the very end, a view Waugh would have thought risible. It is quite possible that Deedes's colleagues, and the legions of *Scoop* connoisseurs, have been looking in the wrong direction: Deedes, perhaps, was never Boot, but Bateson. It is also quite feasible that Deedes knew this perfectly well, but chose to keep quiet so as not to kill an amusing myth that did his career and reputation no harm.*

One of the most inadequate chapters of Deedes's autobiography was the one devoted to Abyssinia. It runs to just eleven pages, much of it quotation from other people's sources. Perhaps Deedes did not wish to dredge up memories from sixty years before; possibly he did not wish to pick a fight with Waugh's children, particularly Auberon, whom he liked very much and who was still alive when the book appeared. Whatever the reason, that chapter's shortcomings left a gap in the market, and six years later Deedes was persuaded by his publisher to write a short memoir of his three months in Abyssinia, *At War with Waugh*.† In many respects it is a charming little book, but still it pulls its punches in dealing with Waugh, despite the punning promise of its title. Only towards the very end of his life, and after prompting from his biographer, was Deedes prepared to acknowledge how much he disliked Waugh.

In both *Dear Bill* and *At War with Waugh*, Deedes offers enough evidence to suggest he had strong reservations. Yet he still emphasises Waugh's qualities rather than his faults. Deedes admired his novels and retained an unrequited interest in him to the end of his life. He owned and had read almost all of Waugh's novels and other writings, his letters and diaries, and several biographies. Deedes regarded Waugh as a brilliant novelist and was particularly haunted by the bleakness of the marital disintegration portrayed in *A Handful of Dust*. He thought Waugh a better journalist than he gave himself credit for. He admired his courage:

---

* The author is grateful to Boris Johnson, who first alerted him to the Bateson–Deedes theory. Johnson enjoyed his share of *Scoop*-like capers in his years on the staff of the *Daily Telegraph* before he became MP for Henley.

† Deedes claimed he was reluctant to write a second book, but had eventually agreed because he was embarrassed his autobiography had failed to earn back its substantial advance.

as Deedes put it, Waugh was not just brave, he was oblivious to danger, and was to prove that point again as a soldier during the war. When the Abyssinian war started and the despised left-winger Emeny and most of the American journalists ran for the hills, Waugh flaunted his contempt for their cowardice and thought it would be hilarious if the Italians came and bombed the journalists' hotels in Addis. Waugh had a natural authority, too, which Deedes, the younger man, found impressive and hard to emulate.

In the end, however, what Deedes could not take about Waugh was his snobbery, both towards those he regarded as his social inferiors but also towards journalists in general. Deedes took the view that journalism was a privileged calling, and that there could be nothing better than being part of that gang. Fellow hacks at the Deutsches Haus or the Imperial Hotel were colleagues not rivals, even if, all other things being equal, you would have had little in common with them. The one journalist in Addis whom Waugh regarded as a true friend was Patrick Balfour of the *Evening Standard*, but he was the future Lord Kinross.

Deedes particularly disliked the way in which Waugh spoke about the journalists he regarded as below the salt, and lampooned them in *Scoop*. 'Shumble, Whelper and Pigge knew Corker; they had loitered of old on many a doorstep and forced an entry into many a stricken home.' Shumble, Whelper et al drive many of the best comic moments in *Scoop*. They were the composite representatives of the grunts of the Abyssinian pack – the freelancers and photographers and back-up men, cockneys and colonials, living on their wits and scraping by on payments from financially precarious papers such as the *Daily Graphic* and the *Daily Sketch*. Waugh despised these men even more than he deplored Emeny and Steer; Deedes found in them the qualities which he later came to value in his non-commissioned officers when he was a company commander in the war.

On the sailing back to Europe from Djibouti, Deedes was taken ill one night with acute stomach pains. He asked a photographer,

Tovey,* to summon the ship's doctor. When the doctor would not immediately attend, Tovey stayed with Deedes to make sure he was all right until he could be properly examined. 'Though ostensibly there was a fierce rivalry between reporters,' Deedes noted in *At War with Waugh*, 'there was also a kinship which Waugh had no wish to share.'

Nothing illustrated the gulf in attitude to the kinship of the trade more than their respective attitudes to the only journalistic casualty of the war, the *Chicago Tribune*'s correspondent Wilfred Courtney Barber. Given how remote the journalists were from the action, Barber's death was appropriately absurd. The scene was earnestly described by an American colleague who had witnessed Barber's final act of reporting at the outdoor Maskal imperial ceremony, supposedly marking the end of the rainy season, at which the thirty-two-year-old reporter caught the chill that was to kill him.

> Barber, a correspondent in morning coat, striped trousers and silk hat, walked out into the mud and rain and water before the Emperor. Taking off his hat, he bowed low and then exposed several films of his camera. Bowing again, he replaced his dripping hat and, soaked through, walked gravely back to the grandstand. He had received his suit only that morning from his wife. It had required two months to reach Addis. But it was a swell exhibition.

This was all too ludicrous for Waugh, who also witnessed Barber's bizarre performance, especially when he learned of his bathetic last words: 'I am going to get better because I have to; I have to cover the war.' He then expired. Waugh wrote to Diana Cooper about the death of 'a very dull chap' who had resigned from the ad hoc correspondents' association in Addis in protest at

---

* Defenders of Waugh might argue that Deedes's point would carry more force had he remembered Tovey's Christian name.

Waugh's flippant reaction 'when a French journalist who is a 5 to 2 [Cockney rhyming slang for Jew] complained he was called a cochon francais by a nigger. Well this American went to maskal in a stove hat and tale coat [*sic*] & did he get wet yes sir so he is dead and we bought a wreath from the bosche legation garden and some of us have black ties and some not . . .'

Deedes, by contrast, was deeply affected. 'We are very depressed today [he wrote to his mother] at the news that W Barber . . . died in hospital this morning after a week's illness.' He detailed at length how the reporter, 'a very pleasant American', had been weakened before he caught his chill by a severe bout of malaria picked up at Harar: 'The Emperor, one of his ministers tells me, is quite distressed.' If Deedes saw anything funny in the whole rigmarole, which is unlikely, he chose not to pass it on to his family.

By temperament, age and background, Deedes and Waugh were too different to be intimates in Abyssinia, or friends thereafter. The young reporter must have held his tongue with mounting irritation as Waugh noisily aired his pro-Italian, pro-Fascist views at the breakfast table at the Deutsches Haus. Several of the correspondents at one of the cinema clubs were appalled when Waugh, in the presence of high Abyssinian officials, began wildly clapping Italian soldiers featured in a newsreel film. One American correspondent feared there could be a violent racial incident, but the Abyssinians sat impassively through Waugh's performance, though they were clearly annoyed.

Waugh did not see himself as part of the journalistic fraternity, but as one who stood apart from it and superior to it, which, given his talent, might not be seen as unreasonable. But Deedes resented this, however much he denied it. Deedes eventually conceded that he had dodged the issue by writing a whole book on his time with Evelyn Waugh without making clear what he really thought of him. 'It's not my nature,' he said by way of explanation, 'life's too short' (he was ninety-two at the time). But he conceded that it was 'a bit feeble' to have written a book called

At War with Waugh without actually revealing where the battle lines lay. Then Deedes belatedly warmed to his theme: 'Waugh was a natural shit,' he said. 'It is true that I never wrote of his deep inner contempt for everyone. *Scoop* shows his contempt for journalism and for the lower classes. He knew he was a pig, he knew of his awfulness, which is why he clung to his Roman Catholicism as it was something he hoped would redeem him.'

This was strong stuff for Deedes, who was rarely one to speak ill of others, or pick fights, or create a scene.* Characteristically, he never told Waugh to his face what he thought of him. 'I think he found me a bore; I found him a snob, but we were very civil, never a cross word,' he said of their three months together in Abyssinia. There was never any question of lunch at White's or the Carlton to discuss their adventures in Abyssinia, though Deedes wrote Waugh a letter of commiseration when his son Auberon contrived to shoot and critically wound himself during his National Service in Cyprus in 1958. Waugh replied with a postcard which read only: 'Thanks awfully. EW.' Deedes got the message. 'Our paths did not cross again,' he noted waspishly in his autobiography.

Waugh's partisanship reached its apogee in his book *Waugh in Abyssinia*, a preposterous justification of the Italian occupation published in 1936 when the absurdities and brutalities of the Italian military undertaking were already obvious.

In her famous denunciation in *Horizon*, Rose Macaulay described it as 'an odd and rather unchivalrous book', before asking: 'What is his motive? Support of a policy endorsed by the Italian clergy. Very probably. Dislike of the League of Nations? Again, likely enough. Or merely sympathy with the big battalions?

---

* As shall be seen, Deedes was much preoccupied with what amounted to a dignified death. In his final years at the *Telegraph*, long after he had vacated the editor's chair, he dismissed questions about retirement by explaining that any former soldier knew the only way to die was 'with your boots on'. Deedes was struck by the fact that Evelyn Waugh died after suffering a heart attack on the lavatory.

If it were that, Mr Waugh should now be crying up the Russian domination, and he is not. This book must be pronounced a Fascist tract.' Deedes rather gleefully quoted the last few words of that review in *At War with Waugh*.

Because Deedes and Waugh were both very English, issues of class inevitably clouded their relationship. As Deedes put it, Waugh was never at his best with people who were posher than him, despite his lofty social aspirations. 'He was a fantastic snob, and though I'd been to a better school, I was of no use to him.' There may have been some professional envy too. Waugh had been able to secure a ticket to Abyssinia only with the *Daily Mail*; Deedes, although lacking Waugh's experience of Africa, was on a good salary with good expenses for the *Morning Post*, the paper for the upper classes.

Deedes deplored Waugh's showy support for Italian actions in *Waugh in Abyssinia*. Waugh dismisses the Italians' resort to poison-gas attacks in a single sentence and footnote, claiming ridiculously and grotesquely that they accounted for 'only eighteen lives'. Waugh was later embarrassed by sections of the book, but Deedes was unforgiving. In none of his writing – fiction or non-fiction – is there any evidence that Waugh understood the wider moral and strategic significance of Abyssinia as a testing ground for totalitarian ambitions to subvert the post-Versailles settlement. Abyssinia paved the way for Franco and Guernica and then later for the invasions of Czechoslovakia and Poland. If Waugh appreciated that Mussolini's aggression in Africa would eventually have consequences for the security of Europe, he chose not to convey this insight to the *Daily Mail*, or the readers of his books.

'The whole Abyssinian war was a disgrace to the human race,' Deedes said many years later, pointing to the use of gas and other atrocities. '*Scoop*, for all its genius, blinds us to this truth, but it was a horrible, horrible war.' Indeed so: the Italian Air Force could fly unchallenged to spray poison gas on Abyssinian columns and civilians; for their part, the Emperor's soldiers took only five Italian prisoners during the entire war. The rest were summarily killed, usually brutally with sword or spear. And on the Abyssinian side there was no provision for dealing with their own wounded, who were left to die agonisingly of their injuries.

There was another factor at play too. Just as it is possible to imagine Deedes's mother thinking racial epithets were common, so there is a strange class aspect to Deedes's views of Waugh. There was a sort of shrieking vulgarity about much of Waugh's non-fiction writing about Abyssinia. C. R. M. F. Cruttwell, Waugh's despised history tutor at Hertford, had spoken more than a decade earlier of his socially affected undergraduate pupil as a 'silly little suburban sod with an inferiority complex and no palate'. Deedes would never have put it in such terms, but he did not disagree with the sentiment. In a slightly perverse English way, Deedes deplored Waugh's abiding snobbery precisely because he though it rather common.

Deedes made it home from Abyssinia in time for Christmas. Waugh reached the Holy Land to hear the church bells of Bethlehem on Christmas Day. Neither had achieved his ambition of hearing a shot fired in anger in Abyssinia. But that is not uncommon in the field of war corresponding, when the only guns journalists see often belong to the men who are paid to keep reporters away from the action. Fleet Street had lost interest in the war just as it was reaching the denouement. Britain and France tried to sanctify the betrayal of Abyssinia with the Hoare–Laval Pact, an effort to buy off Italy with a third of her victim's territory. The British Cabinet endorsed it before a political row erupted, and Sir Samuel Hoare was forced to resign from the Foreign Office.

In Abyssinia, the government's tribal forces disintegrated and the Italians marched on the capital. Haile Selassie fled his kingdom on 2 May 1936, taking the same train to Djibouti that the press pack had used to go home. There, the Lion of Judah was picked up and carried to exile in London by a British warship. As he left, the mob ransacked the capital, destroying the palace and almost all of the other official buildings. Three days later the Italian forces entered Addis Ababa, but only a handful of Fleet Street men were still there to witness the final act, their news desks more interested now in totalitarian challenges closer to home. But fifteen journalists embedded with the invading army were on hand. Herbert Matthews of the *New York Times* broke the news with a cabled intro in the finest hyperbolic tradition of that war: 'ERA OF INDEPENDENCE THAT LASTED SINCE BIBLICAL TIMES ENDED FOUR THIS AFTERNOON WHEN ITALIANS OCCUPIED ADDIS ABABA.'

Before Haile Selassie settled into his new temporary home in England he travelled to Geneva on 30 June 1936 to make one final plea to the League of Nations. As he rose to speak, the Italian journalists in the press gallery began noisily whistling and jeering. In chilling, technical detail, the exiled Emperor explained how the Italians had adapted their aircraft to spray yperite,* an oily liquid that blistered skin, eyes and lung tissue, incapacitating anyone who came into contact with it. 'This death-dealing rain descended uninterruptedly upon our soldiers, upon women, children, cattle, streams, stagnant waters as well as pastures . . . Those who drank the water upon which this poisonous rain had settled or ate the food which the poison had touched died in dreadful agony.'

But the world was no longer listening. Collective security under the League of Nations had broken down. It had been tested by the Italians in Abyssinia, and found wanting, and Europe's other dictators learned the obvious lesson. As he finished his speech, Haile Selassie issued a prophetic warning to the world. 'It is us today. It will be you tomorrow.'

---

* Yperite took its name from Ypres in Flanders where the compound was first used in July 1917. It was generally known as mustard gas because of its smell of garlic and horseradish.

CHAPTER 6

DEATH OF THE *MORNING POST*

'W. F. Deedes, navigating some choppy political sea with blithe dexterity.'

There is a long-standing Fleet Street tradition whereby the news desk puts a returning foreign correspondent back in his place with insultingly humdrum assignments. The more exotic the out of town job, the more mundane must be his first domestic stories. So, in January 1936, Deedes found himself back at his desk at the *Morning Post*, tackling the scourge of the self-knotting telephone flex. Inevitably, the story began with a pun about the GPO facing 'a knotty problem', a joke enjoyed so much by the sub-editors that they also incorporated it in the headline. 'It arises from the irritating habit of all telephone cords, and particularly the latest type of hand-microphone machines,' wrote Deedes, 'to curl themselves into fatal twists, knots and contortions, and ultimately to perish by process of self-strangulation.'

It was characteristic of Deedes that he should have responded to the assignment with stylistic gusto, showing no grandness or reluctance to get back into the home news agenda. For him, there was no greater pleasure than reporting, whether it was about Fascist ambitions in Africa or irritating telephone flexes, and it did not seem to bother him too much that his stories were now shorn of his byline and his special correspondent designation. But soon he was being given stories that reflected his elevated status post-Abyssinia. Occasionally he would be called upon to write about the unresolved Abyssinian situation. He interviewed the exiled Emperor, and showed his admiration for him by topping his article with lines from *Paradise Lost*. Most unusually, the sub-editors indulged the reporter's flourish and did not cut his copy:

> *With grave*
> *Aspect he rose, and in his rising seem'd*
> *A pillar of state*

For his occasional Abyssinian pieces, his byline was restored, and he was labelled 'Special Correspondent lately in Abyssinia'. A 1200-word bylined feature of 9 January 1936 returned to a treasured Deedes theme. 'MUSSOLINI'S GAMBLE WITH THE WEATHER' ran the headline, above a ponderously speculative assessment of how the coming mini rainy season could affect Italy's military performance there. Deedes appeared uncertain, but concluded that one thing was for sure, 'the Ethiopian climate has been, and will continue to be, the most incalculable factor and consequently the most dangerous gamble of all'.

Deedes's cuttings book from the middle of the 1930s reflects the economic trauma in Britain and the looming military crisis in Europe. British defence spending jumped 30 per cent in 1936 as the Cabinet marked the collapse of collective security, the humiliation of the League of Nations and Hitler's increasingly bellicose threats. In March, German troops re-occupied the demilitarised zone of the Rhineland, in a provocative violation of the Treaty of Versailles. Fears of another European war were heightened by the general terror of the bomber deployed so wretchedly by the Italians in Abyssinia. That spring the first civil defence anti-gas training school was opened in response to the awful prospect of yperite being sprayed over British cities. Deedes wrote about the provision of gas masks – in three sizes, for men, women and children – and tussles between central government and local authorities over who should pay for rudimentary air raid defence precautions.

He was also drawn into Edward VIII's abdication, though he did not report the story himself. All the British newspapers abided by an undeclared agreement not to report Edward's affair with Wallis Simpson, or to recycle the increasingly detailed reports appearing in the continental press. The new King seemed oblivious to the looming constitutional crisis, which would develop once his subjects learned of his determination to marry a divorcée, something the Prime Minister, Stanley Baldwin, was determined to resist. H. A. Gwynne, the *Morning Post*'s editor, was anxious to be informed of the matter in his dealings with Baldwin, so Deedes was given the task of assembling a dossier of foreign newspaper cuttings. With the help of Hachette, the publisher and press distributor, Deedes managed to put together a portfolio of articles, which demonstrated that much of the world knew what the British papers were keeping from their readers. The subtext of Gwynne's meeting was that the *Morning Post*, monarchist and conservative, would be the appropriate newspaper to bring the delicate matter of the King's affair with a divorced American woman in to the public domain. Deedes lobbied Gwynne to press Baldwin to give him the green light to publish; the Prime Minister demanded more time and Gwynne was reluctant to run such explosive material without tacit official support.

The press held off until the previously obscure Bishop of Bradford* publicly declared that the King was urgently in need of God's grace; the *Yorkshire Post* took this as an excuse to break its silence and Fleet Street followed the next day. The King's fate was sealed, even when Winston Churchill rallied noisily to his cause and small groups of Communists and Blackshirts temporarily put aside their differences to demonstrate against Baldwin outside Buckingham Palace. Rothermere and Beaverbrook threw the *Mail* and the

---

* As Deedes put it in a letter to his sister Frances, 'the Bishop of someone or other'.

Express behind the idea of a morganatic marriage, but MPs reported solid public opposition to the King marrying Simpson. Baldwin's strong conviction that Edward must abdicate if he insisted on proceeding with the marriage held sway. The *Morning Post* did not distinguish itself in its abdication coverage, and never gave the impression of having an inside track.

The *Daily Telegraph*, under its owner Lord Camrose's shrewd direction, was well-established as the natural read for all-round news, and its circulation rose sharply through the 1930s despite the dismal economic conditions. By the end of 1936, the *Telegraph* was selling 500,000 copies at 1d, more than double *The Times* at 2d. Once the abdication story broke, it was the *Telegraph* that made the running, largely because Baldwin ensured that Camrose, a friend, was fully briefed about negotiations between Downing Street and Buckingham Palace.

With his experience in Abyssinia, and as a resident of the East End, Deedes was the natural choice to report on the antics of Sir Oswald Mosley's Blackshirts in the autumn of 1936. Once again a lodger in his uncle Wyndham's house in Bethnal Green, Deedes only had to look out of the window of number 17 to witness the Blackshirts marshalling in Victoria Park Square. 'So I get plenty of fun for very little trouble,' he wrote to his sister Hermione, adding that covering Mosley was more dangerous than anything he had experienced in Abyssinia.

He was on hand in Cable Street when thousands of Blackshirts mustered to march into the Jewish heartland of the East End. The Commissioner of Police, Sir Philip Game, refused to let them proceed. As Deedes put it to his sister, in language slightly more colourful than he used in the following day's *Morning Post*, '5000 police tried without success to hold the blighters in check' as paving stones were torn up and lobbed at the police lines. Not for the first or last time, Deedes struggled to keep his excitement under control while reporting on the four hours of running battles: 'ever such fun,' he told his sister, before reaching a more sober conclusion. 'Well it's all very serious really, but human life is being endangered, Jews are frightened to walk after dark, hood-lums are on the loose.' He took some satisfaction, however, from word that had reached him on the Fleet Street grapevine that the *Morning Post*'s main rival, the *Daily Telegraph*, had been 'most impressed' with his coverage.

Deedes was given a prized slot on the news feature page to opine at some length on what was billed as 'Political Warfare' in the East End. Deedes was bylined anonymously as a special cor-respondent – a nod to his personal knowledge of Bethnal Green – and given space to contemplate an issue that had long interested his paper: the political loyalties of the British Jew. Given the *Morning Post*'s historic pursuit of the conflicting currents in the soul of British Jewry, Deedes's piece was commendably restrained, though he did clunkingly suggest there was an equivalence between the provocations of the Communists, the Blackshirts and the Jewish East Enders whose shopfronts were being kicked in: 'One of the more disquieting features of the present situation is the way in which the Jews are swelling the ranks of the Communist party in East London,' he wrote. 'The Communists can supply the organisation and driving power; the Jews may supply the money and manpower for an Anti-Fascist drive.'

Deedes's reporting of the Mosleyite mayhem was spirited, par-ticularly by the standards of the *Morning Post*, which by then was showing clear signs of its imminent mortality. But his greatest achievement – and one which would be revived in a different form decades later at the *Daily Telegraph* – was the establishment of the Christmas toy fund of 1936. The charitable impulse was triggered in part by Edward VIII who, towards the end of his brief reign, had visited a derelict steel works in South Wales as part of a royal tour of the 'Distressed Areas'. After an enthusiastic wel-come from the unemployed men and their women, the King said that 'something must be done to find them work'. The *Morning Post* could not do that, but settled on a scheme to help the fami-lies. Deedes was instructed to oversee the immense operation, audacious in its ambition: the paper would strive to deliver a

Christmas present to every child of unemployed parents in those distressed areas – South Wales, West Cumberland and Tyneside.

Even leaving aside the restrictions imposed by the Data Protection Act, it is impossible to imagine, seven decades on, teachers handing over the addresses of their children to a newspaper. But not a single headteacher asked to help offered anything less than full cooperation. Deedes and J. C. Trewin, the ghost writer of his Abyssinian copy, toured the distressed areas seeking human interest stories to tug the heartstrings of the *Morning Post*'s well-to-do readers. As an insurance to make sure the paper did not have to rely on its readers' altruism alone, the *Morning Post* shrewdly published the name of every contributor in the paper in a special daily slot. King Edward VIII sent a cheque shortly before he abdicated on 11 December, as did Queen Mary, who also asked to be kept informed of the appeal. This prompted a splash on the main news page: 'Her Majesty Queen Mary has shown gracious sympathy with our Appeal for children in the Distressed Areas by sending a donation to the Fund,' Deedes reported, without revealing the amount. Queen Mary's patronage was a triumph and priceless in publicity terms and, as Deedes proudly reported in a letter to his sister Frances, the first time 'a show of this kind' had been given royal endorsement.[*] The BBC made tentative moves to get involved with the fund, and the management of the Regal cinema in the West End offered the proceeds of the world premiere of the new Shirley Temple film. But the *Morning Post* turned down all offers, determined to maintain total control of the undertaking.

Department stores were approached to provide toys at discount rates, and most obliged. The Army & Navy Stores once again found itself drawn into supplying large quantities of goods for the young reporter. Selfridge's and the Civil Service Stores

---

[*] Deedes was so caught up in the excitement and exertion of the appeal that in the same letter he only casually mentions that the Wallis Simpson affair had broken that evening. 'Frankly I don't care a hoot,' he told Frances, a rare display of indifference towards a cracking news story.

also cooperated, as did Harrods, though Deedes complained the last was 'damnably inefficient'. The managing director had the temerity to tell Deedes he thought the *Morning Post*'s scheme ill-conceived, a charge which sent him, exhausted by the organisational efforts, into orbit. 'This morning we have been in touch with the Directors and certain departmental chiefs have gone for a six for impertinence,' he reported to his sister Frances. Each gift was to be worth about two shillings and the *Morning Post* stipulated that all must be manufactured in Britain or the Empire. With some £12,500 raised from readers, there was just enough to buy a present for 120,000 children of the unemployed in the distressed areas. Deedes had hoped the Post Office would deliver the parcels free; initially the GPO agreed but the Treasury vetoed the concession, so a further sixpence per parcel had to be found. Staff at the department stores volunteered to stay late to wrap the thousands of packages, while Deedes oversaw the operation to type the addresses, having bought 100,000 labels in rolls of 750. Deedes approached the operation with characteristic rigour, working excessive hours. He was haunted by the thought of the consequences of failure: 'Imagine the nightmare of having to count over hundreds of lists of thousands of children,' he wrote to Frances, 'realising that if one child gets missed, that's a big disappointment for some poor infant on Christmas morning.' Exhilarating as he found it, Deedes was clearly affected by the hardship the fund had identified. As he noted in a letter home, when he asked the headmaster of a school of 440 children in the Rhondda Valley for the names of children with unemployed fathers, no fewer than 419 names came back.

Even if it could not waive the cost of postage, the Post Office did lay on extra staff to ensure that all the parcels were delivered on Christmas Eve and Christmas Day. Deedes and the *Morning Post*'s news editor, Mervyn Ellis, took the train to South Wales on Christmas Eve, sharing a bottle of champagne over dinner on the Cardiff Express. The next day they toured the valleys, making sure the presents had arrived safely. The appeal was an astounding success, not only in bringing a little joy to thousands of deprived children but also in generating positive publicity for the *Morning Post*. It was a personal triumph for Deedes, who had driven the scheme from the beginning, and was recognised in a letter of thanks from the editor. The paper received floods of letters from the children, and until the end of his life Deedes would receive the occasional note from a pensioner thanking him for a present received almost a lifetime earlier.

When the *Morning Post* was folded into the *Daily Telegraph* the following year, Lord Camrose was insistent the scheme be maintained under Deedes's supervision, despite the reservations expressed by senior managers who feared it could become a financial liability. Much richer than the *Morning Post*, the *Telegraph* applied a more professional approach, and with its far greater circulation the Appeal reached a new level. Queen Mary visited the *Telegraph* office on 10 December 1937, where she inspected five hundred presents bound for the children in the distressed areas. One envelope she inspected contained half a crown and an anonymous note:

> *A drop less beer,*
> *A bit less baccy –*
> *Half a crown,*
> *And a youngster's happy.*

Deedes had stumbled upon a truth that still held when the *Daily Telegraph*, many years later, revived the Christmas charity appeal under his leadership: readers get a warm glow inside when they contribute money to good causes, and they like their paper to be involved in doing good as much as they want it to report events.

Shortly after his triumph with the *Morning Post* appeal of 1936, Deedes was promoted into the Lobby as political correspondent and his salary increased to a very respectable fifteen pounds a week. He celebrated with a further upgrade of his wardrobe, buying striped diplomat's trousers, stiff white collars, waistcoats and a formal black coat. He also took to buying a fresh red carnation for his buttonhole each morning, which provided a raffish splash of colour as well as serving the practical purpose of making the *Morning Post* political correspondent instantly recognisable around the corridors of Westminster.*

In those days, gentlemen wore hats, and Deedes favoured an Eden, a black Homburg with a turned-up rim. The Deedes men had traditionally gone to Huntsman in Savile Row, but when their chief cutter, G. Keogh, split to set up on his own at 11 Sackville Street, Deedes and his uncle Wyndham were two of his first clients.[†] Some seventy years later, he had clear recall of his wardrobe of the 1930s. He kept about ten suits on the go at any one time. 'I was a bit dressy,' he recalled, 'I did rather enjoy wearing posh suits.' He clearly relished standing out and dressing true to the social class of his birth. Though journalists would always have worn a suit to work, few of them would have been described as grand, or were flashy dressers.

With free board at Wyndham's house, Deedes now had a substantial disposable income. With his 'guaranteed expenses' – an old Fleet Street racket that gave journalists a tax-free supplement to their salaries – his total income was more than a thousand pounds a year, or forty-seven thousand pounds in 2008 value. After he retired as editor of the *Telegraph*, Deedes would say he never felt as rich as in the last years before the outbreak of war. His main outgoings were beer and his wardrobe – three-piece suits then cost ten pounds at Keogh, and morning suits fifteen pounds. For formal dinners, *Morning Post* correspondents were expected to follow

---

* The fondness for splashes of sartorial colour seems to be hereditary in Deedes men. His son Jeremy, later managing director of the *Telegraph*, was known affectionately around the office as Custard Socks on account of the lurid colouring of his hose.

† G. Keogh thrived, and when the business was forced to move again in 1962 because of redevelopment of Sackville Street, he wrote to Deedes to tell him that he had found an ancient 'frock coat of yours marked "awaiting instructions".' He offered to send

the fashion of the time and wear white tie and tailcoat – preferably not hired from Moss Bros – while black tie would be enough for informal dinners. When not entertaining on newspaper business, Deedes would buy himself a light supper out: in later life he could not recall ever having eaten dinner at home in Bethnal Green during the week.

On top of those outgoings, he dutifully paid his sisters a portion of his salary, for single girls from upper-middle-class families in the 1930s would expect to receive a dress allowance from their father. Deedes took seriously the role as head of the family, which had been thrust upon him by default, and gave away an eighth of his pre-tax income to the three girls: Frances received sixty pounds a year, Hermione forty pounds, and Margaret twenty. He remained an attentive older brother in other respects, too, as he was conscious that home life was not much fun for his sisters because of their father's irascibility. Each August he would take a fortnight's leave and stay in the family home in Marine Parade. He would hire a car and organise the sort of trips that a father would normally lead. Bill and the girls would jump into the car and drive along the coast. Margaret remembers one happy day at Dungeness long before the nuclear power station was built, and they all ran up the steps to the top of the lighthouse. Bill consciously sought to create the fun within the family that his father was incapable of generating.

Despite the general gaiety of Deedes's bachelor life on a perfectly sufficient salary, there was no disguising the parlous condition of the *Morning Post*'s finances as circulation and advertising revenue continued to decline. The consortium led by the Duke of Northumberland, which had bought the paper after Lord Bathurst's death, had fallen apart and the remaining directors were unwilling to sustain the losses of about forty thousand pounds a year, with no sign of relief in sight.

The paper's political outlook was beginning to look eccentric in the mid-1930s, but it was economic forces that sealed the *Morning Post*'s fate. Though its readership was more diverse and

less grand than its own staff liked to believe, its natural core readers among the landed gentry were not doing well at the time. A
high proportion of the *Post*'s income derived from 'situations
vacant' advertising, principally for domestic staff. A three-line
classified advert cost 4s 6d, and ladies who were unwilling to
venture as far east as Tudor Street could avail themselves of the
Morning Post's interview suite in Mayfair Place where they would
meet prospective servants and governesses. In the paper's heyday,
rivers of these lucrative advertisements cascaded down the scrupulously dull columns, starting on the front page, which carried no
news. *The Times* and the *Daily Telegraph* at this point also carried only advertisements on the front, though popular mid-market
papers such as the *Daily Mail* and *Daily Express* did have news
and pictures on page one.

As unemployment rose through the 1930s, country houses
were shuttered and domestic staff were laid off, so the 'Empire's
Senior Daily' began to wobble. Its advertising revenues were
shrinking and there was no prospect for circulation gain because
in every respect – presentation of news, range of coverage, quality of printing – the *Post* was inferior to the *Telegraph*. In July
1937, the consortium abandoned all hope of recovery and sold
out to Lord Camrose, who had owned the *Telegraph* since 1928
and was one of the most astute newspaper proprietors of the
twentieth century.

A self-made man from Merthyr Tydfil, he was one of three
sons of Alderman Mathias Berry and his wife Mary Ann, all of
whom were raised to the peerage. William Berry, who had previously been knighted, was made Baron Camrose, of Long Cross
in the County of Surrey, on Baldwin's recommendation in 1929.
Deedes was in awe of the *Telegraph*'s owner, partly because by
training and inclination Camrose remained a true journalist. He
had started off at the age of fourteen, as a cub reporter on the
Merthyr Times, learning about newspaper layout and printing
before laying the foundations of his future empire with the launch
of a lucrative paper called *Advertising World*. When he bought

the *Telegraph* in 1928, it appeared to be in terminal decline, with a circulation that had plunged from 300,000 at the turn of the century to 84,000 by 1927. Lord Camrose's genius was to understand that price mattered as much as editorial mix. In 1930 he halved the cover price to a penny, the circulation doubled overnight and the *Telegraph* took off, quickly soaring out of the reach of *The Times*, which remained at 2d. Camrose's ambition was to take the circulation to the million mark and establish it as the natural paper of the ascendant middle class. By the outbreak of war in 1939, the *Daily Telegraph* was selling an astonishing 750,000 copies a day and had become the undisputed market leader.

Deedes had sent his mother a ten-page handwritten letter giving her a forty-eight-hour warning of the *Morning Post* sale. He knew that, having watched her husband slide into financial disaster, she would be worried about the prospect of her son losing a salary that was increasingly subsidising the entire family. He crisply summed up the consequence of the yet-to-be-announced sale: 'This may mean two things – Salvation or Disaster, and none of us knows which it is to be.' Writing more, it seems, to reassure her than to convince himself, Deedes suggested that Camrose might keep the *Post* going as an upmarket, distinctive Tory paper, because if he closed it or vulgarised it 'his name would be mud'.

He tells her of his anxieties about the older staff who would never work again should the *Post* close, insisting that he has no fears of his own. 'Unmarried, independent, young, and still keen for adventure, I probably fear the crash less than most in my office,' he wrote, adding that he had been 'approached with a much bigger offer elsewhere, but we won't go into that now'. Deedes, normally a meticulous record-keeper, particularly on details of salary and contracts, kept no written evidence of this overture from a rival paper. It is conceivable that letters were lost, or that the job was offered over a pint of beer, but it is equally possible that he was telling his mother a white lie to spare her further anxiety about the family's financial security.

When the news of the sale broke, a note was circulated to staff saying that Camrose would 'in due course make an announcement of his policy and intentions'. This sent the *Post*'s staff into a frenzy of anxious speculation. For a while, there was hope that Camrose might turn the *Post* into a London evening paper run by his younger son, Michael, the future Lord Hartwell.* But Camrose found no way of making it viable as a separate entity and, sensing that the bulk of its daily buyers would switch over naturally to the *Daily Telegraph*, he settled on closure and the absorption of half the editorial staff at 135 Fleet Street. So the paper that advertised itself as 'independent of everyone and everything' was folded ignominiously into its much richer and more successful rival. H. A. Gwynne walked away a humiliated man – this was the second newspaper to close on his watch as editor – but he was consoled with one of the greatest severance packages in Fleet Street history: a lifetime pension of five thousand pounds, a figure which in 1937 was huge even as a salary.†

Deedes had established a good reputation for himself as a reporter, but he still had reason to worry: he had only recently been made political correspondent at the *Post*, and the *Daily Telegraph* was already fully staffed at Westminster. Perhaps he was distracted by trying to secure a new berth, for his account of the death of the oldest newspaper in Britain is strangely skimpy in his autobiography. His colleague J. C. Trewin missed out on an offer of transfer to the *Telegraph*, despite his keen reporter's eye and rich prose style. He certainly had better recall of the moment the axe fell, as he returned to the *Morning Post*'s office on the evening of 29 September 1937, after dutifully covering a gymkhana at Roehampton:

* Michael Berry was made a life peer by Harold Wilson in 1968.

† This was at a time when a substantial family home could be bought for two thousand pounds, and a new motorcar for less than two hundred.

At six o'clock there was a summons to the sub-editors' room: the entire staff met, most of them still unaware. H. A. Gwynne entered quietly; a minute later we knew from his few words, deeply-felt, that the next day's issue of the *Morning Post* would be its last as an independent journal. Within half-an-hour we knew further, from a distribution of letters in the Foreign Room – a queue outside it was as blithe as a meeting of the Suicide Club – which of us would be crossing to the *Daily Telegraph*, and which of us would leave Tudor Street that night, compensated but unemployed. I was in the second group. Not many wished to go home. People loitered in the corridor, hung about the stairs. The evening's routine passed with the unreality of a dream. In the reporters' room a few cleared their desks; someone pinned on the baize board its last notice, a message, 'Horsey, keep your tail up,' that had been tapped out on the Press Association tape. Just before eleven Littlewood [the drama critic] brought a farewell theatre notice: the play was called, pleasantly, *The Last Straw*.

The reaction from the rest of Fleet Street was sympathetic, with journalists showing the uncharacteristic solidarity they periodically display when any newspaper expires. 'Its demise and the manner of it have been a tragedy for Fleet-street, bereaved by so many similar tragedies in modern times, and a savage blow to that dwindling element of reactionary Toryism which yet deserved a voice, even if it cried in a wilderness,' said the *Saturday Review*. Its leading article of 9 October was broadly sympathetic, though it could not resist making the point that 'modern English flesh cannot be made to creep agreeably by things like the *Protocol of the Elders of Zion*' before concluding that 'a world which has discovered that it is round simply will not pay attention to the band of consistent zealots who still protest it is flat'.[*]

The *New Statesman* was surprisingly sympathetic, even as it

---

[*] The *Saturday Review* would itself expire within a year.

noted that the '*Post*'s point of view had not governed England since the Duke of Wellington'. In general, even left-wing papers and pundits lamented the death of a quirky voice of Tory England: many were unhappy that an independent paper was to be subsumed within the new dominant, commercial, middle-class culture of the *Daily Telegraph*. The *Post*, said the *New Statesman*, had the 'good as well as the bad qualities of the aristocracy; it is not run by its advertisers and does not say what it thinks will please the largest number of people'.

Clearly, the strong whiff of anti-Semitism that had hung over the *Post* since the publication of the *Protocols of the Elders of Zion* had done lasting damage to its reputation as a serious newspaper, judging by how frequently the matter was referred to in newspaper obituaries. Lady Bathurst, who had owned the *Morning Post* from her husband's death until 1924, saw a sinister force at work in the transfer of ownership to Lord Camrose, later speculating that it might have been 'too truthful, too unafraid, too independent, and above all, too *clean* . . . Was any Jewish influence at work, I wonder?' British anti-Semites were oddly obsessed with Camrose's ethnic-religious affiliations. They might conceivably have suspected the name acquired on becoming a peer had a Jewish ring, though this would have surprised old friends of the Berry family of Merthyr Tydfil. (When elevated to the peerage, he took the name Camrose because it was the hamlet from which the Berry family had come in Wales.)

A fortnight after the *Post*'s absorption, the Fascist newspaper *Action* recklessly suggested that Camrose was an unpatriotic Jewish money-man who ran the *Telegraph* in narrow pursuit of his own financial interests. Camrose, whose utter devotion to the interests of the newspaper could not be challenged by any sane person, sought relief in the High Court, where his counsel asked him: 'Are you in any sense a Jew?', to which he replied, 'No, in no sense whatever.' Camrose was awarded £12,500 damages with a further £7500 for the *Daily Telegraph*.

Whatever may have been the truth about his supposed job

offer from a rival, Deedes accepted the chance to stay with the new merged paper and effected the transition to the *Telegraph* seamlessly. On Friday evening he filed his final piece for the *Morning Post*, on the Cabinet's decision to send Mussolini a formal warning about his increasing bellicosity. On Monday, he reported for duty across the way at 135 Fleet Street. The *Telegraph* matched his *Morning Post* salary of fifteen pounds a week, plus the five pounds weekly guaranteed expenses. Young, talented and keen, Deedes had survived the cull of the old guard at the *Post*. But because the *Telegraph* already had its share of political reporters, he reverted to being a general reporter.

His first piece under *Telegraph* colours was about the threat to workmen's cottages owing to slum clearance directives issued under the 1936 Housing Act. Soon he was applying the same level of devotion to the *Daily Telegraph* as had previously been shown towards the *Morning Post*. At the *Telegraph*'s grand head-quarters at 135 Fleet Street, where the doormen wore tail-coats and where reporters were expected to spend the company's money chasing stories, Deedes found a congenial new home. J. C. Trewin, who had done so much to bolster Deedes's career by fleshing out his Abyssinian cables, kept in his mind the final impression of his young colleague, picturing him in those last weeks as the paper expired. 'W. F. Deedes,' as he recalled it, 'navigating some choppy political sea with blithe dexterity.' That blitheness, that dexterity – allied to a boundless natural charm, impeccable manners and a well-disguised determination – was to sustain Deedes for the next seven decades of his life with his new master, the *Daily Telegraph*.

CHAPTER 7

WAR IN OUR TIME

*'Darling, it isn't only a shell around you, it was sometimes
a huge stone wall with glass on top.'*

When the Prime Minister, Neville Chamberlain, flew to
Berchtesgaden in September 1938, Deedes was at Heston
aerodrome with his reporter's notebook to meet him on his
return. Having witnessed the early stirrings of Italian Fascism
in Abyssinia, Deedes knew enough not to share Chamberlain's
confidence that he had bought off Hitler with the carve-up of
Czechoslovakia and the sacrifice of the Sudetanland. Though the
Telegraph never abased itself by welcoming the appeasing of
Fascism as *The Times* and *Daily Mail* had, the paper took the
majority line that it was a decent compromise.

In his dispatch from Heston, Deedes managed to convey his
scepticism. He described in detail how Chamberlain ostentatiously opened a black-edged envelope handed to him by his
private secretary. It was from the King, 'a three-page letter of
congratulations upon his mission, written in His Majesty's own
hand'. George VI's early, indeed pre-emptive, endorsement of
Chamberlain's appeasement diplomacy was ultimately shown
to have been foolish. Deedes raised an eyebrow about this happy
tableau by dwelling in his dispatch on Chamberlain's hapless
enthusiasm. 'Asked how he had enjoyed his journey, he admitted

jovially that his first experience of air travel at the age of sixty-nine showed it to be far pleasanter than he had ever believed possible.' By mentioning Chamberlain's age and nodding at the Prime Minister's unworldliness, Deedes was perhaps subtly conveying to the reader a sense of foreboding.*

Deedes was on hand, too, when Chamberlain returned from the Munich conference brandishing the fateful document endorsing the German occupation of the Sudetenland and declared through the open windows of 10 Downing Street, in words that he immediately regretted, 'I believe it is peace for our time.' Deedes rushed back to the office to write up his report. The production staff at the *Telegraph*, many of them veterans of the First World War, were unimpressed by Chamberlain's claims to have tamed Hitler's ambitions. After shouting a terse instruction for early copy, Bob Skelton, the irascible night editor, aimed a mock punch at Deedes's stomach. 'You young fellows are for it!'

Deedes did not need to be told how dangerous the world had become. Partly as a result of his spell in Abyssinia, he had acquired a profound dislike of casual supporters of Fascism. Having seen the hideously wounded Abyssinians in Harar hospital after Mussolini's mustard gas attacks, he understood the barbarity of the Fascist challenge long before his peers. Most of his colleagues would have to wait for the Second World War to have direct experience of the consequences of totalitarian oppression. In this era, before the indiscriminate bombing of British cities, years before the Holocaust had been uncovered, it was much easier to be complacent about fascism. But Deedes's view had been formed very early, and he was consistent both in his loathing for the big battalions of totalitarianism and for their fellow travellers.

Anxious that the threat should not be underestimated, he

---

* Deedes managed to irritate his mother on this assignment by appearing in the background of a photograph dressed in a pork pie hat, which she thought showed a lack of respect for the solemnity of the occasion.

responded in characteristically practical terms. For the *Telegraph*, he used his expertise of air defence to write a series of articles about air-raid precautions (ARP), which were later turned into a best-selling pamphlet and a money-spinner at 135 Fleet Street. Lord Camrose was sufficiently embarrassed by the profits to send Deedes a royalty cheque, which caused the Inland Revenue to chase him for the tax due for the duration of the war.

His anti-appeasement views drew him into the orbit of two like-minded journalists, Victor Gordon-Lennox, a *Telegraph* colleague and diplomatic correspondent, and Helen Kirkpatrick, an American foreign correspondent, who together ran an anti-appeasement periodical, *Whitehall Newsletter*. Deedes fell heavily for Kirkpatrick, who was a very different prospect to the flighty upper-class English girls with whom he had stepped out until then. She was three years older than Deedes, bustling and self-confident, tall and imposing rather than conventionally beautiful, with high cheekbones and piercing blue eyes. She wanted Deedes to leave the *Daily Telegraph* and work full-time on the *Whitehall Newsletter*. He declined, though was tempted. 'I was deeply attracted by Helen Kirkpatrick,' he recalled in *Dear Bill*, 'but it was not the time to leave mainstream journalism.' Deedes's explanation was characteristically ambiguous. Those words imply a sexual frisson, and perhaps even a sexual experience. Deedes noted in his autobiography that he later went on a double date with Kirkpatrick to watch the Tidworth Military Tattoo, which might not be every American girl's idea of a lively night out. He did not reveal that the other two present that evening were Gordon-Lennox and his wife, or the reason for the double date.

Gordon-Lennox, dashing and self-confident, was having an affair with Kirkpatrick, and the reason the four of them went out together was – Deedes eventually discovered – to give cover for the two lovers to see more of each other. As a further precaution, Gordon-Lennox told his wife that Deedes and Kirkpatrick were sweethearts. The pain of the situation must have been intense for Deedes, but by then he was working not just as the facilitator of

the affair, but had become the *Telegraph*'s deputy diplomatic correspondent. In other words, Deedes was working directly for the
man who was sleeping with the woman he sought. Worse still,
Deedes appreciated how hypocritical was his boss's behaviour:
before he became Diplomatic Correspondent, Gordon-Lennox
had been the editor of Peterborough and had steered the diary
on a course of dreary sermonising, setting himself up as a guardian
of public morals. He denounced the publication of a lesbian novel,
The Well of Loneliness, and was delighted when Peterborough's
campaigning succeeded in getting an exhibition of D. H. Lawrence's
paintings closed down by the police for obscenity.

Displaying his customary facility for compartmentalising
unhappy episodes, Deedes pushed Helen Kirkpatrick out of his
mind. One evening, fourteen months before his death, I asked him
about Kirkpatrick, curious about his ambiguous reference to her
in his autobiography. He was non-committal and appeared
slightly irritated to have been questioned on the subject; he was
always uncomfortable talking about his emotions. But by his
standards, he was in a reflective mood, because it was the night
before a lunch at his home for twenty guests to mark his seventy-
five years in journalism.

The following morning, the day of that lunch, he summoned
me into his bedroom, where he was still in bed, and instructed me,
as was his custom, to sit down in his wheelchair. Perhaps because
he had been thinking about the speech he was going to give that
lunchtime, he had clearly spent much of the night reviewing his
own memories of the 1930s. Without being asked, he confirmed
that he had been, as he put it sadly, 'deeply attracted' to
Kirkpatrick, and that his ambitions had been thwarted by his
shocked discovery that she was having an affair with Gordon-
Lennox. Immediately he had imparted this poignant detail he
rationalised his feelings for Helen Kirkpatrick by returning to her
practical qualities. He liked her spirit and *savoir faire*, but also her
pluck – like several other American correspondents in London –
in emphasising the dangers of National Socialism in Germany

and countering the appeasing telegrams of Joe Kennedy, the US ambassador in London. But of the love affair that never was, Deedes recalled wistfully: 'I'm afraid I just served as what I think you call the gooseberry.' And then he changed the subject, never to return to the matter of Helen Kirkpatrick.

As Deedes had foreseen, Hitler was not satisfied with carving up Czechoslovakia, and by the beginning of 1939 war seemed inevitable to those who would not allow themselves to be deluded into believing in Germany's good intentions. Deedes was encouraged to volunteer for service by Lord Killanin, an Irish peer working at the *Daily Mail*, and who, many years later, became head of the International Olympic Committee. Deedes, who had got to know Killanin after working alongside him on a couple of stories, followed him into the Queen's Westminsters, a Territorial Battalion of the King's Royal Rifle Corps, in which Deedes's father and uncle Wyndham had both served during the Boer War.* The 1st Battalion of the Queen's Westminsters (11 KRRC) had for some months been attracting patriotic City workers and civil servants for weekly drills. As the international situation deteriorated in the spring of 1939, and the government demanded a doubling in the size of the territorials, a second battalion was added. This was a more glamorous outfit, which drilled at Wellington Barracks in Birdcage Walk, perhaps the swankiest military address in the capital. Unusually, C Company of the 2nd Battalion, known as the Day Squad, was allowed to drill mid-morning rather than early evening, in order to accommodate the working patterns of the actors and journalists who filled its ranks. The Day Squad earned a sort of celebrity, slightly resented by the members of the 1st Battalion, who consoled themselves with feelings of superiority because they had joined

---

* Deedes was unaware of the connection between the Queen's Westminsters and the KRRC until he told his father he had joined up. Despite his loathing for the Army and the Empire acquired during his service in South Africa, Herbert was perversely – and secretly – very proud his son had joined the family regiment.

up earlier. Expansion of the armed services was so hasty that there were precious few rifles and even less kit. The 2nd Queen's Westminsters would drill in their work suits, trying not to let the rifle oil ruin their jackets.

Deedes proved himself an assiduous recruiting agent, spreading the word around Fleet Street – so much so that he was summoned to see the managing director and told that the *Telegraph* might not get out if he continued persuading sub-editors to sign up. In the event, such concerns became redundant after the mass call-up in August 1939 following Hitler's invasion of the rest of Czechoslovakia. Deedes and his brother volunteers suddenly found themselves full-time soldiers, subject to the disciplines of the Army Act and the *Manual of Military Law.* What had begun as a jape, a patriotic hobby of weekly drills rewarded with a warm glow and reimbursed bus fares, suddenly became deadly serious. Actors and journalists found themselves liable to be screamed at by regular sergeants determined to eradicate any namby-pamby tendencies in their recruits.

Not so Deedes, who immediately took to military life. He had by this time been commissioned as a second lieutenant and given command of a platoon, while the 2nd Battalion had grown to a strength of thirty-one officers and 634 other ranks. His platoon's first serious mission was to defend the railway bridge at Staines, which was regarded as a vulnerable point and potentially a target for German sabotage. There Deedes upbraided Guy Middleton, a famous West End actor, for chatting up adoring girls while on sentry duty, with his rifle propped between his knees.

In the same platoon, under Deedes's command, was another well-known actor, Tam Williams, who had lately been seen in *The Barretts of Wimpole Street.* Frank Lawton, a stage and film actor, was also in the 2nd Queen's Westminsters, though he was swiftly co-opted by the War Office to make propaganda films, including *Went the Day Well?*, a rather lame fantasy about an English village falling under the boot of German invasion. Lawton remained loyal to his regiment, however, keeping close ties and sending his wife Evelyn Laye, an actress more famous than he, to morale-boosting concerts.

Deedes was the moving force behind a triumphant concert during the phoney war in October 1939, exploiting all the contacts of the Day Squad. Many of the best-known theatrical celebrities of the inter-war years appeared on stage at Greenford, where the local dance hall was transformed by stage carpenters from Moss Empire Theatre. As Deedes reported excitedly to his father, the full bill included screen and stage stars such as Renée Houston, Stanley Holloway, Enid Stamp-Taylor, Turner Layton, Oliver Wakefield, Jack Strachey and Max Miller, who delighted members of the battalion, brigade and divisional headquarters packed in to the hall. Deedes was pleased to see the colonel and his wife in the audience, clearly enjoying themselves. After Max Miller wound up the show, Deedes gave a speech of thanks – which 'nearly killed me', he told his father – before all the cast came on stage to sing *Tipperary* with the audience, followed by the National Anthem. The great success of the afternoon's entertainment enormously enhanced Deedes's standing in the battalion and marked him down as a young officer to be watched and rewarded in the future.

The high calibre of the celebrity cast drawn to the Greenford dance hall was testimony to the cachet of the Rifle Regiment. The KRRC drew most of its senior officers from the better public schools, particularly Eton and Winchester, while the bulk of the riflemen came from the East End of London. Members of the KRRC regarded themselves as the social equivalents of the Guards and the better cavalry regiments, and superior to all of them in terms of soldiering verve. Rifle companies came about in the early nineteenth century as a spin-off from standard infantry units that were trained to fire muskets in rigid formations. Riflemen were expected to peel off from the set piece battle formations and advance to harry the enemy, deploying superior marksmanship and initiative.

Rifle battalions tended to eschew the excesses of square-bashing and boot- and button-polishing, though they were certainly well turned out. By convention, there was no need to shout 'Attention!' to riflemen on the parade ground; they came to attention as soon as they were addressed, usually with a restrained call of 'Riflemen' or 'Squad'. The regimental motto was *Celer et Audax* – Swift and Bold – and in recognition of that it marched at a quicker step than other regiments, which would cause chaos during joint parades. The KRRC song, from Edgar Wallace's 1914 collection of soldier's songs, fails lyrically and melodically, but it does convey the rifleman's singular pride and sense of superiority over rival regiments.

> *You know him at once by the way that he goes,*
> *By his step and his swing and his debonair pose,*
> *By the finicking way he looks after his clothes,*
> *He's as fussy and neat as a flapper.*

And later:

> *He's natty and nippy – his run is a streak,*
> *He honestly thinks his Corps is unique;*
> *That all other regiments are horribly weak*
> *Is the text of his barrack-room sermon.*

As a relatively inexperienced new recruit, Deedes initially enjoyed some advantages. He had been to a decent public school, which marked him down as officer material, but having lived for the past eight years in Bethnal Green he did not find it difficult to get along with the Cockney riflemen, quite a lot of whom were Jewish. He was several years older than most of the new officer recruits, and in Abyssinia and in the distressed areas of Britain he had experiences far beyond those of the callow boys fresh out of their public schools or universities.

Deedes was as keen as any new recruit to maintain the KRRC's grand tradition. Almost eighteen months into his army career, the young subaltern is still recognisable as the slightly Bertie

Woosterish character revealed in his letters home from Abyssinia five years earlier. In a gossipy letter to his sister Hermione, dated 7 December 1940, from a temporary battalion HQ in Newcastle-under-Lyme, Deedes describes how he and a fellow junior officer had been taken up by a family called the Johnsons, whose business was the manufacture of porcelain sanitaryware: 'They're pottery kings – to you, I can confide my dear, lav. kings – and rather rich but terribly kind.' Deedes inevitably christens each of the two Johnson daughters Miss Pots, and tells Hermione how he and his friend had taken the girls out on a double date, first to the pictures and then to a dance in Chester. 'Though born in pots, as it were, the Miss Johnsons have done their Paris and Courts and Seasons, so are not too potty,' Deedes reports to Hermione, sounding rather younger than his twenty-seven years. In the same letter, Deedes addresses himself to the need for vigilance in protecting his battalion's high social standards with the accelerated influx of new subalterns as the war effort geared up. 'Here, we have our internecine strife, caused chiefly, lets [*sic*] be blunt, by the fact that most of the new officers aren't gentlemen and never look like being.' Deedes recounts an indecorous incident, when two of the parvenu officers brought a couple of 'howling tarts' into the bar of the Castle Hotel. Deedes was particularly incensed by the behaviour because the bar was filled with fellow officers and, worse still, riflemen who had to witness their social betters behave so badly. Deedes identifies the problem as the high turnover of young officers, leaving a rump of 'six of us, who remain rather Conservative and we hope well-bred'.

This is an early excursion into the notion that social class determines behaviour. Perhaps, after several years in journalism – the 'mackintosh trade' as he called it – he was exhilarated at being in contact again with men he regarded as his true social equivalents. Previously he had seemed ambivalent about the upper classes. At Harrow, which was fully represented by children of men who had done well out of the Great War, Deedes had always been intimidated by the young aristocrats. Whatever triggered those unusual outpourings to Hermione, it is clear that he slotted comfortably into the cosy, class-conscious atmosphere of the officers' mess.

By this time Deedes was a fit young officer, single and without dependants, ready and willing to serve as his father, uncle and grandfather had before him.* By temperament, he was ideally suited to life as a junior officer, placing his faith in his superiors and winning over the men under his command by his charm and diligent example.

From call up to D-Day, the 12th Battalion led an unsettled existence, moving regularly around the country in search of good ground for training. Rifle companies were designed to fight in support of the main tank units and, though the distinctions had blurred somewhat over the years, they were still expected to practise marksmanship to the point of exhaustion. In the Normandy Campaign, the 12th KRRC was deployed as a motor battalion within what was to become the 8th Armoured Brigade, comprising three tank regiments, the 4th/7th Dragoon Guards, 13th/18th Hussars and the Notts (Sherwood Rangers) Yeomanry. The gunners were the 147th Field Regiment RA (Essex Yeomanry), and for most of the battle across Europe the Brigade was commanded by Brigadier Erroll Prior-Palmer, a splendidly grand figure with an eye for attractive young women.

As a motor battalion, the 12th had to train by moving around at speed in American-built half-track scout cars, lightly armoured vehicles with wheels at the front and short, tank-like tracks on the back axle designed to allow it to move at a reasonable speed on both hard and boggy surfaces. The half-tracks were versatile, but their light side-armour would stop nothing more venomous than rifle fire, and because they were open-topped they were vulnerable to mortars and grenades.

In the early summer of 1941 the battalion moved north to

---

* The 2nd Queen's Westminsters was redesignated 12th KRRC in 1941.

train on the Yorkshire Moors, and was based at Ampleforth public school. Before long, the school challenged the soldiers to an athletics competition at which the battalion suffered a humiliating defeat in almost every discipline. The colonel was furious and bawled out the four company commanders, including Deedes. Morning PT had to be extended by fifteen minutes as a sop to the colonel.

The move to Yorkshire was significant in another respect for Deedes, for it was here he met Evelyn Hilary Branfoot. Hilary, as she was known, had joined the Women's Land Army on the outbreak of war and they met on her smallholding when he was delivering swill from the barracks for her pigs. It was not an easy courtship, largely because Deedes blew hot and cold, pledging his love for her then abruptly withdrawing affection, at least according to the letters that survive.

The Branfoots were a well-established ship-building family from Northumberland who had moved south to Yorkshire during the 1930s to escape embarrassment when Hilary's sister had an illegitimate child. Hilary was a headstrong woman, two years younger than Bill, and she often failed to conceal her obvious preference for the company of animals over human beings. Bill and Hilary's courtship was awkward from the start, and more than fifty years later, when interviewed together for a BBC documentary, they could not agree even on which year they had met. Hilary recalled they had met after she had been shearing sheep, on the day France fell. Deedes interrupted: 'Well, historically, you're one year out, because we actually met in the summer of '41, and France fell in '40 . . . I think it was something more to do with Hitler invading Russia.'

When Hilary persisted, Deedes countered that if there was 'a young man about with his hat in the hall' pursuing Hilary Branfoot on the day France fell it was not him. Hilary conceded that there had been 'quite a few' young soldiers who had got their 'feet under the table' at her parents' home.

Deedes was asked what attracted him to Hilary. 'I thought

rather a practical lady,' he replied. 'Jolly nice house, too,' Hilary cut in, prompting him to concede that young officers in wartime were drawn to girls whose parents had a comfortable home with hot baths, good food and a wine cellar. Hilary then made the point that after meeting Deedes she went to Plymouth and became engaged to another man, who she referred to only as Owen in some of her letters to Bill. She even went so far as to select the hymns for the wedding. Hilary kept a photograph of Owen in a bureau drawer for the rest of her life.

Deedes appeared to have no recollection of this snag in their courtship, or of having to fight to win back the affections of his future wife. The faltering exchange ended awkwardly, with Deedes conceding weakly, 'I'm in no position to contradict her version.'* The awkward tone of this exchange came as no surprise to the Deedes children, who over the years had grown used to the lack of any great rapport between them.

No evidence exists to suggest that Deedes had passionate or physical love affairs in his twenties. His attraction to the American war correspondent Helen Kirkpatrick was unrequited. It is quite possible that Hilary Branfoot was more sexually experienced than Deedes when they met. When talking about sexual behaviour in the 1930s, Deedes would always stress how respectably the two sexes behaved towards each other after a little burst of promiscuity following the First World War. That may have been true of the majority of the population, and it may too have been the norm in the world of journalism, but it was certainly not the case for literary types, as a reading of Evelyn Waugh's *A Handful of Dust*, or indeed of Waugh's letters and diaries about his aristocratic friends, shows. Patrick Marnham's 2006 biography of the writer Mary Wesley, who was born a year before Deedes, shows her to have

---

* This programme, made by Michael Cockerell, contained a segment showing Hilary trying to save England's songbirds by trapping and killing magpies in their garden. For weeks after the film was aired Deedes received hate mail from people describing themselves as bird lovers.

had no shortage of lovers, married or single, in the 1930s. The disruption to normal married life caused by the war, combined with heightened passion because of the general assumption of imminent death in the face of the German onslaught, lowered inhibitions for many.*

The letters Bill wrote to Hilary from this period were destroyed, but he kept some that he received from her tucked away in a drawer in New Hayters, separated from his main filing system. The letters reveal Hilary to have been prone to rapid mood swings and acutely lacking in self-confidence. She is aware that she is not well educated, and she is certainly a poor speller. She frequently expresses regret for her moodiness, apologising for spoiling lunches or dinners with her displays of anger. She was clearly cross that, while Owen had proposed marriage after knowing her for only four days, Deedes dithered endlessly, even after urging her to break the engagement with her new fiancé.

She begins one letter from this time, when she is in agonies of indecision about her rival suitors, with a barb. 'Bill, my dear . . . We are, as you say, overwrought. I may have been hasty in getting engaged in a week, but I do not think it wise to be equally hasty in breaking it off quickly just because in a few hours you decide to change your mind and do something you had no intention of doing when you came south and have had 16 months to think over, and seven weeks seperation [*sic*] to see if we could get along without each other.'

Few of the letters are dated, so it is difficult to know at which particular moments they hit crises in their courtship, but the explosions were clearly frequent. In one generally cheerful letter, written in early 1942, Hilary gently rebukes Bill for his acute

---

* A couple of years after Hilary's death, Lady Aldington, a Kent neighbour, suggested that Lady Deedes had been 'highly sexed' in her earlier life. Lady Aldington offered no specific evidence for this assertion, though the two women had gone on riding and camping holidays with their young children when these sorts of matters might have been discussed.

emotional reticence, which has clearly been a cause of friction between them since their very first dates.

'There are terrible entrys [*sic*] in my diary after several of our outings about the old iceberg stuff still persisting. Darling, it isn't only a shell around you, it was sometimes a huge stone wall with glass on top.' Another undated letter begins: 'Darling, I want to apologise. I am so sorry for all the beastly things I said to you . . .'

There was a strong strand of self-reproach, bordering on self-loathing, in Hilary, and it kept finding expression in her courtship with Bill. His emotional chilliness would enrage her, she would react volcanically and then apologise by letter for spoiling their precious time together. From what Hilary wrote, it seemed her sisters had tried to persuade her to break her engagement to Bill. 'You were quite right about my not making up my *own* mind and about my sisters giving me an inferiority complex. They do but you are the very best cure and do make me feel less of an ass, why I cannot think as you really know me so well and ought to make me feel more of one.'

Despite the inauspicious beginning to their courtship, and the subsequent ups and downs, Bill and Hilary married on 21 November 1942 at the Church of the Holy Trinity in Stonegrave, the Yorkshire village where the Branfoots had settled. Deedes married in uniform, and his best man was his second-in-command, Alan Young. Hilary wore a gown run up by Reg Hubbard, the battalion's flamboyant messing officer, who had worked around the stages of Drury Lane for many years before joining the Queen's Westminsters Day Squad. Hubbard gamely set about scrounging for pieces of cloth and managed to create a perfectly satisfactory wedding dress. Years later, Deedes explained that Hubbard, who was an excellent cook as well as a talented dressmaker, was 'what you'd call a queer these days'. Deedes remained grateful to the memory of Hubbard for the rest of his life, noting with genuine affection, albeit in the unfashionable language of a man born in 1913, 'that's partly why I've always had a soft corner for homos'.

Wyndham travelled back to London on the train from York with the newly married couple. Bill and Hilary then spent two nights at Claridge's, before moving on to a pub near Tunbridge Wells for a week's honeymoon. Apart from these details, Deedes retained no memories of his first days as a married man.

Unlike many couples who married in wartime, Bill and Hilary were not immediately separated by military necessity. As Company Commander, Deedes was entitled to live off base if he chose. Hilary, who, unlike her husband, had family money, rented a house near Ampleforth, where Bill would often stay when not on exercise, although the battalion continued to move around the country. Apart from the prospect of the coming battle in continental Europe, life for a young married officer from 1942 until D-Day was not unpleasant. Training was often hard but, as Deedes would point out, compared with a merchant seaman or RAF crewman an officer in a training battalion had a relatively easy time. Hilary soon became pregnant with Jeremy, who was born in November 1943. Thus the male line was secure before Deedes had to lead his company across the Channel and into the teeth of German military power. Jeremy's arrival caused a row with the Branfoots. Bill was not present for the birth, which was not unusual for that time, but it took him a full four days to get back to Yorkshire from East Anglia, where his battalion was helping with the sugar beet crop, to visit Hilary and their first child. 'Mother-in-law was not at all impressed,' Deedes recalled sixty years later, with a guilty smile. A few months into their marriage there was another minor domestic incident, which passed into Deedes family lore. Bill had sent a parcel to Hilary, which she assumed was a present for her forthcoming birthday. When she opened it on the big day it turned out to be her husband's dirty washing, which he was hoping to pick up freshly laundered a couple of days later.

The joy of Deedes's parents about the birth of their first grandchild was tempered by their strong disapproval of the name Jeremy, which, it seems, they thought lacked grandeur. Over the previous three hundred years or so, Deedes first sons had tended to be called William or Julius, and often the names alternated through the generations. Herbert and Gladys refused to let the matter drop, and the issue was still simmering in the autumn of 1944. Hilary was sufficiently upset to mention it in a letter to Bill, who was in the field and fighting his way towards Germany. 'I rather felt we might get a rocket from the elder Deedes about Jeremy instead of Julius,' Bill wrote back to Hilary, controlling his irritation at his parents' bad behaviour. Bill reminded Hilary of two objections to his parents' preferred name: he knew of a 'very boring and unpopular man called Julius', but, more importantly, 'Julius Caesar was a General and fought and things'.

Deedes was at this point going through some sort of crisis, which found him doubting the ruling class's moral authority to wage war. He was depressed by the realisation that the war was going to continue through the winter, and rather weakly left it to Hilary to sort out the family mess, suggesting she might be able to change the name to Julius if she spoke to 'the chaps in charge of deed polls'. Hilary, who was already finding her in-laws difficult, declined to take up that suggestion. Their son remained Jeremy Wyndham Deedes, and as a belated post-war peace offering, Bill and Hilary's second son was named Julius.[*]

Though there is no specific reference to the condition, it seems clear, from Hilary's letters, that she had general depressive tendencies and that after the birth of Jeremy she suffered from acute post-natal depression. Full of remorse, she writes to Bill after one quarrel: 'I feel you had such a lousey [*sic*] weekend due to my being crabby and depressed.' Her condition had become so bad in the run-sup to D-Day that a Yorkshire neighbour and friend called Peg wrote to Bill in June 1944 trying to

---

[*] Jeremy Deedes had two sons, who were named George and Henry, neither a traditional male Deedes name.

reassure him about Hilary's fragile mental state and to explain how common it was for mothers to suffer a decline after giving birth: 'One doesn't realise how much it takes out of you, and when you stop a sort of reaction sets in and an awful depression, but Hilary has quite definitely got over that now and really is full of beans.'

Bill's last letters to Hilary before embarkation became progressively more affectionate, sometimes gently teasing, as he tried to raise her spirits and reassure that he would be coming home again. They are topped 'Darling', and tailed 'All love, Darling, Bill', or sometimes 'God bless you and all my love'. He signed off one letter with S.W.A.L.K., and when she failed to mention it in her reply he added a P.S. in his next letter to her. Bill explained that one of his young officers, Lieutenant Luxmore, had dared him to put it in as a test because that was how the cockney riflemen signed off their letters to their wives and girlfriends. 'Apparently it means "Sealed with a Loving Kiss"! You don't know what you're missing not being married to a Rifleman, & only to a dull major.'

But as he tried to cheer up Hilary, Deedes's spirits were further lowered by terrible news about his sister Frances. As the eldest daughter, she was closest in age to Bill and closest emotionally, and he adored her. Beautiful and charming, she was plucky too, the daughter most likely to stand up to their father when his behaviour became particularly irrational during their miserable years at Saltwood. She had joined the Voluntary Aid Detachment, trained as a nurse and ministered to the Dunkirk evacuees at a hospital base outside Folkestone in 1940. In early 1944, aged twenty-eight, she became seriously ill and was diagnosed with Hodgkin's disease, a malignant disorder that attacks the lymph nodes, spleen and liver. She was discharged from her nursing role, and as she was unmarried she had no option but to return to Hythe to live with her parents. By this time Herbert and Gladys had been forced to leave their house on Marine Parade, with its views of the Channel, when a six-inch defensive artillery gun was positioned on adjacent land during the height of the fears of a German invasion. Frances's condition was stable for a while, but by D-Day Bill knew full well that his sister's long-term prognosis was poor, and when he embarked for Europe he had no way of knowing if he would ever see her again, even if he survived.

As far as possible, Deedes busied himself with preparing for the land invasion of Europe. Ever diligent, he could become so preoccupied that in the officers' mess he could appear aloof. Deedes's fellow officers in 12th KRRC (2QWR) recalled a highly accomplished Company Commander, while noting that as a man he was difficult to penetrate and had few close friends. Stephen McWatters, one of the many Old Etonian officers in the battalion, found him easy to talk to and often the life and soul of party games in the mess and endless games of billiards. 'He was the outstanding amateur officer of our battalion, a reliable soldier, but more than that I would say he was among the very best I encountered.'

But, despite his admiration for Deedes as a soldier, McWatters was struck by the inscrutable Deedes reserve. Some of the older members of the battalion, who tended to resent the new recruits who came up from the Territorials, found Deedes 'untrustworthy and insincere', McWatters recalled, though he did not share that opinion himself. Nevertheless, he did find it difficult to befriend him: 'There was a barrier there that you couldn't get across. Nobody seemed very close to him.' McWatters confided that he was not at all surprised to find that Deedes had gone into politics after the war.

John Butterwick, an intelligence officer and another Etonian, had a similarly high opinion of Deedes's soldiering skills. 'He was a bloody good company commander – the best we had.' Butterwick remembered Deedes as a soldier with a sense of humour and time to encourage his men and junior officers. However, he raised a trivial point which has intrigued many friends and colleagues over the years. That is, when exactly did

121

the singular Bill Deedes slurring lisp actually materialise? Butterwick was adamant that there was absolutely no trace of it when Deedes wore the King's uniform in the 1940s. 'If you ask me, it's acquired,' he maintained.

CHAPTER 8

SWIFT AND BOLD

*'Darling, it's absolutely loony, or else I am. No I'm jolly
sure I'm not.'*

The 12th Battalion's assault on Nazi-occupied continental
Europe almost foundered before it began when, at the point
of embarkation from the London docks, the men encountered
the iron will of British trade unionism. The battalion had missed
the first wave of the Normandy Invasion on 6 June because there
were not enough boats to take them across the Channel. When
they marshalled five days later, in two groupings at West India
Docks and Royal Albert Docks, they faced an unexpected problem. This was long before the era of roll-on, roll-off landing craft,
and every vehicle destined to take the fight to the Wehrmacht
had to be hoisted by crane on to the two American-built LSTs, or
Landing Ship, Tanks. But the dockers refused to do the loading
work, claiming they were unfamiliar with the American half-track
vehicles and therefore did not know how to classify the load and
what to charge. In blunt terms, they were exploiting the national
crisis to extract extra money from the battalion's cash float.

In later years, Deedes would often describe the baleful dockside
scene in elaborate detail, with a rather unconvincing East End
music hall accent. 'Trouble is, mate, we don't have the Rate,' he
would have the shop steward explaining, and then refusing to

123

budge. At the time, Deedes had been baffled; the riflemen, many of them fellow East Enders and neighbours or cousins of the dockers, had been enraged. Deedes, who was deemed to understand the mind of the cockney because he had lived in Bethnal Green, took charge. He told the dockers that across the Channel Allied soldiers were clinging on to a precarious beachhead and were in desperate need of reinforcements. But the union men were unmoved, and refused even to allow the riflemen to do the work themselves.

In the end, Deedes struck a compromise. The riflemen would load the vehicles, under the supervision of a retired docker, so that strict considerations of workplace demarcation could be maintained. This was not an ideal outcome.

Deedes's riflemen had spent many days meticulously waterproofing the vehicles for their advance through the surf at Normandy. This necessitated complicated applications of webbing and tape, and mechanics had to jerry-build long, vertical exhaust pipe extensions. The 12th's War Diary reveals quite how exacting the preparations were.* All vehicles had to have their carburettors emptied, petrol taps secured in the 'off' position and then securely lashed upright to withstand lurching inclines of forty-five degrees during what was expected to be a rough Channel crossing.

Much of this adaptive work and meticulous preparation was destroyed by the riflemen's inexpert handling of the cranes. Deedes never forgot nor forgave the lack of solidarity in the battalion's send-off from the London docks. He first wrote about the dockers' obduracy in the *Telegraph* on the fiftieth anniversary of VE Day in a piece that argued there had been bad behaviour as well as valour during the war. He received several abusive letters, some accusing him of inventing the incident to do down trade unions and the working classes.

---

* All battalions are required to keep a War Diary when in action. A junior officer would usually be held responsible for adding to it daily, but in practice they were often overlooked and filled in later, so they can be inaccurate or incomplete.

In fact, there was an official bias in favour of downplaying incidents such as this during the war and afterwards, in part to protect morale and give the impression of a nation united against an external threat. Significantly, there is no mention of the dockers' behaviour in the War Diary, which refers to the loading of the vehicles in a straightforward two-line reference without revealing who did the work. Nor did it rate a mention in *Swift and Bold*, a history of the KRRC's campaign in Europe published in 1949, which was co-edited by Deedes. In a privately published memoir, John Butterwick remembered ugly exchanges between the dockers and the riflemen, though his recollection was that the dispute arose when the dockers refused to work because they said their shift had ended. Whatever the precise circumstances, it was clear that officially sponsored images of patriotic workers in reserved trades putting their shoulders to the wheel and willing the squaddies on to fight the Hun were not always as clear-cut as the newsreels and propaganda films of the era suggested.

Hilary wrote Bill one last letter before his departure, which he received in France, in which she was somehow unable to convey much emotion. 'I wonder what sort of crossing you will have today,' she wrote, rather as though he were about to cross the Channel for a few days in Paris. She regretted Bill hadn't taken his camera with him as it 'would have been nice to have some pictures of places you visited'. Possibly she could not bear to put into words her fears about his chances of never coming home again. The letter closes on a mundane note about a hairdressing appointment, before she signs off: 'All love sweetie, Hilary.'

On the evening of 13 June 1944, the battalion set sail in two boats, laden with the imperfectly loaded vehicles that were supposed to help them reinforce the Normandy beachhead, many of their elaborate waterproofings already ruined. That night they anchored in the Thames estuary, sleeping fitfully on their specially issued bundle of straw and two blankets. Each man also kept with him a life belt, as well as 'Bags Vomit, three per man'.

The Bags Vomit were certainly needed, for most of the riflemen had never before ventured on the high seas and there was a heavy swell.

Despite the squalid conditions on board ship, Deedes felt a sense of relief and exhilaration that their mission was finally under way. For almost five years he and his company had been training for this moment. There had been a sense of anti-climax for many of the men when they were unable to be part of the original landing on 6 June. For members of a regiment with such a proud history as the KRRC, it was considered rather shameful not to have been there when the second front was opened up on the Germans. Now most of them were anxious to catch up.

Deedes was afflicted throughout his life by a chronic lack of confidence. But as a soldier, though he often expected things to go wrong, he never doubted his own competence. As soon as he joined the Queen's Westminsters, he found he had a facility for getting on with those above and below him in the chain of command. Transferring from Fleet Street to soldiering, Deedes displayed the same blithe dexterity with which he had navigated cannily to the *Daily Telegraph* upon the *Morning Post*'s closure. He was fit and competent, and physically brave. He fitted in and could lead men, a truth recognised when he was given command of B Company in 1942, taking direct responsibility for its 110 men. By proving himself as an officer, he was validating himself against the measure not so much of his father, who was a failure and in truth something of an embarrassment, but against his uncle Wyndham, knighted, decorated and lauded as one of the youngest brigadiers in the regiment's history.

From their anchorage in the Thames estuary, the two boats set off in convoy on 14 June, passing through the Straits of Dover in darkness. The battalion arrived off the coast of Normandy the following morning, in a swell heavy enough to make the proposed dash through the surf hazardous. The vehicles were winched into landing craft for the final assault on the beach with the waterproofed half-tracks and scout cars. They found themselves near Courseulles-sur-Mer on the right flank of the 2nd British Army landing areas.

As they came ashore on the morning of 16 June, the 12th were met by a young British naval officer overseeing the second wave of reinforcements of the Normandy beachhead. Most of the German guns that had defended the Normandy beaches had been silenced by the first wave of D-Day liberators, so there was plenty of time for the 12th Battalion to wait a little way off shore for the waters to recede and then to drive their vehicles across the beach to dry French land. All the training for the amphibious assault turned out to have been a waste of time.

The beachhead was secure by the time the 12th Battalion arrived. There were dangers for sure – from snipers, mines and stray shells – but their landing was uncontested, because by this day, D-Day+10, the main battle line was already some miles inland. The Allied Beach Masters efficiently directed the incoming traffic in scenes of surprising calm and order. The men were staggered by what they saw when the sun came up. As Major Fred Coleridge wrote in the regimental history it was like '"hundreds and thousands" on a nursery cake, ships of all shapes and sizes covered the waters. There seemed more ships than water.' By this point the Allies had almost complete air superiority over northern France, so at least they did not fear attack by plane. Once ashore, the men dug trenches and defensive positions against a German counterattack. But the relative ease of the 12th's landing did not mean the months ahead would be trouble-free, and in fact the unit was to see action within a week.

The break-out from the hard-won beachhead was bound to be fraught. Normandy made for lousy tank country, because the narrow lanes became easily blocked and the dense bushes and woods offered excellent cover for German defenders, slowing any armoured advance. Hence the need for units such as the 12th KRRC. They advanced in their half-tracks, protecting the flanks of the armoured column and testing the strength of the enemy resistance before the tanks were pushed forward.

127

The 12th was 'blooded' at Tessel Wood as part of the advance on the town of Rauray. Not for the last time, the No. 18 wireless sets – the bane of British radio operators – proved unreliable, partly because German snipers could pick off their conspicuous aerials. The riflemen took a heavy pounding from German Tiger tanks well dug into the woods. The commanding officer, Lieutenant-Colonel R. G. R. Oxley – who was soon to be relieved of his command – wrote a furious denunciation of the 'complete uselessness, nay menace, of the No. 18 set' in the War Diary. A lieutenant and ten riflemen were killed, and several more wounded. It was a costly baptism. 'I don't think I shall ever get to like this,' Deedes wrote home on 30 June. 'I can't imagine any sane person would, but one's nerves get accustomed to it all. The vast waste of material, life, property is, I feel, morbid-making.' Deedes was also struck by the strange apathy of the French peasantry. 'They live quite comfortably in the country, and I don't think greatly care who runs things. I can achieve little affection for them.'

Another letter to one of his sisters – almost certainly Frances – lambasts the politicians who twice in thirty years had said to the nation's young men, 'We have failed and we can no longer do our jobs as statesmen. You must enter the arena and do it for us.' In his tight handwriting, he continues: 'All politicians should be hanged and disembowelled.' But the letter is not generally bitter or downhearted about the fighting. He tells his sister to take care of Hilary, and not to fret about him. 'As part of a crack battalion trained and equipped to a fine edge I am awfully confident. One learns here that casualties are divided between incompetence and bad luck. Bad luck, so called, I leave to the Almighty. Competence one can try to achieve.'

August was the turning point, when the British 2nd Army pressing in from the north squeezed the German force at Falaise hard against the American army under General Patton pushing from the south. Huge damage was done to German armour, and thousands of prisoners were taken. Falaise produced a false optimism that the war would be over by Christmas, a notion Deedes scorned. He was shocked by the level of carnage, the dead bodies and the constant stink of dead livestock that no one bothered to bury. He noted that only two months after their landing in Europe he was the only one of the four company commanders not to have been replaced or invalided out. 'Now I remain the last chap in the battalion in 1939. I should think fate has something saucy for me, what?' (This last observation cannot have offered much reassurance to the Deedes family back home.) Writing to Hilary on 28 August, he conceded that he had been lucky: 'I am always pessimistic, too much so, my officers tell me, but one has to be, and looking for the worst has saved me and them some dirty situations so far.' One of the logistical miracles of the Allied war effort was the reliability of the mail from the battlefield. Letters home would usually reach Hilary in Yorkshire within three or four days, and the service was generally maintained during even the most ferocious battles.

In his autobiography, Deedes extracted from a letter of that same month an incident in failing light in which he almost bumped into two German civilian youths, aged about seventeen, while walking through some woods. They whipped up their hands, shouting '*Kamerad*' (comrade) when Deedes brandished his revolver. But he did not repeat the central observation of that letter: 'I hate all Germans now with fervour and shall not easily change my view.' Even when in uniform, however, Deedes was essentially too humane to retain a loathing for an entire nation and in the months ahead he was to contrast the valour of the German soldier with the vileness of the SS officer.

By late August 1944 the battalion was tearing eastwards across France, sometimes at forty miles an hour. Deedes oversaw the capture of a German lorry with two crates of Martell cognac and six hundred thousand francs, as well as – best of all for the Company Commander – a brand new typewriter. Deedes was thrilled with the progress they were making and the organisational genius of the British army on the move. 'I find my Martell and some aspirin and plenty of cigarettes and the excitement makes one go like a train and I have never felt fitter, fresher, or in better heart than I do tonight. The men of course find taking prisoners a lot better than being potted at.'

On 3 September, Deedes's Company, backed up by a squadron of tanks to provide firepower should matters deteriorate, pulled off an audacious operation by single-handedly liberating Lille, then a city of two hundred thousand people. As B Company led the advance into the centre of town the French poured into the streets, offering fruit, wine and kisses. 'The carriers already looked like harvest thanksgiving. Bottles began to appear and through the canvas roofs of the half-tracks a good deal of stuff was changing hands,' Deedes recalled. Many of the riflemen, unused to wine, were becoming drunk. Young women climbed up on the vehicles, dangling their legs over the windscreens and inflaming the libidos of the men within who had been without wives and girlfriends for months. Deedes, though overwhelmed by the French welcome, was nervous that his men would be sitting ducks if the Germans mounted a counter-attack.

As word spread of the British presence, thousands poured onto the streets, hemming in the tanks and half-tracks as Deedes fretted about the danger of snipers. 'After the first few hilarious moments the welcome got organised. They lifted babies up to the tank turrets to be kissed by grubby and unshaven troopers. Each kiss drew a tremendous cheer and more drink. Many friends of the Allies arrived in due course to present compliments, and quite often a bottle. There were a lot of reminiscences about episodes in 1914–18 and 1940 which had to be heard.'

Members of the Maquis began firing into the air, pleading with the riflemen to come and help them winkle out pockets of German resistance. A uniformed German medical officer demanded Deedes provide help for some of his wounded men, but his riflemen were becoming distracted as more bottles of wine were thrust into their hands. 'Encouraged by a brazen few, modest ladies of all ages sought embraces. "This is revolting," said the

Squadron Leader, watching from his turret as his crews try not very hard to resist these attentions. At the time he had two well-formed cupid's bows of lipstick on his cheek, and smears of rouge from ear to ear.'

John Butterwick, the intelligence officer, later claimed that the brigadier ordered B Company out of Lille and the few miles back to battalion headquarters when he became alarmed by the slurred voices of Deedes's men reporting back on the radio. Deedes's recollection was different: that the giant street party ended abruptly when German guns at the other end of the city announced a heavy enemy presence, forcing the Company into a strategic withdrawal. Either way, B Company's swift and audacious liberation of Lille entered battalion folklore and greatly cheered the men. Crucially, the Germans, impressed by the boldness of B Company and deterred by the warmth of the French reception for Allied forces, did not attempt to re-take Lille.

The strategy of landing in Normandy and taking the fight to the Germans from the beachhead was triumphantly vindicated that summer. After ten weeks of bitter fighting in Normandy, the German forces collapsed in rout and the allies pushed eastwards far quicker than they had dared to hope. Allied commanders had expected to have to fight for every yard of France, but Paris fell without resistance and by early September British forces were streaming into Brussels. On the Eastern Front the Red Army was making even better progress. In eight weeks, from the beginning of July, Russian forces advanced three hundred miles. For a few heady days the soldiers thought it could all be over by Christmas, though in his letters home Deedes never shared this unfounded optimism. 'Well, I can't tell what the future will be,' he wrote on 28 August. 'The bloodiest fighting may well be before us, or maybe we shan't have much more shooting.'

The euphoria of the late summer of 1944 was soon to be crushed by the debacle of Operation Market Garden, Field Marshal Montgomery's grand scheme to bring a quick end to the war by securing the Rhine crossing at Arnhem. Though the mission was conceptually flawed, Deedes had initially been awed by the sight of the drop of the airborne troops, the skies above the Rhine filled with parachutes, and gliders bringing more men and equipment. The 12th KRRC moved towards the Rhine with the 8th Armoured Brigade in the wake of the Guards Armoured Division. But the airborne troops could not hold the bridgehead as the Germans counter-attacked ferociously.

There was a reluctance on the Allied side to admit the operation was failing. On 22 September, five days after the initial drops of the airborne, the 12th were handed some disturbing battle orders. Brigadier Erroll Prior-Palmer, then commanding the Armoured Brigade, ruled that drastic measures were needed to reinforce the Allied defenders at Arnhem, the 6th Airborne Division.

Prior-Palmer's contribution was a hastily drawn-up plan to send the 13th/18th Hussars' tanks to reinforce the Airborne Division and secure the Arnhem bridge; extraordinarily, the riflemen of the 12th Battalion were to ride on the flanks of the tanks in a mad dash to the Rhine. The men sensed immediately that the plan had something of the Charge of the Light Brigade about it; some thought it close to being a suicide mission. John Butterwick recalled watching the vehicles being prepared for the hazardous operation. 'The Colonel [Lt-Col the Hon M. G. Edwardes] and I watched them go past – it was clear that he expected heavy casualties and likely failure.'*

In *Armageddon*, his study of the last year of the war, Max Hastings suggests the battle orders handed to 12th KRRC reflected the 'bizarre delusions' of commanders that Operation Market Garden could be salvaged even when it was obvious it had failed. Deedes kept the order for the rest of his life. It baldly laid out the plans that almost certainly would have led to his

---

* Brigadier Prior-Palmer's son Simon had lunch with Deedes in Kent in 2005 to talk about his father. As Simon Prior-Palmer left, Deedes – who had a very high regard for the Brigadier – said with a smile, 'It's goodbye to the son of the man who tried so hard to kill me!' Then he added: 'I've had sixty years more than I should.'

death, and the destruction of his Company. 'Intention: 12 KRRC will attack and seize the road bridge at ARNHEIM [*sic*],' as though that would prove to be the easiest thing in the world. The idea was that the very boldness of the mission would catch the enemy on the hop. Despite the heavy German presence in the routes into Arnhem, the plan demanded the tanks and the KRRC move at a speed 'flat out from the "off"'. In reality, the Germans had been picking off British and American soldiers for five days, since the arrival of the first airborne troops. After receiving his battle orders, the Company Commander briefed his officers. 'It's VCs for all today, boys,' Deedes told them laconically, leaving no doubt that he believed most of them would be awarded posthumously. Officers and men in B Company began writing farewell letters.

Luckily for the 12th and the tank crews, the mission was called off the next day because German resistance on the road to Arnhem was too intense to give them a clear run. Hundreds of men in that corridor died; revocation of the battle plan almost certainly saved Deedes's life. He later recalled how his riflemen, who had spent a sleepless night writing to their wives, lovers and mothers, affected to be profoundly irritated when told the mission was off. 'We've been buggered around,' Deedes recalled them muttering crossly. Even by its normal laconic standards, the War Diary was characteristically spare when noting the cancellation of the dubious operation. 'The Bn therefore had an uninterrupted evening and a restful night.'

The failure of the Arnhem plan had a terrible effect on Allied morale after the series of successes since the break-out from Normandy. For the troops fighting their way eastwards to Berlin, it meant a whole winter in the field, which they had thought could be avoided. Though he made light of it in later years, Deedes fell into a depressive state and let slip the mask of fixed jollity that, until then, he had maintained for his wife and sisters. On 22 October he wrote to Hilary to apologise for a 'silly and selfish' previous letter, which had prompted in reply a deserved 'tiny sermon' from Hilary about the need to cheer up. At first Deedes dismissed her rebuke and joked that his black mood had been caused by his 'liver, and colder weather on an early middle-aged constitution'. But he was clearly seething, not just about the conduct of the war but about how the newspapers and politicians were lying about it.

Four years earlier, as a young lieutenant, Deedes had told his sister Hermione about the low social calibre of many of the young subalterns joining the battalion. Four months in the field, fighting the might of the German army, had fundamentally changed his outlook and relieved him of his faith in the established pre-war order, so much so that the scion of one of the oldest Kent families was beginning to sound like a socialist.

> I do feel you know that what we have always called the ruling class, I suppose politicians and generals and people have made the most infernal and frightful mess, and I am not sure they are [going] to get it right. They have let the masses down with the most resounding crump which is why they are being slaughtered off out here and elsewhere . . . They refer [to] this steady crumbling of civilization in terms of the most terrific victory, and knight each other like mad and decorate each other's chests. HM [George VI] has been out here racing around HQs swording and accolading Generals all over the place. Darling, it's absolutely loony, or else I am. No I'm jolly sure I'm not.

There was a clear underlying fear that he was succumbing to the eccentricity of Deedes men – 'a family weakness' – that was evident in his own father. Herbert had become even more peculiar since the family left Saltwood Castle in 1925, writing letters to Mussolini and Hitler, and expressing vaguely socialist views. To Hilary, Deedes, for the first and only time, expresses heretical views about Wyndham, who had set him off on his career in journalism and given him board in Bethnal Green. '[A]ll my life I've thought Uncle W daft, because after the last War he got a bit bloody-minded and tucked himself away in BG. I hope sincerely I'm not getting the same sort of trouble. I don't know. It's very muddling.'

Deedes then turned to another hero of his, Lord Camrose, the chairman of the *Telegraph* who had helped to see Deedes right when the *Morning Post* folded in 1937. Previously Deedes had shown his boss the most scrupulous deference, in private and public. But by October 1944, with a bloody and freezing few months in prospect on the battlefield, Deedes was describing Camrose as just another part of the 'fearful dreary politico-propaganda nonsense' cloaking the failures in the prosecution of the war. He tells Hilary sternly that he finds the idea of returning to his pre-war work repugnant. 'My Lord Camrose dresses it up to look like a Christmas cake and serves it to the sorrowing mothers and widows to look like a Christmas cake – with candles.'

On one level, Deedes was probably just blowing off steam. An officer in such a grand Tory regiment as the King's Royal Rifle Corps could scarcely have aired such seditious thoughts in the mess, and certainly not to the riflemen. Deedes had no other outlet for his rage than letters to Hilary. In that same letter Deedes referred scathingly to those who spoke euphemistically, then rather insultingly apologised to Hilary for using 'a word you won't understand'. Deedes would often say that the Edwardian ruling class had lost its moral authority at the Battle of the Somme. Now in the bloody, muddy battlefield of north-western Europe, he was equally scathing of Britain's political and military leaders.

Looking to the future, Deedes no longer wanted to be part of the murky world where politics and journalism intersect – what today would be called the 'Westminster village'. He told Hilary that after the war he wanted to work the land: 'the only honest people left, it seems to me, are those who work the soil . . . people who can't fool nature'. This was a peculiar flight of fancy. Generations of Deedeses may have worked many acres of east Kent over the centuries, but the land had been long since sold off.

Since going to prep school, Deedes had not lived in the country and had lately become a man about town. Perhaps Deedes, who always assumed he would be killed in the war, was offering Hilary the reassuring thought that had he survived he would have come home to Yorkshire to help her out with the animals.

That October marked a low point for Deedes, but by December his spirit had improved. He wrote to Hilary on 3 December that he was expecting leave in the New Year. 'I view this with mixed feelings. I like the idea of seeing you again,' he wrote, with a casualness his new wife might reasonably have found wounding, 'but it seems these plans pre-suppose a longer war and as if we shall be wallowing away next spring.'

Although developments the following month meant all leave was cancelled, Deedes did manage a quick pre-Christmas trip to Brussels with his friend Major Fred Coleridge. For Deedes it was his first break in more than six months – since the Normandy landing. He had not spent a night away from his company and he was physically and mentally drained. At the Plaza Hotel he and Coleridge drank champagne – which Deedes never really liked – before gorging on steak tartare and claret. Then fellow officers lured the pair to a nightclub, where the champagne was 'ridiculously expensive' but the atmosphere festive.

'Fred being Fred and me being married, the girls had rather a thin time,' Deedes wrote home three days before Christmas. 'We lit their cigarettes for them. None of them had any matches! They had to watch us imbibing champagne in a bachelors' duo which maddened them.' The following evening they went to the opera to see *Don Juan*.

Coleridge was a master at Eton, and it was in Brussels that the two men agreed that Jeremy, Deedes's son, would go to Eton rather than Harrow. 'Show some confidence in the future,' Coleridge told Deedes. They returned to their battalion in time for Christmas, a day earlier than planned because of anxiety about the German counter-offensive in the Ardennes. Deedes reported home favourably on the padre's sermon on Christmas Day, but otherwise there was no disguising the bleakness of mid-winter conditions. 'We recce and dig all day and much of the night.'

Deedes had a batman, Gastrell, who took care of his basic requirements, brought him food, prepared his bed and so forth. Like most soldiers, Deedes smoked heavily, Player's cigarettes and an occasional pipe of Player's Medium Navy Cut. Tobacco could be bought from stores, though occasionally Bill would ask Hilary to send out extra supplies. After many weeks on the move, he found it difficult to sleep indoors, even in the middle of winter. He preferred to sleep under canvas, or when there was action nearby under the Humber scout car, on a bed-roll laid out by Gastrell. 'This is regarded by most as sheer lunacy,' he wrote home, but he stuck to it, preferring to 'wake up sometimes bedewed, but fresh and seeing straight'.*

The next big set piece for the 12th KRRC was the crossing of the Rhine in March, but before that there was an important regimental matter to be resolved. The 12th had been challenged by 2nd Battalion KRRC to a game of Eton football. As that year's KRRC annual reported, on 'the eve of the crossing of the Rhine, two Lieut-Colonels, five majors, and other Old Etonians were collected in the same place more or less at the same time to play the Field Game'. It was a measure of the social exclusivity of the KRRC that before an epic crossing of the Rhine, twenty Old Etonian officers could be found for this needle fixture, the remaining two places filled by ringers from Winchester College, who, the match reporter for the KRRC annual generously noted, 'more than held their own'.

The cockney riflemen watched in some bemusement as their officers played out their tribal rituals, clearly thinking their social betters must be mad. 'If they wanted further proof, they got it a few minutes later when their Commanding Officer [Lieutenant-Colonel C. d'A. P. Consett of 2nd KRRC] leapt lightly over a barbed wire fence behind the goal line to touch down a splendid

---

* In later life Deedes felt the cold terribly, as his father had before him.

long rouge, while other men of lesser heart were climbing through or under.' In what was described as an excellent contest, 'much more like Eton football than might have been expected', 2nd KRRC beat 12th KRRC 4–2.

Nothing in that jolly afternoon of sport prepared 12th Battalion for the awful battle that lay just ahead.

CHAPTER 9

THE SADDEST SPRING

*'It's ineffably sad really: the saddest spring
I can remember.'*

If the winter after the Arnhem failure had been bleak and disappointing for the Allied operation in north-western Europe,
spring held a cruel twist for the 12th KRRC. Just as Major Deedes
and his men sensed German resistance was finally beginning to
weaken, B Company suffered a catastrophe. Deedes would carry
the psychological scars of the bungled operation for the rest of his
life.

At the early signs of spring, Deedes's spirits had soared. In letters to Hilary he even praised the German forces for their valour
and determination in the face of the impending Allied victory:
'Secretly, as I think many do, the Huns we meet now are fighting
better than we encountered in Normandy . . . Wearying and sad-
dening though it is, nothing can alter the fact that the German
struggle is now heroic and I hope when he gives in, unconditionally or no, there is a slight pause to accord the usual honours to a
defeated enemy who has gone the last mile and breath before the
British press begin their campaign of odium and vengeance.'

Deedes stressed that nothing should be taken for granted, but
it was clear that he felt the end was in sight. 'All the weeping wil-
lows are out, also some blossom,' he wrote to Hilary in late

March. 'Spring comes after a long and dreary winter just as we prepare to give the Germans a thrashing. I think everyone knows this and morale is awfully high. Higher than I've known since landing. A real sense that after so many disappointments, this thing is within our grasp.'

So it seemed, when the orders came on 2 April for Deedes's company to secure a bridge over the Twente Canal in Holland, close to the German border. European canals are much wider than those in Britain, and with almost all the bridges blown by the Germans Deedes's company was given the task of finding one that was passable south of the town of Hengelo. A damaged bridge, which doubled as a lock, seemed the most promising. There were two spans that met at a small concrete island in the middle of the canal. The Germans had blown a hole in the far span, which would need repairing, but it seemed a reasonable mission.

Possibly because the tempo of the war had picked up again after the Arnhem setback, and there was a sense that victory was in sight, the operation was approached with a casualness unusual for the KRRC. But the principal blame for what followed lay not with Deedes as the commander of the company that bore the brunt of enemy fire. Rather, it seems to have been a battalion-wide failure to scout the area; B Company should simply not have been handed that mission. Deedes spent the remaining sixty-two years of his life wondering if he should have protested more forcefully about the dangers, but, in truth, a Company Commander in 1945 could not second-guess his Battalion Commander. After all, the battalion had accepted Brigade's battle orders for the suicidal Arnhem operation that was eventually called off: crossing a canal seemed, on the face of it, a much less risky proposition than riding on the outside of tanks across the Rhine.

As usual, the War Diary glossed over the scale of what ensued. The report written that evening noted baldly: 'Reports had arrived that the Germans were looting in Hengelo and Deldern, [officers] had stood on the bank of the canal without being shot at and there had been no shelling. It was presumed, therefore, that there would be little opposition to any organised attack.'

That proved to be a very costly assumption. In fact, the 12th KRRC had been sucked into an ambush. The Germans knew that, because the banks on both sides of the canal were steep, it would be impossible for the British to bring tanks in to defend the riflemen's advance. The plan called for Deedes's B Company to lead the advance with C Company held in reserve as back-up.

As B Company's leading platoon moved across the first span of the bridge, withering fire from at least four Spandau machine guns, on fixed lines, pinned down the advancing riflemen. The Spandau fire was soon backed up by accurate mortar fire. Deedes, crawling along the first span of the bridge to urge his men on, was handicapped by a routine radio failure, and Colonel Edwardes could not be reached. Deedes's men fought with exceptional valour, completing the crossing of the first span of the bridge, and then killing the Germans who had materialised as defenders of the island in the middle. Smoke was laid down to offer some cover for the riflemen, but Deedes could find no way to silence the Spandaus or the mortars raining down from the other side of the bank. John Butterwick fired mortars over the canal and some machine-gun covering fire was ordered up, but the far bank was so dense with trees that they were firing blindly and ineffectively. Then further disaster struck, turning a crisis into a massacre. As the War Diary put it, dryly as ever, 'unfortunately, at this moment, the third platoon waiting behind the bank was heavily shelled and lost 90 per cent of its men. The exploiting platoon thus being lost, it was decided to withdraw.'

As usual, the War Diary provided only part of the story. The dead and wounded of Deedes's company lay on the south bank where the platoon had been hit, but others were scattered across the bridge. Deedes knew he had to change the objective from capturing the bridge to a plan for withdrawal of the dead and wounded. He organised small rescue parties that would inch along the exposed bridge to reach the wounded, who were stranded agonisingly out of reach and without any cover. As they moved along the bridge, machine-gun fire whistled above their helmets and mortars dropped all around them.

The initiative was seized by Lieutenant Andrew Burnaby-Atkins, a handsome Old Etonian. He had won a Military Cross the previous month, and had acquired a reputation across the regiment for exceptional valour, bordering on recklessness. He was one of the many KRRC officers who hunted, and, according to Deedes, who did not, they were always the bravest men on the battlefield. Seeing that the leading platoon was still being cut to shreds, Burnaby-Atkins jumped back on to the bridge with his Bren Gun and two magazines, and sprinted across thirty yards of open ground swept by Spandau fire to take up a firing position. There, in full view of the enemy, according to the citation for the Bar to his MC, the twenty-two-year-old lieutenant, 'fired from the hip, emptying the two complete magazines at the Spandaus to cover the withdrawal of the forward platoon. It was his initiative that made this withdrawal possible.'

Burnaby-Atkins may have taken the initiative, but Deedes probably saved his life. Seeing his subaltern hopelessly stranded, Deedes sprinted along the exposed section of bridge through machine-gun fire and detonated smoke grenades to give him the faintest cover. This, according to Deedes's own MC citation, 'greatly assisted the successful withdrawal of the leading platoons'. His conduct so inspired his men that it allowed the company to 'withdraw in good order when ordered to do so'.

That was the British army at its most ingeniously euphemistic in describing how a conceptually flawed operation was closed down. B Company was not effecting an ordered withdrawal but a desperate retreat, and at a terrible cost. Almost half of the company was dead or wounded. Twenty-two men were killed outright, including two of Deedes's young officers, Lieutenant Roger Green and Lieutenant Barry Newton, who had been with him since the Normandy landing. Another officer was wounded, along with another twenty men.*

This was the moment of total despair for a talented and diligent company commander who, in the previous nine-month campaign, had seen his courage rewarded with good fortune. Deedes would later refuse to talk about the day he won his MC. He never gave any hint of the astonishing valour he displayed in running across the exposed span of the bridge to save his young lieutenant. Indeed, it was only possible to piece together what happened that day by talking to other survivors, and by comparing his and Burnaby-Atkins's respective medal citations.†

The numerous medals won by Wyndham hung for many years in a frame in the Deedes drawing room, while his own MC was stashed discreetly in a sock drawer in his bedroom. In part this was a natural modesty but, perhaps more than that, Deedes never wanted to think or talk of the horror he witnessed that day. Though the intelligence failures that did not identify the entrenched Germans defensive positions were the direct cause of the disaster, Deedes was the Company Commander and knew he had to take a share of responsibility. In years to come he talked bitterly of his MC as 'a survivor's medal', and with exaggerated self-effacement would cackle bitterly that he had won his for retreating, adding by way of explanation: 'The Colonel said, "that was a bit of a show, wasn't it? Here's an MC."' As Deedes knew perfectly well, no Military Cross was ever handed out so casually. Being a good officer mattered enormously to Deedes – more, even, than being a good reporter – but he could not begin to take pride in this formal recognition of his valour because men under his command had died.

---

* War Diaries and official regimental histories of the period tended to note only officers killed or wounded and to ignore or underplay other ranks. This omission feels uncomfortable today, but Deedes abided by that convention in his 1997 autobiography, recording the loss of his two young lieutenants while making no mention of the forty-five riflemen killed or wounded on the Twente Canal.

† According to his widow, Caroline, Burnaby-Atkins displayed a similar reticence.

As if to pre-empt tributes to his personal heroism, Deedes later developed a different explanation as to why he survived. He claimed to have noticed that the Germans ceased firing when they realised that he and Burnaby-Atkins were withdrawing the wounded. None of the other officers who survived had any recollection of this, and there is no mention of the ceasefire in the War Diary, or in *Swift and Bold*, the regimental history, or in any of Deedes's letters from Europe. Nor did Deedes refer to it in his autobiography. He first mentioned this surprising German chivalry when offering a favourable assessement of the Wehrmacht (as opposed to the SS or Hitler-Jugend) in 2003, and repeated the claim in an article in the *Daily Telegraph* marking the sixtieth anniversary of VE Day.

On the face of it, Deedes's revised explanation of why he survived seems implausible, not least because Burnaby-Atkins's citation specifically states that he was firing at the Spandau operators to give cover to the team removing the wounded. The German machine-gunners would presumably not have stopped firing when under attack from a recklessly brave English officer firing a Bren Gun at them from his hip. At this distance it is not possible absolutely to rule out the suggestion that the Germans were exceptionally decent that day. But it somehow seems more likely that an old soldier in his nineties, seeking to settle accounts before his death, just wanted to be seen to see the good in his fellow man.

The worst part of commanding a company came when the guns fell silent after the day's battle and letters had to be written to wives and parents. Deedes also wrote up the mini-obituaries of the officers that appeared in the KRRC annual, basing them heavily on the letter he had written to the bereaved in England. The loss at the Twente Canal of Lieutenant Newton, an only son who had been wounded at Normandy only to return to the battalion and be killed at the age of twenty-two, hit Deedes especially hard. Most of the obituary entries in the KRRC annuals of the war years were dreary and spare, offering basic details of place of birth and education, with a few pro forma plaudits of the officer's bravery and a reassurance that his death was not in vain. Deedes's entries were more heartfelt and affectionate, and he exploited his writing skills to convey much more than the mundane details offered by other company commanders. In these dismally frequent tallies of the loss of young life, Deedes achieved a genuine lyricism about the fallen officer and the writing had much more power, there in the heat of loss, than in his subsequent accounts for his autobiography and regular anniversary pieces for the *Telegraph*.

'No duty was too high for him, nor any situation bad enough to prevent momentary pleasure in a poem, a wild bird, a fading sunset,' he wrote of Lieutenant Green, also killed on the canal, aged twenty-one. 'He died, I think, as he had lived his life in action, grudging no effort, giving unflinchingly of his best, but with his eyes on the hills beyond.'

Turning to Lieutenant Newton, killed by Spandau fire a few minutes before his close friend Roger Green, Deedes lauded his boyishness and courage. 'Always he could find contentment for himself and others in the simple things of life. The Young in Heart! Sometimes in England we laughed at him for it. Only on the battlefields of Europe did one appreciate its true value and come to envy him.'

Deedes, a decade older than his subalterns, established with them a sort of connection, somewhere between brotherly and fatherly love, which by his own admission he later failed to find with his own sons. Deedes would certainly have deprecated any cod psychological treatment of the Twente Canal disaster, but it does not seem fanciful to conclude that some part of his limited emotional capacity died along with his men that dreadful April day, just a month before the German surrender. As he wrote of Newton in his regimental obituary, 'When he was killed I think everyone in the Company who knew him felt a few years older, and the funny things in life seemed much less fun.' For Deedes, the loss of these young officers who had been with him since landing did not cause fleeting grief; it was a wound he carried with him for the next sixty-two years of his life.* In his writings and his conversations with his family over the succeeding decades, he never achieved that sort of emotional power, even when struck by family tragedy. Three days after the disaster, Deedes wrote to Hilary, apologising for the long gap since his last letter. He said that recent fighting had been much harder than the advance out of Normandy, explaining that he could not give her any details for operational reasons, though he added: 'In fact, I'd like to say nothing about it, but will tell you all about it later.' It was one of the saddest, bitterest letters he ever sent his wife and all his optimism from the month before had evaporated. He lambasts his own pre-war trade, 'the damned papers', which are full of propaganda and pretend the war is as good as won. 'By golly, it's not. Lots of 16-year-olds keen to die for Hitler.' He was profoundly depressed, as despondent as he had been the previous October following the Arnhem debacle.

Throughout his life Deedes was highly sensitive to the changing seasons. In Saltwood Castle, the end of winter promised respite after months of discomfort in the cold, damp rooms. From his cub reporting days until his last columns written in his nineties, signs of the weather turning were religiously chronicled. As the Allies made progress towards Berlin after the Arnhem setback, the spring of 1945 promised an early end to the fighting.

To witness and experience carnage as nature was bountifully yielding fresh hope was the cruellest touch. 'It's ineffably sad really: the saddest spring I can remember. One feels how superior nature is. Each spring everything is reborn and renewed, while man, when smitten down, goes out. Spring in the battlefield certainly gives me a lump in the throat and a stinging in the eyes.'

---

* Andrew Burnaby-Atkins survived the war despite the extraordinary risks he took. He later became ADC to Field Marshal Montgomery on his appointment as Chief of the Imperial General Staff, and later godfather to Deedes's second daughter, Jill. Though Deedes and Burnaby-Atkins were friendly in the years after the war, they were not in regular contact by the time of the latter's death in 1995.

Bill's formidable grandmother, Rose
Elinor Deedes.

Herbert William Deedes, Bill's father,
about to fight the Boers.

Bill's parents returning 'home' to Saltwood Castle after their marriage in 1912.

Herbert William welcomed home as a hero from the Boer War.

Villagers were given a keepsake of the young squire's coming of age.

"*Facta non Verba.*"

✦ ✦ ✦ ✦

To commemorate the Coming of Age

of

William Deedes.

Saltwood Castle.   *October 27th, 1902.*

'The master of our lives' – Saltwood Castle.

Above: A studious little boy.

Left: Bill with his mother.

With his sisters (left to right) Frances, Margaret and Hermione.

Packed for Africa: Uncle Wyndham can be seen in the background.

WFD with his Sikh driver in Addis Ababa 1935. *(Sunday Telegraph)*

WFD's *Morning Post* press pass for the Abyssinian War.

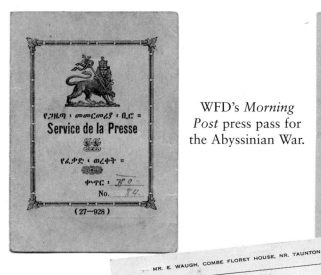

Evelyn Waugh's terse response to WFD's letter of sympathy when Auberon Waugh was close to death in 1958.

'His debonair pose' – Major Deedes of the King's Royal Rifle Corps. (Dorothy Wilding)

The 'day squad' drilling at Wellington Barracks, 1939. The battalion attracted several famous actors of the day, including Frank Lawton, far right, and Guy Middleton, standing next to him. (KRRC Association)

Hilary Branfoot, shortly before their marriage. (Dorothy Wilding)

Dancing with Hilary.

Hilary and Julius in London.

Celebrating WFD's promotion to the Cabinet in 1962: (left to right) Jill, Hilary, Lucy, Juliet and Julius. Jeremy is absent at Eton. (Press Association)

Deedes trounces his Labour opponent in Ashford in the 1955 general election.
(Douglas Weaver)

Very rarely, despite almost daily letters to Hilary from Europe, does Deedes come close to expressing his feelings so openly.

The worst part of the Twente Canal offensive was that it was entirely unnecessary. Finding the way blocked over water, Brigade the next day simply ordered tanks and half-tracks to drive eastwards to Enschede, where the canal stopped. It was an easy road journey, unopposed by the enemy. They drove due east, turned north to round the end of the canal and then came back due west again. By sunset that day Allied forces were on the northern side of the canal, at precisely the point at which they had tried to cross the day before. The entire journey was no more than fifty miles. The Germans who had doggedly protected the northern bank of the canal and had done so much damage to 12th KRRC had scattered in the hours before, conscious that they had carried out their last stand and unwilling to push their luck. On the southern side of the canal, members of Major Deedes's B Company were still burying their dead.

The Twente Canal was the last major battle for the 12th KRRC before the German surrender a month later. With the end in sight, Deedes fretted about the consequences of victory, for he feared his men might lapse into sloppy pre-Normandy conduct once the pressure of war was relieved. Notices were posted warning officers and men of dire punishment should discipline lapse. One drew their attention to a recent court martial in which a man was given six years of 'penal servitude' for 'shamefully casting away arms in the face of the enemy'. Another rifleman was sentenced to two years' imprisonment with hard labour for a self-inflicted wound. Several of the notices, meticulously filed in the War Diary, do point to bad behaviour by British soldiers, a reality far removed from the smoothly efficient image portrayed in war films. One furious notice reported that troops going home on leave were wantonly vandalising the train carriages, as well as 'urinating and excreting in corridors and through the windows'.

The main concern was fraternisation with the enemy, which in practice tended to mean fornication with German women. A fierce reminder was posted at battalion headquarters and company commanders were reminded that they would 'be held personally responsible for ensuring every soldier is aware of the contents of this order'. Fraternisation was classed, *inter alia*, as 'shaking hands with Germans', 'permitting children to climb into motor vehicles', and 'associating on familiar terms, especially with women'. On the whole Deedes's men behaved themselves, with few instances of serious indiscipline, despite the temptation of German girls emerging in the warmer weather in shorter summer frocks. Girls throwing themselves at the riflemen, either out of long-suppressed lust or for a packet of cigarettes, were liable to be locked up by Deedes in the guardroom on bread and water for twenty-four hours, 'so they keep within limits'.

When the end came, many soldiers were too tired to be euphoric. On 4 May Deedes dined well with officers from the 13th/18th Hussars. Before dinner he had reviewed orders for the following morning's business, codenamed Operation Curling. Deedes recalled thinking that the mission 'had a hazardous air about it', so had good reason to be relieved when a message came from the Commander of 30 Corps, General Sir Brian Horrocks: 'Germans surrendered unconditionally at 18.20 hours. Hostilities on all Second Army front will cease at 08.00 tomorrow 5 May 45. NO repeat NO advance beyond present front line without orders from me.'

The officers knew they should be jubilant, but Deedes was struck by the subdued mood. 'There was a certain amount of celebration throughout the Bn,' the 12th KRRC's War Diary noted sparely. Champagne – non-vintage Krug – was opened in the mess and toasts were drunk, but even that did not do much to raise the spirits. 'I find V[ictory] and all that a bit beyond me,' he wrote to Hilary. 'One feels terrific thankfulness but quite unable to express adequate thoughts on the subject.' Now that the guns had fallen silent he felt free to tell her quite how lucky he had been to come through and reported a close call in his final skirmish, two days before the ceasefire. 'I was watching an infantry attack with the Squadron Leader when a large shell fell a few yards from us. It was a dud . . . Luck or Providence has certainly looked after me and particularly in the last few months. I find my thankfulness inadequate.' Deedes was one technical malfunction away from being killed within forty-eight hours of the end.

Forty years later Deedes sought to explain his subdued mood in victory by noting that 'depression is sometimes the companion of exhaustion'.* For him, that was a very rare concession to mental frailty, even if he meant depression less in a clinical sense than simply feeling, as he would have put it himself, a 'bit down'. He had particular cause to feel deflated as well as relieved. Almost half of his fighting force had been killed or wounded at the Twente Canal. A few days later another of his young lieutenants, John Peyton, was killed clearing houses at dusk. It was a shattering time for Deedes, feeling grief, a measure of survivor's guilt, mixed, no doubt with some misplaced sense that he was at fault for their deaths. 'I feel they were much finer fellows than me and less easily spared. All 21 and a lifetime before them.'

Deedes was racked by the fear that, as he put it in a letter home, B Company had not achieved enough on the battlefield 'to balance the loss to England' of the deaths of the precious young officers. Deedes, according to the prevailing ethos of the army, certainly felt the loss of his officers more than his men, which is not surprising given that he would have dined and socialised with them but not with his riflemen. He carried the guilt for ever. 'Naturally, one says to one's self, if they'd been better led they might be still alive. I've always had a conscience about that.'

Casualties for the 12th KRRC were high. On their embarkation for France just after D-Day, the battalion comprised a little more than eight hundred men. In the succeeding eleven months, the

---

* *Spectator*, 27 April 1985. This was one of numerous D Day/VE Day anniversary pieces which Deedes wrote on almost every decade's anniversary, though none of them went into any detail about the Twente Canal episode. Displaying an impressive economy of effort, Deedes recycled much of it, verbatim, in *Dear Bill*.

12th lost eleven officers, four sergeants and ninety riflemen, with sixteen officers and 230 men wounded, and a further ten riflemen taken prisoner. A high proportion of those casualties were sustained agonisingly close to the end. Deedes would later claim to have almost no recollection of the hours and days after the Twente Canal incident; it is possible that he blocked it out. In fact, there is some evidence that he might have suffered a brief mental breakdown. In an undated letter, from the summer of 1945, he wrote to Burnaby-Atkins, then back in England on leave, to tell him in writing what he had not been able to say to his face. By the standards of the formal way men addressed one another in the 1940s, it was a strikingly affectionate hand-written letter, topped 'My dear Andrew'.

He praised his young officer for turning what had been the worst platoon in B Company into the most effective fighting force. But the letter was a more personal message of thanks for helping him through the nightmare of the spring of 1945. 'Andrew, I remember very well (though you do not) that after Roger [Green], Barry [Newton] and John [Peyton] had gone, you and your ways had much to do with preventing me from losing grip. I have rarely been gladder to see the back of anyone than your back when you safely embarked on leave. I think you felt up to a point as I did, so I need not go into it. Without you in the company, I should have felt very down in the mouth.' By Deedes's stringent standards, that was an extravagantly affectionate letter. For this most emotionally reticent of men to entertain the idea that he, as commanding officer, might have been 'losing grip' confirms how profoundly he had been affected by the loss of his men.

This perhaps explains why he had felt no euphoria when his company and his army had finally achieved the defeat of the enemy. Over five years he had shown himself to be a first-class soldier, and in Europe an effective Company Commander. Now the ceasefire threatened to make him suddenly redundant. Journalism before the war had served him well, but it did not come close to the intensity of his life in the eleven months since D-Day. Moreover, Deedes's letters betray no great passion for Hilary, no yearning to be back home with her and Jeremy, and certainly no hint of sexual desire after so many months apart.

Throughout his life Deedes would hint at his personal feelings by making a more general point. Shortly after the end of hostilities he wrote to his uncle Wyndham, who had royal connections, suggesting that Queen Elizabeth might make an address to the nation on the wireless, aimed at the wives of returning servicemen and urging them to show patience to their men. Boys who had put on uniform in 1939 had been turned into fighting men; war had hardened them, brutalised them even. Having had to read and censor his riflemen's letters home, Deedes also knew that many wives had taken up with other men in England and he understood that even when there was no infidelity many couples had grown apart.

A year or so before his death, Deedes shocked his daughter Lucy by telling her that at the end of the war he had come to hate women. It was uncharacteristic for him to be so candid about his feelings, certainly about such extreme feelings. He was a man for whom the phrase 'never a cross word' served almost as a mantra throughout his whole life. He was devoted to his three sisters, who he supported financially and emotionally; he loved Effie, his nanny, who was still part of the family; and he loved his mother all the more because of the nonsense she had to put up with from his father. Though his marriage to Hilary was awkward from the start, he was not the sort of public schoolboy who could never talk to girls. If he did fleetingly come to 'hate' women, that emotion was a consequence of fighting total warfare. A company of riflemen is an inherently masculine and macho outfit bound by ties of comradeship and the suspicion of outsiders, including even other regiments. Deedes formed intense relationships with his young subalterns and was a father figure to the company of more than a hundred men. Women not only had no role in such an environment, they threatened it. In Deedes's mind, wives upset their husbands by burdening them with their domestic problems, while the German girls who tempted the young riflemen into 'fraternisation' were a potentially lethal distraction.

But another factor offers the most likely explanation for Deedes's claim. He shared, albeit vicariously, the anger of soldiers whose wives had taken up with other men at home. He had had to write letters of condolence to the wives of riflemen who had died knowing their wives had been unfaithful. Whatever had triggered this spasm of misogyny, it faded in the post-war years, for in later life he clearly preferred the company of women to men.

Deedes said during an interview three months before his death that 'many of us felt totally estranged from the life we had left in 1939'. As was his habit, he was putting in a general context his own experience. For him the transition back to civilian life was wrenching. Before the war he had lived a contented bachelor's life – boarding in the East End, days at the *Telegraph*, beer in the evenings with fellow journalists, the occasional dance. In the summer of 1945 he faced returning to Hilary and Jeremy, but he showed no urgent desire to do so.

Other soldiers who were similarly exhausted had the compensation of looking forward to seeing family, to hot baths, to sleeping in their own beds at home, to making love to wives and girlfriends. Deedes did not share those desires after eleven months of sleeping in slit trenches. Instead he fretted – about whether he could keep discipline in B Company after the ceasefire. He panicked about the dreariness of life back in Fleet Street, in rationed and shattered post-war Britain. To his consternation, Hilary had used her family money to buy her own home in rural Yorkshire. This was almost certainly meant as a signal of intent; that she, as a north-country woman, with her preference for the company of animals over human beings, would not easily be transplanted to dainty east Kent and the strange Deedes in-laws.

This created a serious problem for Deedes, who worried that he was unsuited to any career other than journalism. Hilary's family's suggestion that he seek a job on the *Yorkshire Post* was dismissed out of hand. Instead, in early July, he wrote from Hanover to the *Daily Telegraph* requesting that he be given his old job back, and was quickly reassured that it was there for the taking. He told Hilary 'the thought of returning to the DT appals me, but it must be, since contrary to Christian doctrine no man is in fact born free in this world'. At this distance it is impossible to know if Deedes was being honest to his wife or if he was seeking sympathy in expectation of her anger at his continuing to live apart from her and Jeremy. But it is certainly possible to imagine that he had less terror of returning to the familiar terrain of 135 Fleet Street than to the unknown burdens of being a husband and father.

Simultaneously, Deedes wrote to Wyndham, wondering if he knew of anyone who could offer him weekday digs in London. This letter shows Deedes had no intention of rushing back and enveloping himself with his wife and new child, and that he was already planning a semi-detached life in London, with weekends in Yorkshire. The previous month Deedes had written to Hilary, noting that in the fifteen months since April 1944 they had spent only ten days together, which is 'not exactly natural or ideal'. Yet at the same time he was working on the assumption of remaining apart most of the week.

There was another development that he kept from both Hilary and the *Telegraph*, even as he appeared to be finalising his return to his old employer. The Army was looking for battle-tested Company Commanders to take the fight to the Pacific theatre. The inducement was promotion from Major to Lieutenant-Colonel, with the prospect of a battalion command in Burma or Japan. Having exhausted his own reserves of good fortune in the north-western Europe campaign, Deedes put his name down for a mission that promised to be even more dangerous – achieving the unconditional surrender of the Japanese. Major Deedes was not going to sink into the slough of domesticity without a fight.

For the time being he was stuck in Hanover, guarding German PoWs and awaiting his battalion's demobilisation. The general election of July 1945 provided officers and men with a distraction and Deedes was alarmed to see that the riflemen were becoming more assertive at the prospect of a Labour victory. His brief dabbling with the joys of socialism the previous October, and his complaint to Hilary about the 'ruling class' letting down 'the masses', had clearly passed. Officers with land and more money than he had were distinctly nervous that the socialists would confiscate the property of the upper classes. Deedes's strange state of mind can be gauged by a juvenile letter he wrote to Robert Stephenson, B Company's second-in-command.

The letter was written in early July, when Stephenson was on leave in England, and reflected Deedes's anxiety that the khaki election was eroding the hierarchal lines within the battalion. 'Down with the rodgering-dodgering proletariat. The general election has made me madly Tory and I realise with a white hot blast of horror how ghastly the lower orders and common people are. Jeezy-weezy I hope we win. My new election slogan is: "The lower orders are overpaid, overbearing, and think they own the earth. The upper classes are underpaid, overtaxed, and think they are lucky to own a butler. Redress the balance! Down with workers and Socialists and left-wing fiends. Vote for Deedes."'

He went on, 'Hope you make some sense of this rubbish. I am in abandoned mood. If the Socialists win all is lost: allus caput [*sic*] I haven't won this war to have my non-existent wealth distributed among a lot of lousy, shiny-suited penny-in-the-slot-philosophising slanderous bastards nor do I intend to take a back seat. On to the BARRICADES!!!! DOWN WITH THE COMMON PEOPLE!!!!!!!'

Deedes was clearly bored – he may also have been drunk – when he wrote this letter. It illustrates quite how tediously exclusive the KRRC officers regarded themselves as being, and suggests that dinner table conversation in the officers' mess must have become exceptionally tiresome once the port was passed. The letter reveals an unbecomingly boorish side to his character. More interesting is that at that early point he was, albeit jokingly, imagining himself

as a political candidate. When he poses as the scourge of the proletariat he is unconvincing. Though it did not stop him in later life
getting on well with men and women of all social classes, Bill
Deedes remained until his death a bit of a snob.

He did not really share other officers' concerns about an
impending socialist terror, partly because there was no family
money left to be appropriated. In one letter to Hilary from
Hanover, he reassured her that the cow and pigs she kept in
Yorkshire were unlikely to be seized by Clement Attlee. He
viewed the Labour victory with mild distaste and surprise, but no
great horror. 'How glad I am I've never been persuaded to take
part in politics seriously,' he remarked.

At the end of July Deedes made the journey back to Britain, his
first leave and sight of Hilary and Jeremy in more than a year. By
the end of his life he had no clear memories of this reunion. The
one thing he did remember was that while he was home the first
atomic bomb fell on Hiroshima on 6 August, followed three days
later by another on Nagasaki and then the Japanese surrender.
The dawning of the nuclear age meant Deedes would not be going
to the Far East after all; it also spared him the awkwardness of
having to tell Hilary of his plans to extend his army career.
President Truman's determination to force an early surrender
from Japan cut off an option for Deedes. He had tried hard, but
he could no longer avoid answering the call of duty as husband
and father.

CHAPTER 10

A TOUCH OF POLITICS

*'I will put Mr Deedes first because I like him
a great deal the best.'*

Jeremy Deedes occasionally told a story about his father, which he swore was true. When he handed in the manuscript of *Dear Bill* the editor at Macmillan said: 'Lovely piece of work, Lord Deedes, but do tell me, did you ever marry?' Jeremy told the story with a laugh, but there was a slight edge to the anecdote. And even if it wasn't quite true, any reader of Deedes's autobiography could have been forgiven for overlooking the references to Hilary, his wife of fifty-five years.

In the first edition of *Dear Bill* there are a couple of passing references to her. He mentions that they met in 1941 when he was based with his battalion in Yorkshire, training for the invasion of mainland Europe, though he adds no further comment about what attracted them to each other.

Hilary merits only one reference in the book's index, where for some reason she is listed as Hilary Brantast. (It was corrected to Branfoot in a later edition.) Jeremy, their first born, merits seven mentions, mostly relating to his work as a journalist and newspaper executive; Lucy, their youngest, gets a single reference, and that in the context of a discussion about Andrew Knight, the *Telegraph* chief executive for whom she had once worked. The other two daughters, Jill and Juliet, are not mentioned and nor is there a single reference in the book to Julius, the second son who fought a terminal blood disease from birth until his death twenty-three years later. By contrast, Max Hastings, who succeeded Deedes as editor of the *Telegraph*, merits ten indexed references; Lord Hartwell, chairman of the newspaper, gets twenty-six; Victoria Combe, the young reporter with whom Deedes collaborated in the later years of his career, has six references.

Deedes was sensitive to the charge that he was a remote and uncaring husband and father; he had heard the accusation many times over the years from those in the family who felt they had suffered this emotional neglect. In a question and answer interview with Naim Attallah in the *Oldie* magazine in 1992 he was asked about his relationship with Jeremy:

> I'm ashamed to this day that my relationship with my son, born during the last war, was more like my father's with me. I was almost the last of that generation who did not feel a great intimacy with his children was part of a father's duty. Today I find that my children share the lives of their children in a way that never occurred to me. Frankly, I was neglectful.

It is significant that Deedes regarded being intimate with his children as a *duty*; also, that he limits his neglect of his children to Jeremy, when his three daughters all felt – to a greater or lesser degree – that their father had maintained a wounding emotional distance from them.

Bill and Hilary never achieved any great intimacy in their marriage. No doubt there were some practical factors at play: they married in 1942, and though they were able to spend some time together before D-Day there was not time to establish a joint routine in the marital home before he had to turn himself into a fighting man, and she experienced the loneliness of life as a young mother uncertain that her husband would return. Both married relatively late for the 1940s, he at twenty-nine, she at twenty-seven, so both had established independent lives. Deedes's life in the 1930s had allowed him total freedom of action. He had a room in Wyndham's house in the East End, but ate no meals there except breakfast: he could come and go as he pleased with no domestic responsibilities or chores.

Deedes only reluctantly dragged himself back to the *Telegraph* and family life in late 1945, though he was relieved at least to find his job had been held open for him. Arthur Watson, the long-standing editor who had joined the staff in 1902, suggested he try his hand on the Peterborough diary column, which was scarcely a prestigious part of the paper. First, however, he was granted a fortnight's leave, in *Telegraph* time, to visit the parents of the young officers of B Company who had not come home. It is not difficult to see why Deedes, and so many other returning soldiers, found post-war life a drab anti-climax. He had commanded a rifle company in the defeat of Nazi Germany, winning an MC in the process, yet he now returned to work for his old employer on a pre-war salary of just under a thousand pounds (plus guaranteed expenses) in a fairly menial role. On the domestic front, Deedes had at least persuaded Hilary to sell the house in Yorkshire she had impulsively bought not long before the war ended, and look for a house in east Kent. She was not impressed by Kent, which she regarded as a dull county compared with the wildness of North Yorkshire and Northumberland, but ultimately she accepted his argument that he could not make a living in the north.

Deedes was drawn back to Aldington, the village of his happy early childhood. Just down the road from Symnells, the pretty family home, they found a rather less lovely house, New Hayters, a six-bedroom Victorian farmhouse with a decent garden and an adjoining wood, which had been owned by the family until one of Bill's father's selling binges. The house was built slightly down the hill from the main village, but high enough to command views across the Romney Marsh towards the coast. A few years later, and on a clear day, visitors using the upstairs bathroom ('the loo with a view') could just about make out Dungeness nuclear power station.

Aldington may not have been a pretty village, but it had attracted more than its share of interesting residents. Joseph Conrad and Ford Madox Ford had lived there, and after the war it came to be known locally as Queensland because it attracted a number of actors and theatrical characters, led by Noel Coward.

Bill and Hilary paid only two thousand pounds for New Hayters, but it was in a terrible state of repair. Aldington was close enough to the coast to have been designated part of the defensive arc in the event of a German invasion; New Hayters had been requisitioned at the beginning of the war as a battalion headquarters and had not been treated kindly by the soldiers.

The garden was overgrown and the house itself required substantial work, including a new kitchen. Trying to renovate a house in 1946 was an ordeal, particularly a house full of damp and woodworm. All building supplies were rationed.* It was almost impossible to buy new kitchen or bathroom equipment. Hilary tracked down a 1929 Aga in a neighbouring village, which was dismantled and re-assembled in the New Hayters kitchen. It was still working, almost immaculately, sixty-one years later when the house was sold.

For Deedes, who was largely oblivious to his immediate surroundings, doing up the house was boring and stressful, and ate up all of his disposable income. His pre-war salary had been more than ample for a bachelor who had free accommodation; the same salary was inadequate for a man with a wife and son, and a large, drafty house to renovate. Hilary took on most of the burden of the renovations while he, establishing the pattern that

---

* Even Field Marshal Montgomery had to pull strings at the very highest official level after the war to secure the materials to rebuild his house in Hampshire.

endured for the rest of their married life, sought refuge in the office in London and around this time began lodging some nights in a Belgravia establishment run by a retired butler.

London in 1945 offered few of the indulgences of Deedes's life in the 1930s; of beer with the boys after work, the odd night club visit and party. The lights had gone out on that world: the talk was not of debs and balls but of food coupons and nationalisation, and of the horror of what had been uncovered in the Nazi extermination camps. Deedes had written to Hilary from Germany that the prospect of returning to work at 135 Fleet Street 'appals me'. His anxieties were well founded, because much of what he loved about his pre-war life had gone. The fact that hundreds of thousands of men were also struggling to make the transition back to civilian life was no consolation.

By the end of the war the *Telegraph* had become an austere place too; 'very twilit' and 'somewhat drear' recalled Malcolm Muggeridge, who joined as a leader writer in June 1945. Lord Camrose, the proprietor, was sixty-six, and Arthur Watson, the editor, sixty-five. The paper was as grey as the staff, matching the times in the bombed-out capital. The dullness of the news columns was not the fault of Camrose or Watson. Severe paper rationing meant the *Telegraph* had to shrink to six pages during and after the war, and even then the circulation had to be artificially capped. News was crammed into the precious columns and stories cut back by the sub-editors, who had strict instructions that everything must be covered, however briefly. Despite the greyness of the columns, and though advertisers were turned away because of a lack of space, the paper was thriving, and in 1947 circulation hit the magic million, which had been Camrose's ambition even before he bought the *Morning Post* ten years earlier. It was an astonishing achievement and, as Camrose boasted in a bulletin to readers, it was the first time 'in the newspaper history of the world that any quality newspaper has achieved a million sale'.

Even if Deedes was less than thrilled to be back at the *Telegraph*, he was lucky to have found a berth as deputy to the splendid Peterborough editor Hugo Wortham, whom Deedes described as a 'tetchy and sometimes tipsy Edwardian, who was both wise and humorous', and who listed his interests in his *Who's Who* entry as 'anything highbrow'. Deedes regarded him as the tutor he might have had if he had gone to university and credited Wortham with doing more than anyone else to ease his transition from war service to civilian life. Wortham had been a leader writer at the *Morning Post* and transferred to the *Telegraph* in 1937 during the takeover, first as music critic before running Peterborough from 1934 until 1959 (and single-handedly during the war years). He wore a grey bowler hat and expected his staff to follow his example. A young staff man who joined the department in 1955 and turned up at 135 Fleet Street in a trilby was taken aside by Wortham and warned sharply, 'On Peterborough, we wear bowlers.'

Wortham laid down the blueprint for the ideal Peterborough item: it should contain one fact, one generalisation and one very slight inaccuracy – and the formula worked. Peterborough carried at least one political item a day – usually written by Deedes – as well as a social paragraph, often about an aristocrat, and something about the arts. Usually the items were of no great news importance – the point was the telling, and Wortham was expert at 'turning' a paragraph to make it readable, arch or simply fun. Deedes learnt a lot from Wortham, not just about writing but also about poetry and about wine, of which Wortham drank a great deal at lunchtime, usually returning late and pickled to the office where Deedes would be labouring to fill the empty page.

Much as he admired Wortham, Deedes was bored by the ritual of providing diary paragraphs but lacked the experience and confidence to write longer opinion pieces, so he took to writing letters to the editor for publication. Using his home address in Aldington, he would sign his name William F. Deedes, with no indication to the reader that he was on the staff of the paper to which he was writing. (No bylines were used in Peterborough at the time.) In December 1946 he was given seven paragraphs to lament how Englishmen were taking a difficult Ashes series in Australia too seriously. 'Many a battalion went into battle in the war to suffer grievously with lighter spirits and a happier countenance than the M.C.C. players and commentators have been able to display so far in Australia.' Cricket lovers who were expecting a much-needed taste of champagne in a 'dreary winter and a naughty world' found they were getting not champagne, 'but a more bitter draught'.

The following month he wrote a letter about the lack of productive zeal in British industry, which he blamed in part on the social upheavals of the war so that promotion was 'looked upon as a matter of getting into the fastest elevator, rather than climbing the right staircase'. The letters were commonplace and, it seemed, designed to pander to rather than challenge the *Telegraph*'s stolidly middle-class readers. By offering his thoughts on issues he regarded as important, Deedes was aping his father who, having moved on from Hitler and Stalin, spent much of his day writing letters to British politicians and newspaper editors.

The possibility of relief came quite by chance at the end of 1946, when he heard that Ashford's MP was to retire at the next election. By his own admission, Deedes had not done 'a hand's turn' for the Conservative cause. Yet the prospect of winning the seat proved an irresistible challenge for the bored thirty-three-year-old. Some disorientated men might have sought comfort in the novel circumstances of his first adult family home, in the arms of his wife or in play with his young son. But this was not Deedes's way. Finding domestic life a trial, he quickly sought a way out of it.

Besides, what he lacked in hands-on experience he made up for in impeccable political pedigree: two of his ancestors, both named Julius, had sat in Parliament for Kent in the seventeenth century and two William Deedeses of the nineteenth century, Bill's great-

great-grandfather and great-grandfather, followed. Few twentieth-century aspiring politicians could claim that their great-great-grandfather had won the endorsement of Jane Austen, who wrote to her sister Cassandra in 1813, 'I do not care for Sir Brook's being a Baronet. I will put Mr Deedes first because I like him a great deal the best.' (Not, of course, that she would have had a vote.)

Bill Deedes was also proud of his great-grandfather William Deedes, born in 1796, a father of twelve, long-serving Member of Parliament for East Kent, and a decent cricketer – 'a fast, under-hand bowler' – who became president of the MCC in 1831. He was popular in the House but, like his great-grandson after him, was not regarded by many as ideologically sound. When Sir Robert Peel died in 1850 Lord Stanley (later Earl of Derby) declined to form a new administration on the grounds that there was insufficient talent in the party. According to André Maurois's *Disraeli,* one of the whips, Beresford, told Stanley there were several sound men waiting at the Carlton club to be summoned.

'Who is there at the Carlton?' asked Stanley impatiently.
'Deedes,' said Beresford.
'Pshaw!' exclaimed Stanley, 'these are not names I can put before the Queen.'

When Bill Deedes launched his own political career he tended to refer in speeches to Jane Austen's endorsement of his great-great-grandfather rather than to Stanley's withering assessment of his great-grandfather. In the early post-war years there was no obligation on the right sort of candidate to prove his determination by chasing a lost cause in the Labour heartland. Deedes was not even a member of the party; nevertheless, because of his close family ties to east Kent, he always had the inside track with the Ashford association, especially with an MC after his name. There were no A-lists in those days, no nagging from

Central Office to find woman or ethnic minority candidates. Individual Conservative associations gloried in their independence of action and Tory activists would always stress that, unlike the socialists, they never suffered the indignity of having candidates foisted upon them.

Only after he was adopted locally did Deedes have to complete a candidate's form for Central Office. In answering the undemanding questions he confessed he had only 'very slight practical experience due to difficulty of practising politics as a journalist', though he claimed a reasonable 'working knowledge in most political subjects'. His lack of experience of politics and apparent lack of ambition for high office were a positive bonus to members of the Ashford selection committee, who in those days expected their MP principally to represent the interests of the Kentish farmer.

The sitting Ashford MP, E. P. Smith, had announced his departure, effective at the next general election just three years after he had won the seat in a by-election. Smith, a successful miller by trade, had achieved a certain fame during the war as the author of two popular plays, *Ladies in Retirement* and *The Shop at Sly Corner*. It was baffling to many of the party officials that he should be announcing his retirement so quickly. But they did not know that Smith kept a mistress in London, for whom he planned to leave his wife, a move that would have been intolerable in a rural constituency in those days. Smith glossed over his infidelity in his letter of resignation to the Ashford association, pompously noting that 'there is something to be said for a man devoting his last act to his home, his family and his more personal and intimate interests'.

Apart from his political pedigree, Deedes had other advantages over rival contenders. Though the Kent press exaggerated the importance of the role of the deputy Peterborough editor, working in any capacity for the *Daily Telegraph* – the paper then read by all Tory activists – was considered glamorous yet respectable. But most important of all, the man who controlled the selection committee was Sir Edward Hardy, an old family friend who immediately set about rigging the process in Deedes's favour. Deedes missed his first appointment before the committee because Hilary's car wouldn't start, but even that offence was overlooked. Cutting it fine after a brisk session trying to get the New Hayters garden into shape, he appeared for the rescheduled meeting in corduroy trousers and tweed jacket.

For form's sake, the selection committee initially let it be known that a young Edward Heath was also a strong contender. Deedes would come to recall that he triumphed in Ashford because Heath appeared for his meeting in a dark blue city suit and stiff white collar, which went down badly in what was then an overwhelmingly rural division. It was one of the little jokes that gave him, and others, harmless pleasure. In his autobiography, Deedes distanced himself from this theory, which he had himself done much to spread, blaming the 'great prankster' Humphry Berkeley, who later became an MP himself, for propagating the story.

Heath – who never carried grudges lightly – disliked the joke enough to deny it in detail in his autobiography, stressing that he did not then own a dark blue suit or a stiff white collar. Rather, he said, he excluded himself from consideration by refusing to accept the Ashford Selection Committee's demand that he resign from his commanding role with the Territorial Army and also to promise not to take a government job in a future Conservative administration.

Under Sir Edward Hardy's firm direction, the Ashford association's selection committee decided that the best way to avoid any unpleasantness was to submit only one name for consideration. Bill and Hilary appeared at the Ashford theatre on 22 March 1947 for his coronation before the full membership. Deedes knew from his experience of reporting political events before the war that a high turnout invariably meant trouble, and he was alarmed to see that the theatre was packed. Heath had already conceded defeat and did not attend, but there was a last-minute revolt from the floor. Some members objected that the selection process was a stitch-up. Somerset de Chair, who had lost his Norfolk seat in 1945 and then moved to live in Kent at Chilham Castle and was actively seeking a safe seat to rebuild his political career, led the revolt and for a while it looked as though he might succeed. Hardy was forced to defend his decision and deftly based his defence of his candidate over de Chair on the grounds of Deedes's relative poverty and the fact that he had to leave Harrow in difficult family circumstances. In Deedes they had a man whose one and only object in life was to serve England and east Kent.

'We put behind us the question of money and decided that we would try to choose the best man, even if he had not a bob in the world,' Hardy told the meeting. Though public funding was increasingly becoming the norm in British elections, rural Tories were traditionally expected to subsidise campaigns and the working of the association out of their own pockets. Deedes, whose ancestor had owned much of east Kent, had grown up in a castle and one of whose family first sat in Parliament in the seventeenth century, suddenly emerged in his most unlikely guise as the 'people's candidate'. E. P. Smith, who was not part of the selection committee, offered his support for Deedes from the floor, though he scarcely sounded enthusiastic: 'I can tell you I like him. I think he will make a good candidate and a good Member, and I can work with him.' Deedes seemed wary of Smith in return, judging by the *Kent Messenger*'s report. In his acceptance speech, he noted that he did not know his predecessor well, 'so it would be impertinent of me to try and express appreciation of him, but I know how well-loved he is in this division and partly why'.

After further bad-tempered debate, Deedes's selection was finally endorsed, but only after he learned that he would not have an easy ride as a prospective candidate until the next general election was called. It was an uncomfortably long period of phoney campaigning; worse, it soon became clear that E. P. Smith was beginning to regret his hasty decision to give up the seat and wasn't going to make it easy for his successor. Deedes, who still had a full-time job at the *Telegraph* and was living in London during the week, was accused – within weeks of his selection – of neglecting the division. Smith was spreading poison about his supposedly negligent successor failing to make his mark. The Conservative Association chairman, Viscount Allenby, became aware of a restive mood, as Deedes recalled in his autobiography:

> He summoned me to lunch and told me I must pull my socks up. There had been a weekend conference for Kent's conservative candidates. An unknown young woman, Margaret Roberts, then Tory candidate in the Labour stronghold of Dartford, had asked intelligent questions and shone. My chairman observed that I had turned up in the wrong clothes – corduroy trousers again – asked no questions and looked bored. I was bored.

Chaotic domestic circumstances did not help the candidate's concentration on the matter in hand. With Deedes away in London for much of the week, Hilary was living in a corner of New Hayters while the rest of the house was being renovated. The Conservatives' new Ashford agent, Sam McCall, was also camping at New Hayters because he and the woman assumed to be his wife – though in fact they were not married – could not find accommodation of their own. Hilary was understandably unhappy, as this was not what she had imagined married life would be once her husband came home from the war. Worse still, McCall was a drunk who frequently crashed the car he was loaned for constituency work – occasionally with the candidate in the passenger seat – and was once arrested by police in Charing Cross Road, having passed out behind the wheel.* Hilary had nightmares about her husband being found dead in the overturned car after another one of McCall's alcohol-induced spins.

---

* 'Drunk in Charge' cases could then be tried by juries which frequently were on the side of the drink driver. Despite the clear-cut evidence against McCall, the jury accepted his defence that he was suffering from 'low blood pressure and a history of concussion', and acquitted him of all charges.

Ashford was then the twelfth largest constituency in the country, with no fewer than 122 villages for the candidate to visit. Much of this had to be done in the evening by driving along narrow Kent lanes, which was tiring and dangerous, even for a sober driver.

Demoralised and distracted by Hilary's mood swings – which seemed to cross the line into a form of clinical depression when exacerbated by her pregnancies – Deedes began to question why he had sought the seat. At any moment he expected E. P. Smith to withdraw his resignation and launch a campaign to take back the nomination. In the two years after his adoption Deedes made the mistake of deferring to Smith, thinking he should remain in the background until the baton was passed during the election campaign, which in 1947 still seemed a distant prospect because the Attlee government was popular and had a large majority.

At the height of his gloom about his prospects as a politician, Hilary's mental condition suffered a further setback, with a development that was to cast a shadow across the rest of their married life. When she appeared dutifully at her husband's side for his awkward coronation as Ashford candidate at the end of March 1947, she had been four months pregnant. When the child, a second son named Julius, was born in August it soon became clear he was seriously ill. Julius was diagnosed as having aplastic anaemia, an extremely rare disorder of the bone marrow, which causes the tissues to generate insufficient quantities of the right type of blood. Though there is still no cure, some variants of the condition can today be treated with bone marrow transplants. But in the 1940s there was no option but to put the infant Julius on a treadmill of monthly blood transfusions.

His prognosis was poor and Julius was not expected to live beyond his teens, or necessarily even to reach them. The transfusions would, over time, damage his liver, Bill and Hilary were warned, and Julius never grew properly. The general outlook was alarming but Hilary, who was already in a fragile mental state after her move to Kent, had extra reason to be devastated. Bill, as ever, responded to the domestic crisis by retreating into his shell and spending even more time at the office. Hilary, however, was determined to establish the cause of Julius's illness and switched between various theories. She held Bill responsible for having called in Rentokil to fumigate the house during the renovations, believing that the chemicals deformed Julius *in utero* in the early stages of her pregnancy. Though exposure to chemicals has been identified as a possible cause of acquired aplastic anaemia, which develops in later life, it is not regarded as a likely cause of the form of the disorder that develops at or soon after birth. Foetuses could certainly be damaged or deformed by excessive exposure to the sort of chemicals used to clean up a house in the 1940s, but they would be extremely unlikely to trigger the small but critical imperfection in the working of the bone marrow. Hilary had other theories, none grounded in medical science, in which she bore the blame: for a while she was convinced she had damaged the foetus through the extreme physical effort required to crank-start the family motor car. Hilary conflated her desire not to move south with her subsequent dislike of New Hayters. Rather as her mother-in-law Gladys Deedes had blamed Saltwood Castle for the respiratory problems she and her daughter Frances had suffered in the 1920s, so Hilary saw New Hayters as the cause of Julius's problems. Long before it became fashionable to go organic, Hilary developed a distrust of all chemical cleaners and agents and refused to have them in the house.

The crisis within the Deedes household was not just emotional and medical, but also financial. The National Health Service was not formally launched until the summer of 1948, a year after Julius's birth, and he had needed blood transfusions from the very beginning because he immediately became highly anaemic. With the family finances already stretched, Deedes resorted to desperate measures. Before going up to London on the train he would rummage through the family silver. There had once been many trunks, stored in the cellars of Saltwood Castle ready to move at short notice in the event of the expected invasion during the Napoleonic wars. Piece by piece Deedes would sort through the

Georgian salvers, cutlery and teapots and take the more valuable ones to London to sell at various silver dealers in order to raise money for the transfusions. Bill and Hilary's other children, who cannot have had personal memories of these exchanges, nevertheless recalled them being discussed subsequently at home as their father's 'blood for silver' runs to London. There could have been no more devastatingly symbolic measure of the decline of the financial fortunes of the Deedeses than that the family silver from the ancestral castle had to be sold to keep the second son alive. Bill Deedes never spoke of this humiliating episode, but it probably explained his lifelong adherence to the principle of socialised medicine. When he suffered health problems he favoured treatment in Ashford's main NHS hospital over transfer to local private hospitals, even though the costs would have been covered by the *Telegraph*'s health insurance scheme.

For Hilary in the late 1940s, the family's relative poverty must have been infuriating because it was unnecessary. Not only had her father-in-law, Herbert, given away or cheaply sold off thousands of the acres he had inherited, he had continued to display his financial incontinence long after Saltwood Castle had been sold in 1925.

By the mid-1930s he had run out of money again, so his brother, Wyndham, took decisive action to put Herbert's family finances on a sounder footing. Though he was only the second son, Wyndham had inherited some family money and lived frugally in Bethnal Green. He came to think his modest fortune was unbecoming for a devout man who had dedicated his life to improving the social and moral condition of the poor. So in August 1937, 'actuated by reason of the natural love and affection I have for my lawful Brother Herbert William', he formally transferred his shares to him 'for his own absolute use and benefit'. The portfolio of shares and gilts included Canadian Pacific Railway preferred stock, Westminster Bank, Peter Walker & Son, Chinese 4½ 1898, and India 3% Stock. The total value of the holding, according to the schedule attached to the settlement document, was £10,137, just about what Saltwood Castle had been sold for twelve years earlier, and about £475,000 in 2008 value.* Given his brother's track record in burning through money, it was a strange decision to entrust him with another injection of funds. Unsurprisingly, Herbert showed no more financial acumen in the 1930s than he had during the decade before, and by the end of the war he was, like his son Bill, again struggling financially.

It can be assumed that Bill knew about this further transfer of funds to his father, but he never mentioned it or betrayed the slightest resentment towards Wyndham or his father. But as he set off to London in the late 1940s with a piece of the family silver in his briefcase to buy blood for Julius, Bill must have cursed the elder generation of Deedeses for where they had landed the family. Hilary never shared her husband's admiration for Wyndham, finding him strange and priggish; worse still, from her point of view, he was a fussy eater who invariably demanded something different from what had been prepared for the table. She also lacked Bill's forgiving attitude to Herbert, whom she thought was scandalously irresponsible with the family money, though she was very fond of her mother-in-law, the long-suffering Gladys.

Neither Bill and Hilary's acute financial problems, nor the anxieties of Julius's illness, slowed the expansion of their family. Their first daughter, Juliet, was born in October 1948, just fourteen months after Julius. Hilary's morale was very low, just at the moment that Deedes was having to work hard to reverse the bad start to his political career. On the day before Hilary gave birth to Juliet she wrote Bill a letter, sealed in an envelope, with the instruction 'open only if I don't get through this time'.† Explaining that women could die having babies, Hilary left one final instruction that, should she succumb, Bill must ensure she was dead

* The document was witnessed by Effie Sinden, Bill's nanny, who was still living in his parents' home in Hythe, described then as a maid.

† It is not clear when Deedes first read the letter, but the envelope had been torn open when the author found the letter at New Hayters in 2007 shortly before Deedes's death.

before the coffin lid was screwed down. 'Ask them to cut an artery or something, please darling.' She apologised for being 'a bore', explaining 'as you know, it has always been a nightmare of mine and I would be much happier now if I knew this would be done'.

After this firm instruction, Hilary began to analyse the state of their marriage, noting that it was six years since their wedding. 'We don't seem to have seen a great deal of each other, but it has been lovely, darling.' But there was a clear rebuke to Bill for his remoteness from Jeremy, who by then was five years old. 'He never saw enough of you when he was small,' which she conceded was aggravated by Bill's enforced absence for fifteen months from D-Day. But she made clear that the distance between father and first son was not merely geographical: 'He is very afecionate [*sic*] and would like to be liked more by you.'

Then, working on the assumption that she would die, she instructs Bill not to let her death interfere with his career. 'I love you more than you will ever know and would like to think of you going on in the high standard you have set yourself. Look forward, not back, always darling untill [*sic*] we meet again, Hilary.' Despite this terrible sense of foreboding, Juliet was safely delivered the next day.

It was a desperately sad, despairing letter, even taking account of the anxieties most women feel just before they give birth. It seems Hilary was using the possibility of her imminent death as an excuse to say things to Bill that she could not otherwise express; the tone of the letter implies the existence of a vast gulf between husband and wife only six years into their marriage. When she tells Bill not to let her death impede his career she is not being reproachful, but she is tacitly acknowledging how his working life had come to dominate their family. Most poignantly, it is easy, even at this distance, to see the truth of Hilary's assertion that she loved Bill more than he would ever know and to sense somehow that her love was not reciprocated.

Bill Deedes remained largely detached from his growing family, justifying his continued absences with the need to get to grips with the division as the general election neared. After two years of indifferent political activity he finally turned the tide in the spring of 1949, partly because of a very strong performance at the Ashford annual meeting. Conservative Central Office sent agents down to each constituency for their annual meetings, and confidential assessments were circulated to a tight group of officials to ensure no safe seats were lost through poor campaigning. The agent who attended the March 1949 meeting, a Miss Cook, reported back to Central Office that the finances were healthy and that membership was strong at 8358.* But she had found an acrid atmosphere around the Ashford division, which she blamed squarely on E. P. Smith.

> He likes being king-pin and has not been too helpful – except on the surface – to Mr Deedes, the Prospective Candidate . . . Mr Deedes was not too popular some time ago. He gave far too little time to the Division and seemed to think that the fact that his family had lived in the Division for 400 years was all the recommendation necessary, though how much of his alleged neglect was caused by subtle propaganda is difficult to estimate. However, the position now is completely changed; he is giving all the time he can afford and becoming increasingly well-known and popular. Mr Deedes made an outstandingly good speech on Saturday, and quite stole E. P. Smith's thunder. This is the first time this has happened, and it was very evident that E. P. recognised his stranglehold on the Association was weakening.

Having won the nomination two years earlier, only now had Deedes claimed the division as his own. With a combination of hard work, his natural charm and growing confidence as a public speaker, Deedes was achieving a popularity in the constituency that he was to retain for the next quarter of a century.

---

* The decline in active participation in all British political parties can be gauged by noting that by 2006 Ashford Conservative Association had just over eight hundred members.

When the election was finally called for February 1950, Deedes was well prepared. Sam McCall may have had a chaotic private life but he was a brilliant agent who organised the division along military lines, befitting a man who had served in the war with the 14th Army in Burma. McCall rejuvenated the activist network and Deedes ran a shrewd campaign, under a slogan that inevitably played upon his name: 'Not Words, but DEEDES'. His main election pamphlet stressed his deep roots in the area, and how his great-grandfather and great-great-grandfather had both represented the division of East Kent, later renamed Ashford.

Bill Deedes the candidate was for 'FREEDOM against the five-year Socialist menace', which shows he had put his brief wartime flirtation with quasi-socialism behind him. The first priority he listed was agriculture (the 'British farmer *must* come first', with promised protection from 'destructive imports') and the third was the Empire, which was created not by words but 'by free men of action and only in this way will it be maintained'. The four-page pamphlet laid out a slightly confusing economic agenda, which reflected the candidate's lack of clear political philosophy as well as his desire to appeal simultaneously to farmers and to manual workers in the small factories around Ashford. On the one hand Deedes pondered, 'HOW LONG the people of this Country can stand giving 8/- in every £ to the Government', while on the other he asked, 'HOW LONG the poor can continue to pay for the better-off?' As well as a portrait of the handsome thirty-six-year-old candidate, the pamphlet carried a separate picture of Hilary with Jeremy, Julius and Juliet.

Though Hilary's delicate mental health added to the tension at home, she was undoubtedly an asset to the aspiring Member for Ashford. He may have grown up in the heart of the rural constituency but he was not really a countryman. His work, and his heart, were in London with the *Daily Telegraph*, not on Kentish farms. Hilary was an authentic countrywoman who kept sheep and cows, snapped the necks of magpies, docked puppy tails and could talk with authority about the prospects for the harvest. During one election meeting an elderly man yelled out a question from the floor at the startled candidate: 'If you know so much, which comes in front on a cow: the ears or the horns?' It required a moment's panicky reflection and a good guess from the candidate, who managed to stutter 'ears', but it was a close shave. Some of the farmers must have sensed that Deedes was a bit of a phoney countryman, despite his corduroys and tweeds. Hilary gave him vital cover from the charge that he was more a London commuter than a true man of Kent.

The election further stretched the Deedes family finances. By 1950 Conservative candidates were no longer supposed to pay their own expenses, an early nod to the party's efforts to broaden its social base. But in practice there were still charges that candidates were expected to meet, above and beyond the subscriptions to local sports clubs and paying for participating in amusements at constituency fetes. In February, he sent a cheque for two hundred pounds to cover various expenses that the Ashford division was incurring. Deedes had to write to the manager of the Midland Bank in Bethnal Green to ask for an overdraft during the coming election campaign.

By the beginning of 1950 Clement Attlee's Labour government was beginning to show fatigue after five years of intense legislative activity. Coal and railways had been nationalised, the NHS established, India granted independence. But there were clear signs of an electoral backlash against austerity and central economic planning, a sense reflected in Deedes's promise of 'freedom against the five-year Socialist menace'. Winston Churchill, having weathered the Labour landslide of 1945, was still Conservative leader, despite having first entered Parliament half a century earlier.

Like most first-time political candidates, Deedes suffered badly from nerves on election day. E. P. Smith had bequeathed him a majority of more than six thousand, which was a comforting buffer. However, much of the Romney Marsh, a Conservative farming heartland, had in the meantime been redistributed to the neighbouring Folkestone and Hythe constituency, adding to

Deedes's concerns on the eve of polling day. The Peterborough staff sent a telegram from Fleet Street wishing him well; his sisters Hermione and Frances – the latter by then gravely ill with the last stages of Hodgkin's disease – wired from Hythe: 'TOMORROW MAY DEEDS [*sic*] PREVAIL'.

Despite his gloomy second thoughts in the two years after winning the nomination, and his last-minute panic about the loss of Romney Marsh, Deedes cantered home against his Labour opponent Neville Sandelson, an amiable London barrister who never quite learned how to talk to Kentish farmers. He held the majority steady at 6147, a reasonable outcome given that the national anti-Labour swing was offset by the loss of a strip of the Romney Marsh. The Conservatives did not win the general election, but slashed Labour's majority sufficiently for another election to be called the following year, which brought them back to government.

The wider Deedes family was thrilled by Bill's success. The new member's father wrote a characteristically eccentric letter of congratulation, addressed to 'Dear Beloved MP' and offering to lend him money – 'No Interest!' – which of course he did not have. Herbert also suggested he and Bill's mother buy him a despatch box 'for carrying Order Papers etc' and requested in return early gallery tickets for them to see their son speak in the Commons. His letter masked his deep unease: Herbert despised the Conservative Party and its attachment to empire and from that 1950 election onward he never voted again. As he said when asked, he could not vote against his own son but nor could he vote for the Tories. Sheaves of congratulatory telegrams appeared at New Hayters: the ever-loyal Effie Sinden, Bill's nanny who was still working as a maid for his mother, wired from Hythe offering 'VERY HEARTY CONGRATULATIONS'. Winston Churchill sent a standard telegram, while, most reassuringly for Deedes, Lord Camrose wired to make clear that he was not unhappy to see one of his employees enter Parliament. Indeed, Camrose seemed to suggest that political advancement reflected well on the *Telegraph*: 'MY HEARTY CONGRATULATIONS LOOK FORWARD TO SEEING YOU ON THE FRONT BENCH = CAMROSE.'

This was the beginning of the arrangement that was to prove of huge value to Deedes over many years, and explained why he remained so loyal to the paper until the end of his life: for the quarter of a century he was an MP, the *Telegraph* kept him on full salary, except for his brief periods in government when Parliamentary rules required him to give up full-time employment. In exchange for providing a daily political item for the Peterborough diary, occasionally briefing Lord Camrose on Westminster gossip and showing willing by working on Sundays, Deedes kept his full *Telegraph* income of £1500. Politics would not make him rich, but with his MP's salary adding a further £1000, Deedes had achieved a level of economic security he had not known since the end of the war.

CHAPTER 11

MINISTER

*'Of course you are not the sort of chap to go out
with a baronetcy.'*

The political career of William Deedes, MP, did not begin with
a bang. In the hours after winning the seat he felt simple
relief that he had not humiliated himself or the memory of his distinguished Parliamentary ancestors.

Once Deedes was elected, two of his mother's maiden sisters
and her unmarried brother offered him a top-floor room in the
house they shared in Eaton Terrace in Belgravia, which was ideal
for getting to and from Westminster in a hurry. Crucially for
Deedes, it gave him a Monday to Friday sanctuary away from the
mounting domestic chaos in New Hayters. He was regarded more
as a lodger than a part of his mother's family, which suited him
just fine. As had been his habit before the war in Wyndham's
house in Bethnal Green, he treated Eaton Terrace as a place to
sleep. Meals would be taken in Westminster, or with old journalist friends around Fleet Street.

Deedes was a highly diligent constituency MP, but he knew he
was never an accomplished performer in the chamber. Within
three years of securing the Ashford nomination, he had turned
himself into a first-class speech-maker and was impressive on
the stump during the 1950 election campaign. That form of

public speaking suited his informal, self-deprecating style, and because he always prepared his speeches meticulously he rarely delivered a dud.

But in the Commons his lack of self-confidence came to haunt him again. He was intimidated by the clever university men around him, who had honed their debating skills at the Oxford and Cambridge Unions and could silence an opponent with a single extempore riposte. That was not his style, particularly as the partial deafness he blamed on too many quinine tablets in Abyssinia often made it difficult for him to hear, and respond to, sly interventions. Though in the early days he attended the Commons assiduously – especially during debates on rural matters of interest to Kentish constituents – he rarely spoke from the backbenches, and when he was a minister he only spoke when he had to. Hilary delivered their fourth baby five days after the election: 'First Baby of the new House of Commons' reported the *Evening Standard* of Jill's arrival, which took the family to two boys and two girls. 'This will even things up, just like the election,' Deedes joked to the reporter.

But within just two months there was to be sad family news when Frances, after a six-year battle, succumbed to Hodgkin's disease at the age of only thirty-four. Already ground down by the news that Julius had a terminal illness, Bill was acutely affected, not just for his own sense of loss but on behalf of his mother. Gladys Deedes's life was difficult enough dealing with her disturbed husband without having to watch as her eldest daughter died slowly of a debilitating disease. Gladys blamed Frances's lifelong poor health on the castle and must, privately at least, have blamed Herbert for forcing the family to move there. Margaret, the youngest sister, said her mother never recovered from the loss; Bill responded in his usual fashion, by declining to talk about Frances after her death, compartmentalising his devastation and concentrating on his new political career.

The year 1950 was a strange interim period in British politics. Labour had run out of steam and was emasculated by the Tory gains in the 1950 election; but it would take the Conservatives another election – the following year – to form a government. In to this transitional political world Deedes stood up to deliver his maiden speech on the afternoon of 4 May, a contribution to an education debate. The new member for Ashford urged the House to think hard about whether school spending needed to be increased: 'It might well be that we have traded too long on the selfless instincts of a great profession,' he said, to polite approval from all sides. Politicians are rarely jeered when they praise teachers.

But, as Deedes was soon to discover, trying to become a Commons star was a fool's errand. Even the *Daily Telegraph* thought its own journalist's debut was worth just two paragraphs. Speaking in the Commons, with all the anxious preparation that was required if you wanted to make a mark, was not an efficient use of time or a good way of getting noticed. This did not worry Deedes too much, because he was shrewd enough to see another way of getting on. Once Churchill was back in Downing Street after the 1951 election, new opportunities opened up. The Prime Minister had recently been to America, where he had seen how television was becoming the important political medium. Deedes soon received a letter from the Whips' office informing him that he had been selected to spearhead the Conservatives' advance into the television age. As an articulate and handsome young MP with a Fleet Street background, he was a natural recruit.

The outcome, in May 1953, was an unintentionally comic moment in television history. Deedes found himself interviewing Harold Macmillan, the Secretary of State for Housing, about the Tory government's progress in meeting its target of building three hundred thousand new homes a year. This was to be the first-ever party political broadcast; Deedes and Macmillan knew all eyes would be on them and they were determined not to fluff it.

For technical reasons in those early days of television, the exchange could not be pre-recorded so the pair attended a couple of coaching sessions at Conservative Central Office. On the big day they arrived early at the BBC's Lime Grove studios for their ordeal, and for hours of rehearsals. The script had been run through many typewriters: Central Office drafted it, but tweaks were made by Deedes and Macmillan and Churchill kept a close eye on progress.

Media training was basic in those days: the two men were required to limber up in front of a 'mock box', a wooden box made to look like a television camera, with a dummy lens attached. 'The whole thing was hilarious,' Deedes recalled, putting it in terms of what was to become known, when he was editor of the *Telegraph*, as a 'Billism'. 'In those days so few people knew anything about television that in the kingdom of the blind, the cock-eyed man was king.'

The classic Billism would be delivered with a slightly exaggerated shushing, and involved a minor deviation from a familiar saying, such as 'one swallow does not make an impression'; 'you can't make an omelette without frying eggs'; or, 'say what you like about Peter Carrington, but he weighs a lot of ice'. Sometimes a Billism could be simply baffling: 'I think we should nail our matchbox to the mast on this one', although occasionally they contained an unintended inner wisdom, such as when he declared he was going to write a leader 'telling the Tories to pull their trousers up'.

Back in the studio with Macmillan, there were no teleprompters or high-tech aids to smooth delivery, so interviewer and interviewee had to learn their lines by heart; the more they practised, the more stilted and tongue-tied they became, so by the final rehearsals the performance resembled a dire school play. The producer of the broadcast was the BBC's formidable Grace Wyndham Goldie, who laid down the rules and would occasionally sharply rebuke all the participants, except for Macmillan. The worst sin was to glance down at the script while the camera was running. After a full day's rehearsal in the airless studio, Macmillan and Deedes were sent down to the basement to lie down for an hour on a pair of camp beds. Macmillan thought it great fun, for the whole experience reminded him of the trenches at the Somme. Going 'live' in the studio put him in mind of going over the top.

Deedes began the broadcast by explaining to the audience that they were watching an experiment, but that television was something that the Conservatives thought should be embraced. 'I hope you will think we were right.' There was a brief cutaway to the Conservative MP Ernest Marples paying a supposedly impromptu call on a Mrs Philpot, a housewife and mother who enthused for the camera about her lovely new house built by the Conservative government.

Deedes showed himself to be a natural television performer, with the true professional's knack for appearing relaxed and authoritative. His diction was crisp, his vowels clipped and there was not a hint then of the distinctive shushing in his voice that appeared in later life. With no trace of any regional influence, Deedes sounded, as did many Tory MPs of the 1950s, like an upper-class Edwardian. Macmillan was more stilted and managed to look faintly ridiculous on a couple of occasions as he delivered his over-rehearsed lines.

'Well, but have I left out anything?' Macmillan asked.

'Well Minister, there was just this,' Deedes replied. 'We are sitting in London but this is a nationwide thing going on. Would you like to indicate that by saying something about Scotland?'

'I'm glad you asked that,' Macmillan replied, reaching the low-point of spontaneity for the entire exchange. He smiled enigmatically before replying that he was not responsible for Scotland, which had its own Secretary of State who oversaw housing there. 'But we work together like brothers and, indeed, we might well do so, for we are brothers-in-law.'

Though Deedes claimed he regarded the broadcast as a fiasco, the reaction from the press and Central Office was positive. Macmillan got the public plaudits – 'The Tories find a TV Star' – declared the following day's *Sunday Express*. The paper's reviewer applauded Macmillan's scripted response when asked by Deedes if the Tories would meet their pledge to build three hundred thousand houses that year: 'It will be a damn close thing, as the Duke of Wellington said at the battle of Waterloo.'

Macmillan and Deedes had much in common despite their nineteen-year age gap. Both were traditional One Nation Tories who were 'wet' on economic policy; both their outlooks had been shaped by battle, Macmillan in the trenches on the Western Front, Deedes during the D-Day invasion thirty years later. But even more than those shared experiences, Macmillan seemed to recognise in Bill a fellow showman with a similar polish and manner. The remarkable thing, looking at that first party political broadcast, was how much both men seemed to be enjoying it, particularly Macmillan, whose slightly smug smile on screen suggested a man who thought he'd cracked it. Deedes said Macmillan approached television appearances rather in the manner of a jolly old man setting about a game of charades in a country house.

If Macmillan won the accolades for their joint broadcast, Deedes put down an important marker for his future career. Macmillan was the progenitor of modern politics of the television age, with its obsession with presentation, and Deedes had shown himself to be an eager and talented accomplice.

Deedes's ease in front of the camera was noticed outside Downing Street, and that autumn he was sent by the Foreign Office on a goodwill tour of America, taking in New York, Washington DC, Miami, New Orleans, St Louis and Cincinnati. Hilary did not accompany him, instead staying at home to look after the children. He was, the *Evening Standard* reported, a great success and he had done so many television interviews that his face had become familiar to millions of Americans. All of his expenses were met by the Foreign Office, but this did not deter his American hosts from trying to press money upon him after his speaking engagements. He learnt to check under his plate at the end of every meal, and would regretfully hand back the dollar bills that had been hidden there.

The party political broadcast was important in other respects, because Conservative MPs, then as now, were suspicious of the political loyalties of the BBC. Churchill thought the Corporation was full of socialists, and particularly detested the director-general, John Reith, whom he regarded as an anti-Conservative prig. The Tory MP John Profumo, a contemporary of Deedes's at Harrow who went on to achieve a certain celebrity, set up a panel of members of the public to monitor BBC radio broadcasts for anti-Conservative bias.

Though Deedes agreed that the BBC was a natural home for leftists, he retained an affection for it for the rest of his life, but he preferred appearing on television to watching it. He always looked good on television, handsome in his youth, kindly and avuncular in his later years.

To his surprise, Deedes was having a lot of fun as an MP and the last thing he wanted, as he played himself in as the new Ashford MP, was to be sucked into a dreary junior government role. But his television performance had raised his profile, and the call of duty came one Saturday morning in October 1954. It was his first weekend at home for three weeks so Hilary, struggling with four boisterous children, was not thrilled when Bill was summoned to Downing Street for a meeting.

It was teatime when Deedes sat down with the Prime Minister, who already had a weak whisky and soda on his desk. Churchill, about to turn eighty, told him he was reshuffling the Cabinet, and promoting Macmillan from Housing to Defence. Duncan Sandys, Churchill's son-in-law, was replacing him and Deedes would become parliamentary secretary of Housing and Local Government. Deedes knew enough about junior government to understand this would be hard, unglamorous work, and he was extremely unkeen. In an effort to soften him up Churchill urged a whisky upon him, but Deedes declined. 'You're not teetotal?' the Prime Minister exclaimed, but Deedes reassured him it was just a bit early for him.

Ever anxious about money, he immediately computed the dire financial consequences of an elevation to ministerial rank. As a junior minister he would be paid his £1250 MP's salary, plus another £500 for his government responsibilities. But upon joining the government he would have to take leave from the *Telegraph* job with its £1500 salary. So, by accepting a job he did not actually want, his pre-tax income would drop by £1000 to £1750. Hilary was pregnant with their fifth child, Lucy, who was born the following spring, and, just to compound the difficult financial outlook, Jeremy was soon to start at Eton. Moreover, there was no guarantee the *Telegraph* would take him back should he fail as a minister – which he assumed he would – or should the Tories lose the next election.[*]

Churchill had spent much of his life chasing his tail financially, so he was sympathetic. He assured Deedes that the Chancellor was addressing the issue of ministerial salaries. Deedes apologetically explained his lack of enthusiasm was caused by his growing family. 'It matters like hell,' Churchill sympathised, 'I know I've been through all the same difficulties.'

No respectable Tory with a good war behind him would have felt able to turn down Winston Churchill, and Deedes must have felt an additional pressure given that they were both Harrovians. So he agreed to do it and miserably accepted the congratulations of the Prime Minister's officials in the ante-room. All that was left was for him to go back to Kent and break the news to Hilary. Aside from the financial worries of his promotion, Deedes fretted that he lacked what he called 'the intellectual equipment' to be a minister. He was not the first MP entering government to find that top civil servants generally have much better brains than politicians. Most journalists are generalists, happier flitting around subjects and stories, hitting deadlines before repairing to the bar. Few claim to have rigorously intellectual minds, and those who do often make second-rate journalists.

Duncan Sandys was no high flyer or intellectual, but he was a

---

[*] There was no problem with the Ashford constituency association when Deedes accepted government office, which suggests Edward Heath had exaggerated, or made up, the local party's hostility to a candidate taking office.

dogged head of his sprawling department and demanded long hours of his minister. Sandys relished Monday evening brainstorming sessions that would go on into the early hours, which Deedes found an ordeal.

Deedes was in awe of the Housing Department's deputy permanent secretary, the redoubtable Evelyn Sharp, alumna of St Paul's Girls School and Somerville College, Oxford. She was a formidable operator who was soon to become the first female permanent secretary, and Deedes knew he had to be on his toes.

Piles of paperwork greeted Deedes every morning, much of it related to planning permission, a key issue as the Tories rushed to build homes and create new towns. Deedes and Sandys addressed themselves to freeing up the planning processes and to strong-arming local authorities into lifting restrictions that stood in the way of the Tories' house-building targets. There had been a row in the popular press when a man named Mr Pilgrim fell foul of local planning regulations in building himself a bungalow, and eventually committed suicide. When Deedes was showing insufficient zeal in tearing up planning restrictions, Sandys would remind him of Churchill's exhortation in the drive for new homes: 'No more Mr Pilgrims.'

Sometimes he would vow to overrule Evelyn Sharp, but because he was new to the business of government every challenge required intense preparation.

For most of his life, Deedes displayed a remarkable fortitude under pressure, during the war and, later, when he was cornered by the Fleet Street print unions and an incompetent management. But only four months into his tenure at Housing, Deedes suffered a physical collapse. Normally blessed with the most robust constitution, he suddenly found himself almost unable to move and feared he might be seriously ill. His doctor ordered complete rest, which he complied with, scared for once by mortality's warning bell.

After four weeks' enforced rest at New Hayters, when Hilary must have been astonished to see so much of him, Bill's health

recovered. He suffered renewed stress at that autumn's party conference in Bournemouth, when Duncan Sandys pulled out of
giving the housing speech because of a crisis in his marriage.*
Deedes was so nervous that he popped a pair of 'purple hearts',
an amphetamine and barbiturate mix that a cousin had procured
for him. His speech was a great success, but he did not repeat this
experience with other prescription drugs.

Despite throwing himself gamely into housing, Deedes knew it
was not really his scene. His faltering ministerial career was given
a temporary boost towards the end of 1955 when Anthony Eden,
who had replaced Churchill as Prime Minister, moved him to the
Home Office under Gwilym Lloyd George. As the Cabinet
became distracted by Suez, Deedes took control of the Homicide
Bill, a short-lived effort to retain capital punishment for murder
by people classed, somewhat imprecisely, as gangsters. The Bill
went the way of Eden after Suez, and when Rab Butler was
moved into the Home Office as part of his compensation for
losing the leadership to Harold Macmillan in January 1957
Deedes's ministerial career appeared to be at an end.

It was important that this be seen to be of his own choosing,
and Macmillan obligingly wrote a letter, making clear the decision was Deedes's. He showed it to his father, who was worried
about the premature end of his ministerial career, for he believed
that his son had the makings of a Cabinet high-flyer. Herbert was
greatly reassured by Macmillan's letter and made a point of
telling all the neighbours in Hythe that his son had jumped of his
own volition.

---

* Deedes ran up against more than his share of Tory MPs caught up in sex scandals.
Apart from his Harrow contemporary John Profumo, Ernest Marples, who had
appeared with Deedes on the Macmillan political broadcast, was later implicated in
a prostitute ring. Duncan Sandys, Deedes's boss, was accused of being the headless
man being pleasured by the Duchess of Argyll in a photograph produced during her
lurid divorce trial. This slur prompted Sandys to undergo a full genital inspection to
prove he was not the man in the photograph – though he was actually sleeping with
her – prompting Bernard Levin in *The Times* to express his amazement that two-
thirds of the way through the twentieth century 'a judge should have been obliged to
ask a doctor to examine the penis of a politician'.

The *Telegraph* had reported that Deedes was one of six ministers to have been 'dropped', though it added tactfully: 'I understand that Mr Deedes has retired from office for personal reasons.' The paper noted that the 'most prominent' casualty of Macmillan's re-shuffle, Henderson Stewart, had been 'consoled with a baronetcy' as he was kicked on to the backbenches. Though he had failed to set the world on fire, there is no reason to doubt Deedes's later assertions that he jumped, relieved, from ministerial office. He was summoned for a farewell interview with the new Prime Minister; they chatted about old times and their joint ordeal on the first party political broadcast three years earlier. Macmillan then said, 'Of course you are not the sort of chap to go out with a baronetcy.' Deedes had no option but to agree, rather ruefully, and later he made light of the exchange, maintaining that the only letters that mattered came *after* one's name.*

Either way, it was a great relief to get out of Whitehall and back into Fleet Street where, as ever, he was welcomed back as a favoured son. Colin Coote, the editor, once again saw him right, immediately offering his old job back when Deedes wrote to him. His restored *Telegraph* salary had been increased by a hundred pounds in his absence, so that his combined income rose sharply when he left government. He was touched to see that, when he reported for his first day back at 135 Fleet Street, his name was still on the door of the Peterborough office.

---

* Jeremy Deedes would tell this story about Bill's exchange with Macmillan with a faintly pained expression, giving the impression that he might be the sort of first-born son who rather wished his father had gone out with a baronetcy.

CHAPTER 12

BLEAK HOUSE

*'He's like the man who always does the washing up in
other people's houses, but never in his own home.'*

Juliet, Jill and Lucy saw so little of their father that they created
a fantasy life for him in London. The flight of fancy seems to
have taken off when Hilary started referring sardonically to Bill
being up in London with 'the mistress', by which she meant the
Daily Telegraph, because that was where he seemed to prefer
spending his time. The girls developed the theme: in their imagination, the mistress became a West Indian woman living – for
some reason never explained – in a St John's Wood bedsit.
Though the existence of a lover would undoubtedly have added
rich texture to a long life fully lived, no evidence could be found
to support the girls' imagining. Bill Deedes was no Lord Lambton,
who was caught in bed with two girls; there was no mistress,
West Indian or otherwise, or indeed any suggestion of female
temptation in London to test his marriage vows. He was a deeply
handsome man, trim in figure and always spiffily dressed, but he
was no flirt – least of all with his wife.

Any infidelity in Bill's marriage to Hilary was emotional rather
than physical. His departure from junior ministerial office in
Macmillan's new administration of 1957 made it perfectly possible for him to spend more time in Kent with her and the children.

He was now just a backbencher with a majority of more than eight thousand. He had answered Churchill's call, impoverishing his family on a junior minister's inadequate salary, and done his bit for his party and country.

True, he was back on the Peterborough diary drawing a *Telegraph* salary again, but that was scarcely onerous work. His twin roles as MP and contributor of political diary items were perfectly complementary and he could move comfortably between Westminster and Fleet Street, often putting in the briefest appearance at either office. Providing a daily political item or two was hardly a challenge for a journalist of his experience and fluency. Yet, as his political duties lightened, Bill would tell Hilary that he had to pay back the *Telegraph* for its loyalty by putting in more hours in Fleet Street. It was not strictly true, but that argument allowed him to continue living his bifurcated life, so that from Monday to Friday his time was entirely his own, without domestic intrusion.

As his family saw it, his normal working week was structured so as to see as little of Hilary and the children as possible. On Monday mornings he would take the train from Ashford to Charing Cross, for working days spent between the *Telegraph* office and Westminster, and nights in his attic room in Eaton Terrace. On Fridays he would catch an afternoon train back to Ashford, where he would usually do a constituency surgery and then have a drink with party activists before driving the fifteen minutes on to Aldington. Often he would arrive at New Hayters after the children had gone to bed and they would not see him until Saturday morning.

The children's memories of their parents were always formed in separate images, for Bill and Hilary lived largely parallel lives, which only occasionally intersected. Lucy would awake in the morning to the whack of iron on golf ball and look out the window to see her father doing his early ritual of hitting a hundred practice shots into a net, 'to give the liver a bit of a jolt'. In the house he would always be working, pounding away at his manual typewriter, either writing a piece for the *Telegraph* to deadline or dealing with his constituency mailbag. Hilary would be in the kitchen or with her animals, milking the Jersey cow or retrieving eggs. As Hilary ironed or cooked, Lucy, perched on the Aga, would read P. G. Wodehouse stories aloud to her. The Aga bore a visible dent in the right-hand steel lid, formed by the pressure of Lucy's bottom over many years.

Even when he was at home, Bill was not really with the family. After breakfast he might spend an hour or two in the garden or play a round of golf. Jill felt so ignored by a father who never picked her up or cuddled her that she would walk behind him as he mowed the grass 'just to be close to him'. When this proved unsatisfactory she enrolled for golf lessons at his club, Littlestone. That way, at least she could spend some time with him in the car there and back and after the lesson she would walk around with him as he played. She wasn't remotely interested in golf. 'I was clutching at straws, I suppose,' she recalled.*

Apart from golf, Deedes's favourite outdoor activities were scything and mowing the lawn, the latter being a particularly good means for a man to indulge in deep concentration while shutting out the world: the telephone cannot be heard and intruding family members can be warned off with a sharp yank on the throttle of the motor mower. A bonfire was a special pleasure in the autumn, though he was particular in refusing to light it until he was convinced it had a 'good bottom', without which it would not burn through. He was also very proud of his scything technique and his ability to hand-sharpen his range of implements. Jeremy's earliest memory of his father was shortly after they had moved into New Hayters, when Bill walked triumphantly into the house, scythe in hand, to announce that he had just found a tennis court under the wild growth in the garden.

Towards lunchtime on Saturdays, Bill would set off for another

* When Jill spent a week at New Hayters in the summer of 2005, during a trip from her home in Melbourne, she noted – without rancour – that her father had not asked her a single question about her husband or children.

weekend ritual of the rural MP, the opening of village fêtes, usually with some or all of the children. If they ever won a prize they would have to hand it back, as they were part of the guest of honour's entourage. Bill would give a little speech, always polished, always respectfully received, and move on to the next fête.

On Saturday evenings Hilary would accompany her husband to a Conservative dinner somewhere in the sprawling constituency. At these numbingly repetitive events, Bill always managed to look as though there were no place on earth he would rather be, but Hilary was less obviously delighted to be supporting the husband who did so little to reciprocate. She suffered anxiety attacks before speaking in public. When she was required to say a few words to introduce him, or to substitute for him when he had to be away, she would often develop a migraine. They would almost never entertain, or be entertained by people in the village, because Saturday was the only night Bill could make and constituency events always came first. Given that he had spent his first six years in Aldington, locals were surprised by how little he was involved in village life. However, he was always loyal to the village store that doubled as a sub Post Office. In later years he worried it would succumb to the nearby Tesco superstore, which he loathed with a passion. He insisted that his daughter Lucy continue to buy his Famous Grouse from the local shop. The owner repaid this loyalty by continuing to take Bill's five newspapers a day to his doorstep each morning, long after home delivery had been withdrawn from others in the village.

On Sunday mornings, he would again absent himself from the family and head into Aldington to teach Sunday school. Given the pressing demands on his weekend time, and an increasingly indignant wife struggling with five children, one of whom was terminally ill, it was astonishing that he devoted his Sunday mornings to the Church rather than his family. As an understated but devout high Anglican most of his life, Deedes would dip in and out of his prayer book but he was not a frequent churchgoer in later years. Because of the daily prayers of his childhood he was familiar with large sections of the Bible and he would pray at night; in his mid-eighties, when he flirted with Rome, he would occasionally attend the Catholic church in Ashford.

Lucy followed Jill's example in taking direct action to secure more contact with their father and signed up for Sunday school simply so she could see something of him at weekends. His teaching themes tended to be more practical than spiritual, offering advice on good manners and sound citizenship, and he was happy to leave Godly matters to the vicar and his wife. Lucy remembers that one of his lessons emphasised the importance of issuing all social invitations by post: it was bad manners to invite people on the telephone because it put too much pressure on them to come up with an instant affirmative reply. Deedes had strong views on another matter, and would lecture girls of all ages that they must on no account lend money to men.

After Sunday school he would infuriate Hilary by heading for the station again to go up to London to do a shift on Peterborough. When Bill rejoined the *Telegraph* in 1945, he would tell Hilary that he had to work Sundays in order to give his older colleagues time with their children; by the time he was well into middle age, with five children of his own, he would explain that the younger men must be given time with their babies. On bank holidays, Hilary would optimistically plan days working together in the garden, only to be confronted by Bill in the hall, with the dreaded briefcase in his hand, heading to the station. As he disappeared out of the house Hilary would mutter, 'the office always wins'.

Tim Heald, then a young journalist doing Sunday shifts on Peterborough, always enjoyed the leisurely ritual of putting the column together with Deedes, the most amiable of colleagues. Most Sundays they would arrive in 135 Fleet Street towards lunchtime and head to a pub off Ludgate Circus for meat and two veg, and a couple of pints of bitter. Refreshed, they would return to the office and go through the 'spike', where the Peterborough editor, Michael Hogg, had put stories from the previous week that he regarded as too risqué. They would resurrect a couple of them, then bang out a few items they had kept from the week before and go through Saturday's post to see if there were any press releases that could be turned into an amusing paragraph or two.

Heald was always astonished that a man with the letters MP and MC after his name thought nothing of doing a Sunday shift on the diary column. He recalled there was absolutely no need for Deedes to work on a Sunday, for one of the younger staffers could easily have been persuaded to come in to help out on what was not regarded as a remotely important part of the paper. The bitter truth for Hilary and the children was that Bill preferred to have Sunday lunch in a Fleet Street pub with a journalistic acquaintance rather than spend the day with his family. Many men are perhaps happier in the company of male working colleagues than their wives, but few are quite so blithe to others' feelings. Deedes would, however, always return to New Hayters on Sunday evening after the Peterborough shift before heading back to London the following morning.

He withheld affection from all of his children, though he would only rarely argue seriously with them: most aspects of raising them, including discipline, were left to Hilary. Occasionally Bill would display what Jeremy called 'little spurts of being an engaged father' and intervene. Bill once banned Jeremy from attending a summer ball at Benenden School for some infraction, but usually he held back from direct involvement in disciplinary matters.

Bill was prone to fits of absent-mindedness and when Hilary persuaded him to come along for Jeremy's fitting for his Eton uniform the three of them managed to board the wrong end of the train at Waterloo, ending up in Weybridge. Jeremy was disconcerted by this inauspicious start to his Eton career and Hilary not much pleased. At that point, Bill hailed a taxi, told Hilary and Jeremy to get in, then looked at his watch and announced he would have to get back to the office. He took the next train back to London while Hilary and Jeremy went on to Eton together to perform the solemn rite of passage.

Jeremy felt the remoteness acutely and recalled that his father hardly ever came to Eton during his years there, not even for the Fourth of June, the social high point of the school year. His father would sometimes say he might come if he was guaranteed a couple of paragraphs for a Peterborough story, but even so he stayed away. In part, Jeremy blamed his father's oppressive sense of duty for the problems at home. He thought this explained why he had volunteered to go to the Far East to defeat the Japanese in 1945. Loyalty to his regiment, duty to King, country and the greater good, came first. 'But of course, that's not the sort of thing a wife with a young son wants to hear,' Jeremy conceded.

Keen on sports as a boy, one of Jeremy's enduring childhood memories was of the pang of disappointment when his father failed to appear to watch him play matches against other schools. He would write to his parents mentioning forthcoming fixtures, but always without result. Despite their shared enthusiasm for golf and cricket, Bill did little to encourage Jeremy in either. He did not arrange golf lessons for him as a boy, which might have turned Jeremy from a good weekend player into something better; he never arranged for him to be put down for membership of the MCC, which Jeremy would have loved. And, as Jeremy would point out, his father was capable of extreme kindnesses to other people's children. 'He's like the man who always does the washing up in other people's houses,' Jeremy reflected in the spring of 2007, 'but never in his own home.'

Of the two boys, Bill was closer to Julius, perhaps because he knew he would have limited time with him. To maximise his time with his father, Julius decided at the age of about ten that he was a committed Conservative and would help his father with his speeches, searching reference books for apt quotations. Julius was a relentlessly cheerful boy, despite the lethargy and headaches that were the symptoms of his anaemia. He set himself the challenge of getting into the *Guinness Book of Records* as the holder of the world record for the highest number of blood transfusions, but the editors were reluctant to establish that particular category.

Deedes was emotionally frozen with his daughters, incapable of extending them any affection or even of touching them. He would never pick the girls up and cuddle them, never kiss them. Jill remembered that if her birthday fell during the week, when he was in London, he would usually forget it. Her godfather was Andrew Burnaby-Atkins, the dashing young lieutenant who only just survived the Twente Canal disaster in 1945. He turned up one day at the front door, when she was three, with a doll called Sarah. Jill adored the doll so much that when Sarah was left too close to the fire and melted she had to be sent to the dolls' hospital and came back with a new head. Jill remembered receiving the doll in vivid detail, more than fifty years later, because it was such a lovely surprise and so unlike anything her father had done for her.

Jill was close to her mother, and not inclined to indulge her father's behaviour. 'The family has suffered, it's affected all our lives,' she recalled. 'We've had to cope with Dad being difficult . . . I just feel I've spent all my life trying to protect Mum.' She conceded that Hilary had been bad at dealing with her father and concealing her indifference to his public life in London. But that was not wilful: 'She did love him terribly, so I think a lot of the time she made excuses for him.' Hilary tried not to be too critical of Bill because his childhood, unlike hers, had been unhappy and he had suffered so much from his father's erratic behaviour. Jill resented how Bill withheld his love from her and was largely absent from the family home, but she thought his obsession with being seen to put hours in at the *Telegraph* sprang in part from a genuine terror that he might be let go. At the *Morning Post* he had seen good men sacked, and his father's financial self-immolation in the 1920s instilled in Bill a lifelong terror of sudden poverty.

Lucy, the youngest child, also felt unloved by him. Bill would never kiss her either; the closest he came to showing love when she went to bed was to incline his head slightly from the shoulder, as a formal man might acknowledge a friend in church. One night when she was about eight – which would have been around 1963 – Lucy was ill and was allowed to sleep with her mother. That was the first time she realised that her parents were no longer sharing a bed, and that Bill had retreated to his dressing room, which adjoined their bedroom. Bill was remarkably untactile all his life, and it is probable that sleeping alone for the last forty-five years or so of his life would have been no great hardship for him. At around the same time Jill remembered that her parents were getting on so badly that she worried they would divorce. The mood was so grim that Jill and Juliet called New Hayters 'Bleak House'.

Of the girls, Juliet was closest to Bill, yet still she felt the iciness of her father's emotional indifference. She thought her mother was partly to blame for the strains in their marriage because she would not really try to engage in his life in an effort to overcome their fundamental incompatibility: 'His life was the world,' she recalled, 'and her life was her animals and her children.' Juliet agreed with her siblings that Bill was a neglectful father, yet she found him easier to get along with than her mother. As the children grew up Hilary became negative and self-pitying. Though Hilary was sorely tested by Bill, Juliet conceded she was very bad at controlling her frustrations with him or constructively encouraging him to change his ways. Juliet put her mother's mental and emotional age at about thirteen.

Even more than Bill, she acutely lacked self-confidence in later life and was convinced she was 'thick'. She was outstanding with animals, but awkward with anyone who had any sort of metropolitan polish. Her goal in life was to achieve self-sufficiency with her livestock. To that end she would keep at least one house cow, which she would milk herself, a couple of bull calves, two or three pigs, several dozen chickens (selling the eggs locally), a goat or two and Jacob sheep, which became her passion. She would spin the wool herself, and make Bill and the children clothes.

197

Hilary resented the way that Bill would swoop into the marital home for short bursts of attention, holding the children spellbound with his tales of political events in London over the supper table. She would start to sabotage his tales, cutting across his monologues with stories about foxes worrying her chickens, or updates about the sheep.

Family holidays followed a set routine, so that every year for the first fortnight of September the seven of them would head to a rented house in Thorpeness, on the Suffolk coast. Bill would drive most of the children while Hilary would take the train with Juliet, who was prone to car sickness. In those days before the M20 and the Dartford Tunnel it was a full day's drive and Bill approached the journey as a military operation. He found being cooped up for many hours with four quarrelling children a trial, so no dallying was tolerated. Pit stops were banned, so Julius, whose bladder function was affected by his illness, would have to pee into a bottle in the back of the car as Bill drove on doggedly, desperate to bring an end to the ordeal.

The children enjoyed the holidays but they were scarcely a break for Hilary. She merely transferred her domestic operation from Kent to Suffolk and did not see a great deal more of Bill. He would do nothing to help with the children, playing a round of golf either side of lunch and frequently taking the train to London for the day, citing essential office chores. By September the sea off the Suffolk coast would be cold, but the children would be expected to swim before lunch. Despite the fortitude he displayed off the Kent coast as a boy when he would dare his sisters to join him in the Channel, Bill now never swam; Juliet recalled that she had not once seen his bare legs. Christmas holidays could be tense, too, because Bill found it so difficult to spend several days at a stretch with the family. Even Christmas Day was a challenge and he would escape in the afternoon to do some logging, or set off alone for a brisk walk while the children waited impatiently for his return so they could open their presents.

Life was hard enough for Hilary, even without the strain of

Julius's illness. She would take him up to London for his monthly transfusions, first at Great Ormond Street Hospital, latterly at St Mary's, Paddington, and would stay at his bedside during his periodic medical crises. For a week or so before each transfusion, Julius became acutely anaemic, which meant he was lethargic and breathless, and prone to blinding headaches. His body did not develop properly and his stomach became permanently distended, partly as a result of a liver swollen by excessive levels of iron from the blood transfusions.

Neglected by Bill, Hilary depended more and more on Julius, who had not followed Jeremy to Eton because he was a chronic bed-wetter and needed regular medical attention. Hilary and Julius became companions. They would take holidays together, in Wales and Ireland. Julius gave his mother the companionship her husband withheld from her, but it was a bitterly sad mother–son relationship, because Hilary knew that he would be taken from her before long.

Lady Aldington, a Kent neighbour and the widow of the former Tory MP Toby Low, saw Bill and Hilary at close quarters. An extremely forthright woman of old-fashioned opinions who smoked untipped cigarettes, Lady Aldington blamed Hilary for almost all of the problems in the marriage. She recalled how Hilary had declined to go a formal luncheon at Westminster for President de Gaulle when all the other MPs were accompanied by their wives. Indeed, most Tory MPs were unaware that Bill was married. Derek Taylor Thompson, Bill's private secretary when he was in the Cabinet, recalled that he met Hilary only on two or three occasions. Lady Aldington said that Hilary would complain to friends around the village of being neglected by her husband while Bill, she maintained, was always scrupulously loyal in public about Hilary.

When Hilary failed to register the faintest interest in Bill's life in London he simply drew further away from her during the limited time they spent together.

Though he would occasionally concede he had been a remote

father, Deedes would also bridle at any suggestion that this had consequences for the children. In 2003, when I was writing a profile for the *Daily Telegraph* marking his ninetieth birthday, I questioned Deedes about his family and tentatively suggested he was distant from them. Geographically, at least, that was self-evidently true, for Juliet and Jill were living overseas and Hilary had by this time moved to Scotland and was living near Lucy, who was running a hunt in the Borders. The smile suddenly vanished and he pursed his lips; the bonhomie that had been generated over a boozy lunch chatting about Boot and Waugh and the *Morning Post* suddenly evaporated in the taxi we were sharing back to the office. 'You've been talking to Jeremy, haven't you,' he said accusingly. 'Oh, all that nonsense about never visiting him at Eton . . .' and he tailed off, visibly irritated. He was cross with me for straying off-side in my line of questioning, and with Jeremy for disloyalty, though Jeremy's observations had been gentle in the extreme.

Deedes composed himself, concentrating rather as though he was going to deliver an important personal manifesto about fatherhood. 'Jeremy's done all right for himself, hasn't he?' he said crisply. 'And my daughters all turned out the right way up, didn't they?' And that was it.

In that awkward moment he revealed more than he realised. What annoyed him, I think, was the lack of gratitude. Sending Jeremy to Eton in the late 1950s, when money was still very tight, had been a considerable sacrifice. But he had been determined to do it. By then Harrow was regarded as déclassé and he had not been happy there anyway. During the war he had observed in the KRRC officers' mess how the Etonians had a polish and a self-confidence that he always felt he lacked. Eton was, and remains, outstanding at conferring this charm and confidence on its boys, especially those who are not very academic. Deedes believed that by sending Jeremy to Eton he was buying his first born an inoculation against the chronic lack of confidence from which he had suffered. What more could a boy want? Like all sons, Jeremy, of course, wanted visible signs of love and evidence that his father was proud of him, whether on the cricket square or later in his working life.

Deedes was an arch monarchist all his life, but he had a very low opinion of the Prince of Wales, whom he regarded as a self-pitying drip. Deedes would never have written about him in such terms, but over lunch at Paradiso or in leader conference at the *Telegraph* he would expound at length on Charles's character flaws. When feeling charitable, he would say of the prince that he was starved of parental love: 'You have to remember he has to make an appointment to speak to his own mother,' he would say. It is interesting that Deedes had a keen eye for the neglect of other parents, and that he recognised that it could have serious consequences. His observation about Charles is all the odder given that Lucy, when planning her wedding, became so exasperated by her father's refusal to talk about the plans at home that she made an appointment with his secretary at the *Telegraph* and went to see him there.

But Deedes was exercised by another factor in the Prince's flawed character, convinced that he had gone to the wrong school. He was adamant that had the Queen put her foot down and sent him to Eton, rather than bleak, dreary Gordonstoun, the heir to the throne might well have turned out the 'right way up'. Deedes particularly enjoyed making the latter point, for it convinced him he had done right by Jeremy.

In almost all ways, Bill Deedes was anxious not to seem old-fashioned. He was pro-European, which, in the 1960s and 1970s, was a 'modern' thing for an Englishman to be. He may have been a member of the Carlton Club, but he was not interested in becoming a stalwart of the institution and was generally allergic to club bores, whether he encountered them around St James's or at the bar at Littlestone. In his seventies he learnt to use a computer; in his eighties he mastered e-mail. But one area in which he showed he was born an Edwardian was in his attitude to parenting. He believed, or he chose to believe, that the nursery upbringing he had experienced during the First World War and into the 1920s was good enough for him and therefore good enough for his children. Because he lived so long, and because he was essentially a humane man who hated causing hurt, he knew in his last years that he had been found out as a father. Periodically he would try to make amends, but because the wounds in the rest of the family were deep his efforts usually misfired. By the end of his life all he could really hope for was that his children would be as forgiving of his inadequacies as he had been of his own father's much graver failings.

CHAPTER 13

JOINING A SINKING SHIP

*'When my gamekeeper shoots a fox, he doesn't go and
hang it outside the Master of Foxhound's drawing-room;
he buries it out of sight.'*

The last thing Deedes sought in the middle of the summer of
1962 was a summons to join Harold Macmillan's belea-
guered administration. On leaving the Home Office in 1957,
Deedes had been flattered to be invited to join the One Nation
grouping of Conservative backbenchers. Its outlook was
what would now be called 'Tory wet', but it drew a catholic
mix of talented MPs from both wings of the party, including
Iain Macleod and Enoch Powell. *The Economist* labelled the
One Nation group as the *premier cru* of the 1950 vintage of
new Tory MPs who saw it as their mission to shake the party
out of its post-war ideological lethargy. They were not so much
egalitarian as seeking to promote a form of Conservative social
policy that would make the welfare state function effectively
and improve the social condition of the population. There were
weekly dinners with guests, which became a highlight in
Deedes's diary, possibly because he knew that otherwise he
had no reputation at Westminster for being a political thinker.
Ian Gilmour, who also attended the dinners regularly, recalled
that Deedes was not a live wire or a major contributor to the

debate over the port, 'just a delightful chap to sit next to, really'. For the final few years of his time in the Commons, Deedes was proud to act as the informal chairman of One Nation.

He was beginning to assume other responsibilities befitting an unambitious backbench MP with a comfortable majority. Rab Butler, Home Secretary, appointed him to the Institute of Criminology at Cambridge University under the inspiring, if eccentric, leadership of Professor Leon Radzinowicz. He was also drafted on to the Historic Building Council for England. Deedes enjoyed committees and, crucially, serving on them gave him the necessary authority to write on the subjects in the *Telegraph*. With his ministerial experience at Housing and the Home Office, Deedes was well-placed to pronounce upon a range of issues, including crime, immigration and the protection of the country-side. It was much easier for him to gain attention for himself by writing for the prime slot on the leader page in the *Daily Telegraph* than by hanging around in the House of Commons to speak in a debate when his contribution would merit a couple of paragraphs down page. From 1960 onwards he began to write more and more in the *Telegraph* under his own name – for which he was paid extra at £20–£25 per article – and devote less time to speaking in Parliament.

Nor was he picky about what he would write about, abiding strictly – as he did throughout his Fleet Street career – by the old hack's maxim, 'you hum it, I'll play it'. In November 1961, during a phase of anxiety about the quality of British manufac-turing output and customer service, he wrote about his battle with his London shirt-maker, whom he chose not to name and shame in print. Deedes noted he had been forced to return three shirts, each with two detachable soft collars, because they had shrunk around the neck. He seems to have been particularly irked by the manager's impudent letter blaming the shrinkage on Mrs Deedes's laundry regime at home in Kent, and her fail-ure to ensure they were 'pulled out to size or ironed while damp'.* To Deedes, this summed up all that was wrong with the British mentality that the 'customer is always wrong', even when he has paid seventy shillings for a shirt. Cunningly, Deedes tweaked the article half way through so that by the end he was making an important political point, which was that with membership of the Common Market looming consumers had a patriotic duty to complain so that manufacturers were kept on their toes as they shaped up to European competition.

As Deedes put it, by the summer of 1962 'even a dull political ear could pick up thunder in the air'. As much as he could, Deedes ignored the rumbles, but it was hard to misread the clear indicators suggesting an imminent end to eleven years of Conservative rule. The Orpington by-election in March 1962, when a Tory majority of more than 14,000 was stunningly converted into a comfortable Liberal victory, rattled the party and increased pressure on Harold Macmillan, who was beginning to look too old and out of touch. John Selwyn Lloyd, the Chancellor, appeared particularly isolated and inept. More problems piled up through the summer and the press talked of a government becalmed.

In July Deedes sought refuge in the most comforting way imaginable by persuading the *Telegraph* sports editor to let him cover one of the highlights of his school days, the annual Eton–Harrow match at Lord's. Deedes clearly relished his new temporary role beyond the boundary rope, and in his debut match report he tested the stylistic limits of sports journalism. Eton managed to hold on for a draw against a superior Harrow team only because of ninety-five runs scored by the captain, M. C. T. Pritchard. 'It was not a poem of uniform metre,' Deedes reported of the match-saving innings, 'but it gave what was badly needed and shone at the end.'

* Not long after this incident, Deedes transferred his custom from Jermyn Street and thereafter bought shirts only from Brooks Brothers, one reason he was always keen to go to America for political conventions. He favoured the classic Brooks Brothers shirt, single cuff and button-down collar, and would buy half a dozen at a time.

Four days after the end of that game, Rab Butler was loose-tongued at a lunch with the *Daily Mail*, revealing that Macmillan had promised to remove Selwyn Lloyd from the Treasury in an effort to restore some vigour to the faltering government. When the *Mail* splashed with the leak the next day, Macmillan realised he could no longer delay action. Selwyn Lloyd was sacked that evening in an awkward forty-five-minute meeting with the Prime Minister. Fearing financial turbulence, it was decided that the reshuffle – which had been triggered early because of Butler's indiscretion – had to be completed the very next day, appropriately Friday 13 July.

Macmillan had panicked, and the perfectly sensible option of moving Selwyn Lloyd sideways to the Home Office was overlooked. Instead, in twenty-four hours, Macmillan sacked one-third of his Cabinet, an episode of blood-letting unprecedented in British political history. Apart from Selwyn Lloyd, Macmillan dispensed with his Lord Chancellor, Minister of Education, Housing Minister and Secretary of State for Scotland. Others followed, and by the time he was finished the diffident, cautious Macmillan had shocked his closest friends with his brutality and inspired Jeremy Thorpe's excellent quip: 'Greater love hath no man than he lay down his friends for his life.'

Deedes claimed to have been caught completely off guard. In his autobiography, he acknowledged that, having read the *Daily Mail* on the Thursday, he knew there was some turbulence at the highest level of government and 'thanked my stars that ministerial office was no longer part of my life'. The next day Deedes was enjoying one of his agreeable hybrid working days, lunching at the House of Commons and then taking the bus back from Westminster along Fleet Street to help out with the Peterborough column. Responsibility for producing the column was split that day between Deedes and Auberon Waugh, the son of Evelyn. As Deedes typed out a story the telephone rang. It was the office of the Chief Whip, Martin Redmayne, inviting Deedes without explanation to report by 3.45 p.m. for a

meeting at Admiralty House, where the Prime Ministerial operation was based during a Downing Street refurbishment. Deedes
claimed in *Dear Bill* that he was 'mystified' by the summons,
but that seems somehow implausible. Selwyn Lloyd had been
sacked some twenty-two hours earlier and Westminster was in
ferment about Macmillan's botched reshuffle. It was disingenuous
of Deedes to suggest that he had no idea why he had been summoned to see the Prime Minister. It is almost as though he didn't
want to be thought to be part of the episode of Cabinet blood-
letting that had triggered the telephone call. There is no evidence
to suggest that Deedes was angling for a return to the government;
all the evidence points the other way, for he was undoubtedly very
happy on the backbenches. It is odd, nevertheless, that he should
have made a point of suggesting he was in the dark when it is
impossible to conceive that he, as a well-connected and gossipy
Tory MP moving freely within the intersecting worlds of journalism and politics, could have been ignorant of such a huge political
storm breaking around him.

According to an aide-memoire Deedes wrote later that day,
the scene in which he was ushered in to see the Prime Minister
was as follows: Macmillan was sucking on his pipe, sipping a
consoling afternoon whisky and soda, and looked watery of
eye. 'No idea how you are placed,' Macmillan said, 'but
wondering if you can help me. Want a minister, in Cabinet of
course, who will not only take over the Information Services, but
without department and can do some of the many jobs that
fall to Cabinet Ministers . . . Political situation very serious.
Considered my own position. Discussed with the Queen. Wishes
me to stay.' He laid out the job as a coordinating role between
departments, presenting the government's image, most crucially with responsibility for selling the Common Market to a
sceptical British electorate. Macmillan stared up at Deedes, and
asked weakly: 'Will you help; will you return to the sinking
ship?' As Deedes wrote in *Dear Bill*, 'What on earth is one left to
say to that?'

Though he did not say so out loud to Macmillan, Deedes later recalled murmuring to himself the words, 'A sinking ship is my spiritual home.' And indeed it was – he had been blissfully happy at the *Morning Post* for the six years he spent there until it expired in 1937. After that experience, a billet in the Macmillan administration was a bagatelle and, financially, it was a mini bonanza.

When he had become a junior minister eight years earlier, Deedes had suffered a disastrous cut in his pre-tax income, but this time he would not suffer for serving in the government. He would get the full Cabinet salary of £5000 plus £750 of his parliamentary salary, even though he would have no department to run. This represented a handy increase to his existing MP's salary of £1750 and the £2000 he then earned from the *Telegraph*. Had Deedes been offered a return to government as a junior minister he would only have been entitled to a much lower salary, and would almost certainly have declined, reasonably pleading that he had done all that and now had five children to raise. But the Cabinet was a different matter: over the centuries, four Deedes ancestors had been in Parliament, but none had made the Cabinet.

Macmillan's tentative, apologetic offer of preferment gave Deedes the chance to dispatch, once and for all, the slur on his great-great-grandfather, of whom Lord Stanley had been so contemptuous. Now, William Francis Deedes had been personally asked by Harold Macmillan to help save the Conservative government, and for his name to be put before Queen Elizabeth. He accepted Macmillan's offer on the spot. As was almost always the case in taking an important decision in his professional life, Deedes felt no need to talk it over with Hilary.

More important for Deedes was to square his appointment with the *Telegraph* and to ensure they would not object to his taking another leave of absence. Colin Coote, the editor, was unimpressed by his decision, but that evening he wrote a leader broadly sympathetic to the reshuffle and laudatory about Deedes's sense of duty. By answering Macmillan's call in the affirmative and interrupting his 'brilliant journalistic career', Deedes had proved he was no 'fair-weather friend' to his political colleagues. It was kind of Coote, but few Fleet Street hands would then have described the career of a man of forty-nine who had risen to the level of assistant editor of Peterborough as evidence of 'brilliant' progress in newspapers. In the Commons and in the press there was a certain bafflement about aspects of the reshuffle, and in particular Deedes's new role. Crossbencher in the *Sunday Express* conceded he was highly popular among MPs but teasingly questioned his credentials for a Cabinet job. 'His cosy, unsigned newspaper column chronicling the daily doings of clubmen and canons was about as slick as a Victorian railway carriage,' it teased. Crossbencher then recalled Iain Macleod's words that the Common Market should be sold 'with trumpets', before adding caustically, 'But Mr Deedes is no hotlips.'

Peregrine Worsthorne, whose *Sunday Telegraph* political column was then essential reading, was more concerned about the ideological tinge of the new Cabinet: 'This, *par excellence*, is a Government of Bow Group favourite fathers, with the Monday Club left very much in the cold.' Worsthorne meant, by that, that the so-called kissing-circle of patrician liberal Tories had been pushed forward at the expense of the ideological right, a fact borne out by the social composition of the new Cabinet. In the 1960s the *Daily Express* printed on its front page the school (though not the university) that every new Cabinet minister had attended. All eleven of the ministers promoted or moved sideways that day were public school boys: five were Etonians, and two – Deedes and Sir Keith Joseph – Harrovians.[*]

Reassured that the *Telegraph* would allow him to take indefinite leave, Deedes took his Friday train back to Ashford to attend, rather late, his weekly constituency surgery. He was there when Downing Street formally released all the names of the full reshuffle,

---

[*] Enoch Powell, not a public school boy, was promoted into the Cabinet though he did not change jobs, remaining Minister of Health.

and a *Telegraph* political reporter managed to reach him by telephone, while he was in the middle of an interview with a constituent. 'My only comment,' joked Macmillan's latest Cabinet recruit, proving there's no pun like an old pun, 'is "deeds not words".'

Deedes was not the first British government spin doctor, or, as Labour members would occasionally brand him, propagandist-in-chief. The practice of a Cabinet minister taking responsibility for presentation had been established by Dr Charles Hill who, as Chancellor of the Duchy of Lancaster, spent most of his time burnishing the image of the government when confirmed in the role by Macmillan in 1957. It had been an easier task in those days, the high point of Supermac and his triumph in the 1959 election. Hill adapted well to the world of public relations, having learned the art representing private doctors during the creation of the National Health Service. He understood the fundamental PR point that information is an instrument of policy, and did much good presentational work for Macmillan. His reward was to be abruptly sacked in the Night of the Long Knives, his exit from the Cabinet eased by a peerage.

Deedes did his best to throw himself into his new job and there was the immediate excitement, three days after his appointment, of being 'sworn of Her Majesty's Most Honourable Privy Council' on 16 July. But in truth the position of Minister without Portfolio, with responsibility for improving the government's image, was a poisoned chalice and would have been even if the Macmillan government had not been dying on its feet. There was an inherent conflict of interest between acting as a Conservative party hack and presenting what was supposed to be something completely different – 'government information'. Too often, it was distinction without a difference, as Deedes himself had uncannily predicted in a *Telegraph* article ten years earlier. 'The idea of a Whitehall machine to do this job [presenting the government's case] appals me. It may be good Socialist theory, but it is bad Conservative practice.' He had been right then, and he found it increasingly difficult a decade later to convince his former journalistic colleagues that he now had a proper Cabinet role that transcended party propaganda.

The Economist was exercised by this point, suggesting that most of his responsibilities could not properly be conducted by a Cabinet minister. What mattered was an improvement in the government's performance, not what Deedes said. 'It therefore remains a bit of a mystery exactly what Mr Deedes is supposed to do,' though the magazine conceded that he was 'a first-rate working journalist'.

Beyond that, Deedes's role put him into a potential rivalry with Harold Evans, Macmillan's press secretary, and indeed with the civil servants in each of the government departments responsible for news presentation. In theory Deedes was Evans's superior, though he was never able to act like a boss, partly because Evans had closer ties to the Lobby journalists but also because he had more direct access to the Prime Minister and his senior civil servants. It was a tall order and, though Deedes's customary tact and aversion to confrontation ensured friction was kept to a minimum, the project was fraught from the start. Ministers and their civil servants resented what they regarded as a ploy by Conservative Central Office to reduce their autonomy and a whispering campaign began against him.

Judged against contemporary government news operations, Deedes's department was modest, fitting into a couple of rooms in Gwydor House on Whitehall. Apart from his private secretary Derek Taylor Thompson, the office staff comprised an assistant secretary, an elderly messenger and a driver called Miss Bussey who drove the minister and his red boxes around London and the country. That was the extent of Deedes's Whitehall empire, and it was the only time in his life that Deedes had a dedicated driver. Taylor Thompson was a familiar type of civil service high-flyer, a clever Balliol classicist with a career background mostly in the Treasury. He was very surprised to find himself working with Deedes, whom he remembered as endlessly pleasant and good-natured. Because he knew nothing of the workings of Fleet Street or of the broadcast media, Taylor Thompson found himself in the awkward position of being unable to brief his minister on any aspect of his job, but they nonetheless struck up an easy working relationship. Taylor Thompson said he had had to think quite hard what the department was for, but he sensed his boss was struggling too. 'At the time, it wasn't entirely clear what he [Deedes] was supposed to be doing.' Soon it became evident that the main priority, so far as Macmillan was concerned, was to sell the Common Market to a sceptical electorate, and much of Deedes's time was spent dealing with the project's most dedicated foes in the Beaverbrook press.

It did not go well from the start, and by the autumn sections of the press were questioning Deedes's role. He would have been wounded by a feature in the *Evening Standard* of 29 November 1962 under the ominous headline 'MR DEEDES LANDS HIM-SELF AN IMPOSSIBLE JOB', with the damning – and increasingly wearisome – pun attached in brackets: 'a mere man of words say his critics'. Robert Carvel, the political correspon-dent, had clearly been briefed by Cabinet rivals and thus questioned the propriety of Deedes's ministerial work and listed a series of internecine Whitehall battles that he had lost. Carvel suggested that for the sake of his future political career he should find a way out of his pointless Cabinet role because it was doomed to crash. 'The accident may be partly the fault of his pas-sengers but he will certainly always get the blame.'

But Deedes ploughed on doggedly, 'providing information' to the public on European matters while not doing anything actively to promote it. In practice, that meant writing and printing a series of pamphlets, aimed at professions and interest groups, with titles such as 'What the Common Market means for Accountants'. He also tar-geted Tory ladies' groups, reassuring them on the domestic aspects of European membership. By Deedes's own admission, it was pretty banal stuff. As the most junior member of the Cabinet, the Minister without Portfolio found himself as the public speaker of last resort at numerous events around the country. His speech at a luncheon at the Institute of Public Relations in December 1962, for instance, yielded a three-paragraph report in the *Daily Telegraph*. Deedes told the audience he would rather speak to a dozen people in what he called 'a village hut' than to five million people via television. The pub, he said, was the stronghold of old-style human intercourse. 'It may well be that a future historian will write of this island that their system of democracy was saved by beer.'

Deedes's input was more valued when he applied his journalistic experience to advise Macmillan on how to use television to political advantage. With a bond forged during their joint appearance in the first party political broadcast in 1953, Macmillan trusted Deedes's views. The Night of the Long Knives had been designed in part to bring in younger men who would look vigorous and dynamic on television. One of the first tasks Deedes completed on his promotion was to prepare a confidential memorandum about the new medium.

'No field of communications offers greater possibilities in the time at our disposal before an election to improve the public mood towards Government than that of broadcasting and television. Their impact on the public mind is immense. Though we have come a long way there is still a tendency in many places to view the resources available with suspicion and to use them half-heartedly.' This view may seem self-evident in an era in which television is so dominant; in the 1960s it was not obvious and many Tories were determined to keep the 'socialist' BBC at arm's length.

This was the heyday of the satirical review *That Was The Week That Was*, which many Conservatives saw as definitive proof of the Corporation's bias. There was particular rage at David Frost's failure to conceal his loathing for Macmillan, and also the general savaging of Tory defence policy. Deedes wrote unofficially to the BBC to complain on at least one occasion, as did other Conservatives, including Toby Low, the party vice-chairman.

But in his paper for Macmillan, Deedes prescribed gentle handling of the BBC, conscious that public rows tend to rebound on the complainant. 'We ourselves should not in this field always be looking for "Pinkies under the Bed". There is scope for horse-trading.' Deedes also shrewdly predicted that ministers would have to break out of the established format of delivering solemn lectures about the state of the economy or the world on television. He said colleagues should be encouraged to move into the field of 'entertainment' programmes, by which he meant those that dealt with matters of human interest. 'Carefully increased ministerial participation in such programmes, thus identifying government with problems people feel and understand, would have advantages.'

The Deedes view prevailed and though there were to remain frictions between the BBC and Conservatives the party overcame its reluctance to engage with the new, coming medium. Deedes himself remained in touch with senior members of the Corporation for the rest of his political career and beyond, and became a seasoned performer in front of the cameras.

Inevitably, the Profumo scandal came to define Deedes's uncomfortable tenure as Cabinet minister responsible for news management, but it was two unconnected events in early 1963 that ensured his short Cabinet career would end on an unsatisfactory note. The first was de Gaulle's January humiliation of Macmillan with his veto of British membership of the Common Market. The *Daily Express* celebrated the routing of the European integrationists, spearheaded in negotiations in Brussels by Ted Heath and in presentation at home by Bill Deedes, by declaring, 'Glory, glory Hallelujah!' While it was true that de Gaulle's veto caused no out-pouring of popular grief in Britain it was devastating to the Macmillan government and to Deedes's role in presenting it as a vigorous administration with a forward-looking strategy. 'All our policies at home and abroad are in ruins,' Macmillan confided to his diary. Deedes's doleful assessment was similar: 'From that moment, we were absolutely becalmed.'

Deedes had the unenviable task of explaining to journalists

why this humiliation was actually a great opportunity for the government. He briefed lobby correspondents on the day of the veto and Harold Evans, the Number 10 press spokesman, unkindly told him afterwards that they remained 'confused'. Deedes retorted: 'Who does not?' He later recalled that this set-back caused him a new crisis of confidence and alerted him to his own limitations. 'It would have taken someone abler than myself to present an appearance of business as usual.'

Nor did Deedes make much impact within the Cabinet. Derek Taylor Thompson thought his boss was intimidated by Macmillan, and certainly Deedes rarely spoke in Cabinet. As was the case when he joined the Housing Ministry in 1954, Deedes found himself at a disadvantage when he came up against the clever men in the top ranks of the civil service. A Rolls-Royce mind may not be needed to be a good journalist, but it helps in dealings with the Whitehall mandarins. 'Bill's memory was not good,' Taylor Thompson noted – the tactful way a civil servant suggests his minister might not quite be up to the job.

Compared to the regime overseen by Duncan Sandys in housing eight years earlier, Deedes's tiny department was easygoing in the extreme. Some days it was quite difficult to fill the diary because other departments were predictably reluctant to accept well-intentioned advice on presentational matters from the Minister without Portfolio. Taylor Thompson decided that even if the department lacked grandeur it was going to have a grand address when, in 1963, it was moved into a couple of rooms at 77 Whitehall, bang on the junction with Downing Street. Taylor Thompson seized on this proximity to order up new departmental stationery with the address 1 Downing Street proudly displayed. Deedes was thrilled and thought there was a splendid ring to his new headquarters. Sadly it was to be short-lived: Tim Bligh, Macmillan's private secretary, sent a tart note to Taylor Thompson, telling him that the only proper numbers in Downing Street were 10, 11 and 12, and that there was to be no more Number 1.

Deedes was later publicly critical of his performance around the de Gaulle veto. But that was an event far beyond his control, and in truth there was nothing he could have done to convince lobby correspondents that it was anything other than an embarrassing demolition of the centrepiece of the government's programme. He was more personally culpable in a much uglier incident, which ruined an innocent man and led directly to the mistakes that allowed the Profumo affair to become such a catastrophe.

Peter Rawlinson, then Solicitor-General, recalled the moment that the director of public prosecutions, Toby Mathew, marched into his office in September 1962 and said genially: 'Sit down. You will need to. We have arrested a spy who is a bugger, and a minister is involved.' The spy was John Vassall, an Admiralty civil servant who had previously been a cipher clerk in the British Embassy in Moscow. There, the KGB had photographed his energetic participation in a homosexual orgy it had staged for his benefit. On his return to Britain in 1956 he began passing copies of Admiralty documents to his Soviet handlers who, in return for about seven hundred pounds a year, which roughly matched his civil service salary, promised not to unmask his homosexual secrets.

The minister ensnared was Thomas Galbraith, a former Admiralty minister, in whose private office Vassall worked as assistant private secretary. This was the height of the Cold War and this episode was not an isolated case of high espionage. The former British diplomat and KGB agent George Blake had been jailed the year before, and Vassall, like Blake before him, was not arrested as a result of counter-espionage activity by British intelligence, but was identified by defectors from eastern bloc regimes. Vassall was a camp homosexual who lived far beyond his civil service salary, yet no one in authority appeared to suspect that he might be a security risk. When Sir Roger Hollis, director-general of MI5, boasted to Macmillan that they had belatedly identified Vassall's treachery the Prime Minister merely looked glum, sensing that it would develop into a political storm. 'No I am not at all pleased,' Macmillan magnificently told Hollis. 'When my gamekeeper shoots a fox, he doesn't go and hang it outside the Master of Foxhound's drawing-room; he buries it out of sight.'

On 22 October 1962, the day the Cuban Missile Crisis erupted in public, Vassall was sentenced to eighteen years in prison. But that did not bring an end to the matter, or satisfy the popular press. The political assault was led by the deputy Labour leader George Brown, which was rich given his own rackety personal life and the frequency with which he was seen drunk in public. The jailed civil servant was 'sick', declared the *News of the World*. 'Men like Vassall don't want to be cured.' Soon the press were hounding Galbraith, who by then had moved from the Admiralty to become Under-Secretary of State for Scotland, and Lord Carrington, First Lord of the Admiralty. The problem for Galbraith was that he had written some slightly unusual letters to the spy, on matters ranging from the office carpets to crockery and paper clips, which were discovered during the investigation into his spying activities. Some of the letters were topped with the words 'My dear Vassall', which was a perfectly normal form of address in the early 1960s, but to the popular press, giddy with a sensational 'buggery-and-spying' scandal, this was clear proof of a wider homosexual ring. Galbraith was later cleared of all impropriety and, as the *Annual Register* put it, the minister was guilty of nothing more than suffering 'a socially pressing and plausible junior colleague a trifle too gladly'.

But that exoneration came too late to save Galbraith's political career, as lurid press headlines trumpeted transvestite activities at the Admiralty. None of the men involved in Galbraith's enforced resignation emerges with much credit. Macmillan was flapping around, worrying how to bury the fox and moaning that governments get criticism, not praise, when they catch spies. He summoned Peter Rawlinson and John Hobson, the Attorney General, to discuss whether the government should accept opposition demands that the internal civil service inquiry be transformed into a full-scale tribunal. Initially, Macmillan had suggested he would hold the line and not allow Labour's jibes to provoke them into a full inquiry. The three men sat by the fire drinking whisky and at the end of an inconclusive, circular discussion Macmillan said enigmatically: 'Very well, we shall retire. But we shall retire to the thunder of the guns.'

That same evening, Deedes was summoned to a meeting at Admiralty House with Redmayne and two of Macmillan's private secretaries, Tim Bligh and Philip Woodfield. Also present was Harold Evans, anxious to brief the lobby correspondents on Macmillan's next move, and who was, according to Deedes, 'slightly overwrought'. Deedes later recalled that he had originally counselled against the sacking of Galbraith. When the question of demanding his resignation was raised at that meeting, 'I murmured "no", because it implied panic.' Redmayne, according to Deedes, agreed, though Macmillan's two private secretaries demurred. Later the four men joined a meeting with Macmillan and reviewed the letters between Vassall and Galbraith, which were about to be made public, in the belief that this would lance the boil.

Deedes then changed his mind, according to a note he scribbled that evening on House of Commons writing paper. Galbraith's letters were 'narcissistic', he concluded, and as more whiskies and soda were produced he switched sides to argue he must go. On the face of it, Deedes's explanation for his volte-face is absurd. His description of Galbraith as 'narcissistic' appears to be just a code word for 'homosexual', implying that, as he was as self-obsessed and strange as Vassall, he was almost certainly improperly involved with him.

To condemn a colleague and hound him out of office on the grounds of 'narcissism', and without in any way suggesting he had otherwise done anything wrong, would be contemptible. It seems much more likely that Deedes simply felt the mood of the meeting swinging against him and wanted to come out on the majority side and not rock the boat. At that point, Deedes,

Redmayne and Bligh repaired to the restaurant Overton's in St James's. Over oysters, the three men honed the resignation letter Galbraith was to be forced to release. Shortly before ten o'clock, Redmayne departed with the letter for Galbraith's Westminster home to tell him that he would be resigning.

Harold Evans, the other man at the meeting directly responsible for the press, was similarly disingenuous in his memoirs, making the dubious claim that 'Galbraith insisted on resigning . . . partly to have freedom to take legal action against those who had libelled him'. Macmillan also later subscribed to the lie that Galbraith wanted to fall on his sword, noting in his memoirs that he only reluctantly accepted Galbraith's 'insistent' offer of resignation. Redmayne, who was regarded in Westminster as one of the undisputed 'shits' in the Commons, was at least honest about Galbraith's demise. Many years later he conceded that Macmillan sent him to a reluctant Galbraith to insist on his resignation. 'It was not my happiest moment. Nor were the wolves diverted for more than a moment.'

In *Dear Bill*, Deedes betrays no sense of remorse about his part in forcing Galbraith's departure. He notes his role in producing a deliberately misleading exchange of resignation letters; indeed, he records with apparent pride his suggestion that, in response to Galbraith's letter, Macmillan should say, 'I would have preferred to wait until after the inquiry, but in the circumstances I accept your resignation.' That was a straight lie; both Deedes and the Prime Minister knew they wanted an immediate resignation. 'In the end it all turned out to be innocent,' Deedes said of Galbraith's conduct in 2004. 'I made a mistake.'

Peter Rawlinson was not so sanguine about this shabby treatment of Galbraith, who did return briefly to office after his exoneration, but whose career was effectively ruined by the non-scandal and whose marriage was put under strain. 'A wholly innocent man had been destroyed by gossip and rumour,' Rawlinson wrote in his autobiography. As Macmillan's circle quietly betrayed Galbraith behind the scenes, they plotted their revenge on the journalists who had encouraged them in the betrayal. A week after the resignation, Macmillan spoke in the Commons proposing the motion for the establishment of the Radcliffe Tribunal, which was ultimately to exonerate Galbraith. Macmillan, livid at the press's impudent behaviour and knowing that many of the more lurid reports about gay sex parties were pure fiction, insisted that journalists' conduct should also fall under the remit of the tribunal. 'Fleet Street has generated an atmosphere around the Vassall case,' Macmillan said, 'worthy of Titus Oates or Senator McCarthy ... a dark cloud of suspicion and innuendo.' Alan Watkins, then of the *Observer*, recalled that Macmillan was heard to say, 'Now we'll get the journalists.' Deedes must have been aware of the dangers of this course of action but there is no evidence, either in his autobiography or in his official papers of the time, that he sought to restrain Macmillan and convince him that attacks on the media generally rebound on politicians.

When Brendan Mulholland of the *Daily Mail* and Reginald Foster of the *Daily Sketch* refused to name their sources for their more sensational stories – notably about who told them Vassall bought women's clothes in the West End – they were sent to prison for six and three months respectively. Fleet Street puffed itself up into scandalised offence at this encroachment of the freedom of the press, although most journalists privately thought their overheated accounts of sex parties were largely, if not entirely, fictional. 'We all assumed it was pretty much all made up,' Anthony Howard, then of the *New Statesman*, recalled. Thus, by going to prison, the journalists were defending their own reputations rather than any high principle of press freedom. Even so, it was essential for appearances' sake that the press publicly and collectively acted as though they were enraged. There was talk of Macmillan's invitation as guest of honour to the Press Gallery's annual dinner being withdrawn, but nothing came of that line of protest. The fact that Macmillan was welcomed at a *Daily Mail* lunch while Mulholland was still in prison suggests that the paper might quietly have had cause to doubt the reliability of his coverage.

In later years, it was generally believed that the Profumo scandal destroyed relations between the Macmillan government and the press, but the real damage was done before any journalist had even heard of Christine Keeler. The Vassall affair could be turned into a case study of the most disastrously bad handling of a sticky problem. Foolishly, Galbraith told journalists he had felt sorry for Vassall, and suspected he had 'a screw loose' and that the interior of his Dolphin Square flat had indeed struck him as 'strange'. Unwittingly, indeed witlessly, Galbraith had thrown petrol on the flames by indicating that he thought an official entrusted with top-secret papers was mad and that he had visited Vassall, a homosexual and a spy, in his own home. Peter Thorneycroft, Minister of Defence, then managed to make matters even worse when he was asked how a junior civil servant could be spending three-quarters of his salary on rent. 'How many of us are living above our incomes in London squares?' he asked, loyally but unwisely. What Galbraith needed badly was for an expert in press matters to step in and take over the news management of the story. Deedes did not become involved, opting to keep his distance.

In his memoirs, Harold Evans recalled how acutely despondent he became at how low relations had sunk between Tory politicians and the press; in his autobiography, however, Deedes was more relaxed about it, though he acknowledged that post-Vassall 'my task of winning hearts and minds in the newspaper world became immeasurably harder'.

In truth, there was little Evans could have done to avert the breakdown in relations, and, despite everything, he maintained a decent day-to-day relationship with the political correspondents. Evans was a civil servant; Deedes was a minister in the Cabinet, specifically charged with improving the image of the government. He could have spoken to Macmillan privately or even raised the matter more formally in Cabinet. There is no evidence that he took any action to avert the breakdown of relations. There were human consequences of this failure, in the humiliation and ruin of an honourable man. After Thomas Galbraith's formal exoneration he won undisclosed libel damages from Beaverbrook and Associated Newspapers, and was restored to junior office. But his marriage later collapsed and he never fulfilled his early political potential. There were to be political consequences, too, for just as the press realised it had overreached itself with Vassall another, even juicier, scandal was dropping into their laps. The lapses committed by Deedes and others over Vassall–Galbraith ensured that the next scandal, when it broke, would be mishandled in a different way but just as gravely, so that when it finally detonated it did so with much more devastating effect.

CHAPTER 14

A WELL-MANNERED SCREW

Oh what have you done, cried Christine,
You've wrecked the whole party machine!
To lie in the nude may be terribly rude,
But to lie in the House is obscene.

Anon

By any sane objective measure, the issue that was to metastasise into the Profumo scandal was a relatively trivial sexual transgression. Had the ground not been prepared by the Vassall–Galbraith episode, it is highly unlikely that the War Minister's brief dalliance with a former topless dancer would have become the dominant political story of 1963. And, had the Vassall incident not already reduced press–government relations to such an acrimonious level, newspapers would almost certainly not have pursued Profumo with such zeal.

John Profumo and Christine Keeler met quite by chance and in comical circumstances on a sticky July night in 1961 at Cliveden, a monstrous neo-Renaissance pile that was the home of Lord and Lady Astor. Profumo and his wife were there for a formal dinner party with the Astors, which was attended by various diplomats, Tory MPs, aristocrats and businessmen, as well as Ayub Khan, the President of Pakistan.

Keeler was part of the louche circle of acquaintances maintained by Stephen Ward, who would today be known in the press as a 'celebrity osteopath' for he tended to the creaking joints of several public figures, including Winston Churchill, Paul Getty, Elizabeth Taylor and Danny Kaye.

Ward was a talented portrait artist and had drawn many famous people, including the Duke of Edinburgh. He also provided girls to well-connected men on terms a jury subsequently found to be pimping, though the evidence suggests that judgment was unduly harsh. He was a dissolute and chaotic figure who slept with countless women and then passed them on to his friends. But he was not driven by money, and would have been too disorganised to run a serious prostitution racket. According to Lord Denning's subsequent report – which betrayed his lordship's interest in the minutiae of sexual practices at the dawn of the permissive society – Ward 'attended parties where there were sexual orgies of a revolting nature'. He had provided many of the female participants at these parties and, before she met Profumo, Keeler – Denning found in his report – had already made herself available to many men, 'sometimes men of rank and position, with whom she had sexual intercourse'.

Ward rented a weekend cottage on the Cliveden estate and was allowed to use the pool. That evening he had four friends down from London, one of them nineteen-year-old Christine Keeler, who was swimming in the nude because her borrowed costume did not fit. After dinner the guests at the Astors' dinner party made their way from the main house to the swimming pool, nursing brandies and cigars. Hearing them approach, Ward playfully tossed Keeler's costume in to the bushes, leaving her standing naked and shrieking by the side of pool just as Lord Astor and John Profumo arrived on the scene. Judging by the contemporary photographs of Christine Keeler, it was no surprise that Profumo – who had a wanton reputation at Westminster – should have been much taken by her.

Profumo's subsequent 'arrangement' with Keeler – usually conducted at 17 Wimpole Mews, Ward's home – was not a straightforward punter–prostitute relationship, but nor was it an affair between equals based on affection or mutual attraction. It was a fairly standard arrangement of the era between a rich man and a suppliant young woman. Keeler was not paid directly for her activities in bed, but did allow Profumo to give her presents, including perfume, a cigarette lighter and twenty pounds 'for her parents'. This was by no means her first outing as courtesan to a powerful man; she did not dispute Denning's subsequent assessment of her promiscuousness and nonchalantly cast her liaison with the War Minister as 'a very well-mannered screw of convenience'.

However, for Profumo there were certain circumstances that would rebound and cause difficulties. First, another member of Ward's catholic circle of visitors at Wimpole Mews was Captain Eugene Ivanov, a KGB spy working under cover as an assistant naval attaché at the Russian embassy in London. Ivanov had become friendly with Ward, who had vague Soviet sympathies, and had come down to Cliveden for a lunchtime swimming party the day after Profumo and Keeler met.* It was a jolly and rather raucous event with much frolicking around in the pool, although all the revellers wore costumes on this occasion. The President of Pakistan participated in much of the fun, though when later approached by the *News of the World* a spokesman at the High Commission in London said the president had 'no recollection' of meeting Christine Keeler in the pool. Profumo famously cheated in a swimming race with Ivanov by using his feet when they were supposed to use only arms. 'That will teach you to trust the British government,' Profumo joked to the vanquished Russian.

But Ivanov was ahead of Profumo in one respect: that evening he drove Keeler back to Wimpole Mews where they drank vodka before slipping into bed. Keeler was impressed by his sexual

---

* There was some consternation at the *Daily Telegraph* when it was later discovered that Ward and Ivanov had been introduced by the paper's editor, Sir Colin Coote, at a lunch he hosted at the Garrick Club, though it seems perfectly possible in arranging the lunch he was acting on behalf of another contact, Sir Roger Hollis of MI5.

energy during their 'real Russian romp', and later described Ivanov as 'rugged with a hairy chest, strong and agile'. Ivanov clearly enjoyed the romp himself but, unlike Profumo, he could see Keeler was trouble. Betraying a snobbery unbecoming in a communist agent, he dismissed her ungallantly as a 'semi-literate, naive provincial girl with loose morals . . . a dangerous creature, sly and treacherous . . . That devil of a girl could seduce any-body!' Though Denning ruled that the War Minister and the Russian spy never overlapped as Keeler's lovers, the fuse was burning even as Ivanov pleasured Keeler that night. Profumo was in single-minded pursuit of his teenage quarry, armed with a tele-phone number provided by Stephen Ward.

Profumo's visits to Wimpole Mews did not go unnoticed by MI5, which kept Ivanov under close surveillance. As was to be confirmed later, British intelligence had a line to Ward; evidence that emerged suggested he was being used to lure Ivanov into a honey trap and to turn him into a double agent. Profumo was warned by the security services of the obvious dangers of his indiscretion: some five weeks into his affair with Keeler Profumo sent her a letter half-heartedly calling it off, which he recklessly topped 'Darling' and tailed 'Love J'. In the event, Profumo found he could not keep away from her and the affair continued until the end of 1961.

As Denning put it, at around that time Keeler was introduced, by Ward, to 'the drug Indian hemp and she became addicted to it. She met coloured men who trafficked in it and she went to live with them.' The problem was that two of her West Indian admir-ers – John Edgecombe and Lucky Gordon – were engaged in a bloody feud to maintain her affections. Edgecombe had slashed Gordon's face, and he decided to go after Keeler herself, arriving at Wimpole Mews one afternoon in December 1962 with a 'hot' revolver, which had been used in a hold-up in Queen's Park. Keeler's friend Mandy Rice-Davies first lied and shouted out of the window that Keeler was at the hairdresser. When Keeler gin-gerly appeared at the window telling Edgecombe to calm down, he fired seven wild shots, doing some damage but causing no injuries.

A shooting in Marylebone in broad daylight inevitably caused a stir and the incident was widely reported in the next day's press. The *Telegraph*'s report was in the finest restrained tradition of the paper's news columns: 'Miss Keeler, twenty, a free-lance model, was visiting Miss Marilyn Davies, eighteen, an actress, at Dr Ward's home,' rather as if it was a vicarage tea party that had been interrupted by the appearance of a stray cat. Keeler panicked and began blabbing to anyone who would listen, not just about Edgecombe but also about her long-defunct relationship with Profumo.

Rumours about Profumo's liaison with Keeler circulated around Westminster and Fleet Street for months after the affair ended. Newspapers nibbled at the story but drew back from full publication for fear of libel. Keeler was fantastically indiscreet and childishly proud of her conquest of the War Minister, and sold her story, including the 'Darling' letter, to the *Sunday Pictorial* for a thousand pounds. Fearing libel proceedings and doubting Keeler's durability as a court witness, the *Pictorial* held off from publication.

Frustrated that the press lacked the nerve to publish, a Labour backbencher named George Wigg, who had previously been humiliated by Profumo during a parliamentary exchange, detonated the bomb when he rose at eleven o'clock on the night of 21 March 1963. Wigg noted that there could not be 'an Honourable member in the House, nor a journalist in the press gallery' who was unaware of the rumours surrounding 'a member of the government front bench. The press has got as near as it could – it has shown itself willing to wound, but afraid to strike.'

As members on both sides of the House considered the implications of Wigg's astonishing allegation, there was a splendidly off-message intervention from Reginald Paget, the hunting and shooting Labour member for Northampton. 'What do the rumours amount to?' Paget asked, as Wigg woke him from his torpor on the back benches, and then he answered his own question. 'They amount to the fact that a Minister is said to be acquainted with an extremely pretty girl. As far as I am concerned, I should have thought that that was a matter for congratulation rather than inquiry.'

Despite that welcome injection of farce, Conservatives in the chamber realised that weeks of rumours, thus far suppressed by fear of libel, were about to burst into the open. Deedes, who had dined that evening with Martin Redmayne, was sitting on the front bench alongside Henry Brooke, Home Secretary, and Sir John Hobson, Attorney General. Deedes later claimed in his auto-biography that, at the time of the Wigg disclosure, he had known of the Profumo rumours 'for about a week, because certain news-paper correspondents came to discuss them with me'. If that memory is correct – and it is difficult to see how it could have been – it would be an extraordinary illustration of his remoteness from the inner workings of the Downing Street machine, and indeed his estrangement from former journalistic colleagues.

Rumours had been circulating around Westminster and Fleet Street for at least three months. As early as 28 January, Sir Peter Rawlinson, Solicitor-General, had grown so alarmed by the per-sistent rumours that he had arranged for John Hobson to cross-examine Profumo. The War Minister emphatically denied there was anything untoward and described the rumours as a malevolent newspaper stunt, which in the aftermath of the Vassall affair some of his colleagues found plausible and reassuring. But Rawlinson was not convinced, even after Hobson took him to Profumo's office and made the minister repeat his denial. 'I said to Hobson, "You can't believe this." He said to me: "I take his word on honour."'

Redmayne briefed Harold Macmillan about the matter on 3 February and, only weeks after the Galbraith resignation, the Prime Minister was happy to give Profumo the benefit of the doubt and did not summon him for a personal grilling. By the beginning of March, as one contemporary account put it, 'the rumour lay around Westminster like a heavy inflammable vapour, waiting only for someone to strike a match to create the explosion'. In these circumstances, it is impossible to imagine how Deedes – as the man responsible for presenting the government's case and who attended the daily briefing with lobby correspondents – could have been ignorant of the main talking-point around Westminster. It is, however, true that Deedes took no active part in the handling of the scandal, except on the night it burst into the open.

Deedes left the chamber to brief Redmayne on the sudden crisis caused by Wigg's accusation. They huddled in a small chamber behind the Speaker's chair and drafted a few non-committal words for Brooke to say on behalf of the government in winding up the debate, then Deedes returned to the chamber. There, Harold Wilson, the leader of the opposition, unexpectedly rose to speak. After indicating that Henry Brooke's comments were inadequate and not the end of the matter, Wilson turned witheringly on Deedes, whose peculiarly awkward role as what he saw as a government-paid party propagandist had long irritated him. This was Wilson at his most sarcastic:

> Whatever our views and our prejudices may be, I would feel that the house as a whole probably takes the view that while we respect the principles which have always animated members of the journalistic profession, all of us think here with deep sympathy of the right honourable Member for Ashford who is sitting on the Government front bench. I do not know what his job is. Is it Minister without Portfolio? Whatever it is, he is the propaganda officer for the Government. All of us understand the difficulties with which he is labouring in these circumstances and we have sympathy for him.

Wilson, the self-consciously gritty scourge of the Tory establishment, had targeted Deedes as one of the more ludicrous accoutrements of Conservative rule. It is easy to imagine that

229

Wilson would have failed to see the point of William Francis Deedes, the scion of an ancient land-owning family from east Kent. For his part, Deedes sat mutely next to Brooke: he made no intervention in his own defence, and nor, according to Hansard, did any of his Conservative colleagues.

Wilson finally sat down at twenty-two minutes past one. Deedes never referred to this exchange in later life, which might seem strange because it must have made a deep impression on him. He would have left the House hurt and humiliated, but as was his custom he would have cast the moment into a separate sealed compartment, never to be revisited. Deedes went back to Eaton Terrace after the debate. Most politicians would have been unable to sleep after being publicly mauled by the leader of the opposition, but within an hour of Wilson's sarcastic outburst Deedes was tucked up in bed in his attic room.

Back at the Commons, Rawlinson, Hobson and Redmayne – after talking to 10 Downing Street – decided the allegations were a perfect opportunity for Profumo to declare his innocence publicly and warn of stiff legal remedies should the allegations of an affair be repeated without parliamentary privilege. It was decided that the lie must be nailed before the weekend, so a junior whip was dispatched to Profumo's Nash house in Regent's Park to bring him to the Commons in order to prepare a personal statement which would be read before the House rose later that day. Deedes was woken by Redmayne at about half-past two and ordered back to the House.

Profumo's home, 3 Chester Terrace, was by then surrounded by journalists so he and his wife – the actress Valerie Hobson – had taken sleeping tablets. In her submission to Denning, Hobson recalled being woken by the emissary from the Whips' office banging on the front door and her husband stumbling around the bedroom trying to fix his cufflinks, and she protested that he had been forced to agree to the wording of a statement while incapacitated.

On his arrival at the Commons, Profumo was told that if he

did not agree to deny the allegations in the House later that morning he would have to resign immediately. The five ministers – Deedes, Redmayne, Macleod, Hobson and Rawlinson – huddled together as they waited for Profumo's solicitor, Derek Clogg, to arrive. Deedes later said that it was assumed that the law officers, Hobson and Rawlinson, were responsible for establishing the reliability of Profumo's truthfulness. Certainly, Deedes had played no part in the affair thus far. Macleod had his own doubts, not least because, like Profumo, he had a rackety private life and was not above writing to girlfriends on ministerial writing paper. He was less inhibited than Deedes and Hobson – both of them, like Profumo, Old Harrovians – and turned to him at one point and said: 'Look Jack, the basic question is, "did you fuck her?"'

This was the essential problem that the five ministers faced. To any objective observer, it seemed implausible that a debonair and sophisticated man in his late forties could have had any interest in a semi-literate 'freelance model' other than for sex. Peter Carrington was one Cabinet colleague who had no doubts at all. 'Everybody knew Jack jumped into bed with anyone; no one believed Jack hadn't slept with Christine Keeler.' But so long as Profumo refused to answer Macleod's key question in the affirmative, there was not a great deal the other ministers could do. With the memory of the forced resignation of Thomas Galbraith still raw, there was extra caution.

Hobson and Rawlinson, along with Clogg, retreated to a separate room to draft the statement for Profumo. Deedes sat drinking whisky with Macleod and Redmayne. In the other room, Rawlinson wrote the statement out by hand. Then the lawyers joined the main gathering and Rawlinson read out their proposed statement. When Rawlinson came to the words 'Miss Keeler and I were on friendly terms', Profumo protested: 'Do I have to say that? It sounds so awful.' The five ministers agreed that Profumo did indeed have to confirm publicly that he had known Keeler. Profumo who, according to Deedes in a diary note, looked 'pretty dapper', albeit 'still under a sleep pill', reluctantly agreed to the wording. Deedes then headed to his Commons office to type out Rawlinson's scrawl.* There was nothing particularly significant in the fact that Deedes did the typing: he was the only man in the group who could type, and there were no secretaries available at that hour of the morning. 'More whisky. Eventually retire with Rawlinson about 4.30 a.m. and try bed again,' Deedes wrote in his diary.

This meeting has since become one of the major points of controversy in the affair. Deedes subsequently expressed remorse for effectively holding a gun to Profumo's head and forcing him to deny the affair, especially as he was feeling the effects of a sleeping pill. Rawlinson, who could never bring himself to forgive Profumo's dishonesty and was irritated by the circle of Conservative journalistic and political acolytes who later lauded 'Jack' for his charitable deeds in the East End, was clear that the War Minister showed no signs of drowsiness. It is difficult to see that they had any option but to require Profumo to deny the allegation at that point. Any vacillation would have suggested guilt, and the Sunday papers would have gone wild.

That said, there were some oddities about the meeting that later added to the general sense of incompetence. It was strange that in a meeting between six members of the government on an issue of such importance no civil servant was summoned to take notes. It is not entirely clear why Henry Brooke, as the senior member of the government present in the House, did not stay on to chair the meeting. Denning recorded that people had subsequently asked why the Home Secretary had not stayed on: 'The answer is that no one thought of it,' which may be true, but it is still odd that they did not.

Since the Maxwell-Fyfe Directive of 1952, the security services had answered directly to the Home Secretary, although this had never been announced and most people, including much of the

---

* That typewriter, which Deedes then kept in his Commons office for his personal use, remained in his study at New Hayters until his death.

Cabinet, thought that the Prime Minister remained in operational control. But even if the five ministers had not known this, it is strange that Brooke, knowing his responsibility for security matters, did not insist on being present. Strangely, Denning exonerated the government on this point on the grounds that Profumo's personal statement to the House 'was not regarded as a security matter, except incidentally'. But this cuts to the heart of the mishandling of the issue. Though Wilson and Wigg were acting out of party political considerations in seeking to damage a weakened government with a sexual scandal, they of course dressed up their anxieties as being primarily about national security. The notion that the evening's meeting could be taken without reference to security considerations is absurd, notwithstanding Denning's casual exculpation; Brooke's absence later made it much easier for Labour to portray the five ministers' session as one of the more ridiculous and suspicious acts of a disastrously managed drama. In a memorandum Deedes sent to Macmillan on 25 September about how to 'spin' the release of the Denning Report, he makes the point that none of the five ministers knew of the Home Secretary's responsibility for the security services and gives warning that Brooke's absence from the meeting would become an issue for the lobby correspondents.

Later that morning, just after eleven o'clock, John Profumo, looking weary and tense, rose to make a personal statement. Harold Macmillan had walked into the chamber just before he spoke and sat down next to him as a public declaration of support. Profumo started off, as liars often do, with a detailed denial of an allegation that no one was making: that he was in some way responsible for spiriting Christine Keeler out of the country to Spain so that she would not have to give evidence in the Edgecombe trial. Then, after dutifully delivering the jarring line about his having been on 'friendly terms' with Keeler, he said the fateful words: 'There was no impropriety whatsoever in my acquaintanceship with Miss Keeler.' This was to become the most famous false denial of adultery in modern politics, at least until

Bill Clinton declared, 'I did not have sexual relations with that woman, Miss Lewinsky.' Profumo finished his statement by warning that he would 'not hesitate to issue writs for libel and slander if scandalous allegations are made or repeated outside the House'.

Initially, it looked as though Profumo's lie would hold the line. Under the headline 'Mr Profumo clears the air', the *Guardian* reported the following day that, with the personal statement, this was now 'the end of the story'. That same day Profumo sent Deedes a barely legible letter scrawled in blue ballpoint pen to his fellow Harrovian and fellow old boy of Wellington House prep school.

> *My Dear Bill*
> *A note to thank you so very much for your help and advice. I*
> *do hope that from your point of view the statement was*
> *alright. Let us hope it will now die. It hasn't been too easy.*
> *Again so many thanks.*
> *Ever Jack.*

But neither the *Guardian* nor Profumo had taken account of the tenacity of George Wigg, backed by Harold Wilson, who viewed the affair as an eye-catching illustration of the sloppiness and incompetence of the Macmillan administration as an election loomed.

The version Denning accepted was that Profumo finally confessed to Redmayne on 4 June, having told his wife over dinner in Venice during a short Whitsun holiday. Profumo told Lord Denning that his wife had said: 'Oh darling we must go home now just as soon as we can and face up to it.'* Denning, who took so many of the submissions to his inquiry on trust, accepted that

---

* One of the unexplained mysteries of the Profumo scandal is why his wife believed his denial, if indeed she did. Given his reputation for philandering, it seems likely that she would have identified the significance of the swimming pool frolics and, having met Keeler, she would surely have doubted that Keeler and her husband were intellectual soulmates.

as a truthful response, though it is much easier to imagine other things Profumo's wife might have said to her husband.

Profumo resigned from the government and applied for the Chiltern Hundreds so that he could immediately cease to be an MP. He was told there would be no farewell audience with the Queen and the seals of office were returned by messenger. On 13 June, Profumo sent Macmillan a handwritten letter from 3 Chester Terrace. The writing paper was headed: 'The Rt Hon John Profumo MP', but 'MP' had already been struck out by pen. The letter was seeking advice about how to remove his prefix.

Dear Prime Minister
I am quite clear I can no longer remain a Privy Councillor,
but how to divest myself of this cherished honour I do not
know. I write to request that you take the appropriate action
with Her Majesty the Queen.
Yours sincerely
Jack Profumo

This sent civil servants into a panic because, as Profumo surmised, no one can simply resign from an honour in the gift of the sovereign. Downing Street was concerned to resolve the issue before it became a press controversy and the right mechanism was quickly found. Enoch Powell, Minster of Health, protested in Cabinet that rescinding membership of the Privy Council set 'an evil and dangerous precedent', but Macmillan slapped him down, saying that it was not strictly a Cabinet matter and that he would resolve it himself. Within a few days, Profumo's personal writing paper had been further defaced by hand and the words 'The Rt Hon' also scratched out. His disgrace was complete.

The abrupt resignation may have marked the end of Profumo's political career, but it inflamed the row over how badly Macmillan and his circle of advisors had handled the matter. For a time it seemed far from certain that the government could survive the shock of Profumo's confession. Powell, who had not believed Profumo's denial in March, was causing mischief. He let it be known to *The Times* that he might resign in protest at Macmillan's cack-handed conduct, and then he refused to deny the report. Deedes was put up to ringing him to cash in chips from their One Nation days. He eventually tracked him down to his Wolverhampton constituency and spoke by telephone, finding Powell 'not explicit but fairly reassuring'. In the end, Powell fell into line, sparing Macmillan what would likely have proved a fatal Cabinet resignation. But the backbenches were seething and turning their fire on those responsible.

Redmayne submitted his resignation but Macmillan refused to accept it, knowing that if anyone should go it was the Prime Minister. He told Redmayne that ministers had 'nothing with which to reproach ourselves, except perhaps too great a loyalty'. This was absurd, as Redmayne himself knew. Senior ministers had acted foolishly, making precisely the opposite mistake to the one they had made over Vassall–Galbraith, this time showing far too much trust in a colleague. Rawlinson, livid at Profumo's 'wicked series of lies', also offered his resignation when Lord Denning's report, published in September, gently criticised the five ministers, but Macmillan rejected it.

Though the government and security services received an almost blanket clean bill of health from Denning he did suggest that Deedes and the other ministers erred when they considered whether Profumo had slept with Keeler, when the 'proper question' was whether 'ordinary people' might think he had committed adultery. That may have been true up to a point, but it still left the five ministers with a terrible problem: how could they force the resignation of a colleague who swore to them that he was innocent, particularly as it was only weeks since it had become clear that Thomas Galbraith had been grossly mistreated in being forced to resign? It was strange that, amid so much official incompetence, Denning rested his criticism on such narrow ground.

According to Derek Taylor Thompson, Deedes's private secretary, Deedes was extremely anxious in the days before Denning's report appeared, fearing he and the other four ministers would be severely criticised. A forced resignation would have been a deeply humiliating end to his brief Cabinet career. But Denning did a good job of shielding the political establishment from the consequences of its folly, directing most of the censure towards Stephen Ward and his girls. The morning after the publication of the report, Deedes's relief was tinged with irritation that the *Daily Telegraph*'s splash headline referred to the government's 'failure'. As Deedes scribbled furiously to an unnamed colleague in that morning's Cabinet meeting, it was 'the only really *gross* newspaper travesty this morning': the word 'failure' had not appeared in Denning's report, but rather in the political correspondent's account of it. The unknown minister scribbled back to Deedes that the same point had been made late on the BBC the night before, 'not that anybody but BFs [bloody fools] like me was up to see it'.

Peter Rawlinson was enraged not just by Denning or the coverage of the report, but by his knowledge that his friend John Hobson never recovered from the shock that someone he had trusted could have betrayed him. Hobson wrote to Macmillan, almost pleading to be allowed to go as 'I do very strongly feel that the right thing is that I should resign'. But Macmillan was adamant in refusing to accept any resignation, not out of loyalty but because if one went they would all have to go, including the Prime Minister himself.

In *Dear Bill*, Deedes quoted the Denning Report saying of him and Iain Macleod that they 'had heard the rumours but had taken no part until this night' of the five ministers' meeting. As Deedes conceded, this did rather invite the question *why* the Minister without Portfolio had not been more involved, given that his role was specifically to deal with the press. John Gordon, in his *Sunday Express* political column on 23 June, picked up on that weakness. Most journalists, he argued, had known of Profumo's philandering. 'It seems almost incredible that Mr Deedes, with his Fleet Street background, didn't know enough to make him very wary about accepting Mr Profumo's assurance without stronger probing . . . Shouldn't he now make retribution by resigning?'

As Deedes put it himself in his autobiography, 'If I had been doing my job properly, I would have made it my business to acquire as well as to impart sensitive intelligence. Instead, I tended to regard the unquenchable thirst of newspapermen for this particular story as a bloody nuisance.'

This is harsh self-criticism, but it is justified. At no point did Deedes take responsibility for presenting the government's side of the story; indeed, he subsequently (and implausibly) claimed that he only knew about it a week before it blew open in the House. He did circulate a briefing paper on the eve of the publication of the Denning Report, which offered straightforward advice for ministers in answering media questions. In many respects this was the forerunner of New Labour's 'talking points' thirty years later, when it was trying to make itself a credible party of government and staying on-message became an absolute necessity for any aspiring minister. Under Deedes's strictures, Cabinet colleagues were advised at every opportunity to stress the point 'that Ministers and officials involved in this affair acted in good faith'.

Thus, in assisting ministers to defend the government's handling of the matter, he was pre-emptively exonerating himself. His claim that he knew of the rumours only a week before they were aired in Parliament should be treated with suspicion. Deedes, it seems, made that claim to exculpate himself, but it is the most damning detail, if true. Equally, he claimed to have known of Profumo's confession when he read about it in the *Daily Telegraph* on 6 June when he was on holiday in Devon. If this is so it is quite extraordinary. At one particularly crucial point in the political storm eleven days later, Deedes headed by sleeper train to a garden fête in Dunbartonshire. There he gave a speech urging voters to keep a sense of proportion, stressing it was 'claptrap' to suggest Britain had become a degenerate nation. 'Today it is not decay but change which we see around us: change at a speed and of a kind which imposes the severest stresses within society. This society is in a tremendous state of fermentation and redesign.'*

It was an interesting speech, rewarded with an eleven-paragraph report in the *Daily Telegraph*. But the fact that addressing a constituency fête in a remote part of the country was deemed an appropriate use of the Minister without Portfolio's time at this critical period suggests that no one in Westminster took his role seriously, least of all Deedes himself. This might explain why at no point did Deedes contemplate following the example of Hobson, Rawlinson and Redmayne by offering to resign.

There was evidence of a certain dissatisfaction with Deedes's performance even before the scandal finally erupted. On 14 May Martin Redmayne had taken the highly unusual step of writing Deedes a letter marked personal and sent to his home address in Eaton Terrace. Topped 'Dear Bill', the letter was gently phrased, but in it Redmayne informed Deedes that he had received a formal complaint from the 1922 Committee that 'the morale of the Party is suffering because Ministers are insufficiently in contact with Members'. Redmayne tried to make the criticism as general as possible, but given Deedes's specific Cabinet role in liaison and news presentation, it would have been impossible not to take it personally, especially when he was urged to 'seek out some of those many Members who are unknown to you'.

As the man who was supposed to serve as the government's chief propagandist, Deedes had grown thoroughly despondent as the news agenda was set by the twists in the Profumo affair. During an idle moment, he sat down and had a rare stab at writing poetry, typing it out on House of Commons writing paper in

---

* Like Uncle Theodore in *Scoop*, Deedes was making use of a line from 'Abide with Me': 'Change and decay in all around I see.'

his office. It is not as good as many of the limericks which were then doing the rounds of Westminster, and his gloomy mood is reflected in a rare obscenity.

> *I'm utterly finally bored*
> *With Keeler, Profumo & Ward*
> *Bored with more shots of Christine in her bath*
> *Bored with Profumo and Parliament's wrath*
> *Bored with the dumb f— osteopath*
> *Enough I entreat you, O Lord,*
> *Of Keeler, Profumo & Ward.*

As with the Vassall–Galbraith non-scandal, there were sad human consequences of the Profumo affair. In what some people regarded as an establishment act of vengeance, Stephen Ward was put on trial for pimping. On 30 July 1963, the night before the jury was due to return its verdict, he took an overdose of Nembutal, leaving a suicide note for the friend in whose flat he was hiding out from the press. Ward asked the friend to delay attempts to resuscitate for as long as possible, and was in a deep coma when he was found. He was still unconscious when the jury returned its guilty verdict and he died four days later. Committing suicide required no guts, he wrote, before adding bathetically: 'The car needs oil in the gearbox, by the way.'

CHAPTER 15

THE GLIMMER OF TWILIGHT

'We did wonder sometimes why he had stumbled into politics, because it wasn't really the sort of thing people of his class did. He lacked the killer instinct; he had the air of an amateur, his heart just wasn't in it.'

Harold Wilson, the new Labour leader, got everything he could have wanted out of the Profumo affair. The Macmillan administration staggered on, discredited and much ridiculed despite the great burst of affluence and the consumer boom the Tories had overseen. Crucially the Prime Minister survived, which served Wilson's purposes well. The mood on the Conservative backbenches was despairing even if the government had comfortably survived the 17 June vote following the Commons debate on the Profumo affair. No one who was in the House that day forgot the intervention of a Conservative member, Nigel Birch, who had grown increasingly contemptuous of Macmillan's inept leadership. Birch began gently, noting that Profumo had 'never struck me as a man at all like a cloistered monk'. He stressed he was not accusing Macmillan of dishonour in believing his denial of an affair with Christine Keeler. Rather, the issue was the Prime Minister's competence and judgment, and Birch's pay-off, in quoting Browning's 'The Lost Leader', was devastating:

Let him never come back to us!
There would be doubt, hesitation and pain.
Forced praise on our part – the glimmer of twilight,
Never glad confident morning again!

'Never glad confident morning again!' said Birch, moving in for the kill, 'so I hope the change will not be too long delayed.'

It was a calculated attack, designed to kill rather than to wound, and to trigger a leadership contest. Macmillan turned round to look at the Conservative benches for signs of support, but he saw only sullen resentment. The Prime Minister stalked out of the chamber, humiliated. Macmillan survived the division after twenty-seven Tories abstained, and the government's majority was reduced to sixty-nine, a figure some MPs thought oddly appropriate. Grievously wounded and nearing seventy, the Prime Minister was nevertheless determined in the aftermath of Profumo to carry on and not be brought down by 'two tarts'.[*]

When he was struck down by a seriously inflamed prostate, just as the party activists were assembling in Blackpool for the October conference, it became clear that Macmillan could not lead the party into the general election, then expected for early 1964. At that time there was no ballot to select a Tory leader; the procedure hinged on a secretive System of Consultation, from which the Earl of Home emerged triumphant to the consternation of many of his colleagues.[†] Under that procedure, the Lord Chancellor, Lord Dilhorne, was responsible for taking soundings from the Cabinet. His records of that process have long been regarded as highly suspect: for instance, he had Iain Macleod marked down as supporting Home, a man he loathed and in whose Cabinet he later refused to serve.

[*] Christine Keeler and Mandy Rice-Davis.

[†] Home would not have been able to enter the Commons and take on the leadership but for the coincidence that the second Viscount Stansgate (Tony Benn) had recently driven through the Act allowing members of the Lords to disclaim their peerages.

Deedes voted for Home, ahead of two old ideological allies Macleod and Rab Butler. Deedes was characteristically puckish in his autobiography about the succession, noting the processes were 'invisible' and 'therefore held by those who disagreed with the choice to be secretive and deceitful'. We know Deedes voted for Home only because of Dilhorne's notes taken in the course of his soundings, though in *Dear Bill* his support is implicit when he says voters needed a man they could trust post-Profumo. 'One of Alec's attractions, at that juncture, was that he *lacked* so many of the politician's attributes.'

Deedes noted that he might have done Butler another disservice – beyond supporting his rival – by passing on to him the heavy cold he had brought up to Blackpool: as a consequence, Butler's speech to conference on the Saturday afternoon was deemed lacklustre, though by then the leadership was already slipping from his grasp. Deedes clouded the matter further in the mini-profile of Butler included in his *Brief Lives*, published in 2004. He said that because of his public relations role within the government, 'I tried to take a detached view, expressing no opinion of my own, but accepting the majority verdict.' That memory is half true in the sense that Deedes does indeed appear to have been swayed by the majority view; but it is not the case that he expressed no opinion, because his preference for Home was observed by Dilhorne and became part of the basis for Macmillan's controversial advice to the Queen that she ask him to form an administration.

It was Deedes's custom to jot down an aide-memoire during periods of political drama, but none relating to this crisis was found in his files. There was a detailed note about Macmillan's final Cabinet on 8 October, in which Deedes observed that the 'very shaky' Prime Minister twice left the room for medication, and that he was drinking whisky to great excess on the day his prostate flared up. But Deedes made no contemporaneous record of his activities or his rationale for backing Home, or at least if he did he subsequently destroyed it. It may be that he later felt guilty about being drawn into the shadowy magic circle of party grandees in backing a rather aloof member of the Lords over one of his own long-standing colleagues in the Commons; it is quite possible, too, that Deedes only decided to back Home when he sensed that that was the majority view of his Cabinet colleagues.

Never one to rock the boat, he might well have regarded Home as the leader most likely to retain his services as Minister without Portfolio. Given his preference for stability and clear lines of authority, he would have been swayed by Macmillan's determination to stymie Rab Butler and promote Home in a seamless transition. Considerations of class might have impinged too: Deedes may have been deprived of the family landholdings, but as a proud member of one of Kent's grandest families – and a bit of a snob – he would have had a certain class affinity with the 14th Earl of Home. Deedes had a realistic view of the limitations of his political career, but the prospect of being humiliatingly sacked from the Cabinet after only fifteen months, and shortly before a general election, was not appetising. As was seen earlier following his exit from the Home Office, it was extremely important to Deedes that when he left the government it should be seen to be on his terms, or as the result of the party losing a general election and therefore not his fault.

Deedes's precise role in the political machinations from which Home emerged triumphant is as murky and confusing as any part of his political career. His files from the period are unusually thin and leave few clues as to what he was up to in Blackpool or the following week in London, and his memory of those events was fuzzy. It is not clear to what extent Deedes was part of the magic circle, or whether he was merely pitching in at the urging of Martin Redmayne, who in turn was showing his normal obedience as Macmillan's enforcer.

Deliberately or unwittingly, Deedes did become part of the operation to ensure Home's succession, particularly in the – as he later described them – 'cloak and dagger' events of 17 October. Deedes was summoned by Redmayne to the whips' office at

12 Downing Street. Over a lunchtime glass of sherry, Redmayne told him that Home had emerged the clear winner from the soundings taken, but that no other Cabinet ministers knew this. This claim of Home's dominance was questionable, even if Dilhorne's polling had been fair and accurate. Home did not score at all among grass roots activists because it was not generally known he was in the running. At that meeting in the whips' office, which Harold Evans joined, it was decided that Macmillan's resignation would be delayed until the following day and Home's succession then presented as a fait accompli.

In truth, Redmayne, Deedes and Evans found themselves as co-conspirators in a plot inspired by Macmillan to 'bounce' the Cabinet into accepting Home as the anointed successor. Deedes, the most junior member of the Cabinet, and regarded as a lightweight, was suddenly in possession of hot information of which his heavyweight colleagues, and the other leadership contenders, were entirely ignorant. The plot was so far advanced that provision had already been made for a fortnight's delay in the opening of Parliament and the Conservative candidate at the pending Kinross by-election had been persuaded to step aside in Home's favour. Iain Macleod, who, as the Leader of the House, should have been the first man to have been told of these procedural matters, was dumbfounded when he learnt about them.

That evening, Deedes was called to a meeting with Home at the Foreign Office. So as not to alert the press he was told to use the tunnel linking 10 Downing Street to the Foreign Office. There, the news management of the Home succession was planned in extreme secrecy. Deedes laid out how the press were to be briefed the following day, once Home had been to see the Queen. He began working on the draft of Home's television broadcast and how Home's entry into the Commons was to be effected. This was a highly unusual situation: the Chief Whip, the Number 10 press spokesman and Deedes were party to an operation so secret that the most senior members of the Cabinet were cut out of it. And, as part of the plot to install Home in Number 10, Deedes had cemented his relations with the next Prime Minister and guaranteed that there would be no humiliatingly early exit from the Cabinet.

Inevitably, word leaked out later that evening – possibly Harold Evans could not resist tipping off friends in the lobby before Deedes did, or maybe it was vice-versa. The anti-Home factions gathered at Enoch Powell's house at South Eaton Place, which was besieged by journalists. The following morning three Cabinet heavyweights and leadership contenders – Rab Butler, Lord Hailsham and Reginald Maudling – agreed to serve under Home, thus ensuring he could form a government. Macleod and Powell refused and returned to the backbenches.

The plot to foist a stealth candidate on the Conservative party thus succeeded. But the sense that Home had been installed in a mini constitutional coup endured, and Deedes never quite succeeded in wiping his fingerprints from the scene of the crime. Journalists became so persistent in their questioning of how Home had 'emerged' as leader that Redmayne sent Deedes a typed memo laying out the 'System of Consultation'. That document did not address the point that Home won no support from activists because hardly any of them knew he was running. Nevertheless, Redmayne exonerated himself and his fellow conspirators in a ringing – if unconvincing – conclusion: 'Any suggestion, therefore, that the Prime Minister's advice was not founded on a balanced and wide view of opinion is quite untrue.'

Deedes used the document to try to mollify suspicious lobby journalists. But the controversy did not die; the specific question of the propriety of Deedes's involvement became a contentious point in the Commons and emboldened those on the Labour benches, who would regularly question the role of the Minister without Portfolio. The normal technique was for a Labour questioner to ask Deedes to release details of his official activities. The trick triggered the following uncomfortable exchange three months after Home became Prime Minister, when Marcus Lipton,

Labour MP for Brixton, asked if Deedes would be more forth-coming about his diary than he had been in the past:

Mr DEEDES: No, Sir.

Mr LIPTON: Is not that answer all the more suspicious as I wanted to ask the Minister on what official activities he was engaged on October 17th last, and whether he, or someone else in the Government information services, told the Press who the new Prime Minister was to be, long before certain of his Cabinet colleagues knew about it? Is this not a grave reflection on the integrity of the Government information services, especially in view of accusations that news management has been taken too far?

Mr DEEDES: I do not accept the implications of that question at all.

Amid laughter [the *Daily Telegraph* reported on 21 January 1964], Mr LIPTON intimated that because of what he termed the 'unsatisfactory reply', he would raise the matter again.

Deedes's role, never constitutionally very happy, became even more confused during the party leadership contest because of his split loyalties. He was a member of the Cabinet yet he also attended the weekly meetings of the Liaison Committee at Conservative Central Office. The Liaison Committee was a party operation and the chairman, Oliver Poole, also sat on it. Deedes claimed in later years that constitutional proprieties were maintained and that he never revealed Cabinet secrets at the committee, though (with a slightly awkward emphasis) he did concede that 'he might have given the party just a little bit of intelligence about problems ahead'.

In the summer before his death, Deedes offered a revealing if not definitive account of his behaviour during the leadership contest.

'I now faintly recall a talk I had with Hilary in the car as we motored to Blackpool, explaining how hopelessly divided I was. On personal grounds I hoped Rab would get it, we were friends. I hardly knew Home, but I was, ridiculously, in charge of "government appearances". I felt a Mr Clean was just what we needed. Oliver Poole, highly influential, had begged me to vote for Home. Feeble-minded as ever that's what I did!'* That explanation supports an image of Deedes in 1963, hopelessly conflicted by the various forces tugging at him as he tried simultaneously to serve the party and the government, somehow always getting caught in between.

When he talked to the press it was never entirely clear whether he spoke for the Prime Minister, the Cabinet or the Conservative Party, and this rankled with his colleagues, with the Labour opposition and occasionally with journalists. There was constant tension with Harold Evans, the Number 10 press spokesman, who maintained his daily contacts with the lobby even though Deedes more often took the main weekly Thursday meeting himself. Deedes also lunched individually with lobby correspondents, though he tried to keep these encounters quiet because Evans jealously guarded his links to journalists. Evans reasonably believed that while he must retain fierce and concentrated loyalty to Number 10, Deedes floated around in a more freelance role, representing the Cabinet one moment, Central Office the next, or indeed his favoured candidate as successor.

Ian Aitken, who was then in the lobby for the *Daily Express*, recalled that Deedes was endlessly affable, the sort of chap a journalist could ring after midnight when the final edition is running to check a story in a rival newspaper. Deedes never minded if his sleep was disturbed in Eaton Terrace or New Hayters, whatever the hour. Aitken said he remained popular, even after he had crossed the divide between journalism and politics, a transition that can cause resentment among former colleagues in the mackintosh trade.

---

* E-mail to the author.

Aitken recalled that Deedes had a tendency in his weekly briefings to get details wrong, so that when the first editions of the evening papers hit the streets Harold Evans would have to intervene to set the record straight.

Aitken was fond of Deedes, but he could not help thinking he was hopelessly miscast as the prototype of the modern political spin doctor. 'We did wonder sometimes why he had stumbled into politics, because it wasn't really the sort of thing people of his class did. He lacked the killer instinct; he had the air of an amateur, his heart just wasn't in it.' Alan Watkins, another veteran political reporter, recalled that Deedes was a delightful sounding-board for government gossip. They would have long lunches at Epicure in Frith Street, though Watkins was occasionally wary of the minister's 'tendency to agree with you' on all points.

Harold Evans learned to stay calm during the very difficult years at Number 10, but when Deedes strayed on to his territory he could be testy. On 10 February 1963, soon after de Gaulle had vetoed British membership of the Common Market, his resentment of Deedes spilt out into his diaries. 'Maudling stands away from contributing. Perhaps Reggie sees himself as the crown prince? He has at least one devoted follower – Bill Deedes – who cuts away his information co-ordination activities as completely as possible from No 10.'*

But the more damaging attacks were made in public, and in Parliament. When Lord Carrington was added to Home's new Cabinet as another Minister without Portfolio on five thousand pounds a year, the Labour benches smouldered with resentment about jobs for the public school boys. A month after Deedes's uncomfortable exchange with Marcus Lipton,

---

* Deedes did support Maudling over Heath when Douglas-Home resigned as Tory leader in 1965, but that decision was neither personal nor ideological. He simply rang as many members of the Ashford Conservative Association as he could track down, and when a narrow majority favoured Maudling, Deedes dutifully voted for him under the new ballot system.

Labour returned to the attack, led by the future Prime Minister James Callaghan, who described Deedes's and Carrington's remuneration and failure to disclose their diaries as 'a scandal of the first order'.

Deedes protested that his department employed only three other people and that he merely provided clear, non-partisan information to the media. 'The press of this country', he said, 'carries its own safeguards against misplaced and misused propaganda from any quarter.' But the mood of the House turned increasingly ugly, with the Liberals joining in, led by Eric Lubbock, the victor in the sensational Orpington by-election who turned to the issue in the House on the afternoon of 17 March 1964. Lubbock started off by saying it was disgraceful that Deedes was paid the full five-thousand-pound ministerial salary when he had no department to run. Certainly Deedes was vulnerable to criticism on this point and he knew it. Junior ministers in the great departments of state had far fuller diaries than the Minister without Portfolio; Deedes had no staff to manage and virtually no MPs' enquiries to answer. But he could not defend himself by pointing to his party responsibilities, for that would only have inflamed the anger about the constitutional proprieties of his role. The only correspondence Deedes had to deal with, Lubbock charged, was the odd letter from constituency chairmen seeking speakers at party events. 'Are we paying him five thousand pounds a year for doing that? If so, it is a shocking state of affairs, which should not be tolerated. Perhaps a firm of consultants could evaluate his work by following him around all day, for he has certainly not told us what he does.'*

That much of the hostility to Deedes was class-based became even clearer when the class warrior Willie Hamilton intervened in a debate in March 1964.

---

* £5000 would be worth about £75,00 in 2008.

I will not detain the House very long, but what we are discussing this afternoon is jobs for the boys, and particularly the
Eton boys . . . [HON MEMBERS 'No'] Most of the men who
qualify for these jobs are Eton boys.

It is not clear from the Hansard record if the honourable members' chorus of 'No' from the government benches was a general
defence of the grander members of the Cabinet, or a hair-splitting
observation that the Minister without Porfolio was not an
Etonian but a Harrovian.

In the following issue of the *Sunday Telegraph*, the question
was taken up in a less than entirely helpful article by T. E. (Peter)
Utley, the great Tory columnist, who conceded that many people
would not really understand the position of his former journalistic colleague. 'Mr Deedes's staff, it is true, is small, but this is
hardly surprising since the task of co-ordinating the Government's
information services would seem on the face of it to be almost
superfluous.' Though Utley loyally defended Deedes for taking his
job seriously, particularly the part which required him to 'mix
freely and convivially with his old friends in Fleet Street', he noted
it was welcome on constitutional grounds that he was winding
down his news management operation as the general election
approached. However, the political assaults continued through
the summer of 1964.

In June George Brown widened the attack outside the
Commons to condemn Deedes. Brown was speaking to members
of the Institute of Public Relations and assured them he had nothing in principle against politicians who tried to master the arts of
what was still a new industry. 'Our objection to the present situation is not merely that money talks and that our opponents are
much richer than we are and have more money to talk with, but
that we have reached the point in this nation that we don't know
whose money is talking.'

On 22 July a Labour backbencher, Arthur Lewis, noting the
minister's infrequent Commons appearances, asked Deedes

bluntly, 'What do you do in your spare time other than make propaganda for the Tory party?' Deedes's nemesis, Marcus Lipton, then joined the assault, noting again how he refused to reveal any diary details.

Mr LIPTON: Is this due to modesty or panic?
Mr DEEDES: Modesty.

Deedes certainly tried to avoid controversy, and settled down behind the scenes to make himself useful to the new Prime Minister, now Sir Alec Douglas-Home since he renounced his earldom. Since de Gaulle's veto of British membership of the Common Market, the Cabinet was desperately casting around for a new theme and settled rather awkwardly and *faute de mieux* on the Modernisation of Britain. It was Deedes's job to come up with a way of projecting this as an exciting new departure for a government that seemed to most observers to be expiring on its feet.

Even Deedes, the man in charge of presenting the overall new thrust, was unconvinced by its merits and disliked the slogan. Some time in 1963 Deedes scribbled a note to an unidentified colleague during Cabinet: 'Before it gets into circulation, do we think "Modernisation of Britain" a very good tag? After 11 years of our government it has a *dispiriting* ring. Should we think of something better?'

No one could come up with anything better so the Tories plodded on with their unconvincing modernisation programme, which on close examination meant no more than the closure of countless branch lines in Beeching's pruning of the railway network and sharp surges in the level of public spending. Deedes, however, urged his colleagues to make the best of it. 'We are able to achieve this unprecedented programme of reconstruction and modernisation because the economy is stronger than ever before, thanks to recent and current policies.'

Deedes's primary responsibility was to produce regular briefings on matters of the moment, to be circulated across Whitehall to all of his Cabinet colleagues. They would usually be headed 'Guidance for Ministers', and were intended to help in preparations for public engagements or media interviews. One dated 8 November 1963 was fairly typical, and under the sub-heading 'Lines of Thought', encouraged ministers to stress the following pluses of the new Douglas-Home government: 'New Prime Minister; first class team, vigorous plans.' The government had not changed course, Deedes reminded colleagues, but rather it had effected a 'dramatic acceleration'. To counter the Labour Party's allegation that the Conservatives were creating private affluence amid public squalor, ministers were told to boast of the 'dramatic acceleration of public and social service spending'.* A hint of desperation about Conservative policies and prospects of winning the coming election can be detected in Deedes's various memoranda. The memos tended to be commonplace and could easily have been produced by a relatively low-level civil servant or – more appropriately – a bright young researcher at Central Office straight down from university. In later life Deedes never spoke of the months of abuse he suffered from Labour politicians in and out of Parliament. Deedes's filing system in New Hayters contained meticulous records of his speeches and positive press reaction to them, but of the attacks he suffered over the propriety of his role in the Macmillan Cabinet there was not a word.

Deedes did score an unexpected hit with a speech about the Beatles, however. In February 1964 he stood in at short notice for a Cabinet colleague unable to keep a commitment as keynote speaker for a Young Conservatives lunch in the City of London. Deedes typed out the speech in the format which he had learnt from Churchill: lines are staggered, some close to the margin, some indented, so that the speech looks like a poem rather than a solid block of text and is therefore easier to read. In the best

---

* If the word 'investment' were substituted for 'spending' in that sentence, Deedes's boast of the Conservatives' stewardship of the public services would be identical to New Labour's claims more than forty years later.

'Modernisation of Britain' spirit, Deedes hailed the Beatles as star representatives of what he called the 'beat group movement', which he accurately predicted would be of lasting importance.

> To be top in the beat business demands
> work, skill, sweat. There is no
>   place at all for the lazy, the
>   incompetent, the slipshod.
>
> For those with eyes to see it, some-
>   thing important and heartening
>   is happening here.
>
> The young are devising their own media
>   through which to express a
>   standard of their own, free of
>   divisions of class or creed.

Predictably, given that the Beatles were then at the peak of their popularity on both sides of the Atlantic, it was by far the most lavishly reported speech of his Cabinet career. The *Daily Express* gave it two columns with a picture of the Minister. The *Evening News* squeezed a follow-up piece out of the speech by contacting Hilary Deedes at home in Aldington, and she did not disappoint. 'The Beatlemania has most certainly invaded this household,' she revealed, noting that the five children owned all the Beatles records. Together they had found a guitar and formed a beat group of their own, led by the 'twenty-year-old Old Etonian Jeremy'.

The most amusing consequence of Deedes's venture into music criticism was the splenetic response it provoked from the polemical journalist Paul Johnson, who was then left-wing and writing in the *New Statesman*. Johnson began by mocking Deedes for having believed Profumo's denial of his affair with Christine Keeler. 'Now any public relations man, even a grand one who sits in the Cabinet, can use a touch of credulity; but even so I remember thinking at the time: "If Deedes can believe that, he'll believe anything." And indeed he does! Listen to him on the subject of the Beatles.'

Johnson deplored the way Harold Wilson and Sir Alec Douglas-Home were competing to identify their parties with the Beatles' popularity as the election loomed; British diplomats at the Washington embassy had been seen jostling to secure the Beatles' autographs during their recent US tour; it could not be long, Johnson fumed, before the Bishop of Woolwich invited them to participate in one of his services. Then Johnson really hit his stride, uncannily anticipating the parodies written a generation later by Craig Brown, who posed as the fictional club bore Wallace Arnold.

Before I am denounced as a reactionary fuddy-duddy, let us pause an instant and see exactly what we mean by this 'youth'. Both TV channels now run weekly programmes in which popular records are played to teenagers and judged. While the music is performed, the cameras linger savagely over the faces of the audience. What a bottomless chasm of vacuity they reveal! The huge faces, bloated with cheap confectionery and smeared with chain-store makeup, the open, sagging mouths and glazed eyes, the hands mindlessly drumming in time to the music, the broken stiletto heels, the shoddy, stereotyped, 'with-it' clothes: here, apparently, is a collective portrait of a generation enslaved by a commercial machine.

Johnson contrasts this hideous 'apotheosis of inanity' with his own cerebral interests when he was a sixteen-year-old: 'Almost every week one found a fresh idol – Milton, Wagner, Debussy, Matisse, El Greco, Proust – some indeed to be subsequently toppled from the pantheon, but all springing from the mainstream of European culture.'

The interesting point to keep in mind about this exchange, which Deedes recalled with great amusement as the moment 'Johnson tried to kick me in the balls', was not just that Johnson should be proved so brilliantly wrong about the durability of the Beatles' appeal: it was that Johnson was fifteen years younger than the minister he was attacking.

There were perks of being in the Cabinet, and Deedes in his private notes often achieved a caustic quality that he never attempted in his journalism. For instance, during a dull dinner for the King and Queen of the Belgians in 1963, Deedes noted that Princess Margaret was badly dressed and – rather brilliantly – portrayed Anthony Armstrong-Jones, by then the Earl of Snowdon, as 'looking more and more like a shop-walker'.

After the withering assaults he had suffered in the Commons, Deedes was working hard on polishing his personal image as well as the reputation of the government. The *Daily Express* received a mysterious tip about a heart-warming detail of domestic life at New Hayters: Hilary had miraculously saved the life of a newborn Jack Russell puppy. 'I suddenly thought how the kiss of life had saved so many human lives,' Mrs Deedes recalled to the *Express* reporter. 'So I lifted the puppy to my face and did a few good, hard blows into its lungs. Suddenly the puppy began to squeak. I knew I had won.' This was not the first example of Fleet Street being spoon-fed insights into the home life of the Deedeses. The *Daily Mail* carried a puff piece about Mrs Deedes and Dianthus, a five-year-old Jersey cow whose prodigious milk output sustained the Deedes breakfast table. Hilary was pictured milking Dianthus, 'who saves me heaps on housekeeping'. When the reporter asked if the Minister without Portfolio ever helped out in the cowshed, Mrs Deedes replied crisply, 'He never milks.'

Despite these little successes, the overall picture remained bleak as the government drifted towards the general election, finally called for October 1964. Deedes began talking to the *Daily Telegraph* again to establish a soft landing after the Tories' almost inevitable defeat. Without telling Deedes, Derek Taylor

Thompson, his private secretary, wrote a memorandum a few days before the October 1964 election for narrow distribution to senior Treasury civil servants. Couched in cautious understatement, Taylor Thompson conceded that Deedes had indeed spent as much time on purely political and party business as dealing with 'specific information problems'. He said that though Deedes had worked assiduously to establish links with the international and the provincial press, this scarcely justified the existence of a Cabinet sub-department with a minister with sole responsibility for information coordination. 'Though these activities are appreciated by the Press and by the Information Class, they are mere frills, brought into being by the existence of the coordinating Minister. In the absence of a coordinating Minister their termination would not disrupt the work of the Information Services.'

Unusually for a senior civil servant, Taylor Thompson was urging his bosses to eliminate the department he administered and suggesting that the modest duties be taken over by a more senior member of the Cabinet who would have greater authority. He forwarded the memo with a handwritten note attached, which revealed he knew he was committing an act of mild disloyalty: 'I should emphasise the note expresses a personal view. It has not been seen by the Minister – for obvious reasons.' Just to cover himself, Taylor Thompson asked that should the Conservatives unexpectedly win the imminent election, meaning that Deedes would retain his Cabinet job, 'I should like to be able to recover any copies of the paper that have been circulated.'

Though Deedes was convinced that the opposition attacks on his role were politically inspired, Labour did at least follow the logic of their criticism when they took office in 1964. The Cabinet information role was not retained, even though Harold Wilson did sound out Tony Benn in July 1964 about 'doing a Bill Deedes' for the incoming Labour government. Wilson told Benn he had thought about offering it to him, but had decided against it. Benn, perhaps thinking of the mauling Wilson had given Deedes in the

Commons while he had done the job, was obviously relieved. 'I told him I was very glad he had as it is a job I would hate.'

Deedes did well in Ashford on election night, maintaining a majority of 9037 over Labour, even with the Liberals fielding a strong candidate. The swing against Deedes was lower than in any other Kent constituency apart from Sevenoaks; clearly, he was not punished personally by Ashford voters for having been in the Macmillan Cabinet or for any errors in the handling of the Profumo affair. Indeed, despite their dismal showing in opinion polls, the Conservatives only just lost the election and would have clung on to power but for a dreadful showing in Scotland.

Deedes's twenty-seven-month Cabinet service came to an end with his farewell audience with the Queen at Buckingham Palace on 20 October 1964. The Queen seemed concerned about what Deedes would do now he was out of government, according to his diary. He explained he wanted to return to the *Telegraph*. 'Have you kept a pen for writing?' she asked him, to which he replied that he had been able to dip in and out of journalism on previous occasions and hoped he could get back in.

There followed a rather awkward exchange. She expressed scepticism about the sudden popularity of opinion polls and asked Deedes if he had ever met anyone who had been asked how he intended to vote. She explained that she didn't know anyone who had been interviewed by a polling organisation and was therefore suspicious of their accuracy. Deedes happened to have spoken to a constituent who had been asked by a polling company how he intended to vote, but this failed to allay her concerns. She was clearly cross with a *Daily Mail* splash headline just before the election that declared, 'We Don't Know', which Deedes told her was probably a sub-editor's play on the high number of don't knows in the late opinion polls. The Queen was not satisfied, suggesting she would have expected better from the *Daily Mail*, and complaining that it had done the Conservative government harm. The two parted after ten minutes, with the Queen and Deedes agreeing how often the newspapers got things wrong.

Deedes had good reason to think he would find a berth back at the *Telegraph*, having been in correspondence with former colleagues there for several months before the election. Though he had made no binding commitment to go back, it was clear that that was in his mind. Yet, when Alec Douglas-Home reshuffled his front bench following the election defeat, Deedes's removal was reported by the *Telegraph* as his having been 'dropped', along with Henry Brooke (Home Secretary) and Frederick Erroll (Minister of Power). Sources cited in the report suggested that Deedes and Erroll were happy to make way for younger men, a contention the reporter found 'strange'. Nevertheless, there is no evidence that Deedes was unhappy to be leaving front bench politics, and quite a lot to suggest that he was keen to accept the *Telegraph*'s welcoming embrace. Most men with more than two years in the Cabinet would have sought lucrative work in the City or industry, but just as he had done at the end of his ministerial career in 1957, he slotted happily into the routine of being a backbench Tory MP and writer of the Peterborough diary column. Deedes was back home at the *Telegraph*, never to seek or take a job in frontline politics again.

CHAPTER 16

BACK TO FLEET STREET

*'If Mr Powell has erred, and I believe he has, by
exaggeration and hyperbole, others have erred by seeking
to gloss over awkward facts and figures.'*

After the Tories lost the 1964 election, Deedes returned to the backbenches with a profound sense of relief. Presiding over government news presentation during two disastrous years of Conservative administration had been stressful and he was in need of a rest. Moreover, life in the Cabinet had distracted him from the abrupt decline in his parents' health and general living conditions. Despite infusions of cash from Wyndham, and occasional subsidies from Bill, Herbert's financial position had weakened so disastrously that he and Gladys could not afford to remain even in their modest rented home outside Hythe. Gladys had developed Parkinson's disease and was struggling to remain mobile, while Herbert's mental state had become dire.

Herbert's disturbed mind was evident in the deranged annotations he made in books of essays or biography, which he would use as notebooks. In 1964 he began scribbling in a fine leather-bound collection of the essays of Francis Bacon, a present from his mother sixty years earlier. Many of the scrawled comments refer to the mess he has made of his life, the loss of the Deedes fortune and the iniquities of the Army and the Empire. A typical observation runs: 'My life of nine years in the army cost me my nerve and my health.'

There are several strange, ambiguous comments about Bill that point to the difficult relationship between father and son. 'Bill is a queer chap, but so am I!' he scrawls in one margin, two pages after an equally mysterious assertion: 'Bill would never have got Hilary in 1942 but for my intervention.' (This seems highly unlikely, given that Bill never informed Herbert of any important developments in his life.) Yet in another ballpoint scrawl, dated 1 January 1965, Herbert shows unrestrained pride in his son, even if it is strangely phrased. 'My son, Bill, is far away the best speaker and thinker the Tory party have, but what does this mean? I DON'T KNOW.'

Having already lost a fortune, Herbert had finally lost his mind. When the money ran out in 1965 there was no option but for Herbert and Gladys to move into Goodnestone Park, the magnificent home of their youngest daughter Margaret, who in 1951 had married the 21st Baron FitzWalter.

Neither of his parents lasted long in Goodnestone Park. In January 1966 Gladys died, racked by Parkinson's and still mourning the death of her eldest daughter sixteen years earlier. Herbert, entirely lost without the woman who provided the only comfort in his tortured life, followed seven months later, surviving against all medical odds in to his eighty-sixth year. Gladys and Herbert were buried side by side within the Goodnestone estate.*

Shortly before his death, Herbert summoned Bill to his side and told his son solemnly: 'When I think of what trouble all the land gave me in my lifetime, I think I have relieved you of a heavy burden.' It was a strange comment to make, because it showed Herbert was oblivious to the enormous grief his incompetence had brought to the family. Most sons who had seen their fathers fritter away a large fortune and many thousands of acres would

---

* In later life Bill Deedes said that he could not remember in which year his father had died, or indeed if he had attended the funeral. His sister Margaret was clear that Bill attended the funerals of both their parents.

be resentful but, characteristically, Bill bore no grudge. Indeed, he would claim his father's financial incontinence spared him a dreary life overseeing dwindling estates and he would suggest he would probably have become 'a quiet alcoholic' had he been miscast – as his father was – as a boring 'landed chap'. But he was certainly scarred by the Saltwood experience, mostly for the toll it took on his mother, and because he thought its tubercular qualities had made her and his beloved sister Frances unwell by the time they left.

By hanging on in the Cabinet for the few months after Alec Douglas-Home succeeded Harold Macmillan, Deedes ensured there was no repeat of the talk, when he had left the government in 1957, of his having been sacked. Still, it would take some adjustment to life in opposition. He lost his driver, Miss Bussey, and no longer were his days organised for him by Derek Taylor Thompson.

He needed a new role. In his most successful speech as Minister without Portfolio, he had praised the Beatles as exemplars of the new pop age. Yet in that same role he had been required to snarl unconvincingly at the BBC when *That Was The Week That Was* poked fun at Tory politicians. Deedes was an essentially deferential man and not as modern as he liked to think. The 1960s were likely to be a challenge for a man of Kent born before the First World War. He was without pomposity or self-importance and never believed politicians, or journalists, should take themselves too seriously. He loved all good jokes and his first instinct was to join the fun, but as the MP for a conservative rural seat, he had to watch his step. 'I felt like a maiden aunt at a fun fair,' he recalled, 'everyone seemed to be on the swings, except me.'

Deedes's politics were always difficult to define. On economic matters he was essentially a Tory wet; he broadly agreed with the post-war, pre-Thatcher consensus in its acceptance of national decline and its aversion to conflict with entrenched interest groups such as the trade unions and the nationalised industries. He never had any time for the economic philosophy that later became known as Thatcherism: it was too ideological and likely to lead to unnecessary confrontation.

But on social matters Deedes as an MP was rigorously conservative, and occasionally reactionary. 'Insofar as I had developed any political philosophy of my own,' he stated in *Dear Bill*, writing about the state of affairs in the mid-1960s, 'it was that in the long run "prosperity politics" would fail to give people lasting satisfaction.' Here was a man who had been an MP for fifteen years, and who had spent two years in the Cabinet, acknowledging that he had developed no serious political philosophy. When Macmillan's government began to attract ridicule, some Conservatives came to blame the hollowness of prosperity politics for the mess that the Party had got itself into. For those Conservatives with a Christian outlook, such as Deedes, the Profumo fiasco was a moral accounting for the greed and laxness which had been taking hold since the late 1950s.

On a wide range of issues, such as immigration, drugs, homosexuality, Rhodesia and South Africa, pornography and hanging, Deedes was on the right of the Conservative Party. As a former Cabinet minister he carried some weight and, no longer needing to toe the government line, he was not shy of speaking up. In the Commons in February 1965 he joined the fight against capital punishment abolitionists, raising the awful spectre of armed robbers giving themselves Dutch courage by taking 'purple hearts' before their criminal missions. 'Guns and pep pills are a deadly combination,' he warned somewhat implausibly, adding that should the ultimate deterrent be removed from the statute book, this nightmare scenario could become common. Deedes chose not to mention in the House his own happy experience when he himself popped two 'purple hearts' a decade earlier to calm his nerves before his address to the Conservative conference, with gratifying consequences.

During a 1968 Commons debate about the Criminal Justice

Bill, Deedes pondered whether it had not been a 'psychological mistake' to abolish corporal punishment in prisons because its absence had undermined the morale of warders, even though it had not been used for six years. That same year, he sponsored a Commons motion signed by 170 MPs – mostly Conservative, but with some Labour and Liberal support – demanding the restoration of capital punishment for the murder of police and prison officers. Again, his standing as a former junior Home Office minister gave some weight to the campaign, which nevertheless failed.

Deedes also complained about the liberal treatment of drug addicts, telling a Commons standing committee in November 1970, 'We are in some danger of allowing a small minority to make mugs of us.' Addicts were free to drift in and out of the facilities provided and were treated better in Britain than anywhere else in the world. 'I think we have got very soft indeed, and are erring in the direction of spoiling.' It is possible that in those days Deedes affected to be more right-wing than he really was. Backbench Conservative MPs are more likely to get their names in the newspapers – including the *Daily Telegraph* – if they adopt such positions. Deedes was always pleased to appear in the news columns of any newspaper and he religiously clipped and filed the stories.

If Deedes took a hard line on illegal drugs, he was bracingly libertarian when it came to alcohol, the preferred stimulant of his twin trades of politics and journalism. He deplored Barbara Castle's assault on drink-driving through the breathalyser, suggesting it was nothing less than an assault on the British way of life. In a well-reported speech in Cirencester he sounded the alarm about Labour's determination to stamp out social drinking. 'The cocktail party is on its way out, and many activities, ranging from the public dinner to darts matches, are going to be curtailed.' He complained that the public was not being made aware by the government 'that a great many of their social habits, which now seem innocent enough, will under this Bill render them liable to prosecution'.

But he was less inclined to live and let live when it came to homosexuality. He was queasy about the Sexual Offences Bill of 1966 which was to decriminalise homosexual acts between consenting adults in private, and he tabled an amendment – which failed – exempting university staff and school masters from any relaxation of the restrictions on buggery. Though he was certainly never reconciled to the mechanics of homosexual activity he was by no means reflexively anti-gay. He always made clear that the riflemen in his company who were known to be 'queers' – a word he used in an old-fashioned way and without conscious rancour – had acquitted themselves bravely under fire and never let him down. He would never noisily or cruelly air anti-gay views and was personally impeccably polite to the campest of homosexuals.

In the mid-1960s Deedes became close to Mary Whitehouse, and a stalwart of her National Viewers' and Listeners' Association, which was to cause so much bother for the BBC. The NVALA was a militantly anti-progressive organisation with a hard Christian edge, drawing support from some churches but very little encouragement from the Church of England. Mrs Whitehouse saw herself as a crusader for morality and a defender of traditional British culture and values against communist infiltrators in the trade unions and the BBC. Her targets for attack were spread widely and included abortion, homosexuality and pornography. She cast her net wide; even *Dr Who* was in her sights for its reliance on 'strangulation – by hand, by claw and by obscene vegetable matter'. Many thought she was dotty, but she was indefatigable and even though the BBC at first refused to give her any sort of broadcasting platform she built up a certain national following.

In later life Deedes rarely spoke of his ties to the NVALA and seemed faintly embarrassed to have been drawn into Mrs Whitehouse's orbit. He explained his support for her on the grounds that, in the 1960s, morals were slipping too far as promiscuity and pornography took hold. '[I]n my book of Tory philosophy, arriving at the right social balance matters,' he explained in *Dear Bill*. 'Nothing in excess, as the Greeks had it.'* He did, however, make light of his association with Mary Whitehouse and the NVALA, noting that he 'did not agree with all she said'. But his role was rather more important than he implied, and he spread the word about Mrs Whitehouse's crusade among his colleagues in the Commons. He had been the keynote speaker at the inaugural NVALA conference in Birmingham in 1966, an event described in an internal BBC report as 'comical', but also 'sinister' and 'menacing'.

His involvement with NVALA marked him down as a social conservative in the House and brought him close to Malcolm Muggeridge, whom he had known on the *Telegraph* after the war. Both had their reservations about Mrs Whitehouse and her Moral Rearmers, and Muggeridge's association with her perpetual campaign against the BBC was surprising given that Hugh Carleton Greene had done so much to boost his television career. They were to join forces for one of the largest anti-abortion rallies in London, in 1974, when eighty thousand protesters marched silently from Speaker's Corner to Downing Street under the banner of the Society for the Protection of Unborn Children. Deedes was selected to hand the letter to Harold Wilson, who was not at home, with a demand to stop 'the unrelenting destruction of unborn children'. The demonstrators took two and a half hours to file down Whitehall past the entrance to Downing Street.

Deedes had been in awe of Muggeridge from the moment he joined the *Telegraph* as a leader writer in 1945. Physically the men were quite similar; both had immense charm, both had distinctive features that they would contort for comic or dramatic effect. Both enjoyed appearing on television, and in 1987 they collaborated on an ITV programme about the churches of the

* Their friendship survived even her turning up one night in the Commons central lobby with a dirty magazine of the type she wanted banned. The lurid, full-colour centrefold showed what Deedes called 'a bonking scene', and while she showed it to him one of the policemen on guard duty started taking an interest.

Romney Marsh. By then Muggeridge was showing signs of dementia and his proposal to save the churches for future generations – by removing them stone by stone and rebuilding them in more populated parts of the country – caused some consternation. It was around this time that Muggeridge wrote to Margaret Thatcher suggesting that Mary Whitehouse be drafted into the Cabinet to lead the campaign against Aids.

Deedes would express astonishment that, with all his natural talent and the brilliance of his writing style, Muggeridge never scaled the heights of journalism. He had been deputy editor of the *Telegraph* before decamping to edit *Punch* in 1953, but he never landed the top job with a major publication. For Deedes this represented a reckless squandering of talent and he would become animated on the subject. Much as he admired Muggeridge, Deedes was a little wary of him and strongly disapproved of one aspect of his chaotic private life: Muggeridge had a long affair with Lady Pamela Berry, the wife of Lord Hartwell, the *Telegraph*'s proprietor, which Deedes thought showed an impertinent lack of respect and gratitude.

Deedes did not allow his political activities outside Parliament to distract him from his increasing workload in the Commons. On his return to the backbenches, Deedes had become an active committee man and immersed himself in the minutiae of immigration policy. He served six years on the Commons Select Committee on Race Relations and Immigration – from 1968 to 1970 as deputy chairman to Arthur Bottomley ('we never had a cross word') and then as chairman until his retirement from the House in 1974.

As a minister in the Home Office he had watched ministers and civil servants attempt to grapple with the influx of Commonwealth immigrants who began to arrive in the late 1950s. When net Commonwealth immigration surged to 134,000 in 1961, Macmillan's government tried to stem the flow with a new Act in 1962, passed over Labour opposition. By the 1964 election, Labour had come round to the idea of limiting numbers and enshrined this in further legislation in 1968, and by 1970 they were boasting – inaccurately – that net immigration had been staunched.

Deedes's time chairing the Committee convinced him there was a strong institutional bias against any effort to compute the scale of the migration, let alone do anything about it. The Committee asked Margaret Thatcher, as Education Secretary in Heath's government, to report on the number of immigrants struggling with language problems in British schools. She found that the teaching profession and her departmental civil servants closed ranks, refusing to collate, never mind release, the information. The result was blistering criticism from the Select Committee about the cover up. '[W]e believe that such obscurantist attitudes may prove disastrous. They could have the effect of concealing the consequences of launching into our society children ill-equipped in language and general education to compete with their contemporaries in an advanced society.' Deedes was sufficiently concerned by the media mauling the report unleashed to write Thatcher a private letter saying that he knew she was not personally to blame, and that wider issues than her civil servants' suppression of information were at stake.

Like most respectable Tories, Deedes publicly deprecated Enoch Powell's Rivers of Blood speech in April 1968, while privately conceding that he had a point. By venting the concerns of millions of Britons about the tide of immigration, Powell had acted against all Deedes's instincts to avoid confrontation and to make the best of a bad job. He was probably correct in suggesting that Powell's intervention and subsequent sacking backed Edward Heath into a corner, and imposed an effective code of silence on the shadow cabinet with regard to the immigration issue. It also pushed the Labour government towards finding palliative relief from the problem by banning a wide range of discriminatory activity, rather than by addressing the issue at root.

For the rest of his life, Deedes was convinced that most of the problems that dragged down state schools in urban areas from the 1970s onwards were the result of decanting hundreds of thousands of immigrants and their dependants into British cities without thinking through the consequences. It was a theme he would return to frequently in his weekly *Telegraph* Notebook in years to come, always referring to his own part in this failure of governance. Derek Taylor Thompson recalled that Deedes had a reputation among civil servants for being a bit of a racist. That may have been so, but it is also possible that civil servants bore him a grudge for highlighting their failure to compute the scale of immigration in the 1960s.

Certainly, by the time he left Parliament in 1974, Deedes was more prepared to admit that he had come round to Powell's pessimism about racial tensions in the cities. The work of the Select Committee ground on under his chairmanship, facing the same official obstruction yet still producing well-researched reports based on extensive travels by him and his fellow officers to the Caribbean and India and Pakistan, all of which were largely ignored.

In one testy exchange in the Commons, during an immigration debate in December 1973, Deedes reacted strongly to Labour interventions. 'I would like less abuse of what Mr Enoch Powell says ... His voice is not diminished by disapproving silence or abuse, it is magnified.' He pressed on, perhaps half-consciously including himself in those he was condemning for taking that easy option of disapproving silence: 'In the past, we have proved ourselves to be ignorant, complacent, and self-deceiving. If Mr Powell has erred, and I believe he has, by exaggeration and hyperbole, others have erred by seeking to gloss over awkward facts and figures. When the Select Committee finished its last report, Mr Powell was entitled to say: "I told you so."'

Deedes was also prepared to challenge the racial consensus as it applied to southern Africa. On Rhodesia, he was persistently involved in the Tory backbench effort to break the bi-partisan approach towards Ian Smith's defiance of the British government.

As Harold Wilson prepared to address the United Nations on Rhodesia at the end of 1965, Deedes joined pro-Salisbury right-wingers such as Julian Amery and John Biggs-Davidson in deploring attempts to impose 'unconditional surrender' upon the white minority. The *Daily Telegraph* reported that the backbench effort to show there was support for Rhodesia was strengthened by the roles as co-sponsors of Deedes and Nigel Birch, 'two experienced "middle of the road" MPs, both former ministers'. Deedes always had a soft spot for Ian Smith, partly because he had had a good war but also because he was similarly unconvinced by the notion of one man, one vote in Africa.* Deedes was one of five former ministers to join forces with Duncan Sandys, Deedes's old boss at Housing, in tabling a Commons motion demanding all sanctions be lifted against the rebel leaders of Rhodesia.

Deedes was sufficiently emboldened by his reputation as a defender of the interests of white Africans to write a personal letter to the South African Prime Minister John Vorster in 1970. In a tactfully worded three-page letter, he urged Vorster to per-suade the South African Cricket Board to call off a forthcoming tour of England which, he foresaw, was certain to cause violent protest and damage to the international game, and to push apartheid up the political agenda in Britain.

Vorster wrote back effectively telling Deedes to get lost, reminding him that when touring teams come to South Africa, 'I will not allow them to be molested or harassed by Communists or demonstraters [*sic*] . . . no Government can ever allow itself to be so blackmailed.' Deedes was not the last British Tory to overesti-mate the Afrikaner leadership's susceptibility to constructive advice.

On one level, Deedes's pragmatic instinct to cave in, pre-emptively, to the legions of Peter Hain's Stop the Tour protest was

---

* Deedes once took Smith to lunch at Paradiso e Inferno in the Strand, where Smith astonished the waiters by talking to them in Italian. He had learnt the language as a prisoner of war in Italy, after his Spitfire had been shot down in the Po Valley.

tactically sound because two months later the tour was duly called off. The Wilson government, with a June election in prospect, bullied the MCC into withdrawing the invitation to the Springboks.

Cancellation did not stop Deedes thundering in the next day's *Telegraph* about Britain's craven behaviour. Calling off the tour might be hailed as a victory for common sense, but this would be dangerous self-deception, Deedes wrote of the tour he had himself tried to have cancelled. 'A majority of people in this country wished the South African cricketers to come. Public instinct was sound,' he declared. 'In short, force – or the threat of force – has prevailed . . . That was the state of mind which Mr Hain and his friends have from the start sought to induce, though they can hardly have anticipated that the government would be supine enough to collaborate.'

Deedes concluded by saying that Colin Cowdrey's charge that the authorities had succumbed to blackmail was 'not a whit too strong'. Cowdrey and Deedes remained cordially in touch until the former's death in December 2000, and it is safe to assume that the great England cricketer was unaware that his friend the Tory MP had tried to torpedo the South African tour two months before the Labour government finally sank it.

Often there was an opportunistic element to the causes Deedes took up. With an eye on the farmers of east Kent, he was happy to serve as the required angry backbencher when in 1967 the *Sunday Telegraph* whipped up a row about the £15,000 that the Ministry of Overseas Development was spending on bringing agricultural students from the third world to a training course in Britain.

'The British farmer is on very short commons,' Deedes obligingly told the paper. 'You really cannot go on asking people to tighten their belts when this sort of exercise is going on.' This intervention somehow seems all the odder given Deedes's subsequent charitable work. When the *Telegraph*'s Christmas appeal was revived in the early 1990s under his leadership, helping the third world – and particularly its farmers – was one of the consistent themes of the fund-raising efforts.

Deedes roamed widely as a backbencher. When the first Concorde aeroplane was unveiled in December 1967, Tony Benn, Minister of Technology, had the awkward task of explaining why he had caved in to the French by allowing the aeroplane to be spelt with an 'e'. The French had absolutely refused to countenance spelling it the Anglo-Saxon way, so Benn decided to concede the point rather than have a row. He tried to make light of the surrender, telling reporters that the 'e' stood 'for excellence, for England, for Europe, and for the *Entente*'.

British technicians present as the first plane rolled out of the hangar in Toulouse were 'startled' by this appalling concession, reported the *Telegraph*'s air correspondent, Air Commodore E. M. Donaldson, because without the Anglo-Saxon engines the plane would never have left the drawing board. Deedes, at that time an arch pro-Common Market man, despite having suffered the humiliation of de Gaulle's veto of British membership, was quick to strike, tabling a Commons motion even before Benn had returned from France. He noted 'with interest the Minister of Technology's attempt to be spry about his latest humiliating defeat at the hands of General de Gaulle and the French aircraft industry'. Eldon Griffiths was sufficiently amused by his Tory colleague's contrived blimpish outrage to write a teasing letter to the *Telegraph*.

> Sir – Concord? With the greatest respect (and admiration) to my old friend Mr William Deedes' spirited defence of Anglo-Saxon usage, may I inquire if he is changing his own name to Deeds in protest?

Deedes enjoyed his freedom on the back benches, even if he failed to develop any sort of coherent philosophy. Ashford was an ideal seat, and not just because it was where the family had settled four hundred years before. It was a comfortable, rural con-stituency with an in-built Conservative majority, yet it was less than an hour from Charing Cross by train.* Representing Ashford from the back benches could comfortably be combined with his duties on the *Telegraph*'s diary column.

As the fifth Deedes to represent Kent in Parliament, he believed an MP had a solemn duty to be accessible to his constituents and to defend their interests. Throughout his parliamentary career, Deedes's home address and telephone number were listed in the local telephone directory and in *Who's Who*, which was useful to constituents but not necessarily ideal for the family, who found that meals were frequently interrupted. All letters would be answered, and if necessary followed up with further letters to ministers or local authorities.

One distressed Ashford constituent wrote to him in 1971 when the local funeral home refused to bury his daughter because he could not pay up front. Deedes telephoned the owner and told him that he was morally obliged to bury the girl, and gave his per-sonal guarantee that the bill would be honoured. The constituent then failed to settle the account, so Deedes, bound by his com-mitment, sent the firm a personal cheque for £51.40. But honour cuts both ways, as Deedes told his constituent when he wrote to him asking how he intended to settle the debt. Deedes posted him a series of stamped, addressed envelopes so that the sum owing could be reduced in easy instalments of a pound a week. It took a whole year, but the matter was finally resolved to Deedes's satisfaction. He kept one of the pound notes on the dresser in his bedroom for the rest of his life as, he said, a warning against lending recklessly.

The episode that brought him the greatest personal satisfaction in his career as an MP arose from a terrible tragedy, the murder of a sixteen-year-old Ashford girl, Yvonne Swaffer. The killer was

---

* Deedes would frequently point out that the Ashford to Charing Cross journey took five minutes longer at the beginning of the twenty-first century than it had taken in the 1960s.

arrested but the prosecution controversially allowed the charge to be reduced to manslaughter, on the grounds that Yvonne was said to have been promiscuous and had led him on. The killer escaped with a sentence of four years and local people were outraged.

It turned out that Mr and Mrs Swaffer were committed Labour party activists, who had jeered Deedes at each of the eight pre-election rallies he had addressed in their village of Great Chart. 'It lent piquancy to my endeavours,' he noted. Still, Deedes pursued the case with determination, firing off letters to the police, the Director of Public Prosecutions and Peter Rawlinson, the Attorney General, whom he knew from his Profumo days. Then, when the Conservatives lost the February 1974 election, he took it up with Sam Silkin, who succeeded Rawlinson.

Silkin wrote to Deedes, formally apologising for the way the case had been handled, stating that a charge of murder should have been put to the jury and that Yvonne's moral character should not have been impugned in court. Silkin apologised personally and as Attorney General to the Swaffers for the additional pain caused by the errors made in the trial. Deedes drove to the Swaffer home to show them the letter, which offered them some comfort in their bereavement. For Deedes, the sorry episode showed that an MP 'can be of service to humankind'.

He would frequently talk about the Swaffer case in later years and kept a bulging file of correspondence to the end. He certainly regarded securing a posthumous vindication of the honour of Yvonne Swaffer as one of the greatest achievements of his twenty-four years in the House of Commons.

When Deedes returned to Peterborough in 1945 he was working under the legendary editor Hugo Wortham, who soldiered on until his retirement in 1959, dying that summer at the age of seventy-five. Many members of staff continued working well after normal retirement age, partly because Lord Hartwell had declined to introduce a proper pension scheme.

Wortham had his weaknesses, particularly for drink, but his

Peterborough had flair. After he left the column declined, and by the early 1970s it was 'stunningly dull', according to Tim Heald, who worked there from 1972. Since he had left the Cabinet in 1964, Deedes had provided the column with at least one political story a day. He would generally do some Commons business in the morning before going to Fleet Street at lunchtime on foot or by bus, returning to Westminster for afternoon or evening sittings. Deedes's primary responsibility was the political item and he usually came up with one that would cause no difficulties for his Commons colleagues. Modern newspaper diaries tend to be arch – or at least try to be – but Peterborough in the 1960s and 1970s was essentially deferential, which was how Lord Hartwell liked it.

Heald regarded the column as shamefully bad, given that in those days it had a full staff of six or seven, including an editor and a deputy, as well as Deedes and Heald and at least one other member of staff, plus the secretary, Dorina Paparritor. She recalled that everyone had fun, taking long, boozy lunches, and that almost everyone smoked, so the fourth-floor Peterborough office was a permanent fug. Most Peterborough staff were public schoolboys but few had been to university.

The staple item was the regimental reunion, and if a bread roll was chucked by a tipsy subaltern so much the better. A typical political story might record a faintly risqué pun at a public meeting, or the marriage of an MP's daughter. Other stories came in as press releases and were lightly rewritten before being handed to the subs. Deedes was regarded as more industrious than most, because he would generally make at least one phone call before writing his piece.

Heald remembered Deedes being an endlessly cheering presence around the office, full of jokes and good political gossip. One day, during the IRA's mainland bombing campaign in the 1970s, a suspect car was found in Fleet Street and the police ordered the *Telegraph* building to be evacuated. Deedes flatly refused to leave and paced around the Peterborough office, instructing

colleagues: 'Don't leave your desks, that's exactly what the terror-
ists want us to do.' The entire Peterborough staff stayed at their
desks, but in a nod to health and safety the blinds were closed as a
precaution against flying glass.

Stories had to be typed with at least four carbons so a copy
could be sent up to Lord Hartwell. At around half-past five in the
evening, Paparritor would take the Peterborough stories up to
Lord Hartwell's suite on the fifth floor and hand it to his butler.
Hartwell would quite often intervene directly, without recourse to
the editor, and demand that a paragraph be dropped if he felt it
showed a lack of respect or decorum.

Deedes also found himself in demand as a regular writer of
signed opinion pieces on the leader page, always under the byline
'W. F. Deedes, MP'. With his junior ministerial experience in
Housing and the Home Office in the 1950s, and his more recent
Cabinet role, Deedes was well placed to pronounce on a variety of
subjects. He was not a star columnist with a regular slot, such as
Peregrine Worsthorne in the *Sunday Telegraph*, but a journeyman
opinion writer, always willing to turn his typewriter to immigration, drugs or crime, or any topic of concern to the editor and the
paper's middle-class readers.

Worsthorne thought Deedes's pieces were competent but
second rate. 'Intellectually, he always stayed in the shallows, and
never dived into the deep end. He was very good on parliamentary tactics, gossip, what ministers were up to, but as a political
commentator he was a lightweight.'

Deedes's columns tended to be constructed along familiar lines.
The basic outline of the issue was laid out in rather pedestrian
terms at the beginning. Deedes would state that there was growing public concern about abortion, or crime, or pornography, or
immigrants, and he would agree that the public had a point. Then
he would ponder whether a new law should be introduced and
usually he would conclude that it would be difficult for the
police – who would invariably have the support of fair-minded
citizens – to enforce it.

Typical of the form was a *Sunday Telegraph* piece in December 1970 about the sudden appearance of what 'Americans politely call skin flicks'. No newspaper opinion piece on censorship would be complete without a passing nod to John Stuart Mill, and Deedes noted it would be absurd to cite his doctrines in order to defend cinematic scenes of bestiality and degradation. 'Change the law?' Deedes asked of his reader. 'Yes, by all means, if we can find the right definitions.' Then the piece simply fizzled out, noting that, at some point in the near future, it might well be necessary 'for the Home Secretary to step in'.

His pieces were professionally constructed and clearly written but they were consistently dull. Lacking any political philosophy of his own, he never acquired a columnar voice; his efforts on the leader page were never intended by him to amuse or provoke the reader, as Worsthorne deliberately set out to do. This faltering, unopinionated opinion writing suited Lord Hartwell, who was no right-wing Tory and deprecated what he saw as the ideological excesses of the leader writers. They, in turn, believed Hartwell's brain had been addled by reading PPE at Christ Church, where he had come under the spell of Keynsians. Hartwell's most damning criticism of an article was that it was 'too viewy', and this was a charge that could certainly never have been levelled at any of Deedes's efforts.

Too often for Bill Deedes, work in London as MP or journalist became a refuge from bad news at home, particularly his son's deteriorating health. Julius could not follow Jeremy to Eton partly because of his chronic bed-wetting. Also, his medical condition meant he had to travel to London for monthly blood transfusions, which would have been incompatible with public school life, as would the extreme tiredness he suffered before each treatment.

After boarding at Pine Hill in Hythe, Julius transferred to the secondary modern school in Ashford where he performed adequately, despite frequent absences caused by trips to London. Though he never grew taller than five foot, and had an increasingly distended stomach owing to liver damage, he left prep school 'quite a useful cricketer', as the headmaster told his father. Bill and Hilary had long known that they would have to prepare themselves for Julius's early death because there were limits to what his body could take, despite his endlessly cheerful approach to life. Bill had grown closer to his second son than he was to Jeremy, who had been away at Eton.

Few sufferers of aplastic anaemia make it out of their teens, but Julius fought tenaciously to live as normal a life as possible though he knew he was dying. He clipped articles from newspapers about the condition, none of which glossed over his inevitable fate. Yet he learnt to drive, and then at the age of twenty – and without telling his father – he applied for an apprenticeship at the *Kent Messenger*. When the paper's owner wrote to Deedes in September 1967 to warn him that his son had been accepted only for a probationary period of three months with no guarantee of a permanent position, Bill wrote back to assure him, truthfully, that it was none of his doing.

> I privately hoped he might settle for something quieter – there is a great scope for someone with his equipment to be a sort of freelance private secretary.* But he is dead nuts on the newspaper idea, I discover, so I hope he makes a go of it. He's bright and can at least write short-hand – which some journalists including his father can't. But I am relieved rather than otherwise to know of the three-month probation. If he finds it too much, that will ease the way out.

In fact, he proved a conspicuous success, earning a full-time staff job and taking to journalism just as easily as had his father. But there was no disguising that Julius was losing the battle with

---

* Julius himself might have been rather appalled by this low ambition, although it was the sort of work that Bill's own father had taken after he left the Army and for which he was himself prepared when he was sent to Clough's Secretarial College.

his own body. On 13 February 1970, Professor P. L. Mollison of the Department of Haematology at St Mary's Hospital, Paddington wrote to Bill alerting him to an ominous development. Julius was showing signs of heart failure, which Mollison assumed was caused by the build-up of iron in his body brought on by the regime of monthly blood transfusions. He added, 'Julius, as usual, makes light of his troubles and we have tried not to convey to him any of the anxiety which we feel.'

Professor Mollison sent the letter to Bill at the House of Commons, rather than at home, which was to have important consequences. The letter was gently worded, but the message was clear: Julius was dying. For whatever reason, Bill decided to keep the news to himself and he did not tell Hilary.

Despite acute bouts of breathlessness brought on by his anaemia and a weakened heart, Julius refused to be defeated. Not only did he secure a full-time job on the *Kent Messenger*, but he was sent to Folkestone to set up a new local edition of the paper that he briefly edited. But, six weeks later, and seven months after the professor's warning, Julius died in the Royal Free Hospital in north London in the early hours of 14 August 1970, four days after his twenty-third birthday. The primary cause of death was non-alcoholic cirrhosis of the liver caused by a lifetime of blood transfusions.

Even though Hilary had spent weeks, probably months, at his hospital bedside over the years, Julius died alone and she was later haunted by this, blaming Bill for failing to keep her informed of the last ominous turn in their son's disease. Jeremy also felt out of the picture: just before his brother died he and Anna, his future wife, had flown to Corfu unaware that Julius's condition had become critical.

Jeremy could not get back in time for the funeral and Juliet, who was working in Wales at the time, was told by her parents not to come back to Kent for the funeral. Later she expressed regret that she had not overruled them and come home anyway. Lucy, then a teenager, was around and was terrified when her parents dashed out of the front door that morning in August, after the telephone rang ominously early. She was told that Julius had 'suffered a collapse', though in truth he was already dead. Lucy retained another memory of that dreadful day: for the first time she could remember her father had actually kissed her.

From that moment, until her death in 2004, not a day passed without Hilary talking about Julius, and often she would speak of her bitter regret that she had not been at his bedside when he died. After the funeral Bill never mentioned Julius, not even within the family, and much later he became palpably irritated with me when I tried to pin him down on the details of Julius's life.

He was incapable of expressing his grief and responded rather as he had after the Twente Canal disaster, by channelling it outwards. Just five days later he appeared on *Day by Day*, a news programme on the local ITV station, talking about his son's abbreviated life and the disease that had killed him. Deedes received a ten-pound fee for the appearance, plus ten shillings expenses.

Six days after Julius's death, Deedes sent a letter to the manager of Jacksons of Piccadilly, where he had stopped on his way to visit Julius for the last time. He had been served by a 'young man with fair hair' who had taken the trouble to select the three best peaches he could find, and put them carefully in a gift box packed with straw.

'The sad point of this story is that my boy has since died,' Deedes wrote. 'The peaches were the last thing he enjoyed and he was very glad to have them, as they came looking rather important from your shop.' Urging the manager not to trouble to acknowledge the letter (which he did anyway) Deedes concluded: 'If you can find the chap in question, foster his interests. I think he is rather a credit to your business.'

It was characteristic of Deedes that he could confide in this way to the manager of a grocer's shop but was incapable of talking to his wife or children about Julius's death. He found it easier to express his grief to strangers and in writing, rather as, twenty-five years earlier, he had expressed his pain at losing his young officers by writing emotional letters to their parents.

After the funeral Julius's body was cremated at Charing Crematorium, not far from Aldington, and for some weeks afterwards there was confusion within the family about what had happened to his ashes. Juliet recalled much later this having been an issue between her parents. The voluminous Deedes filing system provided the answer. Two months after Julius's death, Frank Knock & Co, funeral directors and monumental masons, had written to Bill seeking guidance about what to do with the ashes that had not been picked up. Without reference to Hilary he wrote back, requesting that an employee of the firm scatter them somewhere at the crematorium.

CHAPTER 17

BLITHE DEXTERITY

'I have never given an order on this newspaper, and I'm not going to start now.'

In later life, Deedes was wont to suggest that the editorship of the *Daily Telegraph* dropped into his lap like a ripe plum, but that is not true. There had long been rumours in the *Telegraph* office that Deedes was being lined up as a possible replacement for Maurice Green, the urbane and popular editor who was anxious to retire. As early as October 1972 the *Spectator* diary had reported that Deedes was in the running. 'It is said that the Young Turks on the staff, who idolise Colin Welch [the deputy editor], fear that he may not get the job and favour Deedes as a stop-gap.'

Most *Telegraph* journalists assumed there were two obvious candidates as successor to Green. The popular choice would have been Welch, who was clever, cultured and iconoclastic, a brilliant mimic blessed with an ability to whistle entire symphonies. He had created the Peter Simple column, a whimsical comic fantasy, before handing it over to Michael Wharton, warning him it was a journalistic dead end.

But Hartwell had his doubts about Welch. His private life was rackety and he drank heavily, which occasionally led him into trouble. Moreover, he was unashamedly right-wing, a prototype Thatcherite long before the word was known, which offended the chairman's Keynsian sympathies. Welch had built up the stable of clever young ideological men of the right – notably Frank Johnson, John O'Sullivan, and later Charles Moore – who, in the following years, were to carry the Thatcherite banner in the face of indifference, or actual hostility, from Hartwell and Deedes.

At the beginning of 1974, Green had made it clear to Lord Hartwell that he could not be expected to stay on beyond the end of the year. Deedes got wind of this and it set his mind working fast. Congenial though the life of a senior backbencher was, Deedes had begun to weary of life at Westminster after almost a quarter of a century. When Edward Heath called an election for February 1974, asking the voters 'who governs Britain?' – the elected government or the coal miners – Labour emerged as the largest party, but without an overall majority. This ensured there would have to be another election by the year's end, which gave Deedes a window in which to think hard about whether he wanted to continue serving as Ashford's MP.

Hartwell had let it be known that Welch could not expect to succeed Green because, the chairman told senior staff, he was too argumentative. The other strong internal candidate was Kenneth Fleet, who had been City editor of the Daily and Sunday *Telegraphs* for more than ten years, and was widely respected and impeccably connected in the business world. The City office then operated as a separate fiefdom, its sense of apartness encouraged by having premises further east from the head office on the fringes of the square mile. Fleet was a rather grand figure who guarded his autonomy, and this may have counted against him with Hartwell, who would have feared that he would be difficult to control.

When Heath had called the February election, Deedes repaired to Ashford to defend his comfortable majority against an expected anti-Tory swing. John O'Sullivan, one of the star writers and a Welch protégé, rang Deedes to ask if he would join in a public declaration of support for the deputy editor. Welch's allies, fearful that he would respond to Hartwell's humiliating rebuff by resigning in a sulk, had drawn up a round robin letter urging management to treat the deputy editor with dignity and keep in mind his sensibilities in the selection of the new editor, if it was not to be Welch himself. It was a slightly pompous exercise of the type in which journalists occasionally become involved, and it was difficult to see how it could actively assist Colin Welch's cause.

Deedes, preoccupied with defending his Ashford seat, declined to sign the round robin and there was great irritation in the *Telegraph* office at his failure to show solidarity with Welch. Deedes clearly feared Hartwell would regard a statement in favour of Welch as an act of insubordination, and did not wish to jeopardise his undeclared campaign to fill the editor's chair. Deedes gave a rather pedantic and defensive explanation for his failure to defend Welch in his autobiography, which suggested he felt he might have had a case to answer. 'I felt doubtful if my intervention while absent from the office fighting an election would greatly assist the cause and declined. In the event, he did not resign.' That was true, but Welch never forgot Deedes's failure to show his support.

If Welch was not to succeed Green, Deedes knew he was in the picture as a dark horse candidate. He planned his campaign for the editorship with Dorina Paparritor, the secretary on the Peterborough column and an important ally, when they lunched together in a Fleet Street café on 22 March 1974. Peter Eastwood, the widely detested managing editor who controlled the news side of the paper, walked in on them and, most unusually, asked affably if he could join them. Eastwood mentioned to Deedes – who needed no reminding – that the editor's chair would soon be vacant and that Deedes would be well-qualified to fill it. Deedes knew enough about Eastwood's cunning as an office politician to know his intentions. As Paparritor put it: 'Eastwood was a very devious man. He wanted Bill because he thought he could dominate him.'

Even so, Deedes was quick to spot his opportunity. Three days later he wrote Lord Hartwell a cautiously phrased letter, cannily pitched to appeal to the proprietor's notion of how a deferential editor should behave. Deedes began by pointing out that life as a senior backbencher was quite agreeable: indeed, he stressed that from 'the selfish point of view it is simplest and tempting to go on for another term'.

He couched his job application in the most sinuous terms. Deedes wondered if he 'could be of more help to you if at this point I chucked politics and pulled some more weight in the office'. He doubted that this would be the case, but stressed that he was making the suggestion only because 'your family have been very kind to me over many years, and I have given very little back'.

The soon-to-be-vacant editor's chair was not specifically mentioned, so there was an easy retreat should Hartwell not have considered Deedes editor material. But as he no doubt suspected, Deedes was pushing at an open door. Hartwell wrote back on 4 April, playing for time and pleading the need to consult Maurice Green, who was on holiday. However, he reassured Deedes that he was 'much too modest about your past and present contributions to the paper. There is nobody with whom we could replace you.'

Deedes was handling the undeclared negotiations for the editor's chair with his customary dexterity. And sure enough, at their next face-to-face meeting, Hartwell duly offered him the job. Deedes replied that at his age – he was soon to turn sixty-one – Hartwell might reasonably have regarded him as a stop-gap editor who could swiftly be replaced without embarrassment should things not turn out well. In his letter formally accepting the job, Deedes maintained due deference, joking with Lord Hartwell that if 'you do not know my limitations after 30 or so years with the Telegraph, there is not much I can add now'.

The key to Deedes's success in landing the job lay in Hartwell's criticism of Colin Welch as 'too argumentative'. Over his long association with the *Telegraph*, Deedes had been scrupulous in showing elaborate deference, first to Lord Camrose and latterly to his second son, Lord Hartwell. Deedes's lifelong aversion to confrontation stood him in good stead with Hartwell, who could see that his new editor would be malleable and uncomplaining. Deedes, in retrospect, conceded that he saw the editorial side of the *Telegraph* rather as a well-run battalion in a rather good regiment. For him, being editor was akin to serving as a company commander with the rank of major. Hartwell, chairman and editor-in-chief, was the colonel to whom Deedes would show obeisance and obedience. Indeed, he once said that his role could best be described as 'Lord Hartwell's butler', though his lordship in fact already had a butler presiding over his suite of rooms on the fifth floor of 135 Fleet Street.

Deedes had pulled off a sensational coup under the noses of the astonished staff. Rather in the manner of Alec Douglas-Home 'emerging' as Tory leader and Prime Minister in 1963, Deedes ascended to the editor's chair almost without trace. There was no magic circle at the *Telegraph*, not least because Hartwell took such decisions alone. But, like Douglas-Home, Deedes was assisted in his undeclared campaign by inchoate forces. Douglas-Home had Martin Redmayne, the chief whip, quietly marshalling supporters and, conceivably, lying about his master's level of support. Deedes had Eastwood, the managing editor and the only member of the editorial staff who, apart from Maurice Green, had daily 'face time' with Lord Hartwell. It is safe to assume that Eastwood used these meetings to nourish the chairman's anxieties about Kenneth Fleet and Colin Welch, two potential editors who would have moved swiftly to clip the managing editor's wings.

As Maurice Green was not to leave until the end of the year, Hartwell stressed that the decision must remain secret. With another general election due for the autumn, Deedes could spare his constituency association the bother of a by-election and quietly step down. In May he told his agent and then his committee, as well as the chief whip in the Commons, that he would not be defending the seat. When news began to leak out of Deedes's triumph, there was consternation at 135 Fleet Street. Deedes was regarded as an affable sort, quite up to providing a diverting daily paragraph for Peterborough about life in the Palace of Westminster, or banging out a workmanlike leader page article on prison reform. But the idea of him as editor was astonishing to most members of staff. Welch, however, was extremely decent in the circumstances, telling Deedes that if he could not be editor himself he could not think of anyone he would be happier to serve under.

The *Telegraph* operated along the lines, unusual in Britain but common in North America, whereby news and comment were almost entirely separate. Eastwood, as managing editor, had control over the news operation and the reporters. Deedes was to be responsible for the leaders – the unsigned voice of the paper – and the main comment piece, and to a certain extent the very thin offering of features. He retained some control over the Peterborough diary, too, though Hartwell regarded that as his province.

Eastwood was thrilled when Deedes's appointment was confirmed. He went around the office telling journalists that Deedes was to be a 'writing editor' who would leave the management of the paper to him. He sensed that because Deedes lacked Maurice Green's intellectual heft he would be even easier to dominate. Deedes was well aware of this danger, but understood that in return for taking up the editor's chair he would also be taking on a state of permanent guerrilla warfare with Eastwood. As Deedes noted dryly of his future with Eastwood in an aide-memoire a couple of months before he took over, 'some minor, perhaps major struggle for power ahead here'.

But, for the time being, Deedes had a good excuse to delay any confrontation with Eastwood because the ructions within the Conservative Party culminated in Margaret Thatcher's leadership challenge in February 1975, a severe test just a month into the

new editor's tenure. Frustration with Edward Heath's performance as leader of the opposition was increasing within the Tory
Party, and *Telegraph* leader-writers such as Colin Welch, Peter
Utley and John O'Sullivan did not conceal their contempt. Not
only had the Tories lost two elections in the previous year, but
Heath had reversed key aspects of Conservative policy to embrace
inflationary policies.

Owing to Deedes's golfing friendship with Denis Thatcher, it
has been widely, but wrongly, assumed that Deedes's *Telegraph*
was wholeheartedly behind Thatcher's campaign. Lord Hartwell
was suspicious of Thatcher on ideological grounds; his wife had
the same antipathy, though perhaps more on social grounds.
Word of Lady Hartwell's dislike of Mrs Thatcher got around
Fleet Street. Indeed, a few days after Thatcher's election as Tory
leader, the *Spectator* ran a mischievous paragraph claiming that
Lady Hartwell had been overheard at a party saying, 'God, I see
they've picked that fascist female as leader!' A fortnight later the
Spectator was forced to grovel, unreservedly withdrawing the
purported remark and sincerely apologising to Lady Hartwell for
'this offensive publication'.

The *Telegraph*, nonetheless, was far from enthusiastic about
what would later be known as Thatcherism, and in the run-up to
the leadership election Eastwood, ever alert to the views of his
masters, ensured that the paper offered minimum encouragement
to Thatcher's campaign. The paper, before and since, tended to
support the Conservative leader, whoever he or she may be, until
the party has decided it was ready for a change. Traditionally the
paper did not encourage leadership coups, even when it was
dissatisfied with the leader's performance.

On the news pages Eastwood pulled out all the stops in defence
of Heath's collapsing authority. A day before the poll of Tory
MPs, the *Telegraph*'s redoubtable political correspondent H. B.
Boyne led the paper with the news that Alec Douglas-Home's late
intervention in support of Heath would almost certainly tip the
balance in his favour. 'As a former Prime Minister and Tory leader

who selflessly made way for a successor,' Boyne intoned, 'Lord Home* has a unique place in the affections of the party.'

The message from Deedes's leader pages was less decisive. Rather than embrace any single contender for the party leadership, he created a special feature called 'My Kind of Tory Party', in which the potential leadership contenders were invited to lay out their views. In times of change, journalists like to set up this sort of forum which gives readers the illusion that their paper is going to determine the outcome of a contest. Thatcher's offering was less than inspirational, but did at least present an argument for the party to change direction radically. Heath's, which ran last and on the day before the first ballot, was dire. Betraying his impatience at being constantly asked what the Tories stood for, Heath gave the following answer: 'To that question, the true Conservative does best to put his tongue in his cheek and say, "that depends".'

The leader on the morning of the first ballot, 4 February, was going to be important, given that *Telegraph* leaders at this time were read and deciphered by Tory MPs seeking ideological guidance. The leader bore all the hallmarks of the permanent battle within the leader-writing conference, with the Thatcherites pushing Deedes as far as they could, knowing that he would have to justify too much praise for her to Hartwell.

The leader did not endorse Thatcher, but it was savagely critical of Heath and his lurch towards 'inflationary financial policies out of tune with the party's deep instincts'. It also noted Heath's personal weaknesses, his 'inflexibility, aloofness, and a tendency to surround himself with like-minded colleagues'. The leader seemed to assume that Thatcher would fail in her challenge, so it urged Heath to learn lessons from the contest and 'seriously re-appraise the policies of his late administration before they harden into an orthodoxy. He may be wrong. On some issues, he *is*

---

* Alec Douglas-Home had been made a life peer – Lord Home of the Hirsel – in 1974.

wrong.' That message, though masked by tepid admiration else-where, may well have hit home as Tory MPs prepared to vote later that day.

In the rest of the paper Eastwood was taking no chances in what he also thought would prove to be a comfortable canter for Heath. Boyne was back on the front page with an inside track on the previous day's meeting of the 1922 Committee, which had shown a 'consensus substantially in favour of "no change"'. The front-page picture, a gratuitous photo-opportunity in defence of the status quo, showed a grinning Ted Heath handing over a trophy to a bemused angler who had landed the largest skate caught in British waters in the previous twelve months.

The *Telegraph* looked foolish later that day when Heath was humiliated by Thatcher, by 130–119 votes in the first ballot. Eastwood and Boyne had failed to divine how the mood in the party had shifted sharply against Heath. When Thatcher secured a comfortable victory the next week at the second ballot, Boyne's intro to the splash of the following morning's paper celebrated the moment: 'A radiant Mrs Margaret Thatcher, 49-year-old wife of a business executive and mother of twins, made history yesterday by becoming the first woman to lead a British political party.'

In the main leader – headlined 'Disraeli's Mantle' – she was hailed as a 'bonny fighter' and praised for rising to the top from a modest upbringing. The leader sensed at last a moment when the assumption of post-war British decline could be questioned: 'Let her draw on the experience of her own life and show us that failure is not inevitable.'

Once she had been elected leader, the *Telegraph* instinctively rallied to Thatcher's cause and Eastwood displayed the conspicuous fervour of the convert, ordering the reporting staff to get behind her. Eastwood was a northerner who regarded himself as blunt, but who others saw as simply rude. Short and stocky, he wore his hair short and brushed back. His nickname around the office was 'bottlebrush', and reporters learnt to treat him warily. Eastwood was raised in Batley, West Yorkshire, and educated at grammar school, so his background was different from that of the other senior figures around the *Telegraph*. He had risen through the ranks of the sub-editors' desk to become an accomplished, authoritarian night editor, the man who effectively constructed the following morning's paper. Hartwell's grave error was to promote him to managing editor and give him responsibility for the bulk of the editorial staff.

Because of Eastwood's broad authority over the newsroom, calling Deedes 'editor' was something of a misnomer. The role of the editor under Camrose and Hartwell could more accurately have been described as that of comment editor, answering directly to the chairman and editor-in-chief. Deedes would go to see Hartwell every evening just after six o'clock to brief him on the next morning's leaders. Earlier in the day, at noon, Eastwood would have gone separately to Lord Hartwell's suite of rooms to explain news developments and the shape of the next day's front page. Though Deedes had the more glamorous title and was the undisputed editorial figurehead, Eastwood had much more direct influence on the paper. Hartwell liked it that way, because it gave him the ultimate say.

At the point at which Deedes became editor, the *Telegraph* seemed to be as strong as ever. It was selling more than 1.3 million copies a day, four times the circulation of *The Times*, and comfortably more than the combined circulations of its three 'quality' rivals, *The Times*, *Guardian*, and *Financial Times*. It was packed with advertising, particularly lucrative classifieds – a market it dominated by virtue of its being the unquestioned market leader. But those successes obscured fundamental problems, most of them related to Fleet Street's anarchic industrial relations, though others stemmed from the *Telegraph*'s conservative culture. As Bill Grundy noted in a piece in the *Spectator* a fortnight before Deedes took over, the strength of the paper had been Camrose and Hartwell's knack for knowing precisely what the middle-class reader wanted: 'But it may be that the taste of those readers is changing. It may be that they would appreciate more wit, more humour, more irreverence than they have been getting from the *Telegraph* in the past ... Essential to any journalist, and still the best buy in Fleet Street, it is nevertheless not a paper one opens in a froth of expectation. Mr Deedes will have to do something about that.' Grundy went on to dissect the traditional split authority of the paper between the editor and Peter Eastwood. 'This lunatic policy, clearly an attempt to act on the old tenet "Divide and Rule", has had a disastrous effect. It has resulted in a complete lack of a sense of direction.' Morale was so low that 'you have to go down to the basement to find any'.

Fatally, perhaps, Deedes did not demand any guarantees from Lord Hartwell that he would be supported as editor against Eastwood's incursions. No doubt Hartwell would have refused to offer any: as Grundy suggested, the lines of authority were confused by design, not by default, so as to maximise the editor-in-chief's control. Even before Deedes took over he was bombarded by advice from senior colleagues about how he must show his teeth from the beginning or risk being overwhelmed by Eastwood's relentless campaign to expand his control.

Colin Welch was especially forceful on this point. After a spine-stiffening lunch *à deux* in December 1974 Deedes had sent a 'private and personal' memo to Welch's home, which he asked him not to bring to the office. He spoke of his determination to smash the 'quite disastrous form of diarchy' between the editor and managing editor. He conceded that large parts of the paper, including the City office and the parliamentary staff, have no idea who they should actually report to. Deedes made clear that things 'cannot go on like this'.

But in the same memo Deedes expressed a characteristic caution and reluctance to act decisively, and an implicit rebuke to Welch in his demand that the new editor cut the Gordian knot immediately. 'Much current advice and gossip is that a new editor must at once take the reins and command the ship. This is too simplistic. Clumsily done, it would merely intensify rivalry and empire building . . . Our task is to promote unity, not school house rivalry, though this will be difficult and will take a little time.' In many respects, this argument is a masterly summation of the political credo of a post-war British politician. It is predicated on the assumption that things are bad, and probably getting worse, and that the way to move forward is to strike dubious agreements with rival interest groups.

The weakness of Deedes's cautious approach was that it pre-supposed a certain goodwill on Eastwood's part, which would never be displayed. Moreover, when he wrote Hartwell a memo following his lunch with Welch, Deedes did not mention the issue of the enervating diarchy at all, instead making prosaic sugges-tions about the reorganisation of furniture in and around the editor's office and seeking authorisation for slight changes to the working hours for his secretary.

As Deedes did not strike at the beginning, owing to being pre-occupied by the Tory leadership succession, he left Eastwood free to maintain his practice of constantly picking fights with different sections of the paper. He particularly disliked mini empires within the overall structure and would set about subverting them by undermining their head of department. One day the Manchester office would be in his sights: he might poach the best reporters for the London newsroom and then humiliate the staff who remained in the northern office. The next he would turn his fire on the City department. Occasionally these editorial executives would crack under the constant provocation.

The consequences of Deedes's failure to de-fang Eastwood in the first months of his editorship burst into the open when Kenneth Fleet became so exasperated that, in 1976, he shattered the genteel conventions of 135 Fleet Street by going over the editor's head and directly to Lord Hartwell.

Fleet, who no doubt was still wounded by his failure to succeed Maurice Green the year before, wrote Hartwell a splenetic com-plaint about Eastwood's constant campaign of destabilisation in language that Hartwell must have found appalling. Fleet warned that the traditional spirit of bonhomie among *Telegraph* journalists had been destroyed by Eastwood's guerrilla warfare. 'Where it has not been replaced by low morale and sagging spirits, it has given way to outright hostility.' Eastwood, he suggested, 'would appear to suffer from paranoia or at least to have a destructive urge'.

This letter was an implicit rebuke of Deedes who, while notionally in charge, had clearly failed not just to defeat Eastwood's campaign of aggression, but even to join the battle to dismantle the diarchy. Predictably, Hartwell took no action about Fleet's memo, though it can be assumed that he would have strongly disapproved of his having raised the matter. Fleet left the *Telegraph* two years later for the *Sunday Times*, sadly disappointed but still with enormous affection for the paper and its proprietor. Hartwell regarded his departure as a grotesque betrayal and Deedes had great difficulty in persuading him to attend Fleet's farewell drinks party.

The parliamentary sketch was a frequent cause of friction between Eastwood and Deedes. Though its authorship fell under the control of the editor, it appeared on a news page, which meant that Eastwood could order it to be spiked if he wanted to make a point in pursuit of the permanent campaign. It was understood that the sketch should appear every morning when parliament sat, so Eastwood had to show some discretion in how frequently it was thrown out. The late Frank Johnson, one of the regular sketch-writers of the time, described it as the 'warm water port' of the *Telegraph*, control of which was fiercely contested.

The greatest sin of all, for Johnson, was Deedes's failure to defend the prime newspaper territory upon which the sketch was placed. In a characteristic pose, Johnson described Eastwood's expansionist ambitions in terms of nineteenth-century European statecraft. 'The issue was never resolved in the eight years I worked on the paper. I found it gave a certain savour to life. There was the satisfaction of knowing that in Eastwood one was taking on a worthy foe. Like all aggrieved powers with an age-old territorial claim, he was prepared to renew the struggle, if the moment were opportune, after years of living in relative peace.'

Johnson was less indulgent of Deedes, and actively disliked him. The year before Johnson's death, he dismissed Deedes as 'an oleaginous creep' and a 'good time Charlie who goes along with the powers that be'. Johnson shared the disdain that the right-wingers on the paper held for Deedes on ideological grounds – or, more accurately, for his lack of ideology – but there were more specific reasons for his dislike. Johnson was one of the few authentically working-class members of the leader-writing college and he thought that Deedes was a snob. He was convinced that, deep down, he regarded Margaret Thatcher as a parvenue and shared the distaste of Tory grandees such as Lords Carrington and Aldington. Johnson maintained that, while his career had been actively promoted by Maurice Green, Deedes would never have appointed and then favoured a secondary-modern boy who had learnt his trade on the *Sun*.

Colin Welch, while loyal to Deedes to his face and indeed behind his back, also came to distrust him as a *faux bon homme*. This started with Deedes's failure to back him in the round robin to Lord Hartwell, but the real crisis in the relationship between the editor and his deputy occurred when Welch wrote a pungent leader-page article denouncing the BBC for its anti-Conservative bias, which Deedes passed without demur. Some time later Welch was editing the paper in Deedes's absence abroad and using the editor's office, as was his custom. In a pile of papers on the desk he was astonished to find a carbon copy of a private letter Deedes had written to the director-general of the BBC, apologising for Welch's broadside, which he conceded had been over the top.

He regarded the sending of this letter as an act of betrayal and a typical example of Deedes having it both ways. Welch, who left the *Telegraph* on perfectly friendly terms in 1980 and without airing his reservations about the editor, was further wounded when Deedes failed to invite him to his retirement dinner in Downing Street six years later. Welch subsequently suffered a devastating stroke that left him in a vegetative state for two years until his death in 1997. His family were hurt that Deedes did not come to visit him, or even ask after his welfare.

The skirmishing between Deedes and Eastwood continued right though his editorship. For instance, during the May 1979 general election Eastwood removed jokes from Johnson's political sketch that he deemed unhelpful to Margaret Thatcher's cause and spiked one of his best columns. Johnson responded by withdrawing his services and for several days leading up to the climax of one of the most exciting election campaigns of the twentieth century the *Telegraph* was without a sketch writer. It was an absurd situation: the anarchy on the production side of the newspaper was being mirrored by the paper's senior editorial executives. Though the immediate cause of the impasse was Eastwood's malicious meddling, it was feeble of Deedes and Hartwell not to have acted decisively to sort it out.

Deedes referred to this stand-off in his autobiography as the moment he came 'nearest to a serious quarrel with Peter Eastwood'. He suggested he got his own back on Eastwood by running Johnson's piece on the leader page. Eastwood was, by Deedes's account, livid at this riposte: 'There were volcanic consequences. The flow of Eastwood lava stopped just short of seriously damaging those living near me.'

That was a strange way, perhaps, of assessing a shameful lapse in his own authority. Though by convention Eastwood did control the news pages, there was no real doubt that the editor ultimately outranked the managing editor; had Deedes gone to Lord Hartwell complaining of such obviously bad behaviour by Eastwood, which was robbing the paper of the services of the best sketch-writer in Fleet Street, the chairman would surely have supported the editor. Johnson's memory of the incident was not that Deedes had proved a point by running the piece belatedly on one of the pages he controlled. Rather, he regarded it as no consolation for the fact that, after eight years of skirmishing, 'Eastwood was the victor'.

Johnson eventually wearied of the civil warfare at the *Telegraph* and, ignoring the warnings of colleagues, decamped to Jimmy Goldsmith's short-lived *Now* magazine, which was established principally to settle the proprietor's many scores in Fleet Street. One of his replacements as sketch writer was Stephen Glover, who soon found himself being roughed up by the subeditors. The night editor spiked a Glover sketch in December 1980, returning it to the author with comments scrawled on the hard copy, including 'rubbish' and – most witheringly – 'not funny'. When Deedes did nothing to defend him, Glover wrote him a pained memo. Glover was then only twenty-eight years old so the memo to the editor almost forty years his senior was respectfully worded, but it was implicitly critical of his failure to back a member of staff. Glover's memo missed the point to the extent that the night editor had – on quality grounds alone – been right to spike his sketch, but he was justified in being bewildered by his editor's failure to back him. 'Of course I want and need your guidance, your advice, your correction, wherever I err. But I must also have your support when I fail.'

Trying to be funny in a newspaper is difficult and exposing, and it takes time to hit the right note. Deedes's failure to back his young sketch writer, who was very conscious that he was following in the footsteps of the master of the trade, was lamentable, particularly for a journalist who ever craved compliments for his work. Once, when Glover was trying to goad Deedes into taking decisive action to defend his position, the editor replied tartly: 'Stephen, I have never given an order on this newspaper, and I'm not going to start now.'

Eastwood, who was obnoxious to almost every member of staff at 135 Fleet Street, was invariably ingratiating to the chairman. Hartwell thus closed his ears to the numerous complaints and ignored the obvious damage this was doing to the paper. When reflecting on the weakness of the hand dealt him by Hartwell, Deedes was wont to say that he always thought you should go on court to play tennis, not to argue whether the lines are straight. He had accepted the job of editor in the full knowledge of how Hartwell ran his papers.

There is some truth to this, although others suffered the consequences of Deedes's vacillation, particularly in his failure to stand up to Eastwood. The managing editor's expansionist ambitions grew more, not less, pronounced under Deedes's editorship.

Eastwood was a bully, but like most of his type, he was always careful not to push too far. Nicholas Garland recalled a period under the editorship of Maurice Green when Eastwood began regularly spiking his cartoon, citing lack of space. Garland went to complain rather nervously to Green. The editor listened impassively then picked up a pencil and scribbled a note, which he did not put in an envelope. He told Garland to take it to Eastwood. The note read: 'Once I have passed a cartoon it is to appear in the paper without fail.' Garland took the note to Eastwood, who read it and nodded. Eastwood never again spiked the cartoon.

By writing the note and using Garland to deliver it, Green had not just asserted his authority over Eastwood; he had also humiliated him in front of a member of staff who was unlikely to keep the incident to himself. For years after that moment of reckoning, scores of *Telegraph* journalists could only wish that Green's successor in the editor's chair would show a similar flash of steel.

However, for all the urgency of his original discussions with Colin Welch, Deedes found it very difficult to impose himself on the management. Modest changes were made to the layout of the leader page, but there was no radical redesign. Hartwell was reflexively hostile to innovation and there was a further problem: even the slightest reconfiguration of the pages was subject to endless negotiations with the unions, leading to exorbitant bonuses for the printers.

Deedes failed too in a cherished dream, which he never gave up in his eleven years as editor, of introducing a strip cartoon. Most mass-circulation newspapers ran one, which was usually designed to appeal to a working-class readership. Deedes thought the grey columns of the *Telegraph* could be greatly brightened by such an innovation.

Nicholas Garland was asked to help to find the right cartoon for a middle-class readership. He recommended Bill Tidy, who drew the excellent 'Fosdyke Saga' – about a northern tripe magnate – in the *Daily Mirror*. Deedes could not see the point of it and it is unlikely that Hartwell would have been remotely keen. Deedes then came up with a truly dreadful proposal – a strip cartoon called 'Stringer' – and spent inordinate amounts of time trying to see it through to fruition.

The eponymous hero of the strip was to be a young man employed on a weekly newspaper called the *Toiler*. Stringer would fulfil his journalistic assignments gathering information in the realm of local government, education and public transport. Sometimes Stringer was to become an inadvertent participant in the story rather than just an observer. A memo for circulation around the office laid down the plan. 'The idea is such that the main character is free to react to any new social/political event of particular interest without disturbing the continuity of the current story.' The intention was that many of the topics become rolling themes with the condition that 'each strip will be a self-contained joke'.

The inspiration for the item appears to have been Deedes's memory of himself as a young, inquisitive reporter on the *Morning Post*, ferreting out stories of public interest. With the best will in the world, it is hard to see how Stringer's ambles through issues such as local government or public transport could have been made to seem remotely funny to the average *Telegraph* reader. Judging by the notes Deedes kept of the planning stage, the Stringer strip cartoon seems like an item, designed by committee, for a worthy public service magazine such as *New Society*. Lord Hartwell certainly did his editor a favour by refusing to give the project his approval.

CHAPTER 18

FALL OF THE HOUSE OF BERRY

'We can't just sit around here all day drinking. Let's go
to El Vino's.'

In an age in which journalists are squeezed into purpose-built, multi-media content factories, it is difficult to imagine quite how eccentric life was at the *Telegraph* until the move to Docklands in 1987. The staff laboured behind the grandest façade in Fleet Street, built in 1930 of Portland stone with a base of grey Creetown granite. The building is hard to characterise for it conforms to no known architectural style. Some have described it as neo-Egyptian, and there are classical touches in the columns, but there is also an unmistakeable nod at Art Deco.

Designed by the architectural firm of Elcock and Sutcliffe, the staff loved the building as it managed to be distinguished but faintly modernist at the same time. In feature films that touched upon journalism 135 Fleet Street became the standard backdrop for a newspaper office. The building was commissioned by the first Lord Camrose and cost a quarter of a million pounds. It was designed to reflect the grandness of the ambitions he had for the paper as it entered the 1930s with the hope, then deemed absurd by most industry observers, of circulation hitting the one million mark. Camrose was not going to allow the little matter of the Wall Street Crash of 1929 to distract him from his vast ambitions for the *Daily Telegraph*.

In addition to the building work, Camrose spent the same again on replacing all the presses, which though just five years old were not up to producing the fatter papers needed to take on the competition. In the composing room at the back of the building, fifty-two new linotype machines, which set the text in hot metal, were installed and below them five Superspeed presses of the latest design. The new presses allowed Camrose to print papers with more pages but also, and crucially, of a narrower width than was then the standard. This was designed to appeal to the rising commuting middle classes who found the old *Telegraph* and its rivals too wide for easy reading. The narrower size gave the *Telegraph* a distinct advantage against the ailing *Morning Post*, which failed to reduce the width of its pages because it assumed that its readers lived in large country houses and would not be reduced to travelling in crowded commuter trains.*

The grandeur of the Fleet Street headquarters survived the death of Lord Camrose in 1954. Control of the company passed not to his first son, Seymour, who was a heavy drinker and otherwise unsuited to running a business, but to the younger son, Michael. A visitor who walked from the north side of Fleet Street in to the *Telegraph* building found himself in what was known, in the manner of an Oxbridge college, as 'the lodge'. The area was ruled over by commissionaires, most of them ex-servicemen, who wore white service caps and black jackets with braid. In a profile of Lord Hartwell written for *The Times*, Peregrine Worsthorne described the elaborate ritual of his arrival each morning. The commissionaires 'all leap to attention before rushing to hold the lifts for the great man, brushing aside lesser mortals like flies in paroxysms of deference that visibly cause their reluctant recipient agonies of embarrassment'.

Hartwell presided over the operation from a suite of rooms on

---

* Seventy-five years later, with its real circulation slipping below eight hundred thousand, the *Telegraph* faced another dilemma in contemplating whether to follow *The Times*, *Guardian* and *Independent* in moving to a smaller format.

the fifth floor, complete with office, study, library, dining room, kitchen and butler. There was even a small balcony garden with a narrow strip of lawn and flower beds tended by a gardener, details of which inspired the imagination of Michael Wharton, the writer of the Peter Simple column. Many former *Telegraph* hands have tried to evoke the unique atmosphere of the building, but none captured it as brilliantly as Wharton:

> If it had been possible (and there were times, later on, when I believed it was), there would have been an avenue, terraces, fountains, statues, a walled garden producing peaches and nectarines as fine as any in Fleet Street for a master's table, a lake, a deer park, pheasant coverts, a home-farm and a prospect of rolling, fertile countryside, most of it in the possession of the family.

Fleet Street was generally an eccentric sort of locale, but the *Telegraph* was much the most peculiar newspaper office. Sue Davey first worked for the paper as a teenaged temp before returning, twenty years later, to become the editor's secretary in 1981. She found that in her absence neither the office nor the personnel had really changed at all – the middle-aged men she remembered had become old men, greyer and stooped. She was greeted, after her long stretch away, during which she had borne five children, as though she had just come back to her desk after popping out for a sandwich.

Most of the journalists smoked and drank heavily at lunchtime and before going home. It was regarded as perfectly acceptable to return to the office well-lunched, provided you were not entirely incapable or abusive, and could take your seat without assistance. One lunchtime in the early 1970s, Nicholas Garland, the political cartoonist, recalled Peter Paterson of the *Sunday Telegraph* purposefully banging the table in the Cheshire Cheese pub, and declaring solemnly: 'We can't just sit around here all day drinking. Let's go to El Vino's.' Around this time, Garland recalled, he went one afternoon in to a writers' room on the *Sunday Telegraph* to discover four reporters sitting at their desks, all fast asleep, with half-completed expense sheets in their typewriters. Alan Watkins, who spoke with some authority on the matter, said that the entire Fleet Street ship, 'anchored beside the Thames between the Law Courts and St Paul's, floated on a sea of alcohol'.

Every newspaper had its pub. The *Mirror* pub was the White Hart in Fetter Lane, known to staff as the Stab in the Back, or just the Stab, because of its well-deserved reputation as a location for journalistic duplicity. The *Express* pub was the Red Lion in Poppins Court, a tiny alley running north of Fleet Street, and so the pub was inevitably known as Poppins. The *Guardian* journalists gathered at the Clachan, where Fleet Street's most politicised journalists quietly supped half pints of bitter and behaved in an exemplary manner, looking, as one observer put it, so sedate that they might have been *Telegraph* readers.

The real action, and reliably poor behaviour, was to be found at the King & Keys, a vile bear-bit of a pub where *Telegraph* man was to be found getting sloshed under the watchful stare of the Irish landlord, who, according to regulars, claimed to have served with the IRA. Lunchtime drinking tended to be steady rather than intense: in those days few pubs served drinkable wine so most journalists chose beer and a minority drank spirits. Deedes would often go down and have a couple of pints, rarely more. The evenings would be different, when the drinking would become more manic and violence would occasionally break out.

As Wharton explained, most journalists on the tabloid newspapers took the train home after work to places like Oxshott or Esher while *Telegraph* staff, having finished their sober reports for their middle-class readers, would get riotously drunk at the King & Keys. The resident villain of the pub was Michael Hilton,* a foreign leader writer who, when sober, conformed to the *Telegraph* reader's notion of a *Telegraph* writer. Inside the office he was a cultured and urbane man, who rarely ventured out without his neatly furled

---

* Wharton discreetly hid Hilton's identity behind the pseudonym Philip Weston.

umbrella and who could pronounce with authority on any international crisis. But, after moving next door to the King & Keys and consuming a certain amount of whisky, he would, in Wharton's account, suddenly 'go critical' and become terrifyingly abusive, picking on his victim's weak spot from his stool by the bar. He would constantly goad the printers who frequented the King & Keys, trying to provoke them into violence. They rarely rose to the bait, but once he achieved a victory of sorts by inciting a hefty blonde reporter to take a swipe at him with her handbag, knocking him clean off his bar stool.

Like many serious drinkers, he was a stickler for what he regarded as correct pub etiquette. One evening Maurice Green made a rare appearance just after Hilton had gone critical. Hilton, somehow feeling patronised that an amateur drinker should have come inside the pub to socialise with proper drinkers such as himself, spat at Green to 'get back to your gentleman's club!' Green, who might have organised for Hilton to be sacked or at least reprimanded, simply ignored him.

Peregrine Worsthorne, when he was deputy editor of the *Sunday Telegraph*, handled the monstering he received on loudly ordering himself a whisky less successfully. Hilton let rip, so venomously that Claudie, Worsthorne's wife, had to interpose herself between them, fearing physical violence. Hilton yelled a cruel insult that touched upon Worsthorne's slightly showy demeanour. 'You're a phoney, you're a hollow man! You're a tinsel king on a cardboard throne!' Tears of humiliation flowed down Worsthorne's cheeks. As Claudie, who was French and had a Deedesian capacity for mangling the English idiom, later put it: 'Poor Perry, he was crying cats and dogs.'*

The King & Keys was a magnet for all sorts of chancers and

---

* Worsthorne maintained his endearing habit of involuntary blubbing into old age. At the end of an intense interview with the author in 2006 about Bill Deedes's failure to stand up to Lord Hartwell, Worsthorne abruptly burst into tears. His embarrassment increased when his second wife, Lucinda Lambton, came into their drawing-room at that moment, laughing uproariously at 'soppy old Perry'.

low lifers who wanted to mingle with the most eccentric and bibulous journalists in Fleet Street. On one occasion, a fully grown lioness was walked into the bar on a lead as part of a public relations stunt. She nuzzled the crotch of a printer by the bar and caused general nervous merriment before the landlord announced that she was barred. The beast was then walked next door into the office of the *Telegraph*, at which point the general manager, Hugh Lawson, called the police.

On another evening in the late 1970s there was a commotion in the King & Keys when Christine Keeler was spotted at the bar. 'Bill Deedes, the *Telegraph* editor, was with her at the time, and they were deep in conversation,' Dick Towers, a printer and pub regular, recalled many years later. 'I must say that she caused quite a stir.' Deedes claimed to have no recollection of the incident, but that might have been because he feared that John Profumo, who was then still alive, would have regarded Deedes's socialising with the woman as an act of disloyalty.

Fighting was frowned upon, but not formally disciplined. Perhaps the most memorable punch-up of the 1970s started in the newsroom between a reporter and the estates correspondent, John Armstrong. It was an unusual contest in that Armstrong had lost both hands and an eye to a grenade during the war, but he did not let this get in the way of his drinking, or his skirmishing when drunk. As punches were thrown the bemused news editor called out, 'Shouldn't someone be doing something about this?' at which point Paul Hill, then a junior clerical assistant on the news desk, pulled them apart.

Armstrong's multiple disabilities did not spare him from Hilton's invective in the King & Keys. Having gone critical one night, Hilton began jeering: 'If I were you I'd go home and cut my throat, except you couldn't, could you?' Armstrong took the abuse better than Worsthorne had; Hilton was disappointed if he had hoped to start another fight or make Armstrong cry.

Fun as it was at the King & Keys, there was work to be done at the *Telegraph* headquarters. For the first couple of years of his editorship Deedes styled himself as an energetic moderniser and was constantly talking to colleagues about proposed innovations. But when reality intruded, and he realised that the twin forces of reaction in the shape of the print unions and Lord Hartwell were insurmountable, he settled in to a more easy routine. His working days were long, but they were certainly not a grind, and Deedes appeared to see his primary role as spreading a little sunshine around the fusty, smoke-filled corridors of 135 Fleet Street.

Deedes no longer had his room on the top floor of 7 Eaton Terrace and so would commute daily back and forth from Aldington unless there was a late event to keep him in London overnight, when he might stay at the Carlton Club. He would drift into the office at around eleven o'clock, in summer always bearing a bunch of flowers he had cut from the garden that morning. His secretary would put them in water as Deedes eased his way into his working day.

Until lunch he would do his correspondence, which would frequently involve answering a memo from the proprietor about lack of rigour in a leader or a solecism in a caption in the Peterborough column. Any mangling of a title – military or otherwise – would guarantee a particularly stern rebuke from the fifth floor.* Deedes had no formal role at news conference, which was taken by Peter Eastwood. He would be briefed by Eastwood or the news editor about the main news developments so that he could make provision for subjects for leaders, but otherwise he had no influence over home or foreign news.

Most days Deedes would have lunch with a politician or some other sort of public figure. Always abstemious with company funds, he favoured simple, unflashy restaurants, his clear favourite being Paradiso e Inferno. Deedes frequented Paradiso

---

* During his later editorship, Charles Moore's innate good humour in conference could be demolished by a falsely rendered title. The news editor learned to dread the rebuke which went along the lines of: 'The woman we called Lady Jane Smith on page one this morning was not, last time I checked, the daughter of an earl.'

right through to his final visits to London in the first years of the new millennium, and he always had the same basement booth in the corner, where lunches with Ian Smith of old Rhodesia and Trevor McDonald, the newsreader, were commemorated in framed photographs. Deedes would start with a large pink gin, which the waiter would bring, unbidden, to the table as he sat down. At the end of the lunch he would simply sign the bill that was presented to him and he would then settle his account with the manager monthly by cheque.

Most Fleet Street editors had drivers, but it would not have occurred to Deedes to ask for one, and he only rarely took taxis. Around town he would usually walk, or take the bus if he was in a hurry. If he didn't have a lunch he would go down to the King & Keys for a couple of pints and a sandwich. Even those members of staff who cursed his failure to stand up to Peter Eastwood or Lord Hartwell were impressed by his lack of stuffiness. There was nothing affected about Deedes drinking pints with reporters in one of the shabbiest pubs in London: he was staying true to the habit he acquired in 1931 at the White Swan, where the *Morning Post* reporters would gather at lunchtime. For Deedes, gossiping about politics or the trade of journalism with a pint in his hand was more fun than sipping wine with the great and the good in a St James's club.

After lunch, Deedes's main responsibility was to take leader conference, which was set at the civilised hour of a quarter to four so that leader writers did not need to gulp their claret at the end of lunch 'with contacts'. A leader-writing job on the *Telegraph* guaranteed a splendidly indulgent working life. There was no expectation that a leader writer would appear in the office before lunch. He could 'work from home' in the morning, enjoy a good long lunch at the company's expense with a diplomat or girl-friend then potter into the office. As there were no fewer than eight leader writers, and only three leaders of some 330 words each needed to be produced each day, it was quite possible to get away with a couple of leaders a week without being regarded as a conspicuous slacker. Stephen Glover, who could not believe his luck when he secured a leader-writing berth under the benign Deedes regime, recalled his time with great fondness but later conceded: 'The *Telegraph* of those days was a monument to laziness and general shirking.'

Deedes would preside over the meetings, which were leisurely and good-natured, and generally lasted between forty-five minutes and an hour. Though the atmosphere was thick with cigarette smoke and the whiff of lunchtime wine, the quality of debate was often high. The *Daily Telegraph* then boasted several serious Conservative thinkers, including Peter Utley, Colin Welch, Frank Johnson and John O'Sullivan. Some days Deedes would begin the conference with a burst of ideological fervour. On one occasion he had been enraged to hear of a 'loony-left' scheme of the Greater London Council to introduce parking fees for private motorists. 'Right Colin,' he barked at Welch as he walked into leader conference, 'get your pads on. We'll go for these Socialists.' Welch paused quizzically before replying: 'But Bill, don't you remember that at the *Telegraph* we firmly believe in charging for services?'

The leader writers who were selected to write would frequently leave the meeting confused about the line that had been agreed. Often a second, unofficial caucus would be convened in Peter Utley's room. As he was blind, he had his own secretary to read him the papers, buy his cigarettes and escort him to the King & Keys. Over the years he had a succession of assistants – always young and invariably so pretty that colleagues doubted he was truly blind – who would make tea while the leader writers sat beside him imparting wisdom. He was regarded as the final arbiter of what the line should be or, failing that, which line might be adopted without causing Hartwell palpitations and serious consequences for Deedes the following day.

At shortly after six each evening Deedes would pick up the house phone directly connecting his desk to the proprietor's and say, 'Are you free if I come up now?' Hartwell would reply:

'Would you?' And Deedes would bound up the stairs to see the master. He would not usually take the leaders with him because they were still being banged out on the manual typewriters below. But he would brief Hartwell closely on what was being prepared and if Hartwell objected violently changes would be ordered, either while the leader was on the typewriter, or later when it was being sub-edited.

In the early evening, politicians and diplomats were encouraged to drop by and invariably found the editor's drinks cabinet was open. A typical visit came from a rather sour Ian Smith who was in London for the Lancaster House negotiations in September 1979, four months after the Thatcher landslide in the general election. Deedes marshalled a convivial gathering and broke out the Famous Grouse.

In a diary note Deedes recorded the sympathy he felt for Smith: 'An object lesson in following with your heart what other people's reasoning tells you to resist. Tenacity. Yet accepting the pressures . . . A country surrounded by failures being pushed by HMG into conditions which leads to Rhodesia joining them. There's the bitterness. No mention of – yet clearly felt – the disappointment that Tories had failed to live up to their promises – and were no better than the rest.'

The meeting came about because, on a visit to Salisbury a few weeks before, Deedes had dropped Smith a private note suggesting he come to the *Telegraph* while he was in London for 'an hour among friends'. Smith took him up on the offer, and when he dropped by at 135 Fleet Street for some relief from Lord Carrington and the Foreign Office mandarins he found that he was indeed among friends. In the editor's office Smith was surrounded by men who saw African politics the same way as he did, and just as William Deedes, MP, had done in the 1960s when he sought to subvert the cross-party efforts to impose racial reforms on the white rulers of Rhodesia.

Lord Hartwell would remonstrate with his editors when they showed too much enthusiasm for Thatcherite economic policies, but he was happy with Deedes's line on white Africa. Deedes was sensitive to any public speculation about the limits of his authority as editor, on this or indeed any issue. In January 1981 *The Economist* wrote about Fleet Street's labour problems and Rupert Murdoch's prospects of taming the print unions after a strike at *The Times* which had closed it for a year. The lengthy article made a passing reference to the extent to which Murdoch meddled in the editorial outlooks of his British newspapers, noting that the opinion columns remained pleasingly free of proprietorial pressure, 'unlike, for instance, those of the *Daily Telegraph*'.

It is not clear whether Deedes acted of his own volition or under instruction from Lord Hartwell, but he immediately fired off a 'personal and private' letter to Andrew Knight, the editor of *The Economist*, hoping he would not mind his 'dropping a private line of reproach to you for the rather flip reference to ourselves'. Deedes insisted he could not 'recall a single editorial ordered by, altered by, or subsequently condemned by our proprietor, Lord Hartwell'.

As Deedes knew full well, this was a blatant untruth. Had he had the courage of his private assertion and written the letter to Knight for publication, its appearance would have occasioned gales of laughter within 135 Fleet Street. As Knight pointed out gently in his hand-written reply, Hartwell did not disguise the fact that he was ultimately in charge of the paper, listing himself in *Who's Who* as 'chairman and editor-in-chief of the Daily Telegraph'.

Though Deedes might on occasion have been accused of shading the truth, particularly about how he advanced his political or journalistic career at important junctures, this is one of the few occasions on which he can be seen to have told a straight lie. Deedes's files contained many memos from the fifth floor complaining about leaders. Hartwell was allergic to straight up and down monetarist leaders, many of which were written by Alfred Sherman, whose unpopularity upstairs was compounded by his frequent demands for increases in his retainer.* At other times Hartwell would complain about sloppy thinking, such as in his memo to Deedes dated 2 May 1980 complaining that that morning's leader on trade union reform was 'disappointingly muddled'. Hartwell kept a particularly close eye on any leader about the unions for fear of retaliation from the all-powerful printers. It may be that Deedes wrote the letter to Knight simply so he could subsequently tell Hartwell that he had dealt with the issue and nailed 'the lie', which both of them, in fact, knew to be true.

The Falklands crisis was to prove another test for the leader-writing college. The angry young members of the circle – Matthew Symonds, Stephen Glover and Charles Moore, none of whom had heard a shot fired in anger – were gung-ho. But when the Argentinians invaded on 2 April 1982, Deedes was initially flummoxed at that afternoon's leader conference. 'It's Suez all over again,' he told his young leader-writers, and his immediate assumption was that the islands were lost and that it would be folly to try to retrieve them. For Deedes, the idea of a worthless, far-flung colonial possession slipping out of Britain's hands conformed to his declinist outlook. There was another factor at play: one of Lord Hartwell's daughters was married to an Argentinian, and the proprietor was urging a conciliatory approach.

For a while this view seemed to prevail, but the Tory forces in the leader-writing college rallied and found their voice. The next day's main leader was a restrained but firm reflection on the feasibility of ejecting the invaders. 'The difficulties of mounting military action to evict the Argentinians would be formidable, but not insuperable,' the *Telegraph* argued. From that moment onwards, Deedes had his misgivings about Margaret Thatcher's determination to wrest the islands back, but he left most of the leaders to a clever young Tory, Charles Moore, who was sufficiently self-confident

---

* These letters to Deedes were ingeniously phrased, lamenting how 'inflation caused by the Government's failure to observe our advice' had once again eroded his earnings from the *Telegraph*. Hartwell, a Keynesian, would have been even less sympathetic to his argument than was Deedes.

not to swerve from his instinct that recapturing the Falklands was an essential part of Britain's revival from her post-war malaise.

Five years later, as Hartwell was losing control of the *Telegraph*, Deedes sent him a memo saying that he wanted to run a leader telling readers what was happening to their newspaper. He attached a draft. Hartwell ordered him to strike out two sentences that he disliked but passed Deedes's final paragraph, which ran as follows:

> And since Lord Hartwell does not interfere with the editorial policies of his newspapers, we are free to add these few words more. For 58 years we have been in the hands of a family who have thought it more important to run a newspaper honourably than profitably. We salute that.

Deedes's life as editor was on the whole congenial and extremely social. Denis Thatcher was a frequent visitor to the office though, according to Sue Davey, his loyal secretary who monitored the socialising from her desk in an ante room, Deedes occasionally found him heavy going and would often seem exhausted after his visits.

Wildcat strikes by the printers were so frequent that Deedes often stayed in the office until the presses were rolling with the first edition at around half-past nine. Sue Davey recalled that dealing with the unions probably took up more time than anything else during his editorship. This was also an era of protracted strikes on the railways, which could have disastrous consequences for newspapers as the distribution network was based on rail. It also meant inconvenience for millions of office workers, including Deedes, who lived outside London. Most national newspaper editors who lived out of town stayed at their club, or arranged for emergency taxi cover to get them home at night. Deedes, by contrast, would generally lodge with Sue Davey at her family home in Islington.

Davey, her husband and their five children greatly enjoyed

these emergency stays. Deedes slotted comfortably into Davey family life, was a model house guest, entirely undemanding, and delightful with her children. As Davey recalled, he never cursed the railway unions, partly, she suspected, because when he stayed in Islington, 'he seemed almost to be having a holiday from his own family'. This interpretation would not have surprised Deedes's own children, who had often observed how their father seemed to have more time for children who were not his own. And as they had seen over the years, even if he was in his own home he would soon be heading off to Littlestone Golf Club.

CHAPTER 19

GIN AND GOLF

*'Bill certainly did not invent Thatcherism, but he acted as a
sort of impresario.'*

Margaret Thatcher's triumph in the 1979 general election
brought to life the second great comic creation of the twentieth century for which Deedes could claim to be the inspiration.
Deedes was only the partial model for William Boot, though his
quarter-ton of luggage certainly inspired Evelyn Waugh's imagination. With the 'Dear Bill' letters, the most popular feature in
Private Eye during the years the Thatchers were in Downing
Street, there was no dispute: though a friend called Bill was the
recipient of the fictional letters, their writer, Denis, was in fact
modelled directly on Deedes.

'No one knew anything at all about Denis Thatcher when he
arrived in Downing Street,' explained Richard Ingrams, who collaborated on the feature with John Wells. 'So we just wrote the
letters as we imagined Bill Deedes would have written them.'

Ingrams first met Bill and Hilary in the 1970s when they went to
stay with their son Jeremy and his wife, Anna, in Berkshire. Ingrams
was a neighbour of Jeremy's and came to be fascinated by the
slightly rakish, suburban man of Kent aspect of Bill's personality:
the member in his element at the nineteenth hole at Littlestone in a
pair of loud check trousers, pink gin in hand. Ingrams knew well

that that was only one small part of Deedes's make-up, and that he was just as much the proud scion of one of Kent's grandest families and a man who would certainly have recoiled from anyone who might have been tempted to slap him on the shoulder and ask: 'How's tricks, squire?' But, for comic effect, Ingrams and Wells zeroed in on the Kent commuter with a rolled up copy of the *Daily Telegraph*, even if in his case he happened to edit the paper as well as read it on the train up to town from Ashford.

The inaugural 'Dear Bill' letter appeared on 15 May 1979, within days of the Conservative election victory, and the feature immediately found its voice. Denis laments how Bill, Monty and the Major would be enjoying pre-match snifters without a care in the world while he had been ordered by 'M' to go out and hire the 'full kit' for the State Opening of Parliament.

'The staff at Moss Bros. all appear to be gyppos these days, and there was a bit of a communication problem,' Denis complained. Though Wells and Ingrams could not have known it at this point – no one knew *anything* about Denis Thatcher – that voice is much closer to Denis than to the real Bill. Deedes never used racial epithets, and he most certainly would not have been seen dead in Moss Bros.

Wells and Ingrams did not realise how gravely they had under-estimated Denis Thatcher's political incorrectness until a party was thrown in Downing Street for the cast of *Anyone for Denis?*, a stage play that had spun off from the *Dear Bill* column in 1981. The party was preceded by a special charity performance of the show, the proceeds from which went to the Stoke Mandeville hospital. The idea was to show that Margaret Thatcher had a sense of humour, but it was a tense occasion and Tim Bell, her public relations adviser, later described it as one of the greatest mistakes of his life. Thatcher told Deedes that the director had asked her if she would attend the gala performance in the same outfit as Angela Thorne, the actress playing her on stage. 'Not likely,' she told Deedes, adding she would be wearing 'the first thing that comes off the peg'.

After the Thatchers had suffered through the show they faced the further ordeal of throwing open 10 Downing Street for the cast. As the party got going and the gin flowed, Denis approached Nick Farrell, who had played a plain-clothes policeman in the play, apparently under the misapprehension that he was a real police officer. Denis expressed his admiration for 'you people', before adding his own analysis of the recent racial riots which had broken out in some English cities: 'You get fuzzy wuzzies going on the rampage down in Brixton, you people sort it out in no time at all, but have you noticed one thing: when peace is restored there are no television cameras in sight. I'll tell you why – because the media are closet pinkoes.'

John Wells witnessed this exchange, and was delighted to find that he and Ingrams had uncannily captured the personality of their author. As the world came to learn a little bit more about the real Denis, the letter writer became more closely modelled on him and less on the partial picture of Deedes. Ingrams maintained that they appropriated 'Denis's' distinctive words for a drink – 'sharpener', 'tincture', 'snort' – from Jeremy Deedes who, Ingrams maintained, used them in his normal conversation.

To some, however, Bill and Denis were interchangeable. Deedes had a bizarre conversation with a fellow guest during a Downing Street dinner for the New Zealand Prime Minister, held by mischance on a critical night during the Falklands campaign. A stately New Zealand woman approached Deedes and touched him on the hand. 'I do wish you well; I do feel for your burden,' she told him soothingly. 'Presumably mistaken for Denis,' Deedes recorded in his diary.

The 'Dear Bill' letters were a great boon to both men. Deedes was granted a new burst of celebrity, which proved to be even more fun than serving as the supposed model for William Boot. That the editor of the *Daily Telegraph* featured, albeit fictitiously, in *Private Eye* did something to puncture the paper's reputation for stuffiness. Crucially, so far as Deedes was concerned, Lord Hartwell did not object, probably because he knew there was nothing his editor could have done about it but also perhaps because he was not as staid as he seemed to others. The measure of Deedes's pleasure in being part of the *Private Eye* joke is that he called his autobiography *Dear Bill.**

For Margaret and Denis Thatcher the letters were heaven-sent, for they portrayed Denis as a harmless idiot. As the male spouse of the country's first female Prime Minister, Denis might in other circumstances have been portrayed in the press as the real power in Downing Street. The notion that Denis would be incapable of influencing his wife became all the more important when Margaret Thatcher's resistance to sanctions against apartheid South Africa became a divisive political issue in the mid-1980s.

Denis thought white South Africa was, as he put it, 'God's own country' and was particularly enraged at any suggestion that 'pinkoes' should be allowed to deny the Afrikaners the opportunity to show their skills on foreign rugby fields. Denis was an accomplished rugby referee and was strongly opposed to the international campaign to cut all sporting ties with South Africa. Thus it was far better for all concerned if Denis were to be regarded as a drunken golf club fool rather than a steely Conservative whispering pro-Afrikaner sentiments in his wife's ear.

According to Carol Thatcher, Denis grew into his fictional persona and began to play up to the eccentric image he had been given. At one charity luncheon a fellow guest asked him how he spent his days. Rather than give a standard answer about keeping busy or supporting his wife, he replied: 'Well, when I'm not completely pissed I like to play a lot of golf.'

Because of the fictional correspondence, most people assumed that Bill Deedes and Denis Thatcher were long-standing and extremely close friends, but that was not really the case. Both men were formal, somewhat distant from their children, scrupulously

* His initial preference as a title had been *Is There Much More of This to Come?*, the dispiriting query from the *Telegraph* copy-takers, whose job in the pre-laptop age was to take down correspondents' copy over the telephone.

well-mannered and kindly to others. Their lives were rigidly compartmentalised, so professional friendships and acquaintanceships
were conducted outside the realm of the family. Both men were
intolerant of unpunctuality in others or themselves, and believed
that thank you letters should be written in fountain pen, and
promptly. Both worked hard, were self-disciplined and physically
active. Their real-life letters to each other were affectionate, but
not chatty or gossipy. Only rarely did they stray off the subjects of
golf or politics: there was no talk of their families, no hint of any
true intimacy.

Denis Thatcher was certainly more right-wing than Deedes,
who would only pretend to hate the BBC for harbouring
'pinkoes'. Thatcher thought Africa was full of savages and klep-
tomaniacs; Deedes never believed it was beyond redemption,
though it was undoubtedly true that he was generally keener to
make the acquaintance of Africans south of the equator than in
Ashford town centre.

Carol Thatcher was clear that Bill had been a crucial counsel to
her father when he suddenly found himself in the media spotlight
in 1975. As a journalist and former Cabinet minister, Deedes was
ideally placed to offer advice, which he did freely and which
Denis accepted without question. Not that Carol saw very much
of Deedes at this point. Her father's golfing pals and business
associates were remote figures to her: 'My mother didn't bring
politics home, and nor did my father bring his social or working
life home.'

Deedes and Denis Thatcher had met for the first time at a party
in Harley Street in the early 1950s, but did not see much of each
other until Denis scaled down his working life as his wife's political career blossomed. They played golf and Denis would
frequently write to Deedes on matters of importance. Typical of
the letters was one from October 1978, in which Denis congratulated Bill on his robust put-down of a BBC radio interviewer
earlier that morning: 'What an arrogant s.o.b. he is and how
charmingly you told him so.'

Bill's first contact with Margaret predated her marriage to Denis, and was during a weekend candidates' conference for young party thrusters in 1947 or 1948, during his unimpressive early months as prospective Conservative candidate. Deedes had been contrasted unfavourably to the young Margaret Roberts.

He had kept in vague touch with her while he was still in the Commons, but he was certainly not that friendly with Margaret, partly because he was never in any sense a Thatcherite. He remembered that, on one occasion when she was Education Secretary, Edward Heath had complained to him that she was a 'chatterbox'. When she unseated Heath as party leader in 1975 Bill did, however, do her a good turn by volunteering the services of a young Peterborough journalist, Richard Ryder, to run her office. After a brief interview with Airey Neave, Ryder was offered the full-time job, eventually becoming an MP and Chief Whip.

Though Thatcher had enthusiastic backers at the *Telegraph*, Ryder later recalled that in the 1970s politicians and journalists were not in each other's pockets as they were to be a generation later. Occasionally a couple of the leader writers would go to see her at her Commons office; Lord Ryder (as he later became) thought she might have visited the *Telegraph* two or three times between 1975 and 1979, but certainly no more frequently than that. Deedes preferred to keep Thatcher at arm's length: he was prepared to do her favours but he thought that the more useful way of doing so was to keep Denis amused on the golf course, and he was aware that Lord and Lady Hartwell were never entirely reconciled to Margaret Thatcher.

Lady Hartwell was particularly contemptuous of Thatcher, and would say to Deedes, 'I do wish you would tell that Prime Minister of yours . . .' Desperate to improve relations, Deedes rang Ryder and arranged for the Hartwells to be invited to Chequers for lunch. It was not a success for, as Lady Hartwell subsequently reported back to Deedes, Lord Hartwell's conversation with the Prime Minister was restricted to her asking him, 'Would you care to wash your hands before lunch?'

Richard Ryder thought Deedes was an important figure in Margaret Thatcher's ascent to power, despite Deedes's own ideological misgivings. 'Bill certainly did not invent Thatcherism, but he acted as a sort of impresario,' he explained. To Ryder, Deedes was no political thinker of any note but he thought he was a good editor in the way that Mike Brearley had been a good England cricket captain: Deedes was a steadying influence on Conservatism at a time of wrenching ideological shifts and he gave prototype Thatcherites at the *Telegraph*, such as Frank Johnson and John O'Sullivan, a relatively free rein.

Deedes rarely intervened directly with Margaret Thatcher. Instead, he lunched regularly with Michael Alison, her parliamentary private secretary, who kept him informed of the current thinking inside Downing Street. His involvements tended to be to offer support at times of crisis or stress.

For instance, when in January 1985 Oxford University dons voted against awarding an honorary degree to Margaret Thatcher, a graduate of Somerville College, she and Denis were deeply wounded. Deedes, hearing of their dismay, immediately telephoned to offer his sympathy. Denis wrote to him, enclosing a copy of a bitter letter he had written to Lord Blake, provost of The Queen's College and a Tory historian, the tone of which was all the more remarkable given Blake's devotion to the Conservative cause. 'There cannot be an honourable man in your University that cannot be ashamed. You have diminished yourselves. Sincerely Denis.' To Bill, Denis wrote in bitter gratitude for his support, 'Why anybody takes this terrible job and lives in this awful atmosphere only our God knows. I literally wept. Bless you, Denis.'

Deedes replied the next day, 30 January, assuring Denis that he shared their distress. 'Oxford, alas, is no longer the sort of place where Raymond Asquith took Greats, though she cultivates that illusion and we unwisely cherish it . . . She no longer ameliorates the ills of our society, but simply reflects them; indeed, because of the romantic clouds with which we have enveloped her, magnifies them.' He finishes by apologising for the typed letter, 'but when I am cross my writing wobbles'. The next month Deedes rallied again, answering a request to help draft a speech for Thatcher's address to a joint session of the US Congress. She was to be the first British Prime Minister to be so honoured since Winston Churchill thirty-three years earlier and she was understandably anxious. Michael Alison had asked for just a 'framework of ideas', but Deedes set about the project with gusto and provided a full draft, complete with astute historical references.

Thatcher's speech, on 20 February 1985, made for one of the greatest days of her premiership, and her rapturous reception gave symbolic force to her own special relationship with Ronald Reagan. As well as a standing ovation as she arrived and left the chamber of the House of Representatives, her speech was inter-rupted by twenty-five bursts of applause. *The Times* splashed the next day on the speech, under the headline: 'Triumph for Thatcher's oratory in Congress.' The paper's correspondent in Washington, Nicholas Ashford, did not try to conceal his admiration for her performance. His dispatch began: 'Mrs Margaret Thatcher con-quered the American Congress yesterday with a speech which was Churchillian in tone, Reaganite in its rhetorical flourishes and which contained a message of strength, freedom and economic regeneration that was very much her own.'

Deedes had compared Reagan in his demand for funding for the 'Star Wars' missile defence shield to those men, like Churchill, who had argued for strong defence against the appeasers of the 1930s. 'The war of 1939 was not caused by an arms race,' Thatcher told Congress in Deedes's words. 'It sprang from a tyrant's belief that other countries lacked the means and the will to resist him.'

Two days later, on her return to Downing Street, she wrote to Deedes thanking him for his draft speech. 'As you will have seen, I used it extensively and indeed it set the whole tone for the speech. The language was marvellous and a dream to deliver.' Though like her husband she was a stickler for thank-you letters,

Margaret Thatcher was surprisingly ungenerous towards Deedes in her autobiography. In two volumes, he merited a single indexed reference, recording his willingness to let Richard Ryder leave the *Telegraph* in 1975 to run her office.

Denis, however, felt profoundly in Deedes's debt for what he did for him and for Margaret. He told his daughter that he regarded Deedes as 'one of the great men I have met . . . an educated man, a gentleman with standards, a first class companion and a wonderful raconteur'. Then he added, 'I love him like a brother.' The latter point would have come as a shock to Deedes because that was certainly not the tone of their conversations, or of their letters to each other.

Deedes said to Carol Thatcher of his travels with her father, 'Sometimes he would open up his mind, but never his heart,' which was something that could equally have been said of Deedes. It is easy to imagine how a man of Thatcher's generation and general disposition would have found it easier to tell his daughter of his love for another man than to convey that emotion to the man himself. But perhaps there is a further factor: Deedes never showed a great gift for friendship, especially with men. He did not maintain any close friends from school, or from the *Morning Post*, and he lost close touch with his fellow officers after the war. The people he surrounded himself with tended to be acquaintances and office colleagues, relationships that were the result of circumstance rather than true friendship. In later life he probably saw more of Lord Aldington than anyone else of his own age, but that was principally because they lived in the same village. Rather as he failed to spend time with his own family, so he was generally unwilling to make the effort to sustain his friendships once lives diverged. Bill seemed to enjoy the idea of his friendship with Denis more than he liked actually being his friend; Denis, by contrast, was prepared to admit how much he relied upon Bill and never forgot what he thought he owed him.

Whatever the emotional ambiguities of their relationship,

Two television stars are born: WFD and Harold Macmillan making the first ever party
political broadcast in 1953. (Getty Images)

Embracing the sixties:
talking about the Beatles
with Young Conservatives,
1964.

Gin and golf: (left to right) Denis Thatcher, Ron Monk, WFD, Len Whitting.

Margaret Thatcher plays host at WFD's 'retirement' dinner at Downing Street in 1986. Conrad Black bored the other guests.

Bill Deedes

Nicholas Garland

WFD as *Telegraph* editor, drawn by Garland.

WFD files copy from Luanda, 1997.

(Ian Jones)

Courtier and hack:
at Diana's side in Angola.

(Robin Nunn/Nunn Syndication Limited)

Ministério · Comunicação Social
Centro de Imprensa Aníbal de Melo
CREDENCIAL

Nome WILLIAM H. DEEDES.
Orgão THE DAILY TELEGRAPH
Função JORNALISTA
Emitido a 11 / JAN. / 1997
Valido até 25 / JAN. / 1997

O Director

DR. OLÍMPIO DE SOUSA E SILVA

WFD's Angolan press accreditation.

On assignment covering famine in Sudan, 1991.

With Victoria Combe in Cape Province, South Africa, 1995.

WFD suffered a stroke at the end of this gruelling day in the field, reporting on the devastation after the earthquake in Gujarat, 2001. (Peter Macdiarmid)

A peer is knighted. Outside Buckingham Palace with Hilary, Lucy, and Jeremy, 1999.

In his element: WFD reporting for leader-writing duty in the *Telegraph* office, just turned ninety, 2003. (Rex Features)

'Listening to my mother crying' – return to Saltwood Castle, 2005.

Sixty years on: WFD reflecting on the graves of the young British soldiers who didn't come home. (Rex Features)

Journey's end: on his final assignment in Normandy, 2005. (Abbie Trayler-Smith)

Bill and Denis managed to have a great deal of fun together on the golf courses of Europe and America. Deedes had adored the game since he started playing after his early departure from Harrow, but with Denis there was another factor at play. Deedes felt he had a strong duty to help Denis to relax and, to him, it was almost a matter of civic responsibility to help Margaret Thatcher too. He thought that Margaret could only be happy in her office if she felt that Denis was having a decent time, hence the frenetic pace they undertook on their foreign golfing jaunts.

Their first trip was just before the Tory victory of 1979, with two other keen players, Len Whitting and Ron Monk, who were both in the building trade. The gang of four immediately established a fixed regime. Each would buy their maximum duty free allowance on the way out and they would pool the proceeds in one of their rooms, which was designated as the bar. Considerable amounts of the Scotch and gin would be taken once they were out of their golf gear.

They studiously avoided engaging Denis in political chat, sensing it was his one chance to leave all that behind. They maintained a frantic schedule of eighteen holes in the morning and another eighteen after lunch until Denis and Bill – the senior members of the group – were well into their seventies, when they cut back to nine holes after lunch. They always tried to time their departure from London to allow at least nine holes before dinner. The emphasis was on golf and tinctures; sight seeing and other distractions were frowned upon and wives were certainly not welcome.

Deedes wrote up a diary note about their week-long trip to La Manga in May 1981, just after the golf resort had gone into receivership. The hotel was chaotic, the fairways deserted and the greens uncut. But there was a bonus for four devoted golfers: a youthful Seve Ballesteros had been signed up by the new owners to establish La Manga's glory. Though the four were alarmed to find that Ballesteros drank only water with lunch they were partially reassured when they saw that one of the world's most exciting golfers was a chain smoker.

Over lunch in the barely functioning hotel restaurant, Ballesteros challenged them to a match in which he would play every shot standing on one leg. This was irresistible to Deedes, although Thatcher cried off, worried that such an encounter would attract press photographers to the course.

After a lunch of beer and toasted sandwiches, Deedes, Whitting and Monk arrived at the first tee, having already played a complete round in the morning. Deedes was thrilled to find that despite the earlier exertions, he was striking the ball well and keeping up with the Spanish master.

'Ballesteros examines my driver, points out a missing stud. He plays a shot off one leg and fires it 240 yards. Close match. All square at 8th. The 9th is 490 yards and finishes over a ravine. Ballesteros drives 310 yards, then puts a 6 iron onto the green,' Deedes recorded. 'Seldom played better golf. Beer welcome . . . Nobody else on the course. Unique experience. Ballesteros manners irreproachable. Calm, considerate. Self-confident. Slightly reserved.'

By pure good luck Deedes and his fellow travellers had engineered a round with one of the world's greatest golfers and played it out with no press attention, on an entirely deserted course that, within a few years, would become a thriving attraction for golfers from all over the world. That was a decent achievement in itself, but for Deedes to have kept his end up on his second round of the day against a legend of the game – albeit playing on one leg – just a few days short of his sixty-eighth birthday, was impressive.

Deedes was the best golfer of the four, holding his handicap at around ten. Denis was a decent player with a strange stance which made his bottom stick out when he drove: he would maintain a steady round at a handicap of about fourteen, but would often throw it away in the last few holes with bursts of erratic play. Ten years before the La Manga jaunt, Deedes had thrashed forty-four other players by carding a score of sixty-six to win the cup at Littlestone. The committee met and unanimously agreed his handicap would have to be cut by two, to eight, and Deedes was informed of this by letter. News leaked to the *Evening Standard*'s diary, prompting a writer to speculate about 'the wiry Deedes's secret' for making such a low score. The journalist tracked Deedes down to the Conservative Party conference. 'I watched Arnie Palmer putt at Wentworth and changed my system,' Deedes explained to the paper, 'and it worked.'

Denis's chronic back condition, which often forced him to cancel golf games, was a constant theme of their correspondence. Deedes would urge more rest and relaxation on the Thatchers, for Margaret was notoriously difficult to convince of the benefits of holidays. 'One thing I've discovered in later life,' Deedes wrote to Denis in one of his numerous attempts to urge rest upon them, 'is that when life gets strenuous, nature hits you first in your own weak spot.' He was anxious that they take a summer holiday before the gruelling autumn political season. 'Do try to get something in that tank before the leaf turns.'

Denis eventually had to give up golf and the treasured holidays stopped. Deedes continued to play and until he broke his femur in 2004 he began each morning by hitting at least fifty golf balls into a net at New Hayters. Deprived of their shared enthusiasm, Bill and Denis saw less of each other, though they stayed in touch and lunched regularly. The last time they were out together was at a dinner the *Telegraph* threw for Deedes's ninetieth birthday in June 2003, when they were seated next to each other at the Carlton Club.

That dinner was preceded by a drinks party for the launch of Deedes's book about Abyssinia, *At War with Waugh*, so both men, to use a Deedesian expression, had taken an 'ample sufficiency of alcohol'. As Jeremy Deedes recalled, the pair then began exchanging stories, but because both were slightly deaf they spoke loudly and at complete cross purposes before collapsing on each others' shoulders in helpless laughter. That was the last time Denis went out, and he died later that month at the age of eighty-eight.*

Deedes gave the address at his memorial service, in which he reflected on how the 'Dear Bill' letters had 'marvellously camouflaged his value to the Prime Minister [and] kept the reptiles off his tail'. Deedes then added, to tension-breaking laughter from the congregation: 'That's my profession he was kind enough to designate as reptiles!' The *Private Eye* letters, he continued, looked at 'Denis through the wrong end of the telescope. A lot more than golf and gin and funny friends went to the making of Denis Thatcher.'

Deedes, five months past his ninetieth birthday, was at his best. All his life he had been a superb speaker at formal events. This was partly because of his talent for identifying the distilled human qualities of a friend who was marrying or leaving the *Telegraph* after many years of service or who had died. But his success at such events was no fluke. He meticulously prepared his speeches, thinking hard about past associations and delving into his library for the right reference or historical parallel. Then he typed out the address in exactly the same way he had composed his political speeches, like the stanzas of a poem so he could read it easily and without staring too long at the page.

'He left something imperishable,' Deedes said in his address. 'He left us the memory of a character, a stamp of a man, straight and true, to which every father, whether soldier, man of business, sportsman or reptile might dearly wish their sons to aspire – and if possible attain.'

Once again, Margaret Thatcher found herself writing to thank Deedes. 'Your tribute and memories it brings back give us the strength of spirit to carry us forward in the way that Denis would

---

* Several of the guests remembered another strange moment that evening as Lady Aldington, Deedes's Kent neighbour, was escorted towards the lift when she spotted Lady Thatcher inside. 'I am not getting into that lift with that woman,' she exclaimed loudly, her words echoing around the Carlton Club's walls, covered in portraits of past Tory leaders.

have wanted, and I am sure that somewhere he was listening and raising a glass to cheer all that you said.'

One day towards the end of his life, Deedes began to talk about what he wanted at his funeral and memorial service. By then he was getting around the downstairs of the house only in his wheelchair and was rarely bothering to get dressed. That day he had not shaved. He was showing clear signs of weariness at surviving into extreme old age or, in Denis Thatcher's phrase, 'living in injury time'. For his memorial service he had specified St Bride's, Fleet Street, the journalists' church, but Jeremy had vetoed this on the grounds that it would not be nearly large enough. In his normal self-deprecating way, he muttered that no one could be expected to bother to turn out to see him off. Then, his light lunch finished, Deedes suddenly announced, 'I do hope that I might be granted one modest last request, that I might die early in the day so I make it through the pearly gates in time for nine holes with Denis.' And, with that, he wheeled himself back to his bedroom for his afternoon nap.

One of the difficulties in gauging the true nature of their friendship was that the relationship had been hijacked by the celebrity that the 'Dear Bill' letters brought them both. Bill was always more the showman than Denis, but both started acting into their roles because they had been firmly established in the public mind.

When Deedes said that his last wish was a celestial round of golf with Denis, he was engineering a suitably comic coda to the great national joke of their public friendship. On the face of it that seemed to be a strange priority. His second son, Julius, had died in 1970 at the age of twenty-three and his beloved sister Frances had died in 1950. Most men, contemplating their own deaths, would have thought of flesh and blood first, or if they had not they would have pretended to have done so, for form's sake if nothing else. But for Deedes, showman and connoisseur of celebrity, the joke always came first.

CHAPTER 20

BLACK DAYS

*'I see a beautiful city and a brilliant people rising
from the abyss.'*

By the early 1980s it had begun to dawn on *Telegraph* journalists and printers that the lack of management control and
the resulting industrial anarchy would eventually drive the company into receivership. The shutdown of *The Times* for most of
1979 appeared at first glance to be good news. Its absence pushed
the *Telegraph*'s circulation to new heights: the Monday to
Saturday sale breached the 1.5 million mark, a new press had to
be commissioned to print the extra copies and extortionate new
agreements were struck with the print unions to run it.

Andreas Whittam Smith, the City editor, had made a sensational suggestion at leader conference during the *Times* strike: he
said that if the *Telegraph* improved certain areas of weakness,
such as obituaries, letters and the crossword, readers might not
return to the Thunderer when it reappeared. Deedes was worried
that such behaviour might be 'off side', but agreed that it was
worth raising the matter with the chairman. Hartwell was
appalled by any suggestion of kicking a rival while he was down,
arguing that all of Fleet Street was imperilled by the print unions'
rapaciousness. But when he argued that the main titles should
stand or fall together he was on less certain ground, because in the

years ahead the respective titles made their own arrangements. Deedes reported back that Hartwell would not countenance any move against *The Times* while it was off the streets; Whittam Smith drew his own conclusions about the *Telegraph* management's prospects of surviving in a hostile market, eventually leaving to launch the *Independent* in 1986.

The *Telegraph*'s circulation boost during the *Times* strike masked some serious long-term problems, suggesting that the first Lord Camrose's magic formula, which had seen sales surge to just under the million mark on the eve of the Second World War, needed updating. The presses that had been installed by Lord Camrose were more than half a century old and though they had proved extraordinarily robust they were manifestly inadequate for the newspaper wars of the 1980s. They frequently broke down, and even when running smoothly they produced pages of utter greyness and photographic reproduction was abysmal. The presses could not print enough pages for a modern newspaper, so the *Telegraph* management found itself in the absurd position – as it was during the post-war newsprint rationing – of turning away advertising.

The key to the *Telegraph*'s circulation success had always been its canny editorial mix, based on comprehensive news coverage backed up by a cover price below its rivals. In the second half of 1978, for instance, it was selling 1,372,000 copies a day at nine pence, trouncing *The Times*, which managed just 297,000 a day at fifteen pence. The *Telegraph* was still sticking true to the Camrose strategy of low cover price and high circulation, with the assumption that vast revenues in display and classified advertising would flow to the undisputed market leader.

By the second half of 1982 circulation had dropped back to 1.3 million and continued to slide thereafter, largely because Hartwell had to plug holes in his balance sheet by raising the cover price. Within three years Hartwell had been forced to ratchet the price up to twenty-five pence, so that by 1985 it was the same price as *The Times*. By then the *Telegraph*'s circulation had glided down by another hundred thousand to 1,202,000 – not in itself disastrous – but the gap with *The Times* had narrowed alarmingly. Market-share matters as much to advertisers as headline circulation numbers, and there was no disguising that the *Telegraph* was losing ground by that measure to *The Times*, which had turned more downmarket and therefore closer to the *Telegraph* since Rupert Murdoch had bought it in 1981. Within four years *The Times*'s circulation had climbed from 282,000 to 478,000 as the *Telegraph*'s price rises and *The Times*'s more populist slant took effect. Pricing and poor printing quality were part of the problem, but the truth was that Deedes had failed in his mission to modernise the paper. Features remained skimpy and weak while news – though comprehensive – was set in dreary, tightly edited columns dripping down the page without illustration or much analysis. The paper entirely ignored issues of specific interest to women, or to young readers of either sex; *The Times* and the *Guardian* were offering better all-round packages. Most existing buyers remained loyal to the *Telegraph* but the paper was failing to recruit younger readers, so circulation drifted downwards as the older readers died.

To be fair to Hartwell, he was by no means blind to the need for innovation. His problem was that the company was no longer generating the profits it had reliably achieved since the end of the Second World War, and the main reason for this loss of profitability was the stranglehold the unions had on the running of the business.

Editorial changes were almost impossible to implement because the paper was still being printed according to pre-war procedures at the rear of 135 Fleet Street, known as 'the back of the house'. Printing a newspaper in the early 1980s was still an industrial process, and when the presses began to roll the whole building trembled. Print was set on the banks of Linotype machines and a plate would then be made of the page in lead. It was hot, unpleasant work: printer's ink is thick and noxious and molten lead is inherently dangerous. A huge and belligerent Scotsman presided over the heart of 'the print', taking a vast ladle out of the furnace and pouring the molten lead in to the ingots. It was so hot he would wear shorts and a shirt; his only protection against splashes of the scalding liquid were his metal-capped boots and full-length apron. Paul Hill, a young newsroom clerical assistant, would occasionally be sent over to the print to fetch a page proof. 'You were immediately an alien,' he recalled. 'The staff there, all of them, were suspicious and wary of any editorial staff daring to enter their domain. One rule here: never touch anything. Not a switch, nor a machine, nor a galley, nor a sheet of paper.' Any breach of this rule would be likely to trigger a union meeting to discuss the outrage, in office time, and would thus slow down that night's print run.

As the printers and compositors became more bloody-minded, the paper became fuller of literals and other howling errors. Readers wrote either to Hartwell or to Deedes to complain, and every so often they would be forced to compare notes. When the complaint arose from an editorial mistake, as opposed to a print-ing error, Hartwell could be unforgiving, firing off memos of controlled rage to Deedes. These were often about the most minor indiscretion, a slightly faulty caption on the Peterborough car-toon, or the failure to include a cross-reference to another page.

'I persuaded myself there was wisdom behind Hartwell's sharp eye for small detail. It bore some relationship to the way good commanding officers, when inspecting my company during the war, found tiny and unlikely things at fault – and then somehow conveyed to me that they reflected gravely on my fitness to com-mand.' Even given Deedes's immense capacity for forbearance, this was an indulgent reaction to a picky proprietor who was manifestly failing in his primary duty to maintain the financial health of the business.

These disturbing trends might well have been corrected but for the state of permanent warfare with the print unions. Lord Hartwell's fatal vulnerability in his dealings with the unions was his total dependence on circulation and advertising revenues from the *Telegraph* titles; there were no foreign newspapers earning cash in more congenial industrial environments, no regional British television franchises generating profits to cross-subsidise newspapers in lean times or to keep the company afloat during strikes.

The unions knew this and, armed with the knowledge that an all-out strike cost Lord Hartwell a quarter of a million pounds a day, offered no quarter in the petty, but ruinously expensive, disputes that were steadily bleeding the company dry. The battles in the late 1970s were enervating enough, but Deedes thought Hartwell was never the same after the death of his wife from cancer in 1982. Past seventy, Hartwell was still working punishing hours, driving himself back and forth in a battered Mini from his home in Cowley Street, Westminster.

The year Hartwell lost his wife was particularly bleak inside the office. Twice the unions succeeded in blackmailing the management into giving them space on a page to print a declaration in support of striking NHS staff. As Deedes wrote to Hartwell, if this trend were allowed to continue, 'we shall be on a perilous slope, which will undermine the independence of this newspaper and its editorial integrity'.

There was a special room on the third floor of 135 Fleet Street in which managers would meet the print union extortionists to try to head off wildcat disruptions. Sometimes Deedes would be drafted in to deploy his charm to save a few hundred thousand copies of that night's print run, which was imperilled by some manufactured grievance or other. More often than not, the dispute would be solved with yet another absurd one-off payment. This concession then became enshrined as 'custom and practice' and any shift from that would require further financial inducements. The grim, futile exchanges in the mediation room reminded Deedes wearily of a scene from *Journey's End*, R. C. Sherriff's play about life in the trenches in the Great War, with 'candles trembling on the table, and bottles of whisky for consolation'. Drink increasingly became the lubricant of these encounters and the solace for journalists who would frequently find their stories failed to appear due to strike action.

In the obduracy, greed and lack of sense of duty of the printers Deedes saw the same tendencies he had observed in the dockers who had impeded the loading of his riflemen's armoured vehicles in June 1944. They were the same sort of men, their status as labour aristocrats protected by closed shops until the economic forces consigned them to oblivion. In the short term they played a clever game, deploying maximum belligerence in defence of their indefensible labour privileges; in the long run, following Rupert Murdoch's breakout to Wapping, they lost everything. As they had probably known all along that the gravy train would eventually stop, they took everything they could in the meantime.

The docks and the printing works of national newspapers had another thing in common: they both used a great deal of casual labour, sometimes when it was needed, at other times when the unions said it must be used. Inevitably a man who might have been working the presses one night on the *Daily Express*, the next on the *Sunday Telegraph*, felt no great sense of loyalty or concern that the unions' antics might drive the paper to the wall.

By the mid-1980s, the top print workers had negotiated their way to £500 (an annual salary of about £26,000), putting them on a scale far above almost all the journalists on the paper. The printers' weekly pay packets were just a base: many worked such short shifts at the *Telegraph* — staying just an hour or two after clocking on – that they could go on to do casual shifts on other papers. Most of them had migrated out of the East End and lived in the Home Counties, driving large, high-performance cars. Several doubled up as minicab drivers, further increasing their incomes. Carol Thatcher, the Prime Minister's daughter who was then working in the *Telegraph*'s features department, earned £16,483 in 1985. Even Michael Wharton, one of the paper's stars, earned only £28,418. Wharton was not troubled by the erosion of his differentials: a committed reactionary, he supported the printers in their resistance to any sort of technical innovation.

One particular humiliation stung Deedes for years afterwards. During the 1984 miners' strike word was sent via the *Telegraph*'s industrial correspondent that the editor should meet union representatives to discuss the paper's coverage of the dispute. Incredibly, Deedes went along with it, even allowing Granada Television to film the discussion.

Not that the journalists showed much more loyalty to Lord Hartwell. The National Union of Journalists tightly controlled who could or could not be employed, with only a few exceptions for leader writers and well-bred young men down from university who Deedes would place on Peterborough. Otherwise, management had no free hand in who they could employ on either the editorial floors or in the production departments. The paper was being produced according to an organised form of industrial anarchy.

The company was almost killed off in November 1982 when the Society of Graphical and Allied Trades objected to the management's plan to decommission the printing press that had specifically been put on to deal with the circulation spike when *The Times* was off the streets three years earlier. Some 450 men in the machine room walked out, stopping production and costing the company £1.5 million.

Union militancy was bad enough, but sometimes the company showed itself startlingly efficient at wasting its own money. Some £250,000 was squandered on a state-of-the-art conveyor belt system to transfer the vast reels of newsprint from lorries up to the first floor of the plant on Shoe Lane, at the back of 135 Fleet Street. The exciting piece of equipment was fully built and ready to go before it was discovered that Shoe Lane was too narrow for the lorries to perform the necessary manoeuvres to load the reels, so the entire contraption had to be abandoned without moving a single reel.

When the management made gestures in futile efforts to make

the staff see sense, the goodwill was shamelessly exploited. To the great relief of all the staff large sums were committed to upgrading the subsidised staff canteen, which had become squalid. All of the plates and cutlery were replaced to reflect the more agreeable surroundings where a grilled sirloin steak with tomatoes could be bought for 45p, followed by a choice of puddings at 6p. Yet within four weeks of the new canteen's operation much of the upgraded equipment had been pilfered.

The items stolen included twenty dozen cups, thirty dozen knives and forks, twenty dozen joint plates, ten dozen ashtrays and five dozen salt and pepper pots. The company was being systematically looted, either by staff walking out of the building with canteen equipment or other printing supplies, or by the unions setting ludicrous and larcenous working restrictions. In the 1970s there was a restaurant on the sixth floor with waitress service, and a hellhole of a subsidised bar – worse even than the King & Keys – that the print unions persuaded the management to operate.

The *Daily Telegraph* and *Sunday Telegraph* made combined losses in four of the six years between 1979 and 1985. Hartwell, who was always more attentive to editorial matters than to strategic planning, failed to take action as the financial position deteriorated. As the papers drifted into structural annual loss the management committed to a £105 million modernisation plan, including new printing plants on the Isle of Dogs and in Manchester. The *Telegraph* was to move into a new age in which journalists would directly input their copy in to the main computer system. A further vast amount had to be set aside for the anticipated costs of buying the redundant print workers out of their contracts.

The financial problems were in fact much worse than those in the building feared. There had never been any proper budgets at the *Telegraph*, and expenditure was just nodded through. When accountants were retained to establish some sort of control they found three hundred more men were on the production payroll than the management knew about. In the six months to

September 1985, the company managed to lose £16 million on a turnover of £74 million.

The figures were disastrous, and Hartwell's assumption that the bankers would fund the ambitious modernisation programme proved unfounded. There was no realistic expectation that with the existing management structure the *Telegraph* would even be able to meet the interest payments. In desperation, Hartwell had to turn to a new investor to take a stake in the company to make up the shortfall. Andrew Knight, the impeccably connected editor of *The Economist*, had tipped off Conrad Black, an unknown Canadian financier who was accumulating an empire of small-town North American newspapers, that the *Telegraph* was in serious trouble. Hartwell and two of his managers flew to New York on Concorde on the morning of 28 May 1985 for a meeting with Black at an airport hotel. The meeting was friendly and informal, with no minute taken. It was agreed that Black would put ten million pounds into the company to tide it over its difficulties with its own bankers, in return for 14 per cent of the equity. The *Telegraph*'s finances were so shaky there was a risk Black might have lost it all. But as many people, including Rupert Murdoch, have since acknowledged, it was the newspaper deal of the century. Not only had Black taken a huge stake in a priceless newspaper brand for peanuts, he had inserted a fateful clause into the agreement. He told Hartwell that, in return for his investment, he would require pre-emptive rights in any issue of new shares, or any sale of new shares, should the *Telegraph* need a further injection of cash. Hartwell said, without hesitation: 'I don't think we can resist that.'

When Hartwell flew back to London later that day he may not have known, but he must surely have suspected, that he had given away his birthright. Hartwell had not told even his own sons what he was up to and, needless to say, Deedes was kept completely in the dark too. When news of the deal leaked out Deedes was in the humiliating position of being unable to answer questions from the staff about what was going on.

'I felt no resentment about his reticence; it was part of a compact an editor made with Hartwell. Having appointed you, he left you to edit the newspaper and you left him to manage his business.' In fact, neither of those assertions was quite accurate. Hartwell simply did not leave his editors to run the papers, and he certainly did not manage the business, at least in a way that would allow the newspapers to thrive in a competitive market. Deedes's position outside the loop of important information at 135 Fleet Street fuelled the general sense of an editor who was weak and treated by management with a casual indifference.

As concerns about the viability of the *Telegraph* grew, and journalists feared for their jobs, Deedes's blithe ignorance of what was going on began to cause resentment. In June 1985, Peter Utley, the joint deputy editor with Morrison Halcrow, wrote Deedes a stern letter from his home address, casting himself as the man who had become the 'receptacle of almost all the grievances and anxieties of editorial brethren'.

Utley said he could 'not remember a time when there has been so much grumbling and disaffection abroad', principally caused by management's failure to inform the staff about the true nature of the financial crisis afflicting the company and the likelihood of a change of ownership. Utley was anxious to absolve Deedes of blame for this state of affairs, though it could not be denied that his letter was, at the very least, an implicit rebuke of an editor who had failed to press management to be more forthcoming. Given that Utley had been a pillar and intellectual driving force of the paper for a generation, his deferential approach was extraordinary, demanding only of Deedes that he consider whether it 'would not be a service to the owner to bring this to his attention'.

Deedes chose precisely this moment in June 1985, just when the Conrad Black news came out, to head off to the Philippines to see Ferdinand and Imelda Marcos. The meetings made for lively copy, but some staff felt he should have been more visible around the office at a time of crisis. In December Hartwell inevitably again ran out of money and had no option but to turn to Black, who exercised his right to take full control of the company. Andrew Knight was named as chief executive, running the business on behalf of Conrad Black, who remained in Toronto determined – then, at least – not to mimic other Canadian press barons like Lords Beaverbrook and Thomson in crossing the Atlantic in pursuit of acclaim and the inevitable peerage.

After Knight had addressed all the editorial staff on 20 December, Hartwell summoned Deedes for a full briefing. The two men had discussed Deedes's retirement though no date had been set. He was seventy-two by then, and though Deedes told colleagues he was anxious to step down he proved strangely reluctant to set a date. Hartwell told Deedes – absurdly – that he would be choosing the next editors of the daily and Sunday titles and asked for his thoughts. Deedes had previously favoured Ian Ball, the long-standing New York correspondent, but Hartwell had ruled him out on the grounds that he had been out of the country too long. Hartwell then suggested Andreas Whittam Smith. 'I reply cautiously,' Deedes responded in best 'up to a point, Lord Copper' mode. Deedes did not like or trust Whittam Smith and had thought him impertinent for publicly questioning the abilities of Hartwell's managers. According to the note Deedes made of the meeting, he stressed to Hartwell that the paper must 'evolve – we don't want a revolution. AWS *is* astringent. Maybe the right card, but not a co-operator.'

Instead, Deedes suggested Charles Moore, the twenty-nine-year-old editor of the *Spectator*. Moore was clever and charming, and had impressed older hands when he cut his teeth writing leaders at the *Telegraph*. Moore's appointment would have been especially satisfactory for Deedes, as it would have required a reasonably long interregnum while young Moore learnt the ropes, meaning Deedes's retirement could respectably have been postponed for a year or two.

For Hartwell, who had lovingly nurtured his gerontocracy at 135 Fleet Street, the idea of a man under thirty editing the *Telegraph* must have been extraordinary. To his credit, Hartwell did not rule Moore out on grounds of age, nor demur when Deedes stressed the young man's suitability, emphasising the importance of what he called Moore's 'character'. Nine months earlier Deedes, with Hartwell's approval, had tried to lure Moore back from the *Spectator*, offering him a column and what he described as a 'senior post here'. Moore replied, expressing deep gratitude but pointing out that he had only been editing the *Spectator* for a year, so that to 'leave now would look – and would indeed be – very odd'. That might well have been Moore's principal consideration, but he was shrewd enough to realise that a wise journalist keeps his distance from a newspaper company that is about to expire.*

Deedes's detachment from the currents in the office became obvious at the end of 1985 when news of the imminent launch of the *Independent*† broke in the *Financial Times* a week after his discussion with Lord Hartwell. Even though the three founders, Andreas Whittam Smith, Stephen Glover and Matthew Symonds, all worked at the *Telegraph*, Deedes had known nothing of it. The triumvirate had been working on the plan since June that year.

Given how indiscreet most journalists are, it was extraordinary that Deedes did not get a whiff of it until after Christmas 1985. Nicholas Garland, the *Telegraph*'s cartoonist, had been approached about defecting to the new paper six months earlier. As well as his wife, he had told at least two friends, including Anthony Howard, the deputy editor of the *Observer*. Many people in the City must have known about it, for the founders had been sounding out investors. Sue Davey, Deedes's secretary, had known about it for some time before her boss, and said she felt awful in the run-up to Christmas with people whispering in corners about the new paper but without Deedes or Hartwell having heard about it.

---

* Moore showed equally good timing twenty years later, when he resigned as editor of the *Daily Telegraph* shortly before Conrad Black lost control of the business.

† At this point, it was not clear what the new paper was going to be called. The initial working name had been the *Nation*, and the *Independent* was not agreed until January 1986.

Bill and Hilary had spent Christmas with their son Jeremy and his family and returned to New Hayters on the day after Boxing Day. As they arrived, the phone was ringing: it was Andreas Whittam Smith, calling to find out if Deedes had read that morning's *Financial Times*. Deedes had not, so Whittam Smith read the report to him down the line, with the news that money was being raised from investors for the imminent launch of a new quality newspaper. Deedes always maintained that he never felt the slightest resentment towards the defectors. That may be so, but he must have felt embarrassment at being left in the dark, especially when Lord Hartwell and his brother Lord Camrose both rang him at home that day trying to find out what was going on. Deedes must have felt that the trio's defection to an untried new title was a vote of no confidence in the *Telegraph* for which he bore partial responsibility.

The day after the news broke, Whittam Smith went to see Hartwell to explain why he was leaving. Hartwell was courteous and asked informed questions about the break-even point of the new title; there was no rancour and Hartwell wished the new proprietor well in his endeavour. The atmosphere was much chillier when Glover and Symonds went to see Deedes to explain their decisions to leave. Deedes was not, Glover subsequently recalled, rude or hostile, but nor was he friendly or encouraging. Glover told Garland at the time that he thought Deedes might not have known how to react as at that point he had not known how Whittam Smith's interview with Hartwell had gone: 'With his subaltern's mind, Bill played it as safe as he could.'

Deedes, however, told Glover, Whittam Smith and Symonds to clear their desks immediately, which they did. Around the office the defections served to compound the sense of doom and decline. The year 1986, one of the most momentous in Fleet Street's history, began gloomily at the *Telegraph*. Knight officially took over at the beginning of February; his first action was to fire Hugh Lawson, the monocle-wearing Old Etonian managing director whom Conrad Black had regarded as a risible figure on their first meeting in New York.

From a temporary office on the fourth floor, Knight presided over Black's new empire in uneasy partnership with Hartwell, who remained in his suite one floor above, telling all who would listen that he remained editor-in-chief with his powers intact. This was a fantasy in which Knight was prepared to indulge Hartwell only briefly. John Thompson, who was sixty-five, had been talked out of retiring as editor of the *Sunday Telegraph* by Hartwell, but was now adamant that he wanted to go. At a Downing Street reception Hartwell was heard dismissing any suggestion of change, arguing that 'Bill Deedes has got many years in him yet'. The next twenty years and more proved Hartwell correct on that point, although it was plainly absurd that a man of seventy-two should remain long in the editor's chair at a time of radical change.

After two weeks in charge Knight sent out word to all managers that they were to recognise the obvious – that Hartwell was no longer in charge of the company and that they were to report directly to him. The climate at the *Telegraph* had been terrible for some time, but early in 1986 it was suddenly even more hostile. The launch of the *Independent*, set for that autumn, was a clear threat. As the three founders were *Telegraph* men it was assumed that the *Telegraph* would be worst hit of the established dailies. In the event, *The Times* and *Guardian* suffered more in circulation terms, partly because the *Independent*'s centrist political outlook did not much appeal to the *Telegraph* reader.

The other threat was from east London. *The Times*'s circulation had been creeping up ever since Rupert Murdoch had bought it in 1981, promising to double its circulation and challenge the *Telegraph*'s market dominance. Then, on 24 January 1986, Fleet Street was turned upside down and the unions routed when Murdoch moved all his editorial and production operations to a new site at Wapping. This was a sensational development: in one bound, journalists and management were handed back control of the newspaper, the cost base was transformed and, in the early years at least, there was to be much more money pumped into editorial budgets.

In the medium and long term, Murdoch's break out from the shackles of the print unions offered a great opportunity of future profitability to the *Telegraph*. But in the short term it increased the pressure, for at a stroke not only were *The Times*'s production costs slashed, but its appearance was dramatically improved as it moved from hot metal production to photocomposition. The sacked printers mounted mass pickets outside the Wapping site, but Margaret Thatcher's government made sure the police were present in sufficient force to allow the lorries to get in and out and to distribute the newspapers around the country.

Knight had at first thought he would keep Deedes and Thompson in place for a few months. He had soothingly told Deedes that he wanted 'some glue' and a sense of reassurance on the editorial floor while he sorted out the management mayhem. But as the *Telegraph*'s production howlers grew ever more appalling, and *The Times* perfected its crisper layout, the *Telegraph*'s circulation began to fall too sharply to be tolerated.

Deedes was struggling to stay on his feet under the new regime. With Hartwell, he had known exactly where he stood. He wasn't the subaltern, in Glover's unforgiving phrase, but acted more as a company commander, running his operation as efficiently as he could, and reporting back to Hartwell at Brigade HQ. With Hartwell humiliated, Deedes was lost, unsure who he should report to and indeed what to do. Morrison Halcrow, the joint deputy editor, became exasperated by Deedes's faltering behaviour. 'He used to change his mind every few days,' Halcrow muttered in exasperation. 'Now he changes it every half-hour.'

Knight decided matters could not drift and called Deedes to his office to tell him the bad news. Max Hastings, who was famous in Fleet Street for having liberated Port Stanley during the Falklands War, was to replace Deedes, and Peregrine Worsthorne, aged sixty-two, was belatedly to get his reward with the *Sunday Telegraph*. The new editors had flown in extreme secrecy to Toronto for Black to check them out, and he accepted Knight's advice on both choices. Deedes had been completely in the dark about these manoeuvres, and he was told that both changes were to be made immediately.

In his autobiography and in conversations later in life, Deedes gave the impression he was desperate to step down as editor, but this is not the recollection of those around him at the time. Sue Davey recalls Deedes returning shell-shocked from his meeting with Knight, spluttering balefully, 'They want Hastings.' He told her that he had offered to hang around in a supervisory role as his young replacement played himself in, but that Knight had dismissed that option. He was clearly hurt that he would not, as Knight had implied only a few weeks earlier, be kept around as the glue on the editorial operation. He was shocked, too, that Hastings had been appointed to succeed him without any consultation with him or Lord Hartwell. But, as Sue Davey recalled, after a few minutes of anguished observations about the state of the paper, the Deedes mask was put back on. They repaired to a Fleet Street pub – Davey could not remember which, but it was not the King & Keys – for Deedes to regroup. With a pint of beer in his hand Deedes's spirits revived. 'He started making his plans, and explaining how he would make himself useful to the new regime.' Davey remembered clearly that Deedes had no intention of walking out of Fleet Street and into a calm retirement in Kent with Hilary.

According to *Dear Bill*, Deedes had lunch that same day with Max Hastings. Hastings, however, puts the day of the lunch as his first as editor, in March. Either way, it was certainly – at Deedes's request – at Paradiso e Inferno, which Hastings found deeply unsatisfactory compared to his preferred venues, either Wiltons in Jermyn Street, or his club, Brooks's.

According to Hastings, Deedes then prescribed all the remedies he had been unable to dispense when he was in charge, itemising problems that needed urgently to be addressed and people who should immediately be sacked. 'I did rather wonder, as he confidently listed all the people who needed to be removed, why none of this had been done before I took over.'

Hastings was struck by how sanguine Deedes was in the face of the demolition of the House of Berry, which he had served unswervingly for half a century. He concluded that it must be the reaction of a man who had seen many horrors in the war; he took the news of a change of ownership in Fleet Street as 'he might have done the news of an innings defeat in a test match – the sort of little setback that is inseparable from life's rich pageant'. Deedes did not gloss over the scale of the challenge facing his replacement, warning Hastings: 'I hope it is not a poisoned chalice you are taking on, dear boy.'*

Deedes's seamless transition from editor to roving reporter and columnist was as mysterious as the way in which he had assumed the editor's chair eleven years earlier. Hastings recalled that at lunch he had simply asked Deedes to continue writing for the paper, to which Deedes had replied, by Hastings's account, 'Well, old boy, since presumably I must accept some responsibility for the mess this company has got into, it seems to me that the least I can do is to stick around and try to help us get out of it.' Then, to his utter bemusement and for the only time in his life as editor of two newspapers, Hastings found himself in a reverse negotiation as Deedes demanded a reduction in the size of the financial retainer he was to be paid, on the grounds that he was already receiving a generous pension.

Hastings knew that the legions of loyal readers must be given some reassurance of continuity as the paper was, perforce, radically changed. Keeping the distinctive W. F. Deedes byline would

---

* Hastings is making an error here common to those who attempt to recall Deedes's distinctive manner of speech. Though 'dear boy' is the sort of phrase a man of Deedes's age and background might have used, he never actually did. His preferred form of familiar address was 'old cock', or occasionally, 'mate', the latter delivered in a strange approximation of an East London accent.

serve the purpose of reassuring the elderly readers that the paper was not discarding all of the old.* Hastings had a particular dis- taste for Peter Utley's Orange views on Ulster, and it seemed unlikely that he would stay long. So it was all the more imperative that Deedes be kept on. Hastings seems to have assumed that a man in his seventies, who professed to have been waiting to retire for many years, would contribute to the paper on a freelance basis from home, spending more time with his wife and on the golf course. Deedes, of course, had other plans, which he had begun hatching over his beer with Sue Davey.

Before Deedes could re-build his career there were time- honoured Fleet Street rituals to be honoured. Deedes's last day as editor was 7 March, and drinks and sandwiches were laid on at lunchtime in the basement of the Cheshire Cheese pub. Peter Utley set the ceremony up with a hilarious impersonation of Deedes taking the leader conference. But Utley was just the warm- up act for Lord Hartwell, who was so terrified of public speaking that he had been known to pass out in advance. On this occasion he performed admirably. Given that he had just suffered the wrenching humiliation of losing his birthright and had had to watch Conrad Black move his men into his building, Hartwell's understated delivery won over the journalists crowded into the pub. 'Several times his dry humour had us laughing. It was impos- sible not to feel part of a family or gang,' said Nicholas Garland, the political cartoonist, who at the time was planning his defec- tion to the *Independent*. 'I felt more than ever that I was part of the *Telegraph* and that it was the strangest institution I'd ever joined. It has always been a home for eccentrics and oddballs and it is itself therefore an eccentric organisation. It's why every- one likes it, I suppose; no one hates the *Telegraph*.'

Hartwell presented Deedes with two leaving presents: a hand- some crystal decanter with a silver base and a travelling clock that

---

* Retaining the loyalty, and byline, of Deedes became an equal priority eighteen years later when ownership of the *Telegraph* passed into the hands of the Barclay brothers after Conrad Black's indecorous demise.

doubled up as a fob watch. Deedes mugged up his delight at the presents, making the audience laugh. He concluded by quoting Sydney Carton in *A Tale of Two Cities* – 'I see a beautiful city and a brilliant people rising from the abyss' – which some found odd, as it seemed to suggest that his and Hartwell's Fleet Street had been an abyss. His final words were: 'I wish you all well, and want you to know my heart will always be with you.' He stopped talking, put the piece of paper with his notes back in his pocket, and spoke his last words as editor to his staff: 'That's it.'

Most of those present assumed that that was effectively the end of Deedes's fifty-five-year Fleet Street career. There was widespread sympathy around the office for the rather undignified ending to his time as editor. For eleven years he had been kept in the dark by Hartwell and treated as a factotum who need not be informed of wider issues; now the new management had neglected to consult him about the choice of new editor or to give him enough time for a managed departure. Maurice Green had been granted a full seven months to prepare for his retirement and Deedes was made to wait in the wings until the moment he had wanted to depart. In the end Deedes had, to put it in Fleet Street parlance, 'got the bullet'.

Garland, writing contemporaneously in his journal about Deedes's departure at a time when he assumed the editor was leaving the scene completely, had mixed feelings. As a young man, Garland had worked as a stage manager and theatre director and saw a key part of Deedes's make-up – his theatrical side. His assessment was harsh – even as it recognised his human qualities – for it made points that others always dodged out of fondness for a man of such great charm:

> Facts don't really bother Bill too much. He is an actor and a fantasist and he always casts himself in the leading role. His favourite part is the flannelled fool, the Bertie Wooster sidekick; but in this episode he'll play a different role – probably the grizzled veteran who has seen it all before, who stayed loyal and

true, and stood his ground until the new order swept him aside. Perhaps he'll comfort himself with the thought that the day will come when his editorship will be looked back upon with yearning by the people who leave him behind now. I'm one. I have never suffered particularly at the hands of Bill's fatal unwillingness to make up his mind about anything, or his desperate need to avoid confrontation at all costs. He could not possibly have been more pleasant to work for, invariably amiable and tactful and flattering; but I have watched with a strange remote sort of gloom as the paper has wallowed and yawed and eventually driven herself on the rocks while Bill has grinned and joked and lingered at his desk.

Almost all of Garland's observations were harsh, but they were justified. He was spot on, too, when he predicted that Deedes 'would discover a way of presenting the circumstances of his departure that reflected some sort of glory on himself'. That is exactly what happened. Far from walking away from the scene of the calamity over which he had presided, he was to come back in a new incarnation and Deedes's reputation, inside and outside the paper, was to grow exponentially in the following twenty years. This last phase was to be his greatest achievement, a glittering coda to a long and mixed career in newspapers.

CHAPTER 21

REINVENTION

*'With his instinctive distaste for confrontation, some of
Bill's utterances for the paper could be construed to mean
whatever best suited the reader.'*

Deedes protested to friends that he was to be a reluctant participant, but it was inevitable that Margaret Thatcher would throw a grand retirement dinner for him in Downing Street. There, for the first time, Deedes met Conrad Black, the still-mysterious Canadian proprietor who had usurped Lord Hartwell. Black greeted the departing editor with the words, 'Well, I guess it is hail and farewell,' reflecting a not unreasonable assumption that the seventy-two-year-old would be quitting the scene.

Deedes, who was already planning his new *Telegraph* incarnation and his comeback as a roving reporter, was strangely offended by this entirely unintended insult. For years afterwards he would tell colleagues about Black's greeting, which he regarded as the height of impertinence.* Deedes was never entirely reconciled to Black's ownership of the titles because he regarded the Berry family's fifty-eight-year stewardship as the *Telegraph*'s golden age. For him, Michael Hartwell remained the model Fleet

---

* Indeed, though he was alarmed for the future of the paper when Black lost control of the *Telegraph* in 2004, Deedes was quietly rather satisfied that he had outlasted the Canadian and was still in harness when the paper passed out of his hands.

Street proprietor; the fact that he ran the titles on to a financial reef was almost incidental to the central point, that editorial standards were maintained rigorously throughout and staff were treated with courtesy and respect.

The retirement dinner of about fifty guests was strangely subdued, mostly because of the awkwardness of combining the new and old *Telegraph* regimes under the same roof. Peregrine Worsthorne had written Mrs Thatcher's speech, but he recalled that it seemed to bore most of those present, including its author. Worsthorne tried to create some atmosphere by calling out 'hear, hear' at regular intervals, but he found no one joined him. For many present the lasting memory was of Conrad Black on his first major social outing in London since winning control of the *Telegraph*. The dinner coincided with floodlit Beating Retreat on Horse Guards, and the windows of Downing Street were thrown open so the guests could enjoy the event. It was a magnificent spectacle until Black began a loud and interminable commentary, showing off his encyclopaedic knowledge of the history of the various regiments, even the origins of their uniforms. It was an impressive display of military scholarship, but most guests were infuriated by his oafishness. Charles Moore, who was present, thought 'it was just so boring and pointless'.

Even Deedes's speech was slightly below par that evening and he seemed overwrought with all the recent upheavals and the collapse of the Berry family's empire. He spoke about the relationship between politicians and journalists, quoting Iain Macleod as saying it should be 'abrasive'. As he finished his speech he lay his hand reassuringly on the shoulder of Lord Hartwell, 'who was sitting there like a block of ice. Those two old men together were an extraordinarily affecting sight,' one of the guests recalled.

The public plaudits for Deedes's career concealed a certain disquiet at his record and his responsibility for the mess the *Telegraph* found itself in by 1986. 'Yes, I was feeble, utterly feeble,' he would say about his own performance in the early 1980s when the House of Berry began to totter. Of course, it was that very aversion to confrontation, that feebleness, which proved to be his salvation and the key to his reinvention. Charles Moore once told Nicholas Garland that he could never write a profile of Deedes because if it was to be honest it would be too critical. On the day after Deedes's retirement a laudatory profile, written by Moore, duly appeared in the *Telegraph*, saluting the great natural reporter for his 'effortless charm and unquenchable good spirits'.

Though Garland subsequently upbraided Moore for failing to convey *Telegraph* journalists' reservations about their departing editor, a barb was concealed within Moore's eulogy. 'I hope that I will not be misunderstood if I say that editing is not his first love nor his greatest gift.' Significantly, the profile reads very much as a valediction and there is not a hint within it that Deedes would continue writing for the paper, or least of all keep coming in to the office.

Peregrine Worsthorne found his old colleague personally charming, and was grateful for Deedes's full support when Worsthorne almost destroyed his *Telegraph* career by using the word 'fuck' on early evening television. Worsthorne was briefly suspended by Lord Hartwell, and some colleagues reckoned he was lucky not to be sacked.

Otherwise, he was unforgiving of what he regarded as Deedes's craven behaviour. Worsthorne was scathing about his failure to support Colin Welch, who had been passed over when Deedes became editor. He thought Deedes a second-rate editor, who had been dishonest in allowing Hartwell to think he disapproved of Thatcherism while allowing Welch and the other leader writers to take a Thatcherite line. Deedes then failed to support them in the face of proprietorial disapproval. He would justify his reticence by telling Worsthorne that he was just the adjutant, and couldn't quarrel with the colonel. 'But he wasn't the adjutant,' Worsthorne spluttered at the memory of it, 'he was the captain on the bridge!'

Worsthorne thought this fatal conformist gene might even have cost the Berry family their birthright. He believed that money could have been raised in the City in the early 1980s if men like Deedes had followed the lead of Andreas Whittam Smith and confronted Lord Hartwell with the consequences of his misman-agement. What enraged Worsthorne was that Deedes was about the same age as Hartwell; he was a Privy Councillor and had been awarded the Military Cross, and therefore was of a status that would have allowed him to challenge the chairman.

'At the moment he could have been of great value to that great institution, yet he showed great moral cowardice, and ducked it,' Worsthorne said. 'And then he became the favoured son of the new regime. If Richard Desmond had got hold of the *Telegraph*, Bill would have sailed happily on, and said: "He's just a pornog-rapher, old cock."'*

Some of Worsthorne's accusations are clearly justified, others more dubious. Hartwell was a deeply formal and old-fashioned man who did not confide in his sons or in his most senior man-agers about the commercial performance of the paper, and he certainly would not have welcomed an intervention from Deedes. As Worsthorne conceded, it was impossible to engage Hartwell in conversation about anything for he was master of the long chilly silence: 'Incapable of argument himself,' Worsthorne once explained, 'he gives others enough rope to hang themselves [trans-forming] his own inarticulateness into a dialectal skill.' Hartwell placed greater emphasis on the editorial part of his job than on the dreary business side: he thought dealing with the unions or ordering new plant was his burden as chairman, and was not to be shared with the editors, who had the much more noble respon-sibility of maintaining the editorial excellence of the papers. That said, Deedes knew in heart that his failure to vent his concerns, or to demand more information with which to keep his editorial staff in the picture, did not reflect well on him.

Not that he let that allow him to be distracted from his per-sonal reinvention at the new *Telegraph*. To the astonishment of several colleagues, he began attending leader conference on a

---

* At the time Black took control of the Telegraph Group, Richard Desmond was producing the UK version of *Penthouse* magazine under a 1984 licensing agreement. He built up a large stable of pornographic titles, which he later sold.

daily basis. In his autobiography, Deedes suggested he was dragged back by Max Hastings, who wrote to him on his return from Australia, where he had gone shortly after he stepped down as editor, asking when he might be seen back in the office. Deedes noted that he found 'the pre-emptory tone of the letter reassuring', and immediately increased the hours he spent at the office.

'What I wanted was his name in the paper, as regularly as possible, to reassure readers there was some continuity. But I certainly didn't expect him to come in every day, or start travelling around the world,' Hastings recalled. But soon the new editor came to value Deedes's daily presence as a sane and experienced hand. Hastings found some of the leader writers he inherited eccentric in the extreme, whereas Deedes consistently spoke more sense over time than anyone else. On occasion, Hastings would find that Deedes talked highly critically of the Thatcher government and would ask him to write a robust leader. But when Hastings came to edit the leader he would find Deedes had omitted all the criticism he had aired earlier and so Hastings would put it back in himself. 'Bill just wouldn't put the boot in in print,' Hastings recalled. One of the oddities of Deedes's behaviour in the months after he stepped down from the editorship is that he never acknowledged a desire to remain in the office each day, though it was quite clear to everyone who witnessed his rehabilitation under the new regime that that is what he wanted.

Deedes's efforts to establish himself as an indispensable presence in the new *Telegraph* were boosted when the Hastings editorship immediately flew into heavy turbulence. In April 1986, President Reagan lost patience with Colonel Gaddafi and sent bombers to Tripoli, some of which had flown from bases in Britain. Hastings, backed by his new defence editor John Keegan, and by an unusual unity within the leader writers' college, leapt behind his Atex computer terminal to write a trenchant top leader denouncing the American action.

It was characteristically courageous of Hastings to take that line given Conrad Black's devotion to the Atlantic alliance and his conspicuous admiration for Reagan. To Black's credit, he did not publicly censure his new editor, but Hastings was left in no doubt that he had gravely erred. Andrew Knight, as chief executive, wrote Hastings a long memo explaining why he had fallen short of expectations, contrasting the *Telegraph*'s impetuousness with the performance of *The Times*, which had held back a day and then carried a leader offering considered support for the bombing. Some time later, over dinner, Black compared the pusillanimous Hastings with Peregrine Worsthorne, who had strongly backed Thatcher, Reagan and the special relationship.

Deedes was ideally placed to help clear up the mess. Hastings asked him to write a leader page article the following day, to mollify the more pro-American readers and the hawkish new chairman. It was a classic Deedes opinion piece in that it trotted around the issue without reaching any apparent conclusion. The headline – 'Biggest test, in 40 years, for the Special Relationship' – seemed designed to warn the reader not to bother to read too far. 'Alliances are not comfortable arrangements,' Deedes wrote. 'They lead to debts.' It was not entirely clear by the end of the piece whether Deedes thought Margaret Thatcher had been right to honour the debt and allow Reagan to use the bases in Britain, but the piece was not designed to inform or challenge the reader. Rather, it was a peace-offering from the new editor to Conrad Black, and a means for Hastings to effect a partial withdrawal without signalling a full retreat from the ground he had staked out in his flamboyant leader.

Hastings was rattled by the row, and confided in the leader writers that his perch was wobbling. In *Dear Bill*, Deedes confessed he was cheered that his successor was suffering some of the problems he had been through in his years in the chair: 'The episode gave my self-confidence, which was low, a small boost.' Characteristically, Deedes did not qualify that observation, or elaborate on how his confidence had been undermined by his abrupt departure. In this minor, unqualified admission to having felt low, Deedes confirmed how traumatic it had been for him to have been shown the door so swiftly, and how anxious he was to restore his Fleet Street reputation.

Though initially alarmed by the reaction upstairs to his leader, Hastings began challenging other traditional *Telegraph* causes. From his experiences as a young reporter on the road, he had developed two bogeys: white South Africans and the Orangemen of Ulster. Given that these two groups had traditionally found reliable support only in the centre pages of the *Daily Telegraph*, Hastings was a risky choice as editor. His twin prejudices led to problems with Peter Utley, who was almost as devoted to white rule in South Africa as he was to the Unionist cause in Northern Ireland. Black majority rule, he maintained, would lead South Africa into 'anarchy, barbarism and poverty'. Plenty of commentators and saloon-bar analysts believed precisely that – Deedes among them – but few said it with Utley's vehemence, or indeed said it in print.

Hastings ruled that though Utley could write freely under his own name, he would not be writing leaders giving the paper's view on either subject. Deedes was also taken off writing leaders about the deteriorating situation in South Africa. Most of the top leaders about the state of emergency and the township insurrections were henceforth written by Hastings himself, at his usual breakneck speed.

After one particularly sharp leader warning the Conservatives against being seen to be on the side of white government at a time when black majority rule was inevitable, Lord Hartwell – still clinging on to the title, though not the powers, of editor-in-chief – was moved to send a memo of protest. He told Hastings his piece effectively calling for one-man, one-vote had been 'a little over the top', a stinging rebuke by Hartwell's restrained standards.

Hastings solved the problem by sending Deedes off to South Africa to write under his own name and – in journalistic terms – to put a friendly arm around white South Africans and their supporters in Britain. Once again, a textual analysis of a characteristic Deedes dispatch from Johannesburg in June 1986 yields few clues as to his true thoughts about apartheid and what Western governments should be doing about it. 'History warns and the Government here insists that power for the ANC would lead inexorably to the two-phase revolution, ending with the Communists on top. On the other hand, African history tells us that the Communist plant does not readily take root in the black African mind.'

In an earlier piece, written from London at the end of April 1986, at the moment when Hastings's anti-apartheid line was beginning to infuriate old hands, Deedes was drawn to consider black South Africans' lukewarm response to a concession by the government on the repeal of the pass laws. 'Blacks have loathed apartheid, and with reason,' wrote Deedes, rather as one might record a friend's dislike for eating liver at school.

One of the odd things about Deedes's long attachment to visiting South Africa was how low he shot as a journalist. As a former editor of the *Telegraph*, he could have got in to see any minister he chose, not excluding President P. W. Botha, or, later, F. W. de Klerk. But his trips tended to follow a pattern. He would base himself at the Carlton Hotel, then the most dependable hotel in downtown Johannesburg, or he might stay in the suburbs with the former staff correspondent Chris Munnion and his wife Denise. He would schedule a modest number of appointments, usually with a representative of the Anglo-American Corporation, lunch with the British ambassador, dinner with the resident *Telegraph* correspondent and, always, whisky at the home of Helen Suzman, the voice of the white liberal conscience. These were not strenuous journalistic missions, and Deedes would make no effort to meet radical black opposition leaders inside South Africa or to stop off in Lusaka on the way home to visit the exiled leadership of the African National Congress.

Deedes was not really seeking any great insight into the South African drama, then the dominant international news story. Nor was Hastings expecting it. Deedes's emerging role was to reassure readers, and the chairman, that the paper had not changed beyond recognition. There might be a hot-headed editor just turned forty whose aversion to white minority rule seemed reckless and perverse to traditional readers; Deedes's presence suggested to the core *Telegraph* readership that the world had not simply turned upside down. As Hastings noted dryly: 'With his instinctive distaste for confrontation, some of Bill's utterances for the paper could be construed to mean whatever best suited the reader.'

Once Hartwell had been stripped of his authority, and much of his dignity, Deedes needed a new man he could regard as his colonel. Exceptionally tall, brusque and with a limited attention span, Hastings was mistaken by many for a former military man. So, as Lord Hartwell sat miserably in his fifth floor suite, from which he was soon to be evicted, Deedes transferred his allegiance to Colonel Hastings and his devotion and commitment were total. Deedes would never turn down a request to write anything. No daft idea for a journalistic stunt was beneath him, no subject too trivial for him to pronounce on in a witty third leader. Most leader writers are only prepared to take on a subject if they happen to agree with the line laid down by the editor; not Deedes, who could play it either way and sometimes both ways simultaneously.

Hastings only had to remark at leader conference that developments in South America looked ominous for Deedes to have the flights booked that same afternoon. He never turned down a foreign trip by pleading that holidays had already been booked, for he never took holidays once his children had grown up, though when *Scoop* was turned into a television series Deedes jumped on a plane to Morocco to watch the location filming and roll out his Evelyn Waugh anecdotes.

There was something akin to schoolboy hero worship in Deedes's attitude to Hastings. The new editor had unshakeable self-confidence and an instant opinion on almost any crisis; Deedes was often crippled by self-doubt and generally saw both sides of an argument. Deedes was grateful to Hastings not just for the courtesy he showed to him, as editor to former editor, but for letting him go back on the road again. That sense of gratitude was fully reciprocated by Hastings, who half-expected to be sacked at any moment during his first year as editor. Hastings's desire to keep the W. F. Deedes byline in the paper hardened after Garland – another quintessential 'old *Telegraph*' name – decamped to the *Independent*, adding to the general view within Fleet Street that the *Telegraph* was doomed.

'Given the background of Conrad's takeover, Bill could have made a great deal of trouble for me, but he was absolutely reliable and willing to do anything asked of him,' Hastings recalled. The only time Hastings had faint reason to be irritated with Deedes was in the autumn of 1986, six months into his editorship, when Veronica Wadley, his new features editor, decided upon a complete clear-out of her department. It was bad luck for Hastings that the list included the daughter of the Prime Minister. Hastings summoned Carol Thatcher to his office and suggested that, while there was no hurry, it might be more decorous if she quietly found herself a new job because Wadley could see no role for her. Carol replied, not unreasonably, that if Hastings wanted to get rid of her he would have to sack her. Carol left the *Telegraph* as so many others did at that time, her passage eased with the usual Fleet Street redundancy cheque.

Hastings sensed this could spell trouble for him because at that very moment Conrad Black was assiduously ingratiating himself with Margaret Thatcher, and the signals emerging from Downing Street were not encouraging. Word got back to Hastings that the Prime Minister had told Black she would not personally be heart-broken if he found himself another editor for the *Telegraph*. Hastings spoke privately to Deedes, asking if he might discreetly convey to his old friends Margaret and Denis that there nothing remotely personal about Carol's sacking and that it was a jour-nalistic decision taken by her head of department. But Deedes declined to get involved and told Hastings that he would prefer to keep a clear line between his friendship with the Thatchers and

Telegraph matters. For Hastings, this was the only disappointing episode in his happy association with Deedes: 'My throne was trembling, so I did feel a bit let down by Bill when he wouldn't intervene.'

Attacks from outside the *Telegraph* building over Hastings's reforms caused problems for the new editor and strengthened the hand of his predecessor. Paul Johnson, the freelance journalist and author who had crossed swords with Deedes over his 1963 speech praising the Beatles, intervened with a *Spectator* column denouncing the *Telegraph*'s wishy-washy outlook which, he maintained, was causing concern for Conrad Black and Andrew Knight. Though that claim was true, Johnson's motives in attacking Hastings were open to question – the editor had sacked him as a contributor shortly before.

Johnson overpraised Deedes for his firm hand on the ideological tiller in the old days. This was self-evidently an absurd assertion. But when he praised Deedes's signed and unsigned contributions to the paper they seemed incidental to his main aim of undermining the Hastings's editorship.

Few of the charter members of the Hartwell regime managed to reinvent themselves for a newspaper of the computer age, with features for women, health pages and pretty girls in the front page picture. Peter Utley, contemptuous of Hastings's wet Tory beliefs, was instantly alienated from the new order. In the end, and to Hastings's immense relief, Utley announced his departure to *The Times*, where he became chief obituarist. His final column, on 22 December 1986, generously (and no doubt inaccurately) stated that W. F. Deedes had required 'strong and even brutal encouragement from me' to take the column over.

Taking over the weekly T. E. Utley column was the key moment in the resurrection of Deedes's journalistic career. For the first time, he had a weekly slot that could not be cleared when a news story broke. No more would he have to compete to fill the daily guest opinion piece on a matter of that day's importance. He had his own space for his own thoughts, however whimsical or lacking in news urgency. The column was initially called Commentary, later Notebook, and it slipped down the page in a single column. Utley tended to fill it with a single essay, but Deedes soon turned it into a collection of three separate items.

Thus, observation and an eye for the telling little historical parallel or anecdote became the key to the column's success. There was no need to sustain a single political argument over a thousand words, something Deedes had always struggled to do. Typically the first, and longest, item would relate to an event in the news; the second might be about an anniversary, or the death of a public figure, or an actor Deedes had seen on the stage in the 1930s. The final item would tend to be whimsical, noting an early blossom or the first signs of winter.

The new format ideally suited his style and it allowed him to experiment with humour for the first time in five and a half decades in journalism. He tried voices, and comedic conceits, which might be described as neo-Wodehousian. Just as his letters home from Abyssinian had been self-consciously Bertie Woosterish, so now his column nodded in the direction of that lost world. He even appropriated the idea of Lord Emsworth's love for pigs when Robert Runcie, the Archbishop of Canterbury, boarded some of his Berkshires at a charitable foundation on land adjoining New Hayters.

It is an iron law of journalism that readers love stories about animals, and a passing reference to Harriet, a lively sow, brought a vast mailbag. Hilary had bought Harriet for Bill as a wedding anniversary present in November 1987, an unusual gift as Deedes had never shown the faintest interest in domestic or farm animals. The plan was to keep Harriet in the New Hayters garden with the hens and the Jacob sheep, but she grew so fat and belligerent that she had to be returned to the proper accommodation next door, where Dr Runcie's other pigs were kept.

Harriet's weight gain, her risqué love life and her fights with rivals were periodically recorded, to the readers' increasing delight. Sadly, it was the very media celebrity that Deedes had created around Harriet which was to bring the story to a premature end. For the benefit of a magazine photographer, Harriet was released from her single sty to run around with another Berkshire, called Poppy. There was a hideous fight, after which Harriet expired from a heart attack. Deedes wrote up the event for his column as a parody of a news story-cum-obituary: 'The verdict was death by misadventure. The Archbishop has been informed . . . Innumerable children survive her.'

The little drama was proof of Deedes's impeccable journalistic instincts. From his earliest days on the *Morning Post* filing from Whipsnade Zoo, he knew that stories about animals were guaranteed to register with the reader. He created the Harriet story out of nothing and kept it going with an occasional passing reference to her in his column so that her death became, literally, front-page news when the *Telegraph*'s sub-editors decided the event was too important to be kept in his column and dressed it up with a page one picture of Harriet in her prime.

Armed with a weekly column for the first time, Deedes was hitting his stride and finding the voice that came to define him long after his mixed record as editor had been forgotten. He was enjoying himself more than he had in more than half a century in journalism, and the reputation damaged by his part in the death of the old *Telegraph* was almost completely restored.

His status was further enhanced when Margaret Thatcher decided he must be elevated to the peerage. Deedes was initially reluctant to accept the honour, for he thought it might complicate the resumption of his reporting career and that the management might think it unseemly for a peer of the realm to be jumping in to the back of aeroplanes. William Whitelaw was deputed by Downing Street to talk him round and in the end Deedes agreed, on the condition that he was not expected to be a working peer. When he had been in the Commons, mixing parliamentary and journalistic duties was easy, geographically at least. But with the *Telegraph* moving out of Fleet Street to ugly new premises on the Isle of Dogs, it was going to be much harder because there were no decent roads there and the only public transport link was the appallingly unreliable light railway.

Deedes's neighbour Toby Low had the title Lord Aldington, so he had to settle for Lord Deedes. It was more than a year before he gave his maiden speech, a modest contribution in January 1988 to a debate about the state of the newspaper industry. Godfrey Barker, the *Daily Telegraph* sketch-writer, noted that fellow peers had been disappointed that he had 'brooded awhile' before joining the debate in the Lords. Observing him on the red benches, Barker wrote: 'His is the saintly air of a man who might have studied Divinity at Oxford; his tone one of masterly under-statement.'

This was a time of pervasive anxiety about declining newspaper standards and the excesses in particular of Rupert Murdoch's tabloids. Lord Longford contemptuously read out recent headlines from the *News of the World*, including one – 'Bubbly Diana hits the bottle' – which was a 'disgraceful fabrication'. Lord Deedes, somewhat reluctant to be seen to be disparaging his trade with his maiden speech, took a more con-ciliatory line, though he conceded the public was fed up with the tabloids' excesses. He dismissed the idea of a Council for Press Standards to monitor daily what went into newspapers. What was needed was 'closer attention to how and by whom news-papers are acquired', which was clearly intended as a swipe at Murdoch.

Having done his twenty-four years as an MP, Deedes showed no great desire to get involved in the Lords. He would occasion-ally speak up on issues which came to interest him, such as anti-personnel landmines. So long as he was not travelling he would try to help out the whips by voting on really tight divisions. But he found the Lords a bit of a bore, and was saddened to see politicians who failed to reach the middle rank in the Commons trying to find a second wind in the Upper House. Politics had twice before led him to stray from his chosen trade and he was not going to let it happen again, certainly not with the adventures that lay just ahead.

CHAPTER 22

'NOT LOVE PERHAPS'

'What the world chooses to think about our association
troubles me not at all. Mal y soit . . .'

Bill Deedes and Victoria Combe met at the beginning of 1994, when he was eighty, and she was an attractive, spirited and blonde twenty-seven-year-old Cambridge graduate. Victoria had recently returned from three years in Bangkok as the *Telegraph*'s stringer and while she sought a staff job in the London office she was doing shifts in the newsroom. Trevor Grove, Max Hastings's deputy editor, had the bright idea of pairing off Bill and Victoria as a writing duo. It was a clever stunt that was to mature into a long writing partnership. The energy Victoria injected into their double act prolonged Deedes's reporting career. But their deepening friendship and frequent foreign trips were to have serious consequences for Bill's marriage, and to cause additional strain in his relationship with his children.

Grove's original suggestion was for the duo to travel around five solid Tory constituencies to assess attitudes to the Major government. Bill was to bring his political experience to bear, while Victoria, after her years abroad, would offer a fresh perspective.

The two hit it off immediately and vowed to extend the partnership to wider horizons when their joint debut article, 'Travels through Toryland', was published to approval from the news desk. Some of their pieces in their first year of collaboration were a little contrived: that May they went to Norwich and then to Rouen, twinned cities, and the result was perhaps predictable: 'Twinned but now divided'. Three months later they attached themselves to Customs officers in Folkestone and went on drug busts. That trip took the pair of oddly matched investigative reporters, who must have stuck out like a pair of sore thumbs, for a session in a night club called Bonkers to observe recreational drug use.

Combe suspected that she was unlikely to be given the staff job she sought while Hastings was in charge. She had managed to offend Caroline Waldegrave, a friend of his: she had written a story quoting critics who objected to Waldegrave's recipes for veal in a book she had published, and Hastings sided with his friend rather than his reporter. Working with Deedes offered Combe some prospect of overcoming the disapproval of her editor, for almost any piece to which the W. F. Deedes byline was attached was certain to be accommodated. Some hands, including Hastings, doubted that Combe merited the space she was getting, albeit under a shared byline. Some of the reporters resented what they saw as her preferential treatment.

Though it is true that she was not regarded by the news desk as a high-flyer, there was a sourness and a hypocrisy to the reporters' disapproval. Even if she benefited professionally from her association with Deedes, most journalists get in to Fleet Street, or get on there, via personal contacts. At the *Telegraph* nepotism – a charge that could not have been levelled at Combe – was the more trusted means of advancement.* One of the things that drew the two together, despite their fifty-three-year age gap, was that they both suffered from a lack of self-confidence that they managed to conceal from the rest of the world. This unifying characteris-

* When work experience trainees report for duty at the *Telegraph*, and most other newspapers, the first question they are asked by veteran staffers tends to be, 'How do your parents know the editor?'

tic became one of their main subjects of conversation on their travels. Deedes liked Combe's vulnerability, even the way she had failed, since her teenage years, to stop biting her nails. He claimed to be quite disappointed when, after the birth of her first child in 2000, she stopped: 'Nail-biting showed the true Combe,' he told her.

Their friendship moved up a gear when Deedes planned a trip to southern Africa. He had perfected a hybrid form of journalism whereby he would travel to a famine or civil war under the flag of a charity, which, in return for publicity in the *Daily Telegraph*, would help him to reach trouble spots that were off limits to most journalists. Over lunch at Paradiso, Deedes told Combe of a trip he was planning to Mozambique on behalf of the charity CARE, his preferred aid agency. By the end of the meal it had been agreed that she would come along too. The *Telegraph* would not have permitted her to join him on the foreign desk's account, so she said she would treat it as a holiday and pay her own way. Deedes was thrilled and they set off together to Johannesburg via Rome, on bucket-shop economy class tickets.

The trip was scarcely strenuous. The pair arrived in Johannesburg on 15 February and for the next four days their diary was all but empty, except for social lunches and dinners. Then they flew down to Cape Town for another four days; they took the cable car up Table Mountain, ate lunch at the Waterfront complex and then headed off to the winelands. They swam together in the chilly Cape waters but, by this point, a young man who was showing an interest in Combe had attached himself to them, rather to Deedes's irritation. In his contemporaneous note he made of the visit, Deedes noted that Victoria contrived 'to look her most fetching in a black bathing dress' for the unnamed admirer. 'V. enjoys dazzling men, and I suspect she always will.'*

---

* In these notes, Deedes would generally refer to Combe by either of her initials, 'V' or 'C'.

By this stage of their holiday it is clear that the octogenarian Deedes is himself dazzled by his glamorous young travelling companion. Judging by Deedes's private written account they spent a great deal more time discussing personal matters than they did South Africa's painful advance to democracy. He immersed himself in debates about Combe's potential suitors with a detachment that allowed him to establish himself as a sort of romantic guru.

Finally, on Friday 24 February, after nine leisurely days in South Africa, Deedes and Combe flew to Mozambique for the business part of the trip. When they checked into the Cardoso hotel Victoria expressed alarm at how much the holiday was costing – according to his diary – and Bill made the inevitable gesture of insisting he pay both for her flight from London and her hotel bill in Cape Town. She agreed after first remonstrating, accepting his point that she made the trip much easier for him. 'But, I add, please do not talk about it because people are uncharitable, and those who know I have paid some of your bills will conclude the worst. Silence. So that is settled,' Deedes recorded in his diary.

The following day they set out on some CARE business, visiting water pumps outside what was once a prosperous coastal town, which had been installed by the organisation for the benefit of local villagers. Once again Victoria found herself tailed by male admirers, who insisted that she join them at a local nightclub. Bill went along too, though it was clear the suitors would have preferred her to have come alone. Bill and Victoria finally peeled away, returning late to the hotel, but he was reluctant to go straight to bed. There was a power cut so they were issued with candles. Bill had the best room in the shabby hotel, grandly called the bridal suite. They lingered briefly on the balcony, staring through the darkness at the Indian Ocean. 'I think it is a bit public for restrained larking, which I suspect V would not reject out of hand in these last days of her freedom,' he noted. Victoria later retired to her own 'truly dreadful' room, while Bill bedded down in his suite, no doubt contemplating what might have been, as 'it comes home to me how very attractive she is'.

Bill drifted off to sleep, but before long there was a knocking on his door. He fumbled for a match to light his bedside candle and stumbled to the door to find Victoria standing in the corridor with a torch, 'dressed in a gym vest', asking for the return of her insect spray. Deedes obediently retrieved the spray, handed it to her and returned, alone, to his bed. But he was clearly much affected by the intrusion. 'It occurs to me that she is lucky with her travelling companion – or unlucky, whichever way you look at it.'

At this distance it is impossible to gauge what exactly was crackling through the humid air of the south-east African coast-line in those pre-dawn hours. Journalists working together are frequently drawn close, especially on remote and difficult assignments where relaxation after arduous air or road travel involves expense account dinners and quite a lot of alcohol, conditions in which one thing can lead to another.

It is difficult to take seriously the idea of a passionate physical affair between the eighty-one-year-old and his travelling companion fifty-three years his junior. Though Hilary had found him a neglectful husband, there was never a hint of his having strayed in earlier times, despite the numerous opportunities presented to him by his solitary weekday life in London. Had he been seeking a sexual relationship outside his marriage – as so many of his parliamentary colleagues certainly did – it is likely that this pattern of behaviour would have manifested itself long before he reached his eighties.

Combe certainly inflamed Deedes's desires, and as an attractive young woman who was constantly fending off male admirers it seems unlikely she was entirely unaware of the effect she was having on an old man. Combe has subsequently denied that there was anything remotely sexual or flirtatious about their relationship. But there is no denying that Victoria awoke in Bill a powerful sexual yearning that he had never before acknowledged, if indeed he had ever experienced.

In his letters home from the war to his new wife, Deedes did not once refer even obliquely to sexual longing. He praised Hilary for her practicality, her fortitude, her common sense in her raising of their infant son, Jeremy. But he never talked of the way she looked, or referred to staring at her photograph during bleak moments before dawn operations.

On his travels with Combe half a century later, Deedes constantly scrutinised her physically. His diary noted how she looked in a hat, or a certain dress, or in a bathing suit, how she cut through the surf 'swimming like a fish', how her hair fell across her forehead. On the morning after their diffident 'larking' in the candlelit hotel, he took a photograph of her on the balcony, which he kept in his diary for the rest of his life; it was as though he wanted to bottle that momentary frisson that had passed between them.

But no sooner had Deedes realised that she had roused the romantic, passionate side of his being, he moved to shut it down again. By the time he came to put the episode down in writing he described it in terms of Bertie Wooster grappling with the fairer sex. The Deedes mask was back on: 'Yes, it would have been a nice place for a romantic night, but I am imbued with CARE conventions about never "behaving badly", still less "thoroughly badly" on trips.' Rather than act on yearnings, he bound himself in a code of honour, protecting himself from the risk of rejection and the prospect of being made to feel, and look, like a foolish old man.

As their friendship intensified they both sought new destinations. When Hastings moved to the *Evening Standard* in 1995 he was succeeded as editor by Charles Moore, who gave Combe a trial in the religious affairs job. She was a Catholic and Moore had converted to Rome after growing up an Anglican. Combe soon proved her competence and converted the temporary post into a full-time appointment – and thus had licence to travel in her own right. When possible she and Deedes went away together: twice to Hong Kong, in 1996 and 1997, to Sudan, to Sarajevo to look at the consequences of the Balkan wars, and twice to Rome, once accompanied by Victoria's mother, Angela, whom Deedes liked very much.

That trip, in November 1996, began with Deedes spending the night at Combe's flat in Denbigh Street, Pimlico. Deedes did this quite often after a late night or before an early start in London, and Hilary could have been forgiven for wondering why he should not behave like every other elderly Tory man and stay at his club rather than on the spare bed in the flat of a young single woman. Combe had a dinner appointment that evening so Deedes let himself into the flat and did his expenses, and was sipping whisky and eating toast when she came in at half-past one. They sat up for another half hour, talking about their trip. Together they made up the guest bed for him, and the following morning Victoria surfaced at 8 a.m. in pyjamas.

From Deedes's own account, she had lost none of her allure since their time together in southern Africa. The next day, at Heathrow Airport, they linked up with Angela Combe who had come separately from the family home near Hampton Court. As the three of them walked past a hat shop Victoria tried on an elaborate hat covered with feathers and Bill immediately offered to buy it for her, insisting it be an early Christmas present. Victoria thought the straw version better, so settled for that one. 'C fusses endlessly about her sex appeal, apparently unaware [of the effect her] overwhelming sex appeal has on other people!' Deedes noted.

Combe was bound for Rome to report on Archbishop Carey's ecumenical meeting with the Pope, and Deedes had persuaded Charles Moore that he should tag along. But once in Rome Deedes seemed more interested in gossip and shopping than a new enmity between Canterbury and Rome. According to his diary, Deedes noticed that Combe was not wearing the watch he had bought her the previous year. She confessed she had lost it, and was clearly embarrassed because he had bought it for her during a trip to Liverpool to replace another watch he had bought her on their trip to Folkestone the year before that. When she expressed remorse Deedes remonstrated and asked her sternly 'if she seriously thinks I feel that working with her is not worth one watch a year'.

The following day the three of them attended eleven o'clock mass at the Venerable English College, where Deedes found his lifelong adherence to the Anglican Church under serious pressure. He summarised his religious dilemma in the longest reflection on his beliefs to be found anywhere in his writings or private papers:

> It is a long Mass, but beautifully delivered. Dignity and timing, and I feel drawn more and more to the *reverence* which goes with this Church. I am not by nature an Evangelical. I suppose I am High Church. The smell of incense does not offend me. Moreover with the Church of England accommodating itself to everyone's whims, victim of moral relativism, this one seems the only thing standing out against a moral slide. The more pliable our Church becomes, of course, the more unyielding the Roman Catholic Church appears to be. I simply believe in this Church more than any other.

From that diary note, it seems Deedes was seriously contemplating converting to Rome and breaking with his Anglican upbringing, which had been overseen by his mother, with daily prayers and Bible readings. He would have been aware that such a move would have mildly offended his children and caused greater trouble with his sisters Hermione and Margaret, which may be why he did not follow through.

There at the Venerable English College, Bill Deedes, a lifelong Anglican, for the first time received the host, in breach of Catholic rules, though Anglicans interpret those regulations more loosely. 'I have been to Mass before with Victoria – Rouen, Rome &c but up to now have never taken the host.' On that morning in Rome, in a beautiful setting and in the company of Victoria and her mother, Angela, both Catholics, he was emboldened to take the step away from the Anglicanism of his upbringing. He concluded his reflections on the state of the respective Churches with a final defiant assertion: 'If I believe in the Roman Catholic Church as the best defence against creeping evil, what is wrong with that?' After mass they went to the airport to drop off Combe's mother, who was not staying for the business part of the trip, and on the way back Deedes ordered the taxi driver to stop in the Roman equivalent of Bond Street. The first watch they looked at was promising, but cost the equivalent of £2500. They moved to another, non-designer shop, where they both liked one model that Combe protested was too expensive. 'I press acceptance and win the point,' Deedes recorded, without revealing the actual price. Before they returned to the hotel there was another stop to be made at a glove shop they had passed and they emerged a few minutes later with a 'very fetching' black pair. With those duties completed, Deedes returned to the hotel to compose a leader he had been asked to write about international aid for the third world. 'C makes sensible suggestions about it being too pessimistic.'

Often they would alternate their foreign trips with domestic duties, and Deedes and Combe developed a knockabout 'His and Hers' routine on more trivial domestic stories. When Combe found she couldn't make a soufflé, and Deedes implausibly developed an urge to learn how to cook kedgeree, Raymond Blanc was easily persuaded to open the doors of his new cookery school to show them and then mug about with Combe for the *Telegraph* photographer.

When the Carlton Club was to vote on admitting women members, Deedes and Combe wrote parallel opinion pieces, which provided no definitive evidence of strong feelings from either writer but did yield a six-column photograph of her in a fur hat on the steps of the club. Such stunts, organised by the newsdesk, tended to enrage Combe's younger colleagues in the newsroom, particularly women, who found them self-serving and fatuous. But they amused the *Telegraph*'s older male readers who liked the idea of a pretty young blonde venturing into a gentleman's club with a reporter's notebook in her handbag.

These journalistic missions were all very well, but Deedes preferred long-distance assignments – especially what he called a 'promising famine'. Though pieces were dutifully filed from foreign trips, the notes Deedes took invariably show his preoccupation, when travelling with Combe, with her romantic life rather than with the drama of the events they were covering. It is striking how few senior figures, or off-beat sources, they sought to interview in the course of their travels. When at the scene of a third world famine they were generally happy to be ferried around by the aid agencies, writing the standard form of disaster relief journalism that, but for the W. F. Deedes byline, would almost certainly not have found its way into the paper.

If Deedes appeared to struggle to tame his attraction to Combe in Mozambique, he had controlled it by their later trips. He had become the impartial counsellor rather than the flirty companion and took very seriously the matter of finding Combe the right sort of husband. During lunches and dinners far from home the pair talked about their domestic problems and Victoria would open up to him about her romantic life. 'He is definitely the closest male friend I have ever had,' she recalled later, adding that she felt comfortable confiding in him on the most personal matters.

Deedes offered one of the toasts at her thirtieth birthday party dinner at the Carlton Club in January 1997, an event significant for the presence of an army officer who Combe had been introduced to shortly before. Deedes approved of him and clearly thought a promising military man an excellent prospect.

Deedes's ardour for Combe may have been cooling as she headed towards the safe port of married life, but still the friendship was taking him away from home. He may not have behaved 'thoroughly badly', or even 'badly', under his code, but this did not stop his wife's mounting sense of grievance at his jaunts with the young woman she contemptuously called 'the girlfriend'. There was never any suggestion, however, that Hilary imagined that their relationship was physical.

Hilary had always lived in east Kent on sufferance: she found the county dreary and overcrowded and she loathed the ugly town of Ashford, which had become progressively more unpleasant since the war. She had moved reluctantly from north Yorkshire only so that Bill could resume work at the *Telegraph*. When he gave up the editorship forty-one years later, she might reasonably have assumed her reward would be a return north. Bill, of course, had other ideas.

At first Hilary grudgingly accepted this, but the foreign travels with Combe must have been humiliating. The *Telegraph* was the paper of choice for country people of her type, so everyone she knew would have followed Deedes's progress abroad. Worse still, Deedes would return from his trips with Combe so fired up by their joint experiences that he would regale his wife over the kitchen table with every detail of what they had done, a ritual she came to dread. When Jill, the middle daughter, was visiting Kent from Australia, she and Hilary developed a sign language for Victoria's name and they would privately gesture to each other each time Bill mentioned her during dinner.

For his part, Bill had always acutely felt Hilary's lack of interest in his foreign travels. In his long career on the road, Hilary had never shown the slightest curiosity in what he had done, however exciting had been the mission. She would want to talk about the children or, more often, the chickens and the sheep. When Deedes was commissioned to write an introduction to a special reprinting of Evelyn Waugh's novel *Black Mischief*, he referred to the problem Basil Seal found in engaging his London friends in his experiences in Africa: 'One of the sadder eternal truths is that we are only politely interested in other people's travels, however adventurous; and on return from our own travels we become bores to our families and intimates.' As he did quite often in life, Deedes was casting his own experience in general terms.

New Hayters had been a cheerful enough home when it was full of five Deedes children running around the house and extensive garden. But it became a gloomy place to be alone, especially as for Hilary it contained all the sad memories of Julius. Apart from various hospital wards, it was the only home Julius had known in his shortened life. When Julius died Hilary had wanted to move, but Bill refused.

A crisis was developing in the marriage, yet Bill seemed almost wilfully oblivious. Jeremy recalled one particular flashpoint, when his sister Juliet returned to Kent with a fever from a gruelling trip to Nicaragua. A family event was planned at New Hayters but Bill stayed up in London to keep an appointment with Victoria. Juliet was wounded and Hilary was apoplectic.

Jeremy later conceded that he had been slow to recognise how wide the rift between his parents had grown. He blamed it squarely on his father's relationship with Victoria, whom he referred to as 'this incursion into the marital home'. For all the children, their father's reverential attention to Victoria's life was particularly insulting because they all felt that he had been a neglectful father. Lucy, the youngest daughter who was then living with her second husband and young son in the Scottish borders, felt this remoteness keenly.

The distance between Bill and Hilary grew even wider in 1997 when she was diagnosed with cancer and required an emergency hysterectomy and a programme of chemotherapy. Demoralised by her health setback, she became less forgiving of his absences when he failed to cut back on his travelling. The build-up to Victoria's wedding turned out to be the final straw. On a night when Hilary wanted Bill to be in Kent, he insisted on attending the rehearsal dinner for Victoria's wedding party. Hilary was enraged because she recalled how difficult it had been to persuade him to take the slightest interest in his own daughters' weddings. In the late summer of 1997 – the season of Diana's death and Victoria's marriage – Hilary announced she had had enough and intended to leave the marital home and head north to live close to Lucy. She departed abruptly, within a couple of days of taking her decision, and arranged for her animals and chickens to be transported north with her.

Bill was briefly startled and distressed by this development, though he was also irritated at what he regarded as the indecent haste with which Hilary had moved out. Villagers in Aldington were stunned by the sudden turn in the marriage of their most celebrated residents. He explained to friends that Hilary had moved for purely practical reasons, so that Lucy could offer support during her recovery from cancer. George Deedes, Bill and Hilary's eldest grandchild, recalls that when she left New Hayters the family did not talk about it as a separation or the end of the marriage, but as a practical step that would allow Lucy to oversee the final sessions of chemotherapy. Collectively, the wider Deedes family tried to rationalise the dramatic development.

It is difficult to know Deedes's precise state of mind at this point. In 1997 he was writing long diary notes about his travels with Victoria Combe, but there was not a single reference in his vast filing system to his differences with Hilary. No notes or letters from her from this period survive. Hilary was a letter-writer, so probably he discarded them at the time he received them.

In other ways he displayed his formidable capacity for compartmentalising bad news, and isolated and minimised the emotional impact of the effective end of his marriage. His larger problem was practical: New Hayters had been bought in 1946 with Hilary's money, the proceeds of the sale of the house in Yorkshire that she had bought towards the end of the war, and the house was still in her name. Indeed, Bill initially assumed the house would have to be sold to pay for Hilary's rented home in the Scottish borders, and estate agents were commissioned, valuing the six-bedroom house at £400,000. He was under pressure from family and friends to join Hilary in Scotland, perhaps spending every other week in London. But he would not countenance a life so remote, without the pleasure of going into the office each day and the promise of foreign jaunts. In the end Hilary agreed Bill could continue living in New Hayters if he paid her rent in Scotland.

In interviews and in follow-up letters with the author, Victoria Combe was anxious to make clear that she did not believe she was the reason Hilary left the marital home, and that she had strongly urged Bill to join Hilary. It is certainly true that the problems in the marriage had been apparent long before Bill and Victoria began travelling together – indeed, they were obvious even before she was born. Victoria pointed out that if she and Bill had not gone on trips together, he would have found another companion, and he would certainly not have been sitting at home with Hilary (which is also definitely true). He preferred to travel with women, and all of them – including Anne Allport – were much younger than him, and attractive. (Victoria might have added, too, that there was never a hint of 'bad' behaviour with any of these travelling companions.)

Bill saw less of Victoria after her marriage, but he was made godfather to her son Gabriel ('the sainted Gabriel', as the Deedes daughters ruefully referred to him). Bill took to writing little essays to Gabriel about contemporary events, which Victoria was instructed to keep for him to read when he was old enough to understand them.* Lucy, who found the Gabriel letters infuriating because Bill had shown her four children so little attention, protested to him. A few days later an envelope arrived in the post for Henry, Lucy's younger son. Inside there were papers but it was not a letter to Henry, rather a copy of the latest epistle to Gabriel. Unsurprisingly, having her own son copied in to the one-sided correspondence failed to mollify Lucy.

---

* Deedes possibly had in mind that they might eventually be put together by Victoria and published as a collection.

Victoria was surprised and hurt to hear how deeply the children resented her relationship with their father. She had met Hilary on a few occasions, and said Hilary had always been very civil to her, giving no indication that she resented her presence in her husband's life. Lucy was more sympathetic to Victoria than Jeremy, but she thought Victoria was naive in failing to appreciate how her travels with her father would have upset the family.

Shortly after her father's death, Lucy summed up her thoughts about why her mother left her father. 'The Victoria obsession was infuriating to the family because after a life-time of (slightly) coming second best to his other interests, there he was dashing about doing Victoria's wedding and raving about her children. That's the bit that really got up our noses. You don't miss what you've never had, but you do if somebody else suddenly gets it!' As Lucy pointed out, her father's record as a neglectful husband was well-established, but Victoria was definitely a major contributory factor: after all, some new and severe provocation would be needed to drive a woman of eighty-two, suffering from cancer, to bolt from the family home after fifty-five years of marriage. Woundingly for his own children, Deedes was intensely interested in Combe's family, showing far more concern for her relatives than he had in his own children's lives. Deedes's study at home was crammed with photographs of Victoria and her children. The Deedes children were enraged to discover that he had removed a picture of Julius from an antique frame and replaced it with an image of Victoria.

Each Christmas he would give lunch to Victoria's parents at the House of Lords. He was, as Victoria said in 2005, 'part of the family'. He went to Victoria's grandmother's funeral and to her nephew's christening. He corresponded regularly with Angela Combe on a wide range of subjects. Unsurprisingly, his being part of the extended Combe family caused further resentment with his own children.

Money was possibly also a factor in the family's watchful attitude towards Victoria. Bill was the master of the flamboyant financial gesture. When Lucy's first marriage was breaking down in 1995, Bill had a brief telephone conversation with his son-in-law about the looming problems of school fees, before sending him a cheque for £40,000. When friends got into trouble he would often write a cheque. When his old friend and neighbour Lord Aldington emerged victorious from his ruinous libel action against Count Tolstoy in 1989 – it was alleged that Aldington was complicit in the murder of Cossacks after the war – Deedes took him and Lady Aldington on holiday to Morocco. Although Aldington had won the action and was awarded damages against Tolstoy he had no chance of recouping them and was also saddled with enormous legal costs of his own. Deedes not only organised the trip, which was built around golf, but picked up all the flights and hotel bills. Bill's Coutts bank statements – which Jeremy reviewed after his father's death – revealed a number of substantial payments to Victoria over the years, including one of £10,000 in July 1996, which was a bridging loan – repaid – to help her buy a flat. Victoria said that Bill had also given her a generous sum towards the cost of her wedding reception and a 'substantial' amount to her son Gabriel – Bill's godson – on his birth. Hilary seems to have been aware of these payments, and alarmed and angered by them.

Victoria maintained her friendship with Bill even after she moved to Northern Ireland, where her husband was serving, with her young family. Inevitably, they saw less of each other and she was barred from attending many of his landmark parties: Jeremy refused to allow her to attend Bill's ninetieth birthday party, nor was she invited to an informal lunch party in June 2006 marking seventy-five years since he joined the *Morning Post.**

---

* Strangely, Deedes himself did not invite Victoria to this event. Jeremy would certainly have objected to her presence, but he did not attend the lunch, and Lucy, who was there, generally took a more relaxed line.

When Victoria told him that she was engaged, Bill was thrilled, noting that it marked the beginning of a new life for her 'and in one sense the end of my responsibilities'. He had seen her through some painful times and gently encouraged her in the direction of the most suitable long-term prospect. He had bolstered the confidence of a fellow sufferer from low self-esteem and seen her through her late twenties and the transition from an ex-pat life in the Far East to a marriage to a respectable army officer. Journalism was good enough for Deedes, but not for Combe, he thought, so he was thrilled when she married above their mackintosh trade.

All the notes Deedes made of his trips with Combe – backed up with implausible amounts of paperwork, including even boarding passes – were kept in a trunk in his office in New Hayters with an instruction that they be passed to her after his death. He wanted her to be reminded of his adoration of her in years to come. In a covering note he explained that 'because the world is uncharitable I keep our papers in a cabinet under lock and key'. In fact, there was no lock and the lid of the trunk was left open. Deedes was not ashamed of his relationship with Victoria – indeed, all the evidence suggests he was proud of it, whatever his children thought – and he deliberately left his accounts of their travels together available to his biographer.

Because the only other people who had access to Deedes's papers were his children, that sentence and its reference to 'the world' being unkind can only really be interpreted as a rebuke to his own family for their failure – as he saw it – to understand his relationship with Victoria. 'What the world chooses to think about our association,' he wrote, 'troubles me not at all. *Mal y soit . . .*' Deedes, possibly lost in his thoughts about his misunderstood relationship with Victoria, thus leaves behind a final, posthumous Billism by mangling the famous motto of the Order of the Garter: *Honi soit qui mal y pense.** The paragraph amounts to an unusually defiant statement from Deedes, and it perhaps

---

* 'Shame upon him who thinks evil of it'.

explains why his wife took the extreme step of leaving him. He was perfectly aware that Hilary and the children deeply resented his relationship with Victoria but, in the end, he really did not care enough if it offended them. Because he did not 'behave badly' with Victoria, Bill regarded his conduct as beyond reproach. In June 1996 Bill wrote to Victoria on the eve of his departure, alone, on a potentially risky trip to Afghanistan. He wondered if she would agree to deliver the address at his memorial service, 'always assuming they rate me worth a memorial service'. He explained he was asking her because they had 'shared the joys of being reporters together – the top of the profession in my eyes'; she had made him seem 'a much better reporter than I really am'. Moreover, Victoria believed 'in God and the hereafter, which is important to me'.

At first glance this was an immense compliment for Victoria. For any journalist, eulogising Bill Deedes – one of the most beloved members of the trade – would have been the ultimate honour. But in truth the offer was a hollow gesture. Bill must have known, even as he wrote that letter, that Victoria would not realise that honour because Jeremy would most certainly have vetoed the idea. In asking her to make the address, Deedes was having it both ways, encouraging a young reporter in her devotion to him without taking the necessary measures to follow it through. The courageous way for him to have planned his memorial service, if he truly had wanted Victoria to speak, would have been to tell Jeremy that it was his firm instruction, in a letter perhaps copied to his lawyer. But that would have risked confrontation, and might have provoked a row and an examination of the consequences for Hilary of his globe-trotting with Victoria. He had no wish to take that option and did not take the action that would no doubt have triggered a full and frank discussion between father and son about Victoria.

It is possible – indeed it is easy – for a man to humiliate his wife without sleeping with another woman. Infidelity does not have to be sexual; it can be emotional or intellectual. By opting to spend as much time as he could overseas with Victoria and his other favoured travelling companions, and as little time as possible with Hilary, Bill was causing deep hurt to his wife. Hilary could be a difficult woman, as her children conceded, but for most of her marriage she had been neglected by her husband. For years she and her family had come off second best to the *Daily Telegraph* and the House of Commons. Now, in her husband's supposed retirement, Hilary was coming off second best to a girl ten years younger than their youngest child.

In six decades of marriage to Hilary, Bill had never shown much of a romantic side to his personality. Yet towards Victoria he behaved like a teenager – hanging on her phone calls, observing her physically in the minutest detail, buying elaborate presents for birthdays and Christmas. In July 1996 he sent her a poem by A. S. J. Tessimond, an obscure and syrupy twentieth-century poet who fought bipolar disorder for much of his life, as an effort to convey to Victoria what she meant to him.

> *This is not Love, perhaps,*
> *Love that lays down its Life,*
> *That many waters cannot quench,*
> *Nor the floods drown –*
> *But something written in a lighter ink,*
> *Said in a lower tone.*

The poem touches on one of the consistent talking points between them, their lack of self-confidence. Tessimond talks of how this can be conquered mutually:

> *A need at times to be together and talk*
> *And then the finding we can walk*
> *More firmly through dark narrow places*
> *And meet more easily nightmare faces*

There is even, taking up Deedes's defiant *mal y soit* declaration, a reference to those who fail to appreciate the quality of their love:

> *A need for alliance to defeat*
> *The whisperers on the corner of the streets*

And then the poem concludes:

> *A need at times of each for each*
> *Direct as the need of throat and tongue for speech.*

For her part, Combe agreed that the poem was an excellent way of summing up the 'nature of our friendship – and the love between two hacks with more than fifty years between us'.

Deedes said he kept the meticulous record of his association with Combe 'as a provision against extreme old age, when it will be something to read over and remember how lucky I was'. It is striking that Deedes was so oblivious to the consequences of the way he chose to live his life. He knew he was a neglectful and distant father, yet rarely tried to make amends. In all the files detailing his travels with Victoria, he did not once reflect on how these journeys might have affected Hilary; indeed, he did not once mention his wife. It is possible that he was suppressing those thoughts; but it is more likely that it never really occurred to him to worry.

CHAPTER 23

TRAVELS WITH DIANA

'I find, for the second time that day, my heart is being
wrenched . . . I suddenly feel a great easing of the spirit.
Diana has gone her own way to the stars. Victoria has
a life before her.'

Bill Deedes had long been dazzled from afar by Diana, Princess
of Wales, but he only got to know her in the last year of her
life when Charles Moore, the *Daily Telegraph* editor, decided it
was time to appropriate some of her glamour and bring it to his
newspaper. Moore's *Telegraph* had generally sided with the Prince
of Wales against his ex-wife in their public quarrels; at the end of
1996, Moore heard that Diana wished to build bridges with the
newspaper and Deedes was the obvious figure to reciprocate.
Moore asked Deedes to take her to lunch with a view to persuading her to do a major interview.

Deedes wrote to Kensington Palace and the response was
swift and favourable: lunch was set at Mosimann's in Mayfair
for late January. Shortly after that exchange of letters it was
announced that Diana was to visit Angola on anti-mine business, just before their scheduled lunch. Alec Russell, the
Telegraph's resident South Africa correspondent, had sought
accreditation and was planning to fly across from Johannesburg
to catch up with the Princess's entourage in Luanda. But for

Deedes this was an irresistible combination: an out of town job in the middle of the northern winter with the prospect of establishing ties with the most glamorous woman in the world. Moreover, he had also become involved in the drive to eradicate the scourge of anti-personnel mines left behind after civil wars; he was the obvious man for the story. So he performed a classic 'big-footing' manoeuvre to get his young colleague out of the way: he walked into Charles Moore's office and suggested he accompany the Princess.

Hopping around rural Angola in light aeroplanes and Land Rovers in the mid-summer heat might have been considered an absurd mission for an eighty-three-year-old, but Moore immediately spotted the journalistic impact of a beloved *Telegraph* veteran teaming up with the Princess. He told Deedes to pack for Africa, and Russell was stood down in Johannesburg. When Diana's staff heard that Deedes was going he was asked over to Kensington Palace for his first one-on-one meeting with the Princess. 'Spend 40 minutes telling her about mines while she takes notes sparsely,' he recorded. 'Seems appreciative. Thrilled I am coming with her.'

It was not entirely coincidental that Diana should have been so pleased by Deedes's attention. She was shrewd enough to see the overture from Deedes as evidence of a possible weakening in the *Telegraph*'s support for Prince Charles. Only a few days earlier Deedes had written a laudatory piece about Diana's humanity in taking up the cause of eliminating landmines. Ever attentive to her newspaper cuttings, she clearly had reason to regard Deedes as 'one of us'. For his part, Deedes was smitten by Diana, as were almost all the men who met her. Though he was a life-long monarchist and devoted to the Queen, he had written in the *Telegraph* about his doubts as to Prince Charles's suitability as future king, though not in the hostile terms he used privately of his inadequacies.

Deedes knew it would be a demanding trip, physically and journalistically, but he remained in remarkably fine condition.

Apart from a prostate operation a few years earlier, his health had rarely let him down. Because of Diana's celebrity, her tour of Angola would be covered by all the national titles, so he would be up against some stiff Fleet Street competition, notably Richard Kay of the *Daily Mail*. Deedes knew a great deal about land-mines but, unlike Kay and the other veterans of the royal press pack, he did not know Diana's courtiers. He was careful to prepare thoroughly, reading up on recent political developments. Victoria Combe rang him on the day of departure. Both had been finalising the plans for her thirtieth birthday dinner at the Carlton Club, which Deedes was to host for her later that month, and because of his sudden departure for Africa they would have no chance to meet up before the party itself. Combe lectured Deedes on how he must be careful on the trip, and told him that while she travelled on a story to Israel he would be able to get hold of her via the foreign desk. 'Much cheered by the call,' Deedes noted.

With the *Telegraph* then feeling the financial impact of the grinding price war with *The Times*, Deedes was booked economy class, on a grim routing via Libreville on Air Gabon, the ultimate white-knuckle African airline. 'A first for me,' Deedes wrote a little sourly, 'cheapest route no doubt'. One of the journalists in Luanda was so shocked to find that Deedes had flown on bucket-shop tickets that he leaked an item to the *Times* diary, which noted that the man who held the editorial purse strings at the *Telegraph* was none other than Jeremy Deedes, by then the paper's managing director. The younger Deedes did a good job of deflecting the *Times* inquiry by replying wittily, if not quite accurately, that 'Boot of the *Beast* makes his own arrangements'.[*] He added, correctly, that Deedes senior was always careful with company money, and was 'a catcher of buses, not taxis'.

---

[*] All foreign trips for *Telegraph* journalists were arranged by a travel agency given the strictest instructions to find the cheapest means of getting staff to the story.

Air Gabon dropped the eighty-three-year-old correspondent off at Libreville for the onward flight to Luanda. 'Libreville at 4.00am is not the greatest gift in the world,' Deedes noted. But he made the connection to Luanda without incident, arriving the day before Diana was due, and so was in good time to file a workman-like 'curtain raiser' to her visit.

Diana was travelling under the auspices of the Red Cross, one of the organisations supported by the *Telegraph*'s end-of-year charity appeal, so all copy filed by Deedes was certain to be displayed prominently. The Red Cross was overseeing the dangerous operation to rid large parts of the country of landmines, the legacy of Angola's ruinous civil war between government forces and the South African-backed Unita faction, led by Jonas Savimbi. Deedes's opening piece made the front page the following morning, complete with an explanation of how readers could donate money to the Red Cross and the other two charities selected by the *Telegraph* for the appeal.

Diana's trip received a bonus burst of publicity when Earl Howe, an obscure junior defence minister in John Major's government, was induced to speak recklessly to two journalists, Rachel Sylvester of the *Telegraph* and Alice Thomson, then of *The Times*. With the Conservative government feeling pressure from the anti-landmine rhetoric of Tony Blair's increasingly confident front bench, Earl Howe complained that the Ministry of Defence's position was being misrepresented. Diana's intervention was 'ill-advised' and not at all helpful. 'We do not need a loose cannon like her,' he told the pair of journalists. Both *The Times* and *Telegraph* splashed his comments on Wednesday 15 January, and though neither paper initially named the minister, he owned up the following morning, protesting that he had been inaccurately quoted. Few MPs even knew anything about Earl Howe before his infelicitous intervention over hors d'oeuvre at the Westminster restaurant Simply Nico; one House of Lords colleague described him as a normally discreet fellow 'who has not got a lot to be indiscreet about'.

Deedes was rung by London for a reaction piece from the Princess's entourage, and he promptly filed a loyal defence of her motives and her light, loving touch with the Angolan landmine victims. 'Having followed most of her movements out here, I can testify that the way she has set about her mission of support for the Red Cross campaign against mines has been irreproachable.' Later that day, Diana spotted Deedes and sought him out. 'Lot of fuss, ma'am,' he consoled her. 'Idiot minister,' she replied through gritted teeth, a comment Deedes did not file to London but recorded in his diary. For the rest of the travelling press pack Diana was more diplomatic, telling them: 'This is a distraction we did not need. All I'm trying to do is help.'

But in truth the Earl's clomping intervention was heaven-sent, for it pushed Diana's face, and Deedes's words, on to the front page. With the 1997 general election in the offing it was in the interests of anti-landmine activists to make their cause as political as possible and to force the Tories and Labour to outdo one another in their commitments to a cause popular with the British public. Deedes, as a political and journalistic veteran, knew this as well as anyone: 'I feel rather pleased to be remotely involved with a row with ministers about mines.'

The trip seemed to be going splendidly, both for the Princess and for Deedes, until there was an unwelcome intervention from Barbara Amiel, the wife of Conrad Black. One of the most awkward aspects of Black's ownership of the *Telegraph* had been the position of Amiel as one of the paper's most prominent columnists. Moore tolerated this, though most members of staff, Deedes included, found it an uncomfortable arrangement.

On 16 January the *Daily Telegraph* sent out mixed signals about its attitude to anti-personnel mines. From Angola Deedes filed an effusive account of Diana's progress through the minefield of politics, under the headline: 'A triumph among the dangers of diplomacy'. A few pages later, in the paper's main comment slot, Amiel lampooned the 'woolly thinking' of the Red Cross anti-mine activists – who 'must live in la-la land' – and suggested they could be putting British troops at risk. One of the *Telegraph*'s main columnists was attacking the work of the Red Cross even as Deedes was in Angola with Diana, highlighting the dangers of hidden mines and trying to raise funds for the mine-clearing operation.

Deedes was enraged that morning as the press pack began handing round faxed pages of the newspaper coverage of the tour. 'They include a stupid, sardonic piece by Barbara Amiel on mines and the Red Cross. Diana and I and our kind are called woolly headed and earnest do-gooders. We can look after ourselves, but disparaging stuff about the Red Cross as we conclude our appeal is plain stupid. What a silly bitch she is, but I suppose there was no stopping her.' For Deedes to use the word 'bitch', albeit in a private diary, was a measure of his unbridled fury.

That hitch aside, the trip was a triumph, both journalistically and in terms of Deedes forging a useful working relationship with Diana. He clearly relished being back in the midst of the press pack – 'the lads', as he called them – sixty-two years after his first African jaunt to Ethiopia. Better still, he had become a member of her entourage, as an indispensable adviser on her new cause of landmines. As if to seal his new status as an insider, and perhaps in an effort to clinch the elusive interview with Diana the paper so craved, he wrote a laudatory summing up of her new anti-landmine activism which concluded: 'If the mother of the future King feels drawn in that direction . . . we should stop doubting and carping. We should be glad.'

Deedes was accompanied on the trip by Ian Jones, the *Telegraph*'s royal photographer. Jones was amused to observe the easygoing, jokey relationship Deedes immediately established with Diana, who was obviously clearly and instantly devoted to him. With a comic deference, Deedes called her 'ma'am' – which was also his favoured form of address for secretaries at the *Telegraph* – while she called him 'my Lord', or 'Lord Deedes'.

The royal press pack were intrigued by Deedes, and impressed that he maintained the same pace as journalists a third of his age.

One night reporters and photographers were up on the roof of the press hotel in Luanda, trying to find a connection on their satellite phones to get words and pictures back to London. Deedes had scribbled his copy on an A4 pad and was loudly dictating his story on the telephone. Jones watched as hard-headed members of the royal pack stopped fussing about trying to get through to London and began listening to Deedes's words, amazed by the elegance and simplicity of his prose. At one point a gust of wind swept up Deedes's notes and the other journalists scrabbled on their hands and knees to retrieve them for him.

Ten days after their return to London, the new working relationship between Deedes and Diana was formalised over lunch at Mosimann's on 27 January. 'She is revealing about different things,' Deedes wrote coyly in his diary. He broached the subject of his doing an interview with her, the *Telegraph*'s main prize, and she agreed in principle, subject to timing. He briefed Moore that things were looking good: 'Charles is pleased. Thinks I have done it brilliantly.'

Alas, there was to be another hiccup after the Amiel embarrassment. The day after the lunch Moore summoned Deedes excitedly to his office, where Sarah Sands, the deputy editor, and Robert Hardman, the paper's royal correspondent, were gossiping. Moore had been given a hot tip that Diana was to present her wedding dress to the V&A museum, and to auction another sixty-five dresses for charity. Deedes recalled in his diary that he had immediate misgivings about the story, though characteristically he did not raise them at that meeting, as 'in presence of Hardman, I can hardly check the editor'. That was a rather feeble cop-out: Moore would certainly not have been offended by a quiet intervention at this point from his predecessor but one.

The story, written by Hardman, was splashed on the morning of 29 January, revealing 'a dramatic illustration of her intention to pursue a new role outside the conventional royal mould'. The reaction from Kensington Palace was swift and devastating to the *Telegraph*'s ambitions to woo Diana. She was most upset – or at least she claimed to be – and had had no intention that the story should be published, not least because the V&A had not even known of her plans. 'CM says he hopes it has not upset the main plot,' Deedes noted. 'He says he has grovelled.'

Just to be sure, Moore ordered up a leader for the next day lauding Diana's decision to auction her dresses for charity as 'a characteristically bold gesture. It is also a good one.' Deedes was called upon to join in the grovelling operation, too, and obligingly included an item in his next Notebook specifically sucking up to Diana by praising her touch with ordinary people. 'I think it even money whether editor has upset apple cart. But we shall see.'

Despite the set-back to the *Telegraph*'s stealthy campaign to secure the interview with Diana, she told Deedes that she wanted to keep the momentum going on her anti-mine work and asked him to create another platform for her to publicise the cause. He approached a friend, Clare Crawford of Mines Advisory Group, who set about organising a one-day conference built around Diana's presence. By this time they were corresponding warmly, Deedes topping his typed letters with a handwritten 'Dear Diana' and tailing them 'Yours sincerely, Bill Deedes'. She addressed him, with good manners and due deference to his age, 'Dear Lord Deedes' and tailed them in her round, girlish handwriting, 'With my best wishes, Diana'. It was clear that if she bore a grudge over the dress fiasco her irritation was with Charles Moore, not with her new friend.

The landmine conference was set for 12 June and Deedes formally introduced Diana to the audience, praising her fortitude and common sense during the Angolan trip. He had also written her twenty-minute speech, which was well received by the audience and gained good coverage in the press and on television. When the speaker after Diana congratulated her for the brilliance of her speech, Diana reached over and clutched Deedes's arm, smiling broadly. She wrote to Deedes to thank him for the 'elegant masterpiece' he had written for her. 'Once again, I am *so* grateful for your marvellous help in steering my course for the seminar.'

Deedes had won her trust and her affection; it was now clear that she would be making no move in the area of anti-mine activism without his advice. Better still, future foreign trips with guaranteed demand for his copy were now in prospect.

Over the summer, Deedes subtly stepped up the pressure for the interview with Diana, which had become something of an obsession among *Telegraph* executives at Canary Wharf. He had another chance to press his case when Diana asked him to accompany her to Bosnia in August 1997, which was to be her last working trip. Throughout the summer the European press had been chronicling her affair with Dodi Fayed, so she was anxious to present images of more serious matters to compete with the pictures of her frolicking in the Mediterranean on millionaires' yachts.

Now part of the Princess's inner circle, Deedes did not have to fly steerage with Air Gabon. This time he went in a private six-seater jet lent to Diana by George Soros and the trip was organised by a different pressure group, the Washington-based Landmine Survivors Network. Diana was accompanied by her doting butler Paul Burrell, while a pair of Special Branch protection officers took two other seats.

Diana and Burrell spent most of the flight perusing a backlog of tabloid newspapers brought by Burrell so that the princess could catch up with the coverage of her antics in the Mediterranean. Deedes was somewhat taken aback by the camp spectacle of the pair of them giggling together over a picture of Diana in a swimming suit, or hissing at any reference to Camilla Parker Bowles.

On landing at Sarajevo they drove along Snipers' Alley and straight to Tuzla, where she huddled together with the victims of the Balkan wars. These were emotional, affecting encounters, all open to a small pool of reporters and photographers for Diana, after all, was there principally to make publicity for anti-mine causes. Deedes found himself in a slightly unusual position on this trip. He was no longer part of the pack but a sort of courtier and informal advisor to the princess, and her link to the rest of the press pack. According to Ian Jones, who again was taking pictures for the *Telegraph*, Diana and Deedes palpably enjoyed each other's company and she in particular seemed thrilled to be bouncing in four-wheel drive vehicles along bumpy roads. Despite the physical and emotional hardships both of them faced, they were exhilarated to be working together. Jones never once saw his *Telegraph* colleague, who by then had turned eighty-four, show any physical frailty.

In some ways, Deedes's reports reflected this altered arrangement. Though competent and humane, they reflected the truth that he had become a little too close to his subject, and though it certainly raised the profile of the anti-landmine campaign, Deedes's copy did not achieve any great insight into the Balkan conflict or its long-term humanitarian consequences.

The trip was, however, another giant step forwards in the relationship Deedes was patiently cultivating as he tried to deliver what his editor wanted most – the interview with Diana. A fortnight after his return from Sarajevo, Deedes wrote another letter to Michael Gibbins, Comptroller to Diana, Princess of Wales, to press his case. If Diana wanted to defend the vulnerable on this earth, then her motives 'need to be explained, sympathetically, and perhaps at some length'.

Deedes then explained that he would offer Diana the right to see the 'finished product'. This was something the *Telegraph* was always extremely reluctant to do with any interviewee because it invariably led to endless haggling over stray adjectives. He also made clear that two machines would make audio tapes of the interview, 'one for us and one for her', as a guarantee of fair play. The letter was written on 28 August, but Diana would not have read it because she was killed three days later.

Like most journalists, Deedes heard of the car crash in Paris in a telephone call in the early hours of Sunday morning, 31 August. The BBC rang him at New Hayters at half-past three to tell him that Diana was thought to be seriously hurt, but still alive. A taxi company in Ashford sent a car to pick him up eighty minutes later, and drove him to the BBC headquarters in West London. Five minutes from their destination, the BBC rang the driver's mobile phone to inform Deedes to compose himself and prepare different comments because the Princess was dead. At that moment, Deedes observed that the meter was reading £142 for the BBC's account.

Deedes's diary entry for that day is a masterpiece of acute, rather eccentric observation. On his arrival at Television Centre he noted that, apart from a solitary cleaner, the only sign of activity in the lobby was James Whittaker of the *Mirror*, talking on one of the television monitors in defence of the press. 'I suppose he is the only man they could find awake.' He had to wait twenty minutes in make-up, 'feeling rather tearful', before his appearance. He noted a minister in the new government, unknown to him, hanging around and assumed this must be because the BBC thought it must be studiously balanced, just three months after Tony Blair's election victory. 'He has a woman minder with a satchel. New Labour!' Deedes then did his appreciation with the BBC presenter Martyn Lewis, whom Deedes noted was also tearful. He agreed to do a quick interview with another BBC channel before getting into a taxi to cross London to report for duty at the *Telegraph* by half-past eight. He arrived just before Charles Moore, who had come straight up from his home in Sussex.

As Diana's adviser and travelling companion, Deedes was the obvious man to write the main comment appreciation of her and her charity work. He was set 2500 words, and by twenty past one he had written 1800 of them. His phone in the office was ringing dementedly as journalists from around the world begged the veteran 'royal insider' for a quote or a few words to camera. He allowed ITN into the office for an interview, provided he could continue writing while they fussed around and set up their gear. Charles Moore remembered going round to Deedes's desk to give him encouragement, and seeing tears running down his cheeks as he typed his appreciation.

Nearing the end of the main piece, and despairing of the interruptions, Deedes nipped alone downstairs to one of the few bar-restaurants then open in Canary Wharf on a Sunday, and ordered a gin and tonic – double – which he gulped down as he collected his thoughts. The gin provided the necessary kick towards the finishing line and he pressed the 'send' button by half-past two on 2389 words, much longer than a normal *Telegraph* comment piece.

Instant appreciations written to order to mark a sudden death or human tragedy tend to be banal, but Deedes's meditation on Diana was an extraordinary piece of work. The headline – 'The Princess of Sorrows' – was not his, and was perhaps a shade lachrymose. But the copy was startling and showed that a journalist is as good as the challenge to which he is forced unexpectedly to rise. It did not paint her as a saint, and in Deedes's references to his travels with her he hinted at a neediness and at her contradictory relationship with tabloid journalists and photographers. He predicted, accurately, the imminent storm that was about to break about the paparazzi and tabloid newspaper techniques; the old Fleet Street hand had got in a pre-emptive strike against inevitable demands for a privacy law. Most importantly he captured her qualities in a way that would satisfy those who adored her as well as those many *Telegraph* readers who regarded her as a flibbertigibbet who had imperilled the royal family.

Recognising her own frailty, she was the better able to understand and sympathise with the frailty of others . . . More simply, Diana gave us an example, in this mechanistic world, which we should heed and try never to forget. Her instinct was so right: all those wounded people in Bosnia, crying aloud for someone to hear their tale, to hold their hand . . . We should tell our children and our grandchildren about her. We should say to them, the world you are about to enter remains in sore need of her gifts. Remember her.

With that piece finished, Deedes paused only to receive electronic messages of congratulation from Moore and other executives over the computer system before he sat back down in front of his screen for another 1200 word contribution to the special commemorative supplement the *Telegraph* had decided to produce.

That was finished by six, to the astonishment of the news editor who told Deedes: 'If only all reporters in this building could be so quick.' Then, having written 3600 words during a day which had started with a phone call at half-past three in the morning, and conducted television, radio and newspaper interviews with media outlets across the world, the eighty-four-year-old departed the office at seven o'clock in a taxi ordered by the *Telegraph*, reaching home an hour later. He was tired but satisfied that he had risen to the occasion, albeit on a very sad day. His only regret was that he had missed a call from Victoria Combe and could not raise her because she was travelling.

The following morning he came back to the office, leaving home shortly after nine o'clock and reaching the office, this time by train, around eleven. The *Telegraph* was feeling pleased with itself because its coverage was generally hailed as superb, and superior to that morning's edition of *The Times*. Deedes found on his desk a sheaf of telephone messages requesting interviews. Jeffrey Archer had been on the phone, personally asking Deedes to speak to a television reporter who he billed as New Zealand's David Frost – 'very Palace performance', Deedes noted with wry pleasure. A Belgian television reporter was sent away with a flea in his ear after making impertinent comments about Buckingham Palace's attitude to Diana's death. It was another very busy day, but Deedes was clearly in his element. He was later thrilled when he received – on top of a letter of thanks from Moore – the ultimate 'herogram', a handwritten thank-you note from Conrad Black.

The day of Diana's funeral – Saturday 6 September 1997 – created a logistical and emotional crisis for Deedes. After the funeral service at Westminster Abbey, he had to make his way through gridlocked London traffic to Victoria Combe's wedding at St Bride's in Fleet Street, where he was to give one of the readings. Combe was not the only English bride whose shock at the death of Diana was tempered by the realisation that the funeral was going to clash with her wedding. She was understandably alarmed that, at a time when many thought Britain had gone collectively mad with Diana grief, her wedding would be overshadowed.

Three days before her marriage Deedes wrote to 'My very dearest Victoria', noting that he would never again be addressing an envelope to Miss Victoria Combe. He thanked her for soothing words about Diana. 'You are right. There was no happy future there. Now, I am confident, and we both know, she is in better hands.'

He went on to praise her husband-to-be and to reassure her that the wedding would be a triumph. 'Warn John that for countless reasons I have become deeply fond of you and at my age there is no hope of my changing . . . Thanks for everything. God bless you both, dearest Victoria. It is going to be a wonderful day.'

Deedes was the obvious choice to be the *Daily Telegraph*'s representative in the Abbey. Because it was a Saturday, the *Sunday Telegraph* had its own reporter there, filing for the following day's paper; Deedes had no need to write up his piece – which was to appear in a special commemorative supplement on Monday – until Sunday.

Nevertheless, the Saturday was to prove an absurdly hectic day. In his diary Deedes recorded going about it as he had planned a military operation half a century earlier. Phase One, he wrote, was arriving at Ashford station for the 07.22 train to Charing Cross. There he moved to Phase Two and was picked up by Jeremy's *Telegraph* driver who had been lent for the day. There was an unexpected bonus when Deedes found that a first-class weekend return cost just £16 – 'rather a bargain'.

Deedes's notes of the funeral itself are sparse and unrevealing.

He attended with Sue Ryan, his best friend at the *Telegraph* with whom he collaborated on the Christmas charity appeal, and was pleased to see his sister Margaret and her husband, Lord FitzWalter, there too. He devoted more words in his diary to Sue Ryan's dilemma about whether she must wear a hat than to Earl Spencer's incendiary tribute to his sister. The descriptive piece he wrote the following morning was competent, but lacked the urgency and force of the appreciation he wrote within hours of Diana's death.

Deedes's mind was clearly on an event more significant to him than Diana's funeral. Sue Ryan and Deedes were whisked from the Abbey to the Savoy, via a circuitous route dodging the traffic. Annoyingly for Deedes, Paradiso was closed until two o'clock out of respect for Diana, so they were forced to find an alternative venue for lunch. He and Ryan ate a 'light and expensive' lunch of smoked salmon at the Savoy. After a restorative whisky and soda he took a glass of Chablis, and then the chairman of the hotel, who recognised him, sent over a glass of brandy. Deedes worried that he might slur his reading at St Bride's.

The wedding service itself was clearly a draining experience for Deedes, as his emotions had already been strained by the morning in the Abbey. 'Even behind her veil, Victoria is perfect. Lovely wedding gown. I find, for the second time that day, my heart is being wrenched. All goes just as we have planned in endless discussions. Signing of the register. I suddenly feel a great easing of the spirit. Diana has gone her own way to the stars. Victoria has a life before her. John lifts her veil and she does look the stuff of dreams.'

Victoria had asked him not only to offer a toast at the reception but also to act as a sort of host, greeting the guests as they arrived. After the meal and all the speeches, Deedes felt suddenly exhausted and slipped away quietly before the bride and groom departed, so was not to see her in the going away hat they had bought for her in Bond Street. He made his way not back to Aldington but to Victoria's empty flat in Denbigh Street.

Victoria had left him a note telling him to sleep in her bed and offering a change of sheets in the cupboard. Deedes tumbled gratefully into bed, pondering why he always slept so well under Victoria's roof.

CHAPTER 24

LIVING IN INJURY TIME

'One day it suddenly dawned on me: Bill was a major star
in a way that he simply hadn't been in his earlier years.'

T he autumn of 1997 was to be a traumatic period of adjustment for Deedes. Diana's death had been a terrible shock in
itself, and it had also cut short a promising collaboration over
landmines and the prospect of his becoming her most intimate
media courtier. He remained very close to Victoria after her
marriage, though as she was commuting to the *Telegraph* from
Salisbury Plain, where her husband was based, she was more
pressed for time. And with Hilary's departure for Scotland occurring
almost immediately after Diana's death, Bill found himself living
alone in New Hayters. Initially he was lost because, throughout his
long married life, he had never done any domestic chores; soon he
found a local couple who moved in to serve as housekeeper, cook
and handyman.

Though he was certainly lonely to start with, he was deaf to the
urgings of his children to join Hilary in Scotland. Once he had got
over the shock of his wife's departure he realised he was completely free to travel, without guilt and without Hilary's sullen
recriminations on his return from protracted trips.

Deedes and Combe continued to travel until the birth of her
first child in 2000, and they did a five-part series on the Christian

399

world to mark the new millennium. But with children travel became much harder for her, especially when her husband was promoted and posted first to Northern Ireland and then to Turkey.

As Victoria Combe has pointed out, she was not the cause of Deedes's travelling and when she ceased being available for regular trips he found other partners. During an idle moment while recovering from a medical setback, he drew up a list of all the foreign trips he had taken in the half-century from 1952. He left it in one of his files: I rather think he wanted it to be found, because he was quietly proud of the stamina he showed in later life and always enjoyed brushing aside suggestions that he slow down.

For most of his time as an MP he did not travel abroad very much. He recorded no trips at all in the years 1954 to 1956. The pace picked up slightly in the 1960s. He went to the Königswinter conference in 1962, for instance, and later visited the Caribbean and India with colleagues from the Select Committee on Race Relations and Immigration. From 1975 onwards he used his editor's prerogative to book trips to America for the party conventions in presidential election years, and would take himself off to Rhodesia and South Africa, usually in the depths of the northern winter, to write a leader page piece or two.

As editor, he took roughly two foreign trips a year, but in 1986, his first year of 'freedom' and the year he turned seventy-three, he really hit the road. He went to South Africa, Washington DC for the Iran-Contra congressional hearings, Morocco to write a feature about the filming of *Scoop* for television, and to the Philippines.

As he got into his eighties, the tempo increased still further. In 1994 he made four separate trips to Africa (South Africa, Rwanda, Kenya and Ethiopia), plus a trip to New York to investigate global conventions on the use of anti-personnel mines. In 1998, the year he turned eighty-five, he went to Australia, Russia and Bosnia, and made three further trips to Africa – to Sudan, South Africa and Angola.

Living in Injury Time

The most restless spasm of his life was in the twenty-four months from January 1999 when he embarked on no fewer than twenty overseas trips for the *Daily Telegraph*, seven of them to Africa, plus separate assignments to China, Pakistan and East Timor.

After Diana's death and Victoria's marriage, when she scaled back her travelling, Deedes became more dependent on aid agencies for seeing him safely back and forth. As he reached his mid-eighties there was a view at the *Telegraph* that he should always travel with a sensible companion, preferably female, as a woman might be expected to be more alert to his moods and medical needs.

After Combe, one of his favourite and most regular travelling companions was Anne Allport of CARE International. They had many hazardous adventures together, including a fraught hop around Mozambique during the last few months of the civil war. Allport recalled that Deedes was indefatigable and oblivious to fear, even when the pilot would throw their plane into corkscrew dives to evade small-arms fire each time they landed at bush air strips. Deedes was fearless about flying or rebel gunfire, but he was a strangely nervous car passenger who was not shy of instructing a driver to slow down when he had reason to doubt his competence or sobriety.

He and Allport undertook an extremely risky trip to Benaco camp on the Tanzania–Rwanda border in 1994, where CARE was running a huge food programme for a quarter of a million refugees displaced by the civil war. They were sleeping in the tented camp where the food was stored when a fire-fight erupted one night between villagers and the camp guards. Allport threw on some trousers and sprinted, panic-stricken, to Deedes's tent, where she spent the next few minutes shouting through the canvas to try to wake him from a very deep sleep. In his travels through hell-holes and civil wars, Deedes tended to take the view that if there was a bullet somewhere out there with his name on it, it would probably have found him in France in the summer of 1944.

401

When Max Hastings had taken over as editor in 1986, he had wanted to keep the Deedes byline to reassure older readers, but he had certainly not expected the man himself to spend his seventies and eighties circling the globe. Deedes, he recalled, always 'wrote his own ticket' and invariably was pressing to get on aeroplanes for the paper. 'Frankly, I didn't realise for some years that I had a star on my hands. To start with, we took him slightly for granted, and then one day it suddenly dawned on me: Bill was a major star in a way that he simply hadn't been in his earlier years. The readers wanted to see him out there, and being active.'

One of the factors in his emergence as a journalistic star had been the revival, from the early 1990s, of the Christmas appeal that Deedes had pioneered on the *Morning Post* before the war. Deedes became the face of the appeal, almost its impresario, while Sue Ryan, as managing editor, oversaw the practical challenges of securing space for stories and support from management. Together they would select which charities the paper would support, and he would do a great deal of the writing, travelling to Africa and India to provide the copy that was needed to inspire the reader to donate.

The key to the success of the *Telegraph*'s appeal was that charities were selected only if their activities were interesting enough to generate lively stories. On a Sunday before Christmas, special telephone lines would be set up in the office and readers were encouraged to ring in and make final donations. Most of the paper's better-known writers cheerfully gave up their Sunday to man the phones and tried not to sound too offended when readers almost invariably asked to speak directly to Deedes or, failing him, Matt Pritchett, the *Telegraph*'s adored pocket cartoonist. Deedes was too deaf to take down the readers' credit card details, so he would stay on the phone buttering them up and inducing them to give a little more while a secretary listening on the line saw to the administration. Many of the donors were elderly and apologised for giving only modest amounts, but Deedes was just as effusive with them as he was with the occasional 'high roller' who might be encouraged to give a four-figure sum. These were invariably enjoyable days, with mince pies and mulled wine provided by the management, which left *Telegraph* journalists and readers with a warm glow inside, feeling they had done some good.

Deedes was unusual as a journalist in that he was genuinely interested in the workings and impact of international aid, and in those who worked in the field. Towards the end of his life he had become thoroughly bored by politicians and believed that true idealists were to be found not in politics but in the developing world, trying to make life better for the silenced majority. When Allport moved on to work for AMREF, the medical charity based in Nairobi, Deedes joined her on the board and became an assiduous attender of meetings despite his distaste for procedural matters and his preference to be out where the action was. Deedes brought charities gold dust in the form of publicity in a respected newspaper, but increasingly they also came to value his strategic advice.

After making his escape from London, Deedes most enjoyed descending upon a remote African village, where his white skin and advanced age invariably attracted interest. Often he would launch into a mini-speech, extending the local chief his formal greetings from the United Kingdom. He would tell the bemused villagers that he had once been a Member of Parliament, and make a reference to current political developments in the African country he was visiting. 'He could have been taking part in a debate at Westminster,' said Anne Allport, who witnessed many of these addresses.

Like Diana, he was deeply affected by the conversations he had with the victims of a vicious civil war. Allport would keep some food back for Deedes during arduous day trips from camp, but if he found it he tended to give it to the hungry. He never complained about being uncomfortable on these trips, which were arduous enough to have tested a twenty-year-old, but he would get cross if officials were late and the schedule ran behind. One thing never changed: whatever horrors he had witnessed during the day, once he was back at camp or hotel and the sun went down, he would invite his travelling companion to share some of the whisky he had bought duty-free on the way out.

Deedes never found the intimacy he had established with Victoria Combe with his other travelling companions. Allport said she always felt the closeness you experience with someone when you have been around a few tight corners; he would ask after her children but there was a formality and a seriousness of purpose about their trips together. Certainly there was none of the larking that had marked his trips with Combe, and the work was generally much harder.

There was a persistent fear within the *Telegraph* office that one day some sort of medical catastrophe would befall the paper's octogenarian roving correspondent, but Deedes was ingenious at getting around these concerns. When planning a particularly strenuous trip, he would go to see the editor to get an agreement in principle. To the editor he would imply that the foreign desk was anxious for his reports from some civil war or famine, and Hastings or Moore would stand by their executives. With agreement for the trip secured in principle, Deedes would talk to the foreign desk and imply that, though he was open-minded as to whether the assignment truly amounted to a story, he was under pressure from the editor to go.

As Deedes's copy was so reliably good on these occasions, and because his presence in a war zone at his age was invariably a good enough story in itself, the foreign editor would give further encouragement to the expedition. But though Deedes was polite enough to give the foreign editor the illusion that he was master of his foreign correspondent, he actually set up the pieces with Sue Ryan and kept her informed of his progress and when he would be filing. Deedes would head to the airport and five or so days later an immaculately turned piece would appear in the *Telegraph*'s computer system, often dictated by Deedes on a borrowed mobile or satellite phone.

Most readers thought it was marvellous that a man of his age should be performing so valiantly, but some were critical of what they regarded as the *Telegraph*'s recklessness with their star man. Geoffrey Griffiths, a reader from Essex, wrote more than once to complain about the burdens imposed on him. In April 1999 he chastised Charles Moore, accepting that though Deedes manifestly had 'printer's ink flowing through his veins', he was being over-extended. 'Let him get home in the evenings,' Mr Griffiths wrote, 'to the bowl of soup Lady Deedes has ready in the Aga.'[*]

Moore – ever a stickler for replying fully to readers' letters – wrote back, explaining that there was nothing much he could to stop Deedes travelling. 'I do not send Lord Deedes to do things; he insists on going himself and, when I order him not to, he simply disobeys me. As he is a former editor of great distinction, and I am less than half his age, I fear there is very little I can do about it.'

Moore might have felt deep down that Mr Griffiths had a point, for he forwarded his letter to Jeremy Deedes, then managing director of the Telegraph Group. The younger Deedes, himself aged fifty-five, replied to Mr Griffiths by hand, explaining that he was siding with the editor in not trying to curtail his father's excursions. 'You try and stop him!' Jeremy wrote, adding that at the time of writing his father, just back from Skopje whence he had filed graphic accounts of the refugee crisis in the Balkans, was downstairs in the newsroom writing his weekly column.

Auberon Waugh also jokingly inserted himself into the debate about the welfare of the *Telegraph*'s national treasure. Waugh wrote the Way of the World column and one day turned to the celebrations marking Deedes's eighty-fifth birthday, which had merited a short leader in the *Telegraph* praising the example he set younger men.

---

[*] It was not widely known, even inside the *Telegraph* office, that Hilary Deedes was by this point living in Scotland.

'No Third World disaster can be said to have taken place until he has told us about it,' Waugh wrote, but he expressed mock outrage that Deedes travelled to these global calamities in the back of the plane. 'One does not wish to interfere with the efficient running of the business side, but now Lord Deedes is 85 some readers may feel we should have a Way of the World appeal to upgrade his tickets wherever he goes.'

It was certainly true that on these long-haul trips Deedes would travel economy class and often on circuitous routes. Occasionally check-in clerks, seeing a man in his eighties packed to cover famine or war, would bump him up to business class but, unlike many journalists, he would never ring the airline's press office in advance and try to cadge an upgrade. He was once highly amused, when boarding a plane in Calcutta with Sue Ryan, to observe a prominent Unicef official turn left ahead of him while they bore right towards economy.

Deedes's parsimony stemmed partly from his innate lack of self-importance. But there was another practical point: he feared – ridiculously, of course – that if his travelling expenses got too high his nomadic way of life would somehow be found out, and he might be grounded. It was the same impulse that had encouraged him to negotiate a reduction in the retainer Max Hastings proposed he be given after he stepped down as editor in 1986. He feared too high a figure would attract the attention of the accountants, who might have argued that the man was well past retirement age and already drawing a pension.

Though Deedes worried about money, he was generous with it throughout his life. As a young, single man he set aside cash from his salary to pay his sisters, until they married or started working themselves. After his retirement he gave his pension to his daughters and lived on his retainer from the *Telegraph*. The costs of running and heating New Hayters were high because it was large and unmodernised, but Deedes was innately frugal.

Further evidence of his growing national status appeared when he was ambushed for an appearance on *This Is Your Life*. 'Some people write the headlines, some people make the headlines, and some people do both,' Michael Aspel intoned over the opening credits. 'The man I'm after today is a legend, still working at the age of eighty-five.'

The resulting programme was memorable chiefly for the incongruity of the rather grand guests being shoe-horned into a tired format which was, by then, more often deployed for the family and friends of a star of *Coronation Street*. But the wider Deedes clan played their parts gamely, and even the 21st Baron FitzWalter, the husband of Bill's youngest sister, Margaret, managed to look as though there were no place on earth he would rather have been.

Jeremy had been the contact with the makers of the programme and agreed to do it with an alacrity that was not obviously shared by the subject. The conceit of *This Is Your Life* was that the victim must be unaware, or at least must pretend to be unaware, of what is going on until Michael Aspel springs the trap. The cover on this occasion was that the *Telegraph* needed Deedes to interview the French footballer David Ginola about his role as a goodwill ambassador for the Red Cross. As the two men chatted in a back room at the Tottenham Hotspur training ground, Aspel burst through the door with his red book. Deedes adopted his familiar look of theatrical astonishment, which he would break into at parties when presented with a gift; the expression was designed to convey surprise and the sense that he regarded himself as wholly undeserving of the honour. Deedes's mouth was fixed open, his head inclined slightly backwards, an expression he maintained for most of the subsequent recording in the studio. At this distance it is difficult to know if his suprise was genuine or not. He confided to Anne Allport that he had his suspicions he was being set up during the laboured interview with Ginola and he later, and rather ambiguously, told the *Daily Telegraph* reporter covering the event, 'I had no serious inkling anything was afoot.'

He managed not to show it, but his main reaction to the

ambush was fury – towards Jeremy for putting him through the ordeal, and Sue Ryan, who had arranged the interview with Ginola. Deedes icily told Aspel to leave the room while he completed the interview with Ginola, and was only partially mollified when he was assured that the article about the Red Cross was wanted and would actually be appearing in the paper. After subjects are ambushed they are generally taken by limousine directly to the recording studio so they do not get cold feet and pull out of the programme. Deedes refused to do so, and insisted on returning to the office: he wanted to write up the Ginola interview and he had Clare Hollingworth, the *Telegraph*'s famous Second World War correspondent, coming for tea. He was certainly not going to let down an old journalistic pal for the sake of a television programme. It was the only time in their sixteen-year association that Ryan experienced Deedes being genuinely angry with her, and she felt wounded that he was taking it out on her rather than confronting Jeremy, who had originally accepted on behalf of the family. Ryan sent Deedes a message on the *Telegraph*'s Atex computer system making that point, and he swiftly apologised.

Meanwhile, matters at the studio were deteriorating as the guests waited impatiently for the star of the show to arrive. Because of some alcohol-fuelled bad behaviour in the past, the green room serving *This Is Your Life* was dry, by order of the producers. After toying with glasses of fizzy water while the studio was made ready and the audience warmed up, Denis Thatcher and Auberon Waugh grew increasingly disgruntled. Eventually they formed a formidable alliance: protesting at the programme makers' bad manners, they said they would leave unless proper drinks were produced. After a certain anxious consultation the green room regulations were swiftly amended, a bottle of gin materialised and good humour was restored. At around this time Sue Ryan, still feeling some iciness from Deedes as she accompanied him to the studio, rang ahead and warned a production assistant to ensure a strong whisky and soda was ready for his arrival. Thus the *This Is Your Life* alcohol ban, which had survived intact through countless programmes, collapsed under a sustained assault from Fleet Street veterans.

The programme was odd in another respect, for it was made only a year after Hilary – whose cancer was then in remission – had left the marital home. Obviously no reference was made to this on the show, but it was strange that Jeremy had agreed to the making of a programme showing Bill surrounded by his reverential family at a time of crisis between his parents. To those outside the family who knew what had happened in the marriage, the programme seemed artificial and faintly absurd, especially when Hilary – who had been specially brought down from Scotland for the programme – related rather stilted anecdotes about their courtship during the war.

Deedes seemed not to care too much about that on the night. The star mystery guest was his daughter Jill, who had been flown over from Melbourne with her family by Thames Television. As she moved in to hug him Bill's voice could be heard over the audience applause, asking urgently, 'Did they pay your fare?' and then repeating the same question to her husband.

Auberon Waugh gave a rather rambling account of working with Deedes on the Peterborough diary in the early 1960s, and Max Hastings, looming over all the guests like an elongated cavalry officer, spoke of Deedes's exploits as an octogenarian reporter. Lord Runcie appeared via a video link-up, talking about the Berkshire pigs that had run around New Hayters, and the producers had even persuaded a rather bemused Jack Nicklaus to speak by satellite about their joint admiration for Bobby Jones.

The comic and emotional highpoint was achieved when Denis Thatcher walked through the sliding doors and seemed close to choking up as he recalled his golfing exploits with Bill: 'Golden years Bill, and you're a golden man to play with.' Deedes looked slightly wary at the emotion in Denis's voice – conceivably the gin had done its work – and replied: 'No, no, do you remember we didn't always get off the first tee so we gave ourselves a Mulligan?' By then the emotional force had gone and the two had reverted to a comic double act. 'That was because of the night before,' Denis shot back, as the studio audience began to enjoy the exchange between two elderly men who were fully conscious of their comic potentials. 'I wouldn't have put it that way, but you are quite right,' Bill replied, to more laughter.

This Is Your Life took Deedes's celebrity far beyond the traditional middle-class confines of the *Daily Telegraph* and marked an important step in his transformation from a Fleet Street character to a national figure. The W. F. Deedes 'brand' was getting into parts of the national consciousness that the *Telegraph* could not reach.

The programme also gave a wider audience the opportunity to ponder a matter that had long fascinated Deedes's colleagues – his Churchillian lisp which resulted in a distinctive shushing of the letter 's'. Deedes's frequent broadcast performances allowed a rolling assessment of the development over the years of his impediment – if that is what it was – captured in the *Private Eye* joke when he was editor: 'Shome mishtake, shurely – Ed'.

There was no hint of the lisp in his childhood, nor in his television appearances of the 1950s. John Butterwick, who had been an intelligence officer in Deedes's battalion in the war, noticed how his voice had changed over the years. There had been no shushing when Major Deedes was shouting orders to his rifleman, or over drinks in the officers' mess. Yet when Butterwick saw his comrade on television in later years he noticed that it was there. Butterwick thought the sudden shushing had been deliberately acquired.

Deedes always affected to be puzzled himself as to how it developed. In a television profile by Michael Cockerell broadcast in 1997, Deedes was unforthcoming. He claimed that when stopped by a policeman in his car, the breathalyser was always produced on the assumption he had been drinking. 'Occasionally I get abusive letters, saying why can't you pronounce words properly? I'm encouraged by the thought that Winston did it. But there is nothing I can do about it.'

Some colleagues at the *Daily Telegraph* rather doubted that latter claim. Peter Utley was fascinated by the Deedes personality and by his ascent to the editor's chair in 1975. In a 1986 Radio 4 programme about the *Telegraph*, Utley pointed to the happy coincidence that Deedes's natural charm was intensified by his eccentricity of speech.

'He slurs his "s"s. I've never known exactly why. This suddenly happened to him in middle life and I don't think it was due to any great dental operation or anything of the kind, but it has given him a great air of geniality, and also of elder statesmanship.' Utley was by no means the only colleague to think he put it on, and that Deedes, ever the actor, was fully aware that it added to his appeal as he got older.*

As his celebrity spread he began to relax self-imposed restrictions. Over the years, successive producers and presenters of *Desert Island Discs* had tried to convince Deedes to appear on the programme but he resisted, until 2002 when Sue Lawley managed to land him. He had put it off partly because he couldn't think of eight records he would want to listen to, but also for fear that he would be asked personal questions about his family and his feelings. In the event, Lawley did press him about how the war had affected him, but steered clear of any personal matters. There was a passing reference to Hilary, but no mention of Julius.

The programme's researcher who had gone to pre-interview Deedes at the *Telegraph* had a dreadful time, as the notes handed to Sue Lawley before the recording reveal. Deedes was half an hour late for the appointment, 'weighed down with an enormous sports bag, groaning that he hated talking about himself'. He rejected the researcher's request that they move into a private office where they could have talked more intimately; Deedes insisted they stayed in the newsroom where he could play selectively deaf if he found any of the questions off-side. 'So as an attempt to draw secrets and revelations from him it was a bit of

* The author's best guess is that Deedes slowly acquired his shushing in the late 1960s when his clipped, upper-class way of speaking fell out of fashion, even for Tory politicians. It was a defence mechanism against the 'anti-toff' attacks from the Labour benches when he was Minister without Portfolio.

411

a flop,' the researcher reported, conceding defeat in penetrating the Deedes reserve, adding that the subject had at least promised to 'play up on the day'.

Deedes's sister Margaret helped him to pick some favourite singers who might cheer him up on the island, including Flanagan and Allen, Noel. Coward and Vera Lynn. The most regrettable choice was the toe-curling 'Goodbye England's Rose', Elton John's dirge at Diana's funeral, though there was some mitigation in that Deedes had at least been present in Westminster Abbey. The most characteristic was 'Here Sir!', one of the Harrow songs that reliably reduced Winston Churchill to tears. For a book he opted to take – along with the Bible and Shakespeare – his Prayer Book, 'the original one, no amendments,' he emphasised. His luxury was aftershave and hair lotion from Trumper in Jermyn Street.* The one record he selected to be saved if all were washed away was the African hymn 'Nkosi Sikelel' iAfrika' – God Bless Africa. Overall, his performance was low-key and rather blood-less, and there was no obvious rapport with Sue Lawley. He answered several of her questions by repeating, almost verbatim, whole passages from *Dear Bill*.

Deedes had been less than thrilled in 1986 when a life peerage was thrust upon him, partly because his elevation to the Upper House was to raise the question of the validity of the arms and crest the family had used since the seventeenth century. In 1653, during the Interregnum, Robert Deedes, a direct ancestor, was granted arms, which produced a handsome family crest of 'three martlets counterchanged' framed by an eagle with wings raised skyward, and wanted to continue to use it when raised to the peerage. The crest was still borne on one of the external walls at Saltwood Castle long after the family had moved out. As

---

* Deedes stayed loyal to Geo. F. Trumper's Eucris lotion all his life, despite blaming its irresistible aroma for once inducing a bee to sting him on the head and cause an extreme allergic reaction. He ordered his last consignment, a 500ml travel bottle, in the summer of 2004, a month before he broke his femur and his globe-trotting days came to an end.

Telegraph editor he would be asked to write formal letters of accreditation for correspondents travelling in the third world, and he would seal the letter with wax, stamping the Deedes crest on the letter. It would bemuse and delight immigration officers who would generally treat the *Telegraph* correspondent with new respect.

The College of Arms, which oversees such matters, approaches all new peers, anxious that they avail themselves of its services – at no less than a thousand pounds a go – in creating a crest. Bill Deedes wrote crossly to Jeremy, saying the Garter King of Arms acts like a man 'trying to sell double-glazing' as he has 'a dozen or so from art school embellishing parchment – at a price – and they like to keep them busy'. Deedes simply wanted to incorporate the 1653 arms into his baronial crest, but there was a snag. All arms granted during the Interregnum were declared null after the Restoration of Charles II. Successive generations of the Deedes family simply ignored the prohibition and continued to display their illegitimate arms proudly. 'So I suppose strictly we have been living in sin for about 325 years,' Bill wrote to Jeremy shortly after he was made a life peer.

There was no such complication thirteen years later, when a letter arrived from Downing Street advising Bill Deedes of his nomination as Knight Commander of the Order of the British Empire. To him this was a proper honour, earned by a lifetime's sweat, 'for services to journalism and humanitarian causes', not some bauble chucked at him according to a tariff designed to reward failed politicians. He accepted without hesitation and wrote excitedly to Hilary, 'I've heard of knights being made peers, but not peers being made knights, certainly not at my age, so it is kind of Blair.'

He suspected that Charles Moore had put in a word for him to reward his front-page stories about the Balkan refugee crisis. He was chuffed about the reference in the citation to his humanitarian role for, as he put it to Hilary, 'Uncle Wyndham would have been pleased'. He closed his letter by telling her of another forthcoming trip to Albania, which meant he would be out of the country when she had a back operation and would also miss a birthday lunch that their old friend Lady Aldington had planned with his sisters Margaret and Hermione. 'She will be cross, very cross. But the *Telegraph* want some dramatic account of the refugee plight, so I really have no option.'

Deedes, of course, did have the option of declining the trip but he was a master at blaming his failure to honour domestic or social commitments on the pressure of duty. His enthusiasm shone through in his pay-off, ordering Hilary's silence until the Queen's Birthday Honours were to be published three weeks later. 'Blimey! Don't talk in your sleep!' Bill and Hilary were by this point on calm and relatively easygoing terms. The rancour that had surrounded her departure had abated in the intervening two years. They were not exactly close, but they were friendly, and Hilary would look forward to the occasional visits he made to stay with her in Scotland, usually three or four times a year.

Lord Deedes, of Aldington in the County of Kent, was knighted on 15 December 1999 and, rather as he had before Diana's funeral, he planned the day with military precision. Removed from the tensions of New Hayters, Hilary was detached enough to be proud of her husband's achievements. There was no question that she would come south to witness him receiving the honour.

'Awkward event in that it involved hauling wife and youngest daughter down from Scotland,' he recorded in his diary. The Carlton Club was full the night before, so Deedes, then eighty-six, had to leave New Hayters early to drive himself to Ashford station to catch the train around seven o'clock. He arrived at the Carlton early enough to nip next door for a haircut at Truffitt & Hill, and was then driven to the Palace. He described the moment of dubbing thus: 'March up, left turn, fancy I manage an instinctive bow. Down on the pad. Right shoulder, left shoulder with some famous sword. Up. Did they say stand left or right of the pad? Can't remember. Stand right, bow head, as they told us to do, so Queen can slip KBE ribbon over head . . . I think they said four steps back, which at my age would be perilous. Bow again, and march off. Thank heaven it's over!'

In fact, as the closed-circuit television footage which is taken of these events proved, Deedes had performed impeccably. His back was ramrod straight as the Queen dubbed him: he certainly had the bearing of a soldier, but not of one who had last put on his uniform half a century earlier.

After two gins and tonic with the Lord Chamberlain, 'an old pal', and a chat with the other guests who had received honours, he was driven from the Palace with Hilary, Jeremy and Lucy for celebratory oysters at Wilton's in Jermyn Street. Lunch over, Bill inevitably headed back to the office for leader conference. 'I go to the office every day,' he told the *Telegraph*'s court correspondent, who wrote a detailed report of the event in the next day's paper. 'I love it.'

Generous coverage in other newspapers reflected how Deedes had grown out of his narrow role as the *Telegraph* reader's favourite columnist into a fully-fledged national treasure. The *Mirror* gave his knighthood almost a whole page, under the headline 'Knighthood for a Legend Still Young at 86'. It listed '20 intriguing bits of news we've got about Dear Bill', including the fact that he still hit fifty golf balls every morning, and that he had been to the Balkans twice in the previous nine months.

His celebrity was reinforced with his appearance on the BBC's satirical quiz show *Have I Got News for You*, in its last episode of the old millennium. He was paired with the *Private Eye* editor Ian Hislop, facing the comedian Paul Merton and the novelist Will Self.

The youthful production team were nervous that Deedes would be too slow to keep up with the pace of the show, but he was at the top of his game, cracking one-liners assisted by Hislop, who generously fed him many of his best lines. The show as broadcast seemed an almost Wildean riot of off-the-cuff humour, but Deedes's diary shows that the recording session had been rehearsed and scripted, just like his 'interview' with Harold

Macmillan in the first party political broadcast in 1953. He and Ian Hislop were sent off before the recording session with a list of the questions they would be asked during the broadcast. 'Hislop and I return to my room, order tea, and go through the questions for 20 minutes. Solve one or two, discuss what to say when don't know the answers, think up one or two witticisms.'

Deedes was struck again by how television companies failed to offer proper drinks to their performers, and gloomily surveyed the soft drinks and the sandwiches covered in cling film. He asked Hislop about the guest performer on the opposing team; he had not heard of him and in his diary referred to him as 'Wilfred Self'. Hislop divulged that Self had taken drugs on John Major's plane, 'which raises my morale a bit. A background of disreputable incidents is liable to lead to deep embarrassment on this particular programme.'

Deedes was amused to discover that the recording, which was more fun than expected and less dangerous, went on for three times longer than the broadcast time so that judicious editing would allow all the participants to appear spontaneously witty. As he was driven back to Kent in a studio limo, he concluded that he had earned his thousand-pound appearance fee. Hislop recalled that the genius of Deedes on the show was the way he used his age to comic advantage: 'He always knew where the jokes were.'

Deedes regularly featured in the pages of *Private Eye*, and not just as the fictional recipient of the Dear Bill letters. He was frequently lampooned as the journalist who had broken the news of the invention of the wheel, or as a soldier who had fought at the Battle of Waterloo. ('Arthur Wellington was my commanding officer, some years after I had been his fag at Eton, or it may have been Harrow.') But the satire was always scrupulously affectionate, despite the fact that when he attended *Private Eye*'s fortnightly lunches Deedes invariably failed to provide any titbits for the following week's magazine. Hislop concluded that Deedes was a great man, but a lousy gossip.

Looking towards his ninetieth birthday, Deedes sensed that his travelling days would come to an end before long, and 1999 and 2000 were his most nomadic years. He mounted no fewer than twenty foreign trips in that time but, predictably, his body eventually rebelled. The medical emergency that *Telegraph* colleagues feared occurred in February 2001, four months short of his eighty-eighth birthday. A huge 7.9 earthquake had flattened parts of the Indian state of Gujarat, and Deedes arranged for himself to be taken there by Unicef to write about the relief operation and to raise some money for the survivors from *Telegraph* readers.

On Sunday 4 February Deedes was taken on a gruelling all-day tour of the disaster area. His party travelled by helicopter, as it was the only way to get around the devastated region. He was working with Peter Macdiarmid, a *Telegraph* photographer who had flown out with him from London, as well as two Unicef staff. Deedes had advised the news desk that he would file that evening. Filing for Monday's paper usually guarantees a reporter a good show because so little happens on a normal Sunday, and Deedes would have had his eye on a full page of coverage.

As happens on these trips, they fell behind schedule and Deedes, ever a stickler for punctuality, grew flustered at the prospect of filing late. They got further behind schedule when they stopped to refuel, and Deedes, unusually, had a very strong cup of coffee. Finally they took off to fly back to Ahmedabad, from where Deedes was to file his graphic account of the humanitarian consequences of the disaster. He began scribbling his story in his notebook when the Unicef staff noticed he was having difficulty turning the pages of his notebook with his left hand. Over the racket of the rotor blades the pilot was told to radio ahead so a car was waiting for them at the airport to rush Deedes to the nearby Rajasthan hospital.

There a scan quickly confirmed that he had suffered a stroke, though because he received prompt attention the damage did not appear too serious. Deedes had not finished his story in the helicopter so, as he was prepared for his scan, he dictated the rest of it to Macdiarmid with instructions that he send it on to London. Though the piece could perfectly easily have been held over for a day or two, Deedes was adamant that he was not going to start missing deadlines seventy years into his reporting career.

I was foreign editor of the *Daily Telegraph* at the time, and was immediately informed that the medical catastrophe which had long been dreaded had occurred on my watch. I was booked on the following morning's flight to Delhi, while Paul Hill and Patsy Dryden, who ran the paper's foreign operation, persuaded an Indian diplomat to meet me at the High Commission that Sunday night to issue an emergency visa.

By the time I reached Deedes's bedside the following evening, recovery was under way. Deedes had been profoundly depressed in the first few hours after the stroke because his left hand was immobile and he could not walk. Fearing he would be permanently disabled, and therefore unable to work, he descended into a funk.

But he rallied the moment the Indian doctors gave him the news that he would make a full recovery so long as he took six weeks' complete rest. For some reason, Deedes became convinced that he was in an exclusive private clinic, when in fact it was a well-run but far from prosperous hospital in one of India's poorer state capitals. The doctors were skilled and the nurses kindly and attentive, but parts of the hospital were squalid and visitors learnt to avoid the lavatories.

The hospital administrator, conscious that he had under his roof a journalistic celebrity, was anxious that 'Mr Lord Deedes' should avail himself of one of the hospital's private rooms. Deedes vetoed that immediately on the grounds that he would be bored, and had already struck up a rapport with the staff who were attending to him in the general ward. Indian hospitals employ male orderlies – 'ward boys' – to do the more menial tasks such as emptying bedpans. To their evident bafflement, these lowly staff would be addressed as 'old cock', while the nurses learnt to answer to 'darling', as in: 'you are doing that drip beautifully darling, no pain at all'. For their part, the nurses called Deedes 'Uncle' and treated him as they might a beloved member of their own family.

Soon Deedes had established a sort of court in his ward, from which patients who were not so fortunate would occasionally be removed to the mortuary, discreetly covered in sheets. To the consternation of his doctors he quietly organised a bedside press conference of Indian journalists, including a team from the television arm of the Associated Press. Through these journalists he offered advice to the Indian government on how to structure the relief operation.

As his condition improved, and the physiotherapist worked to rebuild strength in his weakened limbs, Deedes's spirits soared. An emergency flying doctor was sent from London by the *Telegraph* to ensure Deedes was fit enough to come home. Only on his last night in the hospital did Deedes's faith in the Indian health system desert him. He was in a filthy mood when the British doctor and I arrived at his bedside to prepare him for the journey home. He claimed not to have slept at all the previous night and grumbled that he had suddenly been abandoned by his devoted nursing staff.

In fact, overnight there had been a huge aftershock – measuring 5.3 on the Richter scale – which had sent all the nurses, and the patients who could struggle out of bed, into the street where they spent the night. Deedes, who claimed not to have slept a wink, had in fact dozed right through both the seismic event and the panic-sticken evacuation of staff and patients.

Deedes affected to be indignant that the *Telegraph* had sent two people out to bring him home. 'When I was editor of the *Daily Telegraph*,' he announced with mock gravity, 'it was considered that the foreign editor had better things to do than go half way round the world to see a foolish old man who has overdone it.' On the other hand, he explained that for someone of his generation it was infinitely preferable 'to go down in action than to fall over on a golf course'. The key, Deedes reminded all his visitors, was this: 'You want to die with your boots on – that's the thing, with your boots on.' As usual when Deedes uttered solemn thoughts, it was a bit of a joke; but there was perhaps a part of Deedes that made him wish he had died with the dust of Gujarat on his boots.

He had a theory about why he succumbed to the stroke in India. Ever since he acquired the taste in Abyssinia, it had been his custom after a strenuous day's reporting to wind down with a couple of stiff whiskies and soda. Out of deference to Mahatma Gandhi, who was born in the state, Gujarat was dry. Even foreigners with access to dollars or sterling could not secure alcohol unless – quixotically – they could produce a doctor's certificate stating they were genuine alcoholics, in which case they would be granted a bottle on medical grounds. Deedes had not sniffed alcohol since his arrival in Ahmedabad and was convinced that this had added to the pressure that built up in his brain with such disastrous consequences.

The journey home passed without incident, except for Deedes's rapture at being allowed gins and tonic at Delhi airport after his enforced abstinence. On landing at Heathrow Deedes was driven to a private hospital near his home in Kent, and though doctors ordered six weeks' recuperation, he was agitating to get back to the office after a month.

Four weeks after his stroke he wrote to Charles Moore informing him that the 'top heart man' in Kent had told him he was in fine fettle, and far healthier than the new American vice-president, Dick Cheney. Moore accepted Deedes's early return to the office with equanimity, but grew alarmed three months later when he learnt from other sources of his intention to go to Bosnia, and then the Sudan. 'I would not want the *Telegraph* to support anything unwise or premature,' Moore wrote in a memo. 'Could we discuss?'

Deedes fended him off deftly, writing straight back and deferentially stressing he would do nothing without Moore's approval. He blamed his stroke in India on a missed blood pressure test, which would have given warning of coming trouble. Now, with a course of pills, his blood pressure was 'consistently 130 over 60, which your own medical adviser will tell you is pretty satisfactory ... the nurse who took it described it as lower than her own!'

Deedes promised to keep Moore fully appraised of his medical bulletins and travel plans. Naturally, he went both to Bosnia and the Sudan, also squeezing in a quick cross-Channel trip for the anniversary of the Battle of the Somme which he predicted would make a 'good Monday Notebook'. It had been a close shave in Gujarat, but he had bounced back from the stroke and was travelling almost every month.

But as his ninetieth birthday loomed, he planned an ambitious African trip with Sue Ryan to observe the human consequences of the war in Darfur. They based themselves at Lokichokio, an air base in northern Kenya close to the border with Sudan, from which international aid agencies try to feed the victims of Africa's various civil wars.

Deedes wanted to see for himself how the food was delivered, so he and Ryan undertook a hazardous three-day journey, capped by a mile-long march through the bush in stifling heat. They watched from the ground as the pilot circled over the drop zone, then threw the plane's nose up and yanked open the rear hatch: the sky was suddenly filled with sacks of grain, the only form of sustenance the starving of southern Sudan could expect for weeks.

Ryan was aware that the bush camp in which she and Deedes were forced to spend the night lay in the geographic centre of Sudan's civil war. Aid bases had been attacked by the various tribal factions and Ryan had asked Deedes if he was sure it was worth the risk. They had sat through a terrifying security briefing to be told that, in the event of a full armed assault, they would have to muster at a point three days' walk away and wait to be airlifted out. The walk was reckoned at three days for a fit young relief worker.

'Is this wise?' Ryan asked Deedes. At this, he produced a crude map with arrows that he had whipped at the end of the security briefing the night before. 'I can lead the way,' he said. In fact they were very lucky: three hours after their plane took them out of that camp it was overrun and burnt down, the aid workers were evacuated and some of the local civilians killed.

Deedes's self-contained existence was threatened in 2003 with the breakdown of the marriage of Lucy, his youngest daughter. Lucy left her husband behind in the Scottish borders and moved south with their son. Hilary, by then eighty-eight and suffering with a chronic bad back, could not stay on her own so moved with her. An unfortunate stand-off ensued: Hilary wanted to move back into New Hayters, but since she had left for Scotland six years before a local couple had been living in the house, keeping it clean and secure during Deedes's frequent foreign travels. They occupied the downstairs wing that Hilary wanted to take over because of her bad back.

Deedes was reluctant to evict the couple, Eddy and Wendy, whose presence had allowed him total freedom of action, rather as when he lived with his uncle Wyndham in Bethnal Green before the war. In a letter to Hilary from 2003 in response to her request that the couple move out, and she move back in, he showed his exasperation at her suggestion that his routine be changed.

'If Aga goes wrong – and the old thing has been playing up lately – they fix it . . . if cellar gives trouble, Eddy deals with it. If New Hayters needs painting outside, or new draught-proof windows, a friend of Eddy's turns up . . . Car always in safe good order, tyres up . . . Eddy makes sure my computers work. All the food is bought for me.' In other words, the couple were giving Deedes the domestic life he wanted – practical and impersonal, allowing him to come and go as he pleased.

Hilary pressed the point and moved back in to New Hayters in the spring of 2004. It was a difficult time for them both; her health was visibly declining, and by then she was showing signs of possible dementia. Hilary then started to feel intense pain. A scan revealed that her cancer had returned and was far advanced. There was nothing to do but to move her into a hospice between Ashford and Aldington. Juliet, who had come over from America, was with her when she died a few days later at breakfast time. Bill was at home at the time, but was driven over immediately. As usual, the famous Deedes reserve betrayed not a hint of what he was feeling. He did not go into the office on the day she died, but it was business as usual the following morning, and on arrival at Canary Wharf he thanked colleagues for their condolences, but made clear he did not wish to dwell on the subject of his wife's death.

The following month, Deedes went on a trip to Normandy with the photographer Abbie Trayler-Smith. She had made numerous trips around the world with him and always looked forward to his genial company, but on this journey she found him unusually reflective and emotional. He talked to her about Hilary and their life together. Trayler-Smith recalled that it was very clear that he was deeply affected by her death. Bill and Hilary's sixty-two-year marriage had been difficult from the start; in fact, their relationship had been fraught from the earliest days of their courtship in 1941. They both seemed to understand they were fundamentally ill-matched: she would not engage with his public life; he could never be troubled to show any interest in her animals. He had neglected her, as he had neglected his children. The neglect was fundamental and entrenched, for Hilary had first complained of it in 1948 when she gently rebuked Bill for not showing enough love to the infant Jeremy. But despite such provocations, his manic travelling in later life and the humiliations of the Victoria Combe era, they maintained an affection and respect for each other that endured for the six years she was in Scotland, and there was never any talk of divorce. The amity was threatened only at the very end when she moved back into New Hayters, and they found tensions built up when they were under the same roof again.

Shortly before she died, during that final unhappy period when Bill was resisting her moving back in, Hilary changed her will.

Previously everything she had – really just New Hayters, which remained in her name – had been left to Bill. But she amended the will so that the house was left to the four children and Bill was granted only a life interest in the house. The children believed she changed her will in case he was tempted eventually to bequeath the proceeds of the house to Victoria Combe, or possibly to his own charitable foundation. Given the financial generosity he had shown his children over the years, that notion seems somehow fanciful, but Hilary was by this time in a confused state of mind. The change to her will meant that for the last three years of his life Bill Deedes, who was born to be squire of Saltwood Castle and its thousands of Kentish acres, did not own even the house in which he lived, or the two-and-three-quarter acres of land in which New Hayters lay.

Hilary's death did not reduce the tempo of his travelling, and in fact he was acting more and more like an old man in a hurry. After his return from Normandy he set off in July for Darfur again, to observe the refugee crisis created by the savage policies of the government in Khartoum. The trip had been a success, produced good copy, and had raised his spirits that a man who had just turned ninety-one could stay on the road.

A couple of days after his return, he was walking out of the kitchen door into the garden at New Hayters with a satchel of papers slung over his shoulder when he tripped on a slight ridge in the concrete, fell headlong, snapping his femur and ended up in the William Harvey hospital in Ashford. Deedes immediately understood that this would bring an end to his globetrotting. He sank into a deep gloom at the prospect of enforced immobility, as he had after his stroke in India. At one point it seemed the shock might kill him, and for several days after the operation to repair his leg he seemed to lose the will to live. After surgery he was placed in a grim general ward, next to a heavily tattooed motorcyclist who had also come a cropper and broken his leg.

Jeremy Deedes wanted his father to be transferred to a private clinic to recuperate from the operation. The costs would have been covered by the *Telegraph*'s health insurance scheme, but Bill was adamant that he did not want to move. He took great pride in pretending to think he was receiving magnificent care and was adamant – as he had been in Ahmedabad – that private rooms were boring. He was being attended to by the 'top leg man in Kent', he would declare when the suggestion of a move was made. There was another factor, too: he retained an affection for the NHS as a reaction to the awful memories of having to sell the family silver to pay for Julius's blood transfusions. So he stayed put in the ward, next to the hobbled biker and a deranged old man, who sat up most of the night, shouting abuse at the nurses. 'Sometimes one is grateful to be pretty deaf,' Deedes told visitors, riffling through the newspapers looking for items for his column, which of course continued without interruption throughout his hospital stay.

CHAPTER 25

'A STINKING MOB'

*'Only when most of you are producing a newspaper more
like the* Daily Mail *shall we have the paper we want.'*

By the beginning of 2003 Conrad Black's shareholders were
losing patience with the way the majority of the company's
profits seemed to be funding his lavish lifestyle. The 'corporate
governance zealots', as he termed his shareholders who were
beginning to ask where their dividends had gone, no longer
accepted his flippant dismissal of their complaints. The answer to
the riddle of the missing money was to be found in Black's 2007
trial on multiple charges of fraud: he and his wife Barbara Amiel
had embarked on a fantastic ten-year spending spree, behaving
like their billionaire friends with the profits of Hollinger, the
Telegraph's publicly listed company, which Black controlled via a
cunningly constructed minority holding. In advance of the trial an
independent investigation into the funding of their private jets and
three homes and staff found that Black had operated what
amounted to a 'corporate kleptocracy'.

Publicly Deedes had always shown elaborate deference to
Black, but privately he was never entirely reconciled to him as an
appropriate successor to Lord Hartwell. Black never really got the
point of Deedes either, and he did not merit a single reference in
Black's bombastic and inadvertently hilarious autobiography, *A*

426

Life in Progress. Deedes did not own a copy of that book, which was not published in Britain, but he was aware that it contained some gratuitous attacks on individuals within the old management structure, and that Black had been gloatingly unpleasant about Hartwell and his son Nicholas Berry.

Deedes did not seem entirely heartbroken that the chairman who had tried to send him packing in 1986 – 'well, I guess it is hail and farewell' – would in fact be leaving the scene before his evergreen columnist and roving correspondent. That personal satisfaction aside, there was no denying that any change of ownership was destabilising; every journalist believes that the people who buy a newspaper company always turn out to be worse stewards than those they have bought it from.

By coincidence, Black's last public appearance at a *Telegraph* event was at Deedes's ninetieth birthday dinner, at the Carlton Club in June 2003, for which he had flown over from New York with Evelyn de Rothschild in the latter's private jet. On their arrival in London, the two men were dismayed to find the London papers that day were full of predictions of Black's demise and speculation about the future of the *Telegraph* group.

A month after that dinner, Deedes was thrilled to be invited to tea by Barbara Amiel at the Stafford Hotel in St James's. The invitation seemed to confirm his status as an important figure in the newspaper's hierarchy, as opposed to a relic of the past, and Deedes wrote a full diary entry about the encounter.

Amiel wanted to gossip and also to seek his advice on the growing discontent over the fact that her column was continuing to appear in the *Daily Telegraph* while her husband was being accused of siphoning off the profits. Amiel was frustrated that she could not get a straight answer from Charles Moore about whether her column was still wanted. 'We are always glad to print your pieces,' he would tell her, but Amiel though this sort of endorsement was not satisfactory.

'I confirm it is NOT satisfactory,' Deedes reported himself telling her, with unusual forthrightness, 'not because of her or

Conrad or Moore, but because the well-informed know of her connection with Conrad and this reduces the influence of what she says. All journalists want to make an impact. Her impact is weakened by the connection. I perceive that has convinced her.'

In fact, Amiel did not heed Deedes's advice. She told him that she could not write for a Murdoch paper because of the price war he had started with the *Telegraph*, which had done her husband such damage. Deedes encouraged her to secure a deal with Veronica Wadley, whom he liked and admired, to beef up the *Evening Standard*'s leader page. In the event, Amiel stayed put at the *Telegraph*, testing the patience of Moore and his successor Martin Newland, even after Black lost control of the group and had been expelled as chairman by his company board. The final break came in March 2004 when Amiel wrote that Martha Stewart, the television lifestyle expert who had been caught insider trading, had fallen victim to the 'tall poppy syndrome' currently afflicting corporate America. Her column appeared just a week after Conrad Black had been denounced in a Delaware court judgment and, though she made no reference to her husband in that column, readers were implicitly invited to view them as a matching pair of corporate martyrs. The *Telegraph* management decided that Amiel's routine was laying the paper open to ridicule, and her column was dropped.

Moore's departure the previous October had been a shock to staff, particularly when his successor was named as Martin Newland. Newland had been a well-respected news editor of the *Telegraph* before he was sent to Canada to help set up Black's new daily, the *National Post*. Most staff in London were astonished that he had been appointed by Black over so many ostensibly better qualified candidates, notably Dominic Lawson, the editor of the *Sunday Telegraph*, and Sarah Sands, Moore's deputy on the daily.

Newland was dealt a bad hand, for immediately he took over as editor it became obvious that Black was going under. After an acrimonious public spat with Hollinger International, the public holding company, the Telegraph Group, including the *Spectator*, was auctioned. On 30 July 2004, Sir David and Sir Frederick Barclay, secretive twins who had made their fortune as property developers and lived on the private island of Brequou in the Channel Islands, secured the titles for the enormous price of £665 million.

Deedes was initially relieved that the Barclays had emerged as the winners, because two private equity outfits had expressed an interest and he feared there would be mass job cuts and asset stripping if they prevailed. Jeremy had also reassured him that the twins were probably the best of the bunch of bidders. They seemed to be amply rich, and it was put about that they had a profound affection for the paper and its culture. Nevertheless, there was the inevitable sense of drama around the *Telegraph*'s premises in Canary Wharf which always accompanies a change of ownership.

Deedes, who had been through precisely the same agonising uncertainty as editor when the Berry family lost control in 1985, instinctively tried to bolster Newland, who was a fitness fanatic with a physique which suggested he need not be intimidated by any new owner. Deedes sent him encouraging letters, telling him that mental toughness was necessary for an editor at a time of change.

But privately Deedes had some misgivings even before the Barclays took control. During a lunch at Paradiso in February 2004, he was in a sulphurous mood about the condition of the paper. Newland had moved leader conference from its civilised mid-afternoon slot to noon, which made it difficult for leader writers to get to lunch in the West End on time. Worse still, Newland was regularly failing to attend leader conference himself, an unforgivable omission for Deedes partly because, in his day, running the leaders was one of the editor's few specific responsibilities.

Deedes was protective of Newland in public, but after his second pink gin he betrayed a deepening sense of gloom. 'What else is he [Newland] doing, what else?' To the suggestion that he was probably mired in meetings with management and the marketing department, all the chores that are the burden of the modern newspaper editor, he replied: 'Oh for God's sake, that old nonsense, fucking waste of time, they used to get me in, all this fucking nonsense about twenty-one-year-old readers.' It was unusual for Deedes to swear like that and he was obviously highly animated. Asked if the *Telegraph*, as a title as opposed to a business, had ever been in worse condition, he pondered gravely for a few moments and said, 'No.'

Deedes was also scrupulously loyal, as one old editor should be to another young editor, despite his misgivings. When Newland asked him to write a signed piece to reassure readers that the paper's future was secure, Deedes cheerfully obliged, deploying a protracted metaphor of the *Daily Telegraph* as an aeroplane. He reminded readers that many years before he had joined the *Morning Post*, a newspaper which was not suited to flying at '30,000 ft along with Rothermere's *Daily Mail* and Beaverbrook's soaring *Daily Express*'.

The metaphor moved relentlessly on, with Deedes recalling how, when he was editor in the 1980s, the print unions were so anarchic that 'even the cabin staff were belted into their chairs every night!' Pressing on further Deedes suggested that Conrad Black's takeover in 1985 allowed a sense of complacency to set in – 'we loosened our seatbelts; drinks and dinner came up' – until the aircraft encountered this latest turbulence. He predicted confidently that 'we'll land safely' even if 'some of the passengers are looking a bit solemn. Time I took a walk down the aisle. Turbulence? Alongside what I have known, this plane's a rock!'

It was certainly one of the odder pieces Deedes wrote. The metaphor of a plane trying to maintain altitude was not a great success, and few *Telegraph* journalists were reassured to read they were working for an organisation with the aerodynamic qualities of a rock. Nor did the article entirely mask Deedes's private misgivings. Immediately the Barclays won the auction, it became obvious that the price of £665 million was far too high and that operating costs would have to be drastically reduced to earn back the capital outlay.

Deedes's own anxieties multiplied when the Barclays appointed Murdoch MacLennan of the *Daily Mail* as the new chief executive. He had been regarded as a competent manager at Associated Newspapers, but he had never been allowed near the editorial floor. At the *Telegraph* he at once started imposing himself in editorial matters. Though Newland was not sacked as editor, he was undermined and surrounded by hostile forces. Without telling Newland, MacLennan recruited Simon Heffer from the *Daily Mail* as a star columnist and the voice of a raucous, populist strand of Conservatism alien to the *Telegraph*'s culture, and anathema to Deedes's One Nation sympathies.

Other executives took the same route from the *Mail* to the *Telegraph*. The executive editor was removed and replaced by Lawrence Sear, who had been much disliked at the *Mail* and was not taken entirely seriously at the *Telegraph* on account of his peculiar moustache. He was a dead ringer for Saddam Hussein, and he was soon known simply as Saddam around the office. One day as Deedes, walking on a stick, headed out of the office Sear rushed ostentatiously across the newsroom to shake his hand and assure him that it was an honour to meet 'a *Telegraph* legend'. As Sear headed back to his glass box Deedes swivelled towards the leader writers' desk with a look of theatrical horror on his face and said in a stage whisper, 'A palpable shit!'

The second half of 2004 was a depressing time for Deedes. Having broken his femur on his return from Darfur in July, he was coming to terms with the end of his long-haul travelling. Feeling physically vulnerable, he also began to worry, absurdly, about his own job. Deedes had witnessed his first cull of journalists shortly after he joined the *Morning Post* in 1931, and ever since then he always feared he was about to be sacked, even when he was established as the *Telegraph*'s most popular writer. Jeremy knew how to read the signs of his father's bouts of insecurity, and asked Martin Newland to write to him to cheer him up and reassure him that his position was secure. Newland, a devoted admirer of his predecessor but two, was happy to oblige, though he thought it an eccentric and unnecessary exercise.

On top of anxiety about his own position, at around this time Deedes began to feel profound gloom about the future of the *Telegraph*, the central institution in his long life where he felt more at home than in New Hayters. His diary entry of 10 December 2004 noted a poor turnout at the office carol service, where he delivered his customary brief address. Sue Ryan was especially gloomy. The directors of advertising and marketing had just been replaced. 'Martin Newland, editor, arrives and sits between me and Ryan, murmuring to me, "Well, *I'm* still here!" in a not very confident tone of voice. My little contribution goes okay; but you learn if you speak as often as I have done to get vibrations back from your audience – yes, even in church. The vibrations today are sombre.'

Deedes was beginning to think that his worst fear might be coming true – that he was regarded as a relic, part of the *Telegraph*'s past rather than its future. Two days later he noted in his diary that the new management had ripped out the old boardroom and Conrad Black's grand office, as if to purge the *Telegraph* of its past. He wondered what they would do with the portraits of past editors, including the one of him, painted by Festing. 'Dare say they'll throw the portrait back at me; nobody more embedded in the past than me.'*

Then Deedes moved into a full denunciation of the failings of the new management, confiding to his diary in terms he would never utter in public:

---

* His fear was unfounded on that count. Shortly after his death the Festing portrait was hung in a prominent position in the *Telegraph*'s new headquarters in Victoria.

Knowing the Telegraph intimately, as I do, Daily Mail/Associated Press methods won't work at the DT. They will walk out, plenty of takers. There is everyone says a lack of communication. Nobody sees Murdoch whatever his name, the new boss. Nobody gets anything but a terse comment from the owners. Even in the last days of the Berry family I don't remember lower morale. I had hopes of Jeremy being a bit of an ambassador, but I suspect they have sidelined him. They want to run the show their way. Well, if they do to editorial what they did to advertising, I shall walk. Draw comfort from that.[*]

Word of Deedes's unhappiness seems to have leaked to the Barclays, for in March 2005 a letter arrived out of the blue inviting him to lunch at the Ritz – which the family also owned – with Aidan Barclay and his brother Howard. Aidan had the title of chairman and was said to be in ultimate control of the *Telegraph*, though his father, Sir David, kept a close eye on the group, occasionally intervening in editorial matters by fax from Monaco or Brequou. Though Deedes was deeply suspicious of the Barclays he was ever vulnerable to flattery and was thrilled and excited by the invitation. He asked Victoria Combe to light a candle for him in church on the day of the lunch. He was intrigued, too, that the letter of invitation from Aidan Barclay contained a schoolboy grammatical error, and by the detail that a five-line lunch invitation sent to his home address was marked 'Private and Confidential', with the envelope stamped 'Strictly Private and Confidential'.

The lunch was not a meeting of minds and did nothing to reassure Deedes of the Barclays' suitability as stewards of the *Telegraph*. Given Deedes's celebrated love of a gin or whisky before lunch, it was odd that the Ritz waiters were not instructed to offer him a pre-prandial drink and characteristic of him that he

---

[*] Murdoch MacLennan soon began purging editorial as thoroughly as he had cleared out the advertising and marketing departments, but Deedes did not walk.

did not ask for one. Nor was wine served at lunch. Deedes told several people of this omission, adding his traditional condition when imparting mundane gossip that it should be treated 'in strictest confidence'.

Apart from an abundance of fizzy water, Deedes's main memory of the lunch was that Aidan was extremely short, that his brother Howard scarcely said a word and that neither conveyed much knowledge of the editorial content of the *Daily Telegraph*. Deedes wrote a bread and butter note to his host, quixotically addressing him as 'Sir Aidan Barclay'. 'Anyone who has drawn a living from this newspaper as long as I have owe [*sic*] you, as the Aussies would put it, "their best hit". Will do my best.'

That was no hollow promise, for soon Deedes was planning one last journalistic hurrah. In the spring of 2005 Sue Ryan conceived of a highly ambitious trip to cap his career: she would drive him along the entire route he had taken as soldier, from D-Day to VE Day, for him to write a week-long series of articles about the defeat of Nazism. It was a bold suggestion: they would set off after Deedes had turned ninety-two, and was in effect confined to a wheelchair as he was still finding it difficult to walk on his sticks. He knew that one more fall and broken limb would probably kill him. Ryan, however, did not know that by then Deedes had lost full bladder function and was dependent on a catheter, which was greatly to add to his discomfort in travelling long distances by road.

Nevertheless, he quickly accepted Ryan's plan and became so set on the idea that when she began to have second thoughts and to worry about the medical implications of the trip he refused to contemplate calling it off. For him, part of the attraction of the trip was working with two of his favourite travelling companions of the post-Combe era, Ryan and the darkly glamorous Abbie Trayler-Smith.

The emotional highpoint of the trip was the return to the bridge over the Twente Canal where Deedes had lost his men, and won his MC. They found the exact spot with extreme difficulty;

Deedes had been ready to abandon the effort but Ryan showed her journalist doggedness and eventually they came upon it. All that day Deedes had been tense and bad-tempered at the thought of returning to the point of carnage, and his misery was apparent when he stood momentarily on the bridge for Trayler-Smith to take a few pictures. When he climbed back into the car he was completely silent on the drive back to the hotel. Sue Ryan's mobile phone rang: the office in London wanted to know if Deedes could knock out a quick piece defending the memory of Denis Thatcher after someone had attacked him. Ryan knew that he was in a black mood by the way Deedes immediately refused. She had never once known him to turn down a piece, on any subject, let alone on Denis. The gloom didn't lift until the three of them found their way back to the hotel, where Deedes had two stiff whiskies and soda. Immediately his mood brightened and he started talking about the war and the young subalterns he had lost that day on the canal. 'Once he started, he couldn't stop talking,' Ryan recalled. But he remained in a dark mood about the state of the *Telegraph*. While they travelled across Europe, secretaries were being made redundant as the new regime extended its purge of the staff it had inherited. When they had a drink Deedes would propose an ironic toast to Saddam – Lawrence Sear, the moustachioed executive editor.

Then the trio pressed on to Hanover, where Deedes had ended his war guarding German prisoners. Deedes had been appalled in 1945 by the terrible suffering of German civilians and how cities had been flattened by the RAF and the US Air Force. He went to look at a memorial to the dead German civilians, and then he announced he wanted to visit Hanover Cathedral. There, he lit a candle for the civilian dead. Sue Ryan hung back, but from a distance she scrutinised his pained features and saw to her surprise that tears were rolling down his cheeks. Ryan had not seen him cry before and did not see him cry again.

He was in a heightened emotional state, partly because of the memories the trip had revived, but also because he knew from the

435

toll it was taking on his body that he could not travel again for the paper. On the last night of the trip, in their Hanover hotel, he cheered up again at cocktail hour. He insisted on ordering champagne for Ryan and Trayler-Smith because he enjoyed the thought of Saddam combing through the bar bill in horror. Deedes stuck to his usual whisky and soda. Ryan recalled that he was highly emotional, though not downhearted. Most of all he seemed relieved that he had physically survived the trip and not let the *Telegraph* down by having had to abandon the mission half way through. The following morning they boarded the flight home from Hanover and, as the plane took off, Deedes knew that seventy years after his first out of town job, he was heading home, never to leave British shores again.

In his absence, the *Daily Telegraph* was no closer to settling down. Martin Newland staggered on without any proper direction or support from MacLennan. Shortly after his lunch with Aidan and Howard Barclay, Deedes had begun telling colleagues that 'those Barclays are going to lose a pile of money on the *Telegraph*, mark my words'. When Sarah Sands, the deputy editor, moved across to be editor of the *Sunday Telegraph* in June 2005, Newland was not allowed to appoint her successor. He eventually ended up with two deputies because the management could not make up their minds on a single candidate.

Deedes let his concerns about this muddle be widely known, and according to Kim Fletcher, then editorial director and still clinging on to his job as a holdover from the old regime, Murdoch MacLennan was 'paranoid' that Deedes might resign. MacLennan had a problem because Sue Ryan had already been identified as the next senior executive to be sacked. 'I had warned him of the danger that Bill might resign if Sue was pushed, and for MacLennan it became an obsession that his leaving would be a disaster, like the ravens leaving the Tower of London.'

MacLennan organised a further lunch for Bill Deedes, and Jeremy was invited along too. It was held in the *Telegraph*'s executive dining room, and wine was offered at the table in breach of the alcohol ban that had been imposed by the Barclays. Despite the fuss he made of not having been given a drink at the Ritz, Deedes did not accept a glass; only Jeremy took any wine.

Deedes said he wanted to establish from the lunch whether the Barclays were consciously purging the *Telegraph* of the culture of the old regime. According to Deedes's account, MacLennan emphatically denied this and assured him that the twins, Sir David and Sir Frederick, had enormous affection for the paper, which was why they had bought it. MacLennan said that the sackings and redundancies were necessary because – as Deedes had known from the beginning – the Barclays had paid far too much and had to cut costs out of the business. Despite the chief executive's reassurance, Deedes remained convinced that there was a conscious cultural purge going on. *Telegraph* journalists were constantly hearing from the management floor of the new team's intolerance for what it called 'the country club culture' of the newspaper they had bought.

The general sense of drift and bewilderment hardened considerably in November 2005 when management announced the appointment of an editor-in-chief, the clearest indication yet of a lack of confidence in the two editors, Martin Newland and Sarah Sands. Few at the *Telegraph* had heard of John Bryant, who had worked latterly at the *Daily Mail*, where he had been part of a small group of venerable executives indulged by Paul Dacre, the powerful editor. Peter McKay, who wrote the Ephraim Hardcastle gossip column in the *Mail*, had given these executives names from the television series *The Last of the Summer Wine*, and Bryant – who was a by no means youthful sixty-two by the time he came to the *Telegraph* – was known as Compo.

Deedes reacted with dismay to the creation of yet another layer of managerial confusion. In private talks and in public declarations he tried to buck up Newland, but it was clear that the editor's authority had drained away. After a few days considering his options, Newland resigned, convinced his position had become untenable.

Newland wrote to Deedes an hour before he told staff of his resignation, poignantly apologising to him for failing to show what Deedes had told him was the necessary level of 'mental toughness'. Deedes was scandalised that an editor could be treated so appallingly by management. Sands was sacked from the *Sunday Telegraph* shortly afterwards and the purge of Charles Moore's executives gathered pace. Neil Darbyshire, who had overseen the *Telegraph*'s news operation, left when a new deputy editor was appointed from the *Daily Mail*. Sue Ryan's departure was a particularly heavy blow to Deedes, as she had 'run' him during most of his later foreign trips and he regarded the manner of her sacking as particularly shabby. John Bryant dithered so long before telling her the news, even after Ryan's replacement had been recruited – once again, from the *Daily Mail* – that half the building new of her imminent sacking when MacLennan finally summoned her to his office. Deedes claimed, on hearing of Ryan's demise, to be considering resigning in protest, but as usual this sort of tough talk came to nothing. He told the author in a telephone conversation on 24 February 2006 that he had been persuaded not to resign after reading a batch of recent readers' letters that made him realise, he said, that he was an important bridge for loyal readers. But he bitterly concluded that his beloved *Telegraph* was now being run by 'a stinking mob'.

In theory, the editorial direction of the paper fell into the hands of Bryant, but in practice it was not clear whether he or MacLennan was in charge. Bryant spent most of his day not in the editor's chair on the twelfth floor, but on the fifteenth in an office next to MacLennan's. As his secretary on the editorial floor, he inherited a highly intelligent former school-mistress, Frances Banks, who had worked happily for Newland though her true loyalty remained to Charles Moore. Having become accustomed to Moore's circle of peers and top Tory politicians, Banks was deeply unimpressed by the low calibre of the names in Bryant's contact book.

Bryant may not have seemed a dynamic personality, but he

was an experienced newspaper executive who had had long spells on *The Times* and the *Daily Mail*, as well as the defunct *Sunday Correspondent* and the *European*, which had been owned by the Barclays until they shut it down when its losses became intolerable. Bryant went down to New Hayters to pay his respects, and though Deedes was sceptical of anyone who joined the *Telegraph* from the *Mail*, he was partly reassured to find Bryant had been around Fleet Street a while.

By Easter 2006, Deedes, no longer able to come into the office, had almost no friends left at the *Telegraph*. He still craved gossip from Canary Wharf, but increasingly there was no one he knew there to keep him informed. Instead he brooded about how the Barclays were destroying the civilised culture of the company and coarsening the pages of the newspaper. Cautious to the end, Deedes recoiled from any further correspondence with the Barclays or Murdoch MacLennan. Instead, he wrote a long memorandum expressing his dismay about the state of the *Telegraph*, his beloved home for almost all of his working life.

Nobody from the editor downwards has been sure where they stood. Received wisdom was that the Barclays enormously admired the *Telegraph* and so would pay any price for it. Such feeling has been well concealed from the existing staff. An impression was immediately imparted that they were inadequate, too 'clubby', too fond of drink and were in effect spoiled children of the disgraced Conrad Black regime.

The 15th (management) floor proclaimed this. It was swiftly stripped out. The custom of offering guests to an editor's lunch a glass of champagne before lunch and a white or red wine with the meal was abruptly and embarrassingly halted. Ostensibly to pay for a new print plant, redundancies were declared essential* . . . Most replacements came from the *Daily Mail*. The

---

* The print plant was never built, and management set on the cheaper option of renting capacity at News International's new state-of-the-art presses.

secretaries (on £25,000 a year) were included in the clear-out ... The depressing feature of this exercise was its impersonal character. Existing staff felt like pawns moved by an invisible hand.

Deedes noted that, for the first time since the Berry family had taken control of the *Telegraph* in 1928, the paper was being directed 'not by its owner, but by a manager'. The younger generation of Barclays, Aidan and his brother, whose name Deedes could not remember from their lunch at the Ritz, continued to operate out of their headquarters in St James's. Murdoch MacLennan, Deedes said, seemed no worse than many of the bad managers who had been employed over the years. But when he had been at the *Mail*, MacLennan operated 'in the tradition of newspapers excluded from editorial matters. At the *Telegraph*, he took charge of them.' Deedes remained convinced that the worst single aspect of the Barclays' takeover was the power it gave MacLennan, whom he regarded as lacking any subtle political or journalistic instincts.

Deedes reserved his most caustic comments for the Barclays themselves:

Clearly the feeling that we were an inadequate lot, especially in the top echelon, conveyed the feelings of the Barclay family. This was a newspaper they were ready to pay £660 million for, but it was being produced by an unsatisfactory staff. Not a word of encouragement or praise came the way of the journalists who produced this high-value newspaper, though reason suggested they must have had something to do with what the Barclays had paid. On the contrary, through redundancies &c came the message, only when most of you are producing a newspaper more like the *Daily Mail* shall we have the paper we want.

It struck me that what the Barclays saw in the *Telegraph* was an asset that in the right hands could be turned into a more profitable business. That was their role in life. To make this feasible, a different staff had to be imported by degrees and this [was] justified by making it clear to the existing staff that some of them, especially at the top, were simply not up to the job.

The costs incurred were not small. Furthermore the intention to change the nature of the *Telegraph* into something more profitable had to be shielded from readers who loved it most for its unprofitable qualities which they saw as a stand against the vulgarity of the red tops.

Deedes then turned to a fear he had expressed privately to his family and friends, that he was being kept on by the Barclays not for the intrinsic quality of his weekly column but because he reassured elderly readers that their paper was not changing too much.

On this I was called upon to play a minor role, which I accepted. As a somewhat shabby *Daily Telegraph* mascot with an excessive number of years with the newspaper, I offered a certain reassurance to some readers in doubt about the Telegraph's future intentions. On the face of it, it was ridiculous to keep a 92-year-old man employed who could not even attend the office, and to sack people like the managing editor Sue Ryan. But he served as part of the cover plan, and she did not. It was the style in which she was dismissed after 15 years of devoted and useful service that led me – and others – to doubt whether the *Telegraph* and the Barclays were compatible.

For someone as cautious and as loyal to the *Telegraph* as Deedes, this was extremely strong stuff, even if he knew it would not be published until after his death. It was clear from the way Deedes solemnly handed a copy of his considered reflections to his biographer that he wanted his thoughts about the state of the paper to be publicly recorded. Perhaps he thought he had been feeble over many years in failing to speak up about successive management failures and thought he could make amends posthumously. Conceivably he felt 'survivor's guilt' that he was still there after Martin Newland, Sue Ryan and others had been forced out.* The Barclays were certainly not his sort of people; though he never said as much, Aidan and Howard perhaps reminded him of the spoilt sons of the nouveaux riches he had encountered at Harrow in the 1920s, and Deedes never entirely managed to raise himself above occasional displays of snobbery. What is certain is that as Deedes contemplated his own mortality and the destruction of the newspaper he loved, he wanted belatedly, even posthumously, to get his revenge on the Barclays and to do them damage.†

While he was alive Deedes would not admit publicly to any reservations about the *Telegraph*, so keen was he to stay in harness to the very end of his life. Word of Deedes's unhappiness had, however, spread around Fleet Street and Bill Hagerty came to interview him for the *British Journalism Review*, a small-circulation quarterly read by a few journalists and 'media analysts'. Deedes was on guard, because even the most gentle criticism of the Barclays would assuredly have found its way into the media pages.

Speaking for the record, Deedes set off by endorsing the need for change: 'You can't expect to be static, you've got to move along,' he said, before reflecting on the heavy human toll of recent redundancies. But Deedes would not be drawn into public comment on the Barclays' stewardship of the paper.

'To me, it's rather like my own home, which is reliable regardless who runs it or what they do. I have a deep-lying affection for the *Telegraph*. After all, I've known it for seventy years and I never discuss its affairs.' Deedes also reflected on his traditional theme of how being on the road was the highest form of

* The author was shown the door in September 2006, which further darkened Deedes's mood.

† Deedes would occasionally talk as though he wished he were still writing for the *Morning Post*. In the summer of 2006, the author found him at his desk grappling with the complexities of death duties. 'It's my *middle-class* item,' he explained, suddenly sounding rather Edwardian. 'I try to get one in every week.'

journalism. 'I know the editor is above you, but getting a good story is to me the most satisfactory experience one can undergo. It's better than sex.'

Hagerty had arrived at New Hayters having heard on the grapevine of Deedes's disquiet but he left without any scoop, just the normal engaging reflections on Deedes's charmed life in journalism. 'It has been an admirable and largely successful display of stonewalling by Lord Deedes,' he wrote. Hagerty was no journalistic novice, yet he had been thoroughly outmanoeuvred by an old professional who had shown, once again, that you don't stay in Fleet Street for three-quarters of a century by publicly criticising the management, at least not from this side of the grave.

CHAPTER 26

TIME ENOUGH TO SLEEP

The latter years of Bill Deedes's long life were punctuated by ever more implausible anniversary and celebratory events. There had been his supposed retirement dinner in Downing Street in 1986; five years later, most of the editorial staff of the *Telegraph* foregathered at the Cheshire Cheese in Fleet Street to mark his seventy years in journalism; and in 2003 there was a dinner at the Carlton Club for his ninetieth birthday, which most present assumed would be the last of the big anniversary events.

One spring morning in 2006, Deedes casually mentioned to his daughter Lucy that 'another silly anniversary' was pending: in June it would be seventy-five years since he joined the *Morning Post*. Lucy decided that three-quarters of a century in journalism required proper celebration, at which point Deedes, having alerted his daughter to the milestone, affected to be unwilling to do anything to mark its passing.

There was indeed a practical problem. He was still seething at the Barclays's editorial executives for the manner of Sue Ryan's sacking three months earlier, and he did not want the 'stinking mob' to be invited to any social event he was hosting. But nor did he want a celebration to cause any public unpleasantness. Thus it was decided that a relatively small lunch would be held at New Hayters, and it would be termed a strictly private family

444

event in case word of a snub leaked out to the newspaper media diaries.

Lucy acted as hostess and oversaw the preparations for twenty guests. Bill's sister Margaret attended, as did Lucy's elder son, Drummond Money-Coutts, then an undergraduate at Leeds University.* To the surprise of some of the guests, Jeremy Deedes did not attend, citing a prior racing engagement. Richard Ingrams, the former *Private Eye* editor who had played the organ at Lucy's wedding in 1978, was there, as was Jane Clark, the widow of Alan and chatelaine of Saltwood Castle. Ion Trewin, the editor of Clark's diaries was there too, not for any Saltwood connection but because he is the son of J. C. Trewin, who was on the *Morning Post* when Deedes joined in 1931. Michael Howard, the former Conservative leader and a Kent neighbour, also attended.

The remainder of the guests were strictly 'old *Telegraph*'. Sue Ryan, the veteran political cartoonist Nicholas Garland, Neil Darbyshire, the joint deputy editor, Simon Scott Plummer, an erudite foreign leader writer, and the comment desk secretary Penny Cranford were there. It was an unusual gathering in that Charles Moore was present, but John Bryant was not invited. Nor was Murdoch MacLennan or any member of the Barclay family. On the other hand, to show there were no hard feelings over their defection to the *Independent* twenty years earlier, Stephen Glover and Andreas Whittam Smith were both invited, though neither could attend.

For two days before the lunch Deedes went into virtual hibernation, rarely emerging from his bed. Lucy was concerned her father might not be up to playing host to so many guests, but in fact he was merely conserving his energy for a day he desperately wanted to go well. Once everyone had gathered to drink champagne, Deedes was pushed in to the room in his wheelchair to

---

* On hearing that his grandson was to be called Drummond, Deedes had asked laconically, 'How many bank names can you give a boy?'

welcoming cheers. He had recently given up any attempt to walk again, but was immaculately dressed in blazer, his usual Brooks Brothers button-down shirt and – as a raffish touch – he wore the gold, black and orange tie of the I Zingari Cricket Club, of which he was a non-playing member.

The lunch was a triumphant success, capped by Deedes's funny and evocative speech, delivered without notes, about his first day of work at the *Morning Post*. In simple, conversational style, he transported his guests from a glorious summer's day in Kent to the vanished world of London two years after the Great Crash. He recalled how he had been so nervous that his grandmother had to take him on the bus for his first day of work; and how the chief reporter S. R. Pawley took the young cub reporter on a tram to Elephant & Castle to speak to a timber merchant about cheap Soviet imports, or 'red timber', as the true-blue *Morning Post* called it.

Then, with theatrical solemnity, he said he must put right a great journalistic wrong that had preyed on his conscience for seventy years. Gesturing towards Ion Trewin, he recalled that the only reason his Abyssinian dispatches had any merit was because J. C. Trewin had turned his telegrams into magical prose. In fact, Deedes had acknowledged Trewin's contribution years earlier in his autobiography, but he was never one to let a trivial detail spoil a charming anecdote.

Even by his own high standards, it was an uncannily well-pitched speech, and one that delighted the table. Deedes knew how to gauge whether a speech had hit the mark, and his exhilaration at his guests' reaction kept his fatigue at bay. By the summer of 2006 he was not getting out of bed for long stretches, but that afternoon he stayed with the guests until he had spoken individually to every one, as good manners dictate.*

---

* The guests assumed he was speaking extempore. In fact, on the evening before the lunch he had invited his biographer to his bedside where, over whiskies and soda, he had told the same anecdotes in identical language. What had seemed like a chat over a drink was in fact the final rehearsal for the following day's bravura performance.

The next big event in his life was the publication in September of *Words and Deedes*, an 822-page selection of his journalism. Deedes had not been well enough to take charge of the project so the pieces were selected by the publisher, Macmillan, with no great discernment. The articles were not annotated, no background information was provided for many of them and Deedes merely provided brief introductions to the chapters. He was depressed when he saw the resulting volume, thinking that his loyal *Telegraph* readers would feel short-changed after paying out twenty-five pounds for a rather shoddily produced collection. He complained privately that Macmillan, having done well with his previous book, *Brief Lives*, was squeezing rather more than was seemly out of the W. F. Deedes byline.

With a certain sense of trepidation, Deedes headed to a book signing at Hatchard's in Piccadilly, and what was to be his last trip to London. He travelled in a privately hired ambulance and sat inside the shop signing books for his loyal fans, sipping a strong whisky and soda thoughtfully provided by the manager. Then he was wheeled through the heavy lunchtime traffic to the Traveller's Club in Pall Mall for the official launch party. Macmillan had seemingly botched the invitations because many friends and colleagues – even those who worked at the *Telegraph* – were unaware of the party, which was thinly attended. Still, Deedes gave a good speech, offering witty general reflections on the state of journalism. This was to be the last time he spoke in public.

The party was memorable to Deedes mostly for a peculiar incident involving John Bryant. He had met Deedes previously only once on his 'editor's club' visit to New Hayters the previous year. In the ambulance on the way back to Kent after the book party, Deedes remarked to Lucy that it was surprising Bryant had failed to turn up. Lucy remonstrated with him, pointing out that Bryant had not only been present but had kneeled at the side of Deedes's wheelchair while the pair had a fifteen-minute conversation.

Deedes, lying down to rest in the ambulance, winced and said 'Ahhh' with heavy emphasis. He explained that because of

Bryant's general hangdog demeanour, and perhaps as a result of two large whiskies, he had assumed the editor-in-chief to be one of the sub-editors who had recently been made redundant. Therefore he had told Bryant, attempting to be sympathetic, that no one in authority at the *Telegraph* had a clue what they were doing and that the new management was driving the paper on to the rocks. 'I may have been a bit pissed. I told him they were mad.' Thus, W. F. Deedes, that most cautious of men who had never spoken ill of the *Telegraph* – at least not in public or to anyone in authority – had unwittingly launched a frontal attack on the management of the group. More than that, he had delivered it to the man who had been installed by the new owners to assist in purging the clubby culture of the old *Telegraph*, a culture that Deedes embodied.

Deedes looked momentarily alarmed as the realisation of what he had done sank in, but then – according to Lucy – he seemed quite pleased that Bryant had been given a full blast of censure. 'He did seem to be pleading for my understanding,' he said. Then he lay back, chuckling mischievously to himself, before falling asleep as the ambulance carried him out of London for the last time, setting course for the M20 and the Kentish countryside.*

That book party in September 2006 marked Deedes's final direct contact with the *Telegraph*. John Bryant was himself shown the door three months later, without achieving his ambition of being made up from acting editor to editor proper. Will Lewis, a former financial journalist with spells at the *Financial Times* and *Sunday Times*, was made the third editor of the Barclays' brief but eventful tenure.

Deedes felt increasingly isolated and disenchanted with the way the paper was moving perceptibly downmarket under the direction of news and features executives recruited from the *Daily*

---

* Jeremy Deedes had a similar embarrassment with Bryant. Arriving for an appointment with Murdoch MacLennan at the *Telegraph*'s Canary Wharf offices, he assumed the man tidying up the chief executive's stash of magazines in his ante-room was a cleaner, rather than the group's editor-in-chief.

Mail. With each passing month he felt more the 'shabby mascot' he had described himself in his bitter memorandum of the previous Easter. He complained that the *Telegraph*'s news coverage had become so thin that he had to pick his way through the *Guardian* to find out what was going on in the world. Around this time he also cancelled his subscription to the *Spectator* and switched to the *Tablet*, the Catholic weekly. He explained the change by complaining the *Spectator* had become vulgar, and that the *Tablet* provided more useful material for his weekly Notebook. But it may also have been that, as he contemplated the imminence of his own death, he felt the need for a weekly read about religious matters.

He had been quietly proud in November 2006 when he was included in a list compiled by the trade magazine, *Press Gazette*, of the forty most influential journalists of recent times. Murdoch MacLennan sent a bottle of champagne down to New Hayters, which thrilled Deedes almost as much, even though, as his colleagues knew, he never touched the stuff. It was no ordinary champagne, but Louis Roederer Cristal, which Lucy told him was favoured by the wives and girlfriends of Premiership footballers. It was a particularly expensive vintage, 1986, the year Deedes had supposedly retired from the *Telegraph*. It came in a special presentation box and Deedes kept the bottle on the kitchen table for several days, inviting guests to examine it, rather as if it was a pygmy head recovered on an expedition to the South Seas.

'I'm reliably informed Mrs Beckham will drink nothing else,' he would tell visitors. The bottle was eventually opened in May 2007, when all three daughters – Juliet, Jill and Lucy – were briefly together in Kent. Deedes lay in bed sipping his customary whisky and soda, laughing and repeating how they were all getting a little glimpse of how footballers and their wives lived the high life. 'Those footballers earn five thousand quid a week,' he cackled, underestimating their remuneration by a factor of about ten.

He continued to attend to the huge volumes of correspondence he received, acknowledging routine letters from readers but struggling to his desk to compose proper answers to more important communications. For instance, when Marilyn Tweddle – the widow of Alec, one of Deedes's riflemen – wrote to him at some length, he took trouble to reply properly, because he was spending a great deal of his day lying in bed thinking of the war and the men he lost.

'We were very lucky to survive. It was a pretty hairy 12 months because we led the whole Army so often. Always remember, Mrs Tweddle, we were considered to be 'crack' troops – the best – and I have always been proud of that. So should you!'

In the last months of his life Deedes also made efforts to raise his game, as he might have put it, with his grandchildren. He knew he had been an inadequate grandfather, as he had fallen short as a father, and in his own way he tried to make amends, encouraging them to visit him more frequently. The results were mixed: George Deedes, Jeremy's first son and Bill's eldest grandchild, was greatly saddened that his grandfather could not share his treasure trove of memories and experiences because he simply could not communicate with his grandchildren.

His body language was awkward, George recalled. Bill would shake hands with his grandchildren – even with the girls – rather than hug or kiss them. Sometimes he would try to convey affection, but often it would misfire. When George broke his jaw playing cricket his grandfather wrote him a sweet letter, but the force of it was ruined because he signed off 'Yours, Bill'.

George said that he and his younger brother, Henry, had benefited from that aloofness, so he was indulgent of Bill's shortcomings. 'My father always made sure he was a good father in every way that grandpa had been crap as a father,' he recalled. Having suffered the disappointment of never seeing his own father come to watch him play cricket, Jeremy, accompanied by his wife, Anna, would go almost without fail to watch George play in Saturday cricket matches at Eton.

Otherwise, Deedes struggled to keep up with rapidly changing events in London. He was bemused by the talk of new 'digital platforms' for the *Telegraph*, and never really saw the point of the vogue for 'podcasts', in which columnists read out their efforts, which could then be downloaded from the paper's website. But after his unhappy experiences in the early 1980s, when all change was obstructed by the print unions and sclerotic management, he readily accepted the need for innovation, though he worried about the business logic of newspapers giving themselves away free to online readers. 'The Barclays will have to sell, I'm sure of it when they find it won't make them any money,' he predicted in early 2007.

Sensing that Deedes was feeling alienated from the new *Telegraph*, Nicholas Garland wrote to him in Kent expressing sadness about the changes and the sacking of so many mutual friends. In his own memoir of the last days of the Hartwell regime, Garland had been critical of Deedes for his vacillation as editor, but no ill-feeling lingered. Deedes, now confined to his home and mostly to his bed, wrote back: 'How closely we think alike. I see some of the casualties down here; it is sad to see the effect on friends of being told suddenly, in effect, "we have no further use for your services". It is a great blow to self-confidence, so vital to us all.' Deedes praised Garland for his work and contribution to the past success of the *Telegraph*, before adding: 'Bullying does not produce happy newspapers – and the readers notice it!'

He was also concerned about the new populist right-wing voice of the paper, and particularly its scathing attitude towards the Tory leader, David Cameron. Traditionally the *Telegraph* had been loyal to the Conservative leader, whoever that was. Certainly the *ad hominem* attacks from Simon Heffer and Janet Daley, the two main political columnists, did not chime with the paper's ancestral voices or his own notion of fair play. Deedes assumed that the political tone was ultimately being set by two generations of the Barclay family, all of whom were thought to be right-wing

Tories with an enduring devotion to Thatcher. Deedes remained personally loyal to Margaret Thatcher, but he was clear that the moment of Thatcherism had long since passed. He warned Will Lewis that if the *Telegraph* remained so hostile to Cameron the paper would not be forgiven by readers if the Tories narrowly lost the next general election.

When Simon Heffer was eased out of his role as comment editor in May 2007 and replaced by the non-ideological figure of Richard Preston, Deedes was delighted. He was fond of Heffer but deplored the tone of his column, which he thought was unsuited to a broadsheet newspaper. Deedes celebrated this shift in power by turning his Friday Notebook into a strong endorsement of David Cameron's decision to water down the Tories' support for grammar schools. It was a classic Deedesian argument in favour of avoiding confrontation and accepting the inevitable, true to best One Nation thinking. Will Lewis seized upon Deedes's offering with relish, seemingly determined to send a public signal that the *Telegraph* was having another look at the Conservative leader. Lewis ordered up a huge page one 'blurb' flagging the Deedes column inside: WHY CAMERON IS RIGHT ABOUT GRAMMAR SCHOOLS. Deedes was delighted by this revenge of the Tory wets.

Deedes was becoming increasingly frail as he turned ninety-four on 1 June 2007. He hadn't tried to walk for some time, but now he was frequently staying in bed all day, even for meals. He could only work for about half an hour at a time so he started to write his weekly column in instalments, tapping away on a laptop perched on his tummy in bed.

On Saturday 7 July he awoke feeling terrible, and calmly told Dee, his South African carer, that he was dying. He asked her to summon Lucy back from Sussex, where she spent her weekends, and for Aldington's rector, the Reverend Richard Love, to come by to address unfinished spiritual business. He then shakily signed some cheques, including one to the Inland Revenue because his income tax was due and he was worried his bank account would be frozen upon his death, causing bother for his children. He decided the 'intro' to his next column on the state of the NHS was rather weak so he dictated two new paragraphs, with clear instructions for the office about how the changes were to be made. He dozed through the afternoon, talking intermittently to members of his family, and assuming he was about to die. The retired local doctor was called, but only for Deedes to say thank you and goodbye. Then Peter Herbert, his gardener of forty-two years' service, was summoned to say farewell, a nicely feudal touch that would not have seemed out of place at Saltwood Castle a century earlier.

In his last years Deedes had contemplated converting to Rome, but he stayed true to the high Anglicanism of his upbringing. Mr Love hurried to his bedside, and found Deedes very calm and resigned. 'He had his focus on God, there was a holiness and reverence,' the clergyman recalled. 'He asked me to read from the Prayer Book. Then he said he wanted to thank God for His grace, and for all the other things in his life, his home and his family. He was relaxed and open; he had a clear certainty of where the physical becomes the spiritual, and he was ready.'

Mr Love had only got to know Deedes three years earlier, but from the start he had been struck by the strength of his faith, and his knowledge of the Prayer Book and the scriptures. 'He knew his Bible as literature, but it was engraved on his heart.' Some parishioners and clergy could be competitive in showing off their knowledge of the Bible, but Mr Love joked of Deedes: 'I never caught him out on anything.'

Mr Love had come prepared from his last church service, and he asked Deedes if he wanted to take communion. Deedes nodded, and took the bread and the wine. Then Mr Love anointed him on his forehead with oil blessed by the Archbishop of Canterbury; Deedes lay back in his bed and prepared to die.

There is no doubt that Deedes at that point was convinced he had hours to live, but to his obvious astonishment he rallied. It turned out he was suffering from some sort of stomach virus, for after a violent attack of diarrhoea he woke the following morning feeling much better. He was deeply embarrassed by the false alarm and all the bother it had caused for others. Soon he was back to reading the newspapers, hunting for items for his column. Dee gently rebuked him, saying that as a Christian he should have known it was not for him to decide when he was going to be called.

His recovery was momentarily threatened by his disapproval one morning when the *Telegraph*'s main page one story, the splash, was devoted to a brutal murder at Harrow School. It was a sensational story, and certainly worthy of full coverage in a paper like the *Telegraph*, which never stinted in detailing grisly crime cases. There was no doubt an element of his being protective about his old school, but he complained that splashing with the story, rather than running it in all its gory detail on page three in the traditional manner, was to surrender to tabloid impulses. 'We are moving from the gutter into the sewer,' he muttered darkly.

Soon he began to decline again and I drove down to New Hayters on 2 August 2007. Since his birthday two months earlier, he had rarely got out of bed and would greet visitors in his downstairs bedroom. I arrived towards lunchtime, and Deedes was lying in bed in his dressing gown, sipping his customary pre-prandial whisky and soda, but that day it was very weak. He instructed me to go to the kitchen and pour myself a drink. 'Make it a stiff one,' he called through, 'you're going to have to edit my column.' Usually any visitor from London would be cross-examined for journalistic gossip, but on that day he waved aside my efforts to engage in chit-chat, insisting there was work to be done.

As his health had deteriorated in his last months, it was his practice to write his Friday column through the week, a couple of hundred words a day, before filing it to the office by e-mail on Thursday morning. But that Thursday he woke early, with the crisis in Darfur on his mind, and scrapped the column he had all but finished the day before. He set off on a completely new column from scratch. By the time I arrived, he was visibly exhausted by the effort, and anxious that I should read it immediately and then e-mail it before he drifted off to sleep.

I sat at the end of his bed, reading the column. It was astonishingly good; in fact, it was one of the most powerful pieces he had written in all his years in journalism. A man of few firm or fixed views, Deedes had never been at his best turning out opinion pieces. His Notebooks were generally measured, occasionally puckish, but this one was a pungent denunciation of Western policy towards Khartoum and of Islamic influence at the United Nations. Having liberated Hanover in 1945 and run a prison camp there containing many hardcore Nazis, Deedes declared his fitness to pronounce without apology that Khartoum's genocide in Darfur was on the same moral plane as the atrocities of Nazi Germany.

> Women and children were hunted like wild animals, raped, robbed and left for dead. What has been happening in Darfur is unspeakable; and much of the world has simply shrugged its shoulders. They are an unknown people in a far-off land. What business is it of ours? It is very much our business, because behind this ghastly inhumanity lies the iron will of Islam in Khartoum.

As a journalist who had witnessed Mussolini road-testing totalitarian techniques by inflicting terror on Abyssinian civilians in 1935, Deedes was warning complacent Western leaders that they could not justify their inaction by claiming ignorance. 'When details of the Holocaust came to light, many – and not all of them Germans – took shelter behind the assertion: "I did not know." That offers us no escape route from the shame of Darfur. We've known, wrung our hands and done nothing. It's going to take some living down.'

As I read the piece I could sense that Deedes was watching me closely to gauge my reaction. Occasionally I would peer up and catch him averting his gaze back to the view out of his window across the Romney Marsh. When I finished, I told him I thought it was a superbly powerful piece of writing. He pretended to be oblivious to my reaction, but I knew that, like most journalists, Deedes had an almost physical craving for praise of his writing. 'You know it's bloody good, too,' I said. He didn't reply, but screwed up his face so it resembled a crinkled paper ball. And he nodded, acknowledging that he knew that I knew it was a very good column.

As I e-mailed the article to London, it occurred to me why he had put his all into the Darfur polemic by rewriting the whole thing in one burst: this was to be his last column. What I did not know at the time was that the previous day he had abandoned the course of antibiotics he was taking to deal with a chronic chest infection. The pills made him feel so rotten that he had decided he would not be able to write the column if he continued taking them. Without the pills there was no chance of the infection clearing up. But he told Lucy that he could not be bothered with medication any more.

For Deedes it was an easy calculation to make. He hated being dependent on others for his basic needs; life without the prospect of a convivial lunch or supper with gossipy old friends from journalism was not worth the bother. He had been ready to die for a few months so he cheerfully sacrificed his remaining few days for the sake of writing one last column.

After I sent his final, completed Notebook down the line to London, he stayed awake only long enough to check that the office had received it. Then he fell asleep, exhausted. I ate my lunch in the kitchen and drove back to London later that day, after bidding him farewell, apologising that I had something on that evening and could not stay for our normal early evening whisky. 'That is sad,' he said to his nurse after I had gone, 'I shall never see Stephen again.' As usual, he was right.

Though he was better some days than others, there was no

doubt that he was fading away. On 10 August there was no Friday column, and *Telegraph* readers were told in a note below the substitute column that 'W. F. Deedes is away', as though he were on a golfing holiday with pals in East Anglia. In fact, for the first time in his life he could simply not summon up the energy to write. To have stated the truth, that 'W. F. Deedes is unwell', would have provoked a tide of anxious letters and phone calls from his devoted readers.

Increasingly Deedes was finding life, confined to bed, a terrible chore for himself and – he worried endlessly – for those around him, particularly Lucy. All newspaper readers are conned to a lesser or greater extent by the picture bylines that now accompany almost every column. Deedes's byline picture showed him a good fifteen years younger than his true age, and few readers realised that he had been unable to leave his home, except for essential medical check-ups, for a year before his death. When he turned ninety-four in June 2007 and was hardly getting out of bed, the *Telegraph* had marked the milestone with a photograph of him taken almost twenty years earlier, nursing a pint of beer in a Docklands pub. There was no point in the paper shattering the readers' illusion that Deedes was constantly out and about, reporting as in days of yore.

His sense of frustration mounted and he explained that, though he felt he had lost the will to live, he worried there was nothing specific that might carry him off. One of the nurses who had been hired to help Dee had to be let go after she called him 'Billy Boy'. Deedes explained: 'She asked me what I'd prefer to be called, and I said: "How would Lord Deedes do?"' Deedes was never particularly grand about having been made a life peer, but losing his dignity in becoming wholly dependent on others was taking its toll on his morale.

On Wednesday 15 August he made one final effort to complete a column after the previous week's enforced absence. He began tapping at his laptop, pausing occasionally to stare out of his bedroom window. He got about two-thirds of the way through before it defeated him. His main item, on the row about footage in a BBC trailer purporting to show the Queen storming out of a photo session, was not his best effort. The second item petered out as he wrote about Robert Mugabe's strange appeal to the South African president Thabo Mbeki. The very last words of the millions he wrote in his seventy-six years of journalism were: 'He is striving to broker a deal between Mugabe and the opposition MDC . . .' Later that evening Lucy noticed that her father seemed downhearted at his failure to finish the column, and that the resigned look in his eyes suggested he knew he would never again summon up the energy to write.

Two days later, Lucy realised the end was near. A nurse had been summoned and he was put on oxygen. When asked if he wanted to go to hospital he shook his head defiantly. By now he could only whisper, and Lucy bent over to hear him speak as he clutched his stomach in obvious discomfort. He whispered to her, asking if there was anything she could give him, as he put it, 'to help me go'. Lucy misunderstood, thinking he was asking for a laxative. (A few weeks later she could laugh at the misunderstanding.) When she realised her father was talking about helping him on his way, she stared solemnly at him in gentle rebuke.

Lucy squatted at the side of the bed while Bill raised both his hands before his chest for her to grasp, and he clenched and unclenched his fingers around her arms, drawing her closer to him. Bill had scarcely touched his youngest daughter when she was a child; Lucy didn't think he had ever kissed her until the day her brother Julius died when she was fifteen. Now he craved the comfort of her body as he prepared to die.

By mid-afternoon it was clear he was going. Lucy decided to summon the rector, but by mischance she had mislaid his telephone number. So she jumped into the car and drove the two minutes up the hill to the rectory. Mr Love said he would follow her in a few minutes. But by the time she returned a few moments later, Theresa, the agency carer from Poland who had followed Dee, met her in the passage in tears. Bill Deedes had died, peacefully in his bed, with its views across the lands occupied and owned by his ancestors over five centuries.

He had achieved one key ambition of his later years which was to avoid the indignity of a death attached to machines in a hospital ward. He narrowly failed to achieve the death he really wanted, with his boots on, and covered in the grime of some third world hellhole or amid the rubble of the earthquake devastation of Gujarat. The melancholic side of Deedes's character, which became pronounced after the war, always hinted at a vague desire to have died younger, if not in combat then armed with a notebook. But even if he died in his pyjamas rather than his boots, when the end came he was still in harness as a working journalist, grappling with words for a newspaper.[*]

Aldington was at its prettiest for the funeral the following Wednesday, on a lovely late August day at the end of a dismally wet summer. Jeremy Deedes gave the address at the Church of St Martin. He explained to the congregation that the funeral had been designated private because, over the years, the family had felt so often that they had come second best to the *Telegraph*. Indeed, the only people present still employed by the *Telegraph* were Penny Cranford, the secretary on the comment desk, of whom Deedes was very fond, and Charles Moore, the former editor and latterly a columnist. Sue Ryan, whose sacking had enraged him two years earlier, was there, as was Abbie Trayler-Smith.

Jeremy's address was witty and affectionate, but very slightly barbed. He recalled how the children learned from an early age that they were going to have to share their father with a much wider family 'made up from *Telegraph* readers, constituents, golf partners, African despots and saloon bar bores. He embraced them all and was incapable of ever saying no to them.'

Jeremy spoke about Julius, the son blanked out of Bill's life

---

[*] Lucy Deedes was irritated that when she registered her father's death, the registrar wrote down as his occupation 'retired journalist', a pardonable error given his date of birth, but one that would have rankled.

story, who would have turned sixty the week before their father died. Not a day had passed without his mother talking about Julius, and Jeremy said he was sure his father thought about him every day too, even if he never spoke of him. 'It is one of life's little contradictions that for someone who had such marvellous gifts of communication, Dad was least comfortable when speaking about his family to his family. To us children, he could never quite bring himself to say what he felt.'

Jeremy ended on a flight of fancy, describing the last time he saw his father: 'He was still wearing a plastic hospital bracelet from an earlier visit. I offered to take it off. "I am keeping it on," he said. "It reminds me of how much I appreciate being at home, in my own bed where I can see the trees and the chickens with people I love." He very nearly said it.'

But Bill did not say it, of course, and nor would Jeremy have expected his father to say it. And with that Jeremy took his seat. Only one factor threatened, briefly, the restrained solemnity of the occasion. The funeral notice had stressed that the service was to be strictly private, with no flowers. Yet Victoria Combe had arrived at the church with a flower in a pot, which she said was from her son Gabriel, Deedes's godson. While most members of the family were on the way to the church from the New Hayters garden, where they had had lunch before the funeral, Combe approached the coffin and put the flower pot on a chair by the side of the coffin, which bore a single wreath from the family.

The funeral proceeded, with the rest of the family unaware of what had happened. But after the coffin was borne from the church to the hearse for the short drive to the crematorium, Victoria Combe told the undertaker to go back to collect the flower and to place it on the coffin. George Deedes, Jeremy's son, remonstrated with her. He was concerned that Jeremy, who was at this point unaware of what Combe was trying to do, would explode in rage if he saw she was trying to have her flower conveyed with the coffin. The commotion caused a slight delay in the departure of the hearse and the immediate Deedes family who were to attend the actual cremation, while the rest of the mourners headed for New Hayters for tea. Victoria's flower pot was taken to the crematorium, where it was laid out by the undertaker next to the family's wreath. Combe had succeeded but, seemingly distressed by the family's reaction to her behaviour, she withdrew in tears and did not go on to the house for tea.

Within five days of the funeral, estate agents were summoned to New Hayters to value and market the property. Lucy Deedes, who like her mother had never really liked east Kent, was anxious to move to Sussex with Henry, her youngest child, as soon as practicable. Her two sisters, Juliet and Jill, both lived abroad and had no desire to take on the house. Jeremy had no intention of moving from Berkshire to the home in which he had grown up. Thus the Deedes presence in east Kent, which could be traced back to the days of Thomas Deeds, a contemporary of William Caxton, was finally at an end.

After generations in which Deedes men served only as landowners or soldiers, W. F. Deedes had struck out at the age of eighteen, and become the first member of his family in five hundred years to take a job. By the time of his death seventy-six years later, the Deedes family, like all wise dynasties, had diversified away from land, the original source of their wealth. Jeremy had been the managing director of the Telegraph Group, and how Bill had laughed on the day in 2003 when Jeremy retired: 'I'm going to have to look after him in my old age,' he joked as he headed for the airport on yet another out of town job.

Also present in the Aldington parish church that day were Jeremy's two sons, George, a classified sales manager at the *Daily Mail*, and Henry, a diarist on the *Independent*. Lucy's elder daughter, Sophia Money-Coutts, was there, and just about to begin her career on the *Evening Standard*. Saltwood Castle and its thousands of acres may have gone the same way as all the ancestral lands that surrounded Aldington and ran down to the coast at Hythe. But

William Francis Deedes, who always preferred the mountebanks of his mackintosh trade to 'landed chaps', died knowing that a new dynasty based on words, not land, had been created, and that the line was secure.

Sources Cited

As well as the documents held at the libraries mentioned in the Preface, I have drawn on many published sources in researching this book. For background details about Deedes's schooldays, I am indebted to Christopher Tyerman for *A History of Harrow School 1324–1991*. Philip Knightley's *The First Casualty* was indispensable in chronicling the absurdities of the media operation in Abyssinia in 1935. Nicholas Rankin's *Telegram from Guernica* is brilliantly researched and manages to show how high the stakes were in Abyssinia, despite all the high jinks captured so raucously by Evelyn Waugh in *Scoop*. No future history of the *Telegraph* will surpass Duff Hart-Davis's *The House the Berrys Built*; no memoir of a newspaper in crisis will be as deliciously indiscreet as Nicholas Garland's account of the *Telegraph* in the mid 1980s, *Not Many Dead*. I drew from two privately published memoirs: John Butterwick's *Through the Wrong End of a Telescope* was useful in describing the KRRC's progress across north-west Europe, and Dick Tower's *The Jobbing Shop* offered rich detail about the industrial lunacy in Fleet Street in the pre-Wapping era. Marilyn Tweddle, the widow of Alec, kindly sent me his unpublished diary of his war experiences in the KRRC.

I also found the following titles useful:
Dear Bill, *At War with Waugh* and *Brief Lives* by W. F. Deedes; *Swift and Bold: The Story of the KRRC in the Second World War* edited by W. F. Deedes and Sir Hereward Wake; *The Annals of the King's Royal Rifle Corps* (volume VII) by G. H. Mills;

Banana Sunday by Christopher Munnion; *Live From Number 10* and *Sources Close to the Prime Minister* by Michael Cockerell; *Waugh in Abyssinia* by Evelyn Waugh; *A Study in the History and Politics of the* Morning Post *1905–1926* by Keith M. Wilson; *Below the Parapet* by Carol Thatcher; *Editor* by Max Hastings; *Paper Dreams* by Stephen Glover; *Will This Do?* by Auberon Waugh; *A Short Walk Down Fleet Street* by Alan Watkins; *A Dubious Codicil* by Michael Wharton; *Tricks of Memory* by Peregrine Worsthorne; *Women of the World: The Great Foreign Correspondents* by Julia Edwards; *Never Had It So Good* and *White Heat* by Dominic Sandbrook; *Evelyn Waugh: A Biography* by Selina Hastings; *A Price too High* by Peter Rawlinson; *Downing Street Diary* by Harold Evans.

Index